The Rise of
Afrikanerdom

The Rise of Afrikanerdom

Power, Apartheid, and the
Afrikaner Civil Religion

T. Dunbar Moodie

UNIVERSITY OF CALIFORNIA PRESS
BERKELEY   LOS ANGELES   LONDON

University of California Press
Berkeley and Los Angeles, California
University of California Press, Ltd.
London, England
Copyright © 1975, by
The Regents of the University of California
First Paperback Printing 1980
ISBN 0-520-03943-2
Library of Congress Catalog Card Number 72-85512
Printed in the United States of America

1 2 3 4 5 6 7 8 9

To my parents

Contents

Introduction to the Paperback Edition

This study employs a methodology which is foreign to the majority of sociologists today, who are trained in a positivist tradition. Ironically, although I write as a sociologist, the book has been better received by historians and theologians than by those in my own discipline. What I should like to do in this new introduction is to outline briefly the sociological perspective out of which this study grew. This will bring us to focus on an aspect of Weberian classical tradition and my development of it. I shall set this discussion in the context of the research undertaken for this book in order that the reader better understand the purpose for which it was written.

I

Sociology studies social reality. But social reality is inexhaustible—a melange of meanings, misunderstandings, anxieties, exploitations, exigencies, complacencies, purposes, paradises and purgatories. Sociology seeks to make sense of an "infinite multiplicity of successively and coexistently emerging and disappearing events" (Weber). The question is, then, how is sociology possible? Max Weber's greatness lies precisely in that he recognized the fundamental nature of this problem. His solution was vested partly in a neo-Kantian notion of causality and partly in what he called "the method of the ideal type." It is with the latter that I shall deal herein.

Weber was convinced that any sociological study is a part of the very reality which we seek to explain or understand. No methodology can lift us out of that reality to some firm source of certainty from which we can survey the plethora of sociality

---

*Much of the substance of the argument in this introduction and indeed certain passages are culled from my University of Witwatersrand inaugural lecture *On Doing Sociology* and are used here by kind permission of Witwatersrand University Press.

laid out before us. Instead, Weber urges that we construct "ideal types" to serve like "piles driven into the mud" (Lakatos) as temporary footholds. Such ideal types must be built upon our values and interests in order to enable us to control for them.

We undertake analysis, Weber said, because it is relevant to the interests of our own cultural generation (which may include our class interests). Such interests may be moral, practical or scholarly. We may, of course, also be guided by personal commitments, but our work becomes sociologically relevant only if it applies to wider concerns as well. Let me illustrate by examining my own motives in undertaking the work which resulted in this book.

When the National Party came to power in South Africa in 1948, I was 8 years old. My father was an officer in the South African army. During the next twelve years I watched him suffer discrimination as a result of D. F. Erasmus's Afrikanerization policy. It seemed quite natural to extrapolate the burning sense of injustice aroused over my father's treatment to the wider and more severe suffering of my Black fellow-countrymen. I became a liberal, a member of the National Union of South African Students. While an Honours student, I dated the daughter of an eminent Afrikaner in Pretoria and found myself involved in intense debate over separate development policy. I became convinced that it was possible to provide moral justification for separate development as an idea, despite the despicable practices associated with its execution and its complete impracticability. Furthermore, I began to see that such justification for separate development was rooted in the history of Afrikanerdom and in the Afrikaner's own attitude to the English.

When I arrived at Harvard to work on a doctorate I became fascinated by the Puritans of the seventeenth century. I decided to return to South Africa and study my own brand of Puritanism at home. If Max Weber had shown the importance of Puritanism in the rise of capitalism, why should I not show the importance of Afrikaner Calvinism in the development of apartheid policy and, of course, in the outcome of the 1948 election which had had so marked an effect on my own life?

Thus, my work was situated by the general interests typical of my generation of liberal-minded English-speaking white South Africans: resentment of Afrikaner political domination and identification with black African misery. Interwoven with these general interests was a desire to contribute to that sociological tradition which stresses Calvinism as a causative factor in social change.

For Weber, personal and cultural values, such as those I describe above, necessarily direct the inquiry of every social scientist. The construction of ideal types is derived precisely from such values and interests. The sociologist must come to the situation which he wishes to analyze armed with an ideal type by means of which he is able to select with rigorous consistency those aspects of social reality which he proposes to explain. Such a construct, by focussing the analyst's interests, can control for his own values and also can consistently grasp the values of his subjects. Thus, while the method of the ideal type necessarily limits the scope of a study to a narrow focus, bounded by the values of the investigator, nonetheless, within that scope, "objectivity" is possible.

When I began my research the notion of "civil religion" had recently been revived by my mentor, Robert Bellah (1970), and it seemed a particularly useful ideal-typical way into Afrikaner social reality. (See Chapter 1.) Perhaps in research, things are never so simple as one at first imagines. In the *Ossewa Gedenkboek* (1940), I found ample support for my initial exploratory ideal type in the speeches of leaders made between August and December 1938 and reprinted there. When I plunged into the historical events of the period between the Boer War and 1948, however, I soon came to realize that the civil religion which I had chosen as my independent variable changed as much as the other variables which I found myself forced to introduce. I had always imagined that social reality was malleable, opening up different aspects to different ideal-typical perspectives. Imagine my perplexity when the ideal type which I had constructed to make sense of Afrikaner history began to change as I used it. Social reality, however protean, had a facticity which I had never expected.

My problem at that point was two-fold. On the one hand, if my ideal type itself changed in the course of my investigation, then even that measure of consistency, that relative "objectivity," was proven uncertain. Not even the ideal type could provide even a tentative source of certainty without distorting social reality. On the other hand, it was the very facticity, the perverse unexpected consistency of social interaction, which was forcing me to modify my ideal type. It is as though Afrikaner history had a meaningful order to which my ideal type had granted me access but whose logic of development refused to conform to that type. The very structure of Afrikaner efforts to cope with the exigencies of their own social situation caused them constantly to reinterpret their civil faith. How was I to proceed?

II

I read every Afrikaans newspaper published between 1929 and 1950, student journals, journals of voluntary associations, local parish magazines, local party minutes, school magazines, diaries (where I could get them) and Afrikaans literature—besides a mass of secondary literature on the whole of Afrikaner history. I struggled with the writings and speeches of Dr. Malan, General Hertzog, General Smuts, Joon van Rooy, Nic Diederichs, L.J. du Plessis, Hans van Rensburg, W.W.M. Eiselen, Oswald Pirow, and many others, until they were like old friends. Then I went out and spoke to their friends and enemies, persons who had known them, loved them, despised them. I strove to reconcile their memories with my own impressions.

There were groups that had to be understood too—the Broederbond, the National Party, the Federasie van Afrikaanse Kulturrverenigings, the Afrikaanse Nasionale Studentebond, the Mineworkers Union, and the Ossewabrandwag, not to mention the three Dutch Reformed Churches. Within each of these organizations there were factions and schisms, rifts about ideologies and personalities, maneuverings and conspiracies. By the time I came to interview Afrikaners who had lived through the period, my knowledge was better than their memories, and hence often they told me more than they believe they were saying.

There were disagreements among Afrikaners about the very notion of Afrikanerdom itself. I watched the Afrikaner civil religion come into being after 1881, and I confronted innumerable variations in its formulation and different usages by different groups and individuals. Then, behold, it began to echo back to me in various forms, from political and economic, ecclesiastical and educational events, not as a causal factor, certainly, but as the medium through which causes became effective in interaction. The Afrikaner civil religion was not so much an ideal type which I had imposed on events to measure them accurately; it was rather a perspective, shared by the actors themselves, which provided an everchanging horizon of meaning for their actions. To borrow a term I have since discovered in the phenomenologists, the civil religion *constituted* reality for Afrikaans-speaking white South Africans during my period—and to an extent, it still does.

Thus, in the midst of my research, to my initial exasperation and then growing excitement, social reality came to life; it began to answer me back in unexpected ways. Instead of my ideal type opening up reality to me, reality altered my ideal type. It is this radical notion of ideal types as changing in the course of research which is, I believe, my own contribution to the business of doing sociology. What it means is that one cannot eliminate "values" from social research by controlling for them by means of an initial, admittedly "value-relevant" ideal type. Values and interests continue to be an integral part of all social research.

The process of sociological discovery is always a dialogue, an interaction in which we cannot but involve ourselves. This involvement in the very interaction we set out to study must not be deplored as an unfortunate consequence to be avoided as far as possible. Such involvement should be welcomed as the only basis for scholarly study of human interaction. We have to make decisions about the persons we study—decisions related to the explanations we seek to make about them and the explanations *they themselves* make of the way they act or have acted. Their life becomes a part of our life and we must live in their social reality.

Alfred Schutz has argued that all of us constantly use "types" in the course of everyday life. After all, each of us every day has to break anew into the multiplicity of social interactions; we construct types in order to interact at all. Social actor's role expectations, for instance, are necessarily typological. Our expectations of how a woman will act may differ depending on whether we see her as a doctor, a lab technician, a dentist, a pharmacist, Jewish, preppy, a mother, and so on. But unless such typological generalizations in everyday life are continually checked against individual particularities and altered by them in the course of interaction, they become stereotypes, morally repugnant fixations. If we are not bigots, everyday ideal types are modified in the course of interaction. I suggest that sociological types are even so— tentative assumptions about action situations which change in the course of their application. If the sociologist does not alter his typological concepts in the course of analysis, the concepts are liable to distort the reality which he seeks to understand, even as the anti-Semite never sees beyond his stereotype of Jewishness.

III

Ideal types as they were used in writing this book, then, are tentative models for interaction which change in the course of analysis and over time. Of course, the method can be used more widely than in the study of Afrikanerdom or in the analysis of ideas. In this study I have concentrated on conscious or implicit meanings held by actors themselves. This approach is open to one very fundamental objection. What of structural factors (urbanization and power structures, demography and poverty are scattered throughout this book), and, more important, what about Marx's "false consciousness" and what Ricoeur calls "interpretation as exercise of suspicion?" Can social reality be understood, let alone explained, purely in

terms of the conscious meanings of social actors? Can we
ignore social structure? I do not believe so.

This study has indeed tended to focus on ideal types of ideas
and ideals. In so doing it perhaps subordinates ideal types of a
different sort—those of structure. These deal with structural
constraints upon interaction. The most influential ideal type
of structure is that proposed by Karl Marx, who believed that
in working upon nature, human beings establish structural
contexts within which action takes place. Most important is
the fact that various class groups are differentially related to
the forces of production. Whether or not that particular nexus
is as important as Marx believed, sociologists have long been
aware of the effects of social structure upon individual actors.

The impact of such factors was fundamental in causing
reformulation of my initial ideal types. Some would say this
did not go far enough. That may be. I shall be satisfied if those
now writing on Afrikanerdom from a structural perspective
will wrestle with Afrikaner ideals, even as I have with situa-
tional factors. Writing this book was a lesson to me in how the
structured initiatives of historical actors force social analysts
to struggle, not in despair, but toward an ever better understanding of the intersection of consciousness and history.

Preface

What constitutes social and political reality for the majority of Afrikaners in South Africa? What are the symbols of this reality, their origins and the manner in which they both mediated and were altered by different social philosophies and social, economic, and political events and personalities in the years before 1948? This book attempts to come to grips with these issues.

As a backdrop for my analysis, I first provide the reader with an ideal typical exposition of the Afrikaner civil faith.[1] This civil religion is grounded in the Afrikaner sacred history, which was publicly stated at least as early as 1899 and expressed in a civil ritual with a standard liturgical form. I also attempt to outline what may be called the mainstream civil theology, although, as we shall see, interpretation of the Afrikaner civil faith has always been a matter of ideological debate between protagonists of different systems of social metaphysics. The roots of the Afrikaner doctrine of election grew out of the Calvinism of Paul Kruger and the experience of the Boer War, and the young shoots of Afrikaner nationalism were nurtured in the post-Boer War language movement. The divine agent of the Afrikaner civil faith is Christian and Calvinist—an active sovereign God, who calls the elect, who promises and punishes, who brings forth life from death in the course of history. The object of his saving activity—the Afrikaner People—is not a church, a community of the saved, however; it is a whole nation with its distinct language and culture, its own history and special destiny. This Christian heresy managed to achieve a theological and practical *modus*

[1] In the Theoretical and Methodological Appendix, I define the terms *civil religion*, *social metaphysics*, and *ideology* as used in this study.

vivendi with the avowedly orthodox Dutch Reformed churches in South Africa.

It was in the cultural sphere that a consistent ideology firmly based on the civil faith began to be institutionalized in the late 1920s, largely through the efforts of the Afrikaner Broederbond. The major tenets of the civil faith, especially republicanism, gained political import only with the National party schism of 1934. During this period young Afrikaner intellectuals were returning from Germany with a neo-Fichtean social-philosophical framework and steering the Broederbond into economic as well as political and cultural activity. Yet, until 1938, the major tenets of the civil faith were not overtly accepted by the majority of Afrikaners. With the centenary of her covenant vow with God, however, civil-religious enthusiasm seized Afrikanerdom. Ordinary Afrikaners were swept wholesale into the mainstream of Christian-National myth and ritual. The civil faith now became a guaranteed effective ideological agency of social, political, and economic mobilization. Two new and very powerful organizations sprang into being on the strength of this new mass appeal. One was the O.B. (Ossewabrandwag), the other the R.D.B. (Reddingsdaadbond). The O.B., particularly, seized upon the Second World War as an excuse for propounding a far more militant and less mystical version of the civil religion which reinterpreted the sacred history to justify political subversion of the state. The defeat of Germany spelled the end of the O.B., however, and left the field to the National party. I discuss the major issues of the 1948 election campaign insofar as they incorporated the civil religion and Christian-National ideology.

Lastly, I analyze the policy of separate development as an attempt of sincere Christian-Nationalist Afrikaners to impose ethnic nonracial pluralism on black African and white voter alike. Given the class position and vested interests of the Afrikaner elite that supports separate development on moral grounds, the theory may be simply interpreted as an opiate for sensitive consciences. For some of this elite, such rationalization is obviously true. For the rest, however, hypocrisy is too superficial an explanation. Indeed, from the corresponding English-speaking South African elite who have equally vested interests in the status quo comes whatever meaningful liberal opposition to racism that continues to exist in white South Africa. Class interest alone does not account for the extent to which the principle of separate development is rooted in the Afrikaner's own struggle for ethnic apartheid from the English in South Africa. However, the number of Afrikaner true believers in a nonracial version of separate-development policy is now small, and most Afrikaner voters appear quite unwilling to make personal sacrifices on behalf of the ideal. Having argued the present bankruptcy of the policy, I go on to speak briefly of current developments in Afrikaner politics, where ethnic exclusivism seems to be giving way to a common white "anti-Co-munist" authoritarianism. Whether a new civil religion will emerge to sustain this racist ideology remains to be seen.

Throughout this book, unless otherwise stated, the translations from Afrikaans are my own. It was most difficult to find an adequate English rendering of the Afrikaans term, *volk*. To leave the term untranslated might have implied an association with the tradition of German Volkism. Since the original meaning of the Afrikaans term was closer to Rousseau than to Hitler (although the latter sense became significant in the 1930s,) I have translated *volk* throughout as "People." The capitalization is meant to emphasize the essential importance of the term for Afrikaners without necessarily implying Nazi overtones. The adjective *volks* has been translated as "ethnic."

Since this book was originally conceived as a doctoral dissertation, it implies a short lifetime of intellectual obligations. At Rhodes University, a small group of remarkable teachers, in particular the late Professor James Irving, and an unusual set of fellow students helped make possible for me a liberal education in my illiberal homeland. Then, at Oxford, I was able to read theology under tutors who sympathized with my sociological interests. John Baker's lectures and tutorials on the Old Testament gave me the key to understanding Afrikaner civil religion. I worked closely with Robert Bellah at Harvard: and after he left for Berkeley, he continued to provide friendly advice and encouragement, while Michael Walzer kindly assumed formal supervision of my thesis. My earliest formulations of the proposed research were fruitfully criticized by Professor Leonard Thompson and by Peter Hilldrew. Newell Stultz and Arthur Dyck, who served with Michael Walzer on my dissertation committee, added their worthy share of comment.

My research in South Africa during 1968-1970 was financed by a Foreign Area Fellowship. The University of Massachusetts at Boston also assisted in the writing up, with a grant for the summer of 1970. I rewrote the whole study while I was a visiting member at the Institute for Advanced Study in Princeton during 1972-1973. None of the institutions above, however, may be held responsible for my conclusions, however indebted I feel to them for their generosity. The same holds true for those many Afrikaners who so graciously gave their time to discuss with me their memories of earlier days.

Finally, my wife Meredith alone knows the human cost of this book. She has given of herself unstintingly as companion and critic, postponing her own academic and singing career, willingly coping with innumerable moves while bearing three children and rearing them in places far from home. At the end, she devoted hours midst serious illness to review in closest detail the style and argument of the entire study. Those obscurities of language and logic which have escaped our common critical eye, she maintains, testify to the paltriness of even the best-intentioned human effort. I have no words to express my indebtedness to her.

I

The Afrikaner
Civil Religion
An Ideal Typical Description

In the Afrikaner civil religion,[1] God imbues all history with
ultimate meaning. He rules sovereign over the world and
works His will in the affairs of nations—most visibly of
Afrikanerdom. Dr. D. F. Malan voiced the sentiments of his
People when he said, "Our history is the greatest masterpiece
of the centuries. We hold this nationhood as our due for it
was given us by the Architect of the universe. [His] aim was
the formation of a new nation among the nations of the world.
. . . The last hundred years have witnessed a miracle behind
which must lie a divine plan. Indeed, the history of the
Afrikaner reveals a will and a determination which makes
one feel that Afrikanerdom is not the work of men but the
creation of God" (Pienaar, 1964, pp. 235-236).

Sacred History

In order to acquaint the reader with the major events that
Afrikaners have chosen to regard as revelation, I shall briefly
sketch the sacred saga of Afrikanerdom.[2] For the telling of

[1] The only other work in my acquaintance which deals specifically
with the civil religion as such is an article by F. A. van Jaarsveld
(1963, pp. 1-32). See also Degenaar (1960).

[2] In order to impart as accurately as possible the flavor of the
original sources, I quote verbatim from Afrikaner writings wherever
possible. Although I have used the earliest sources, van Jaarsveld

this story, I rely heavily on the speeches of Paul Kruger (in du Plessis, J. S., n.d.), as well as on a pamphlet issued by the Transvaal government in 1899[3] (Reitz, 1900).

For Afrikaners the century between the British occupation of the Cape in 1806 and the execution of Jopie Fourie in December 1914 was the period of revelation. During that era, God made known His will for the Afrikaner people. Prior to that period events were unimportant except to the extent that they delineated a scant "myth of origin." Thus every Afrikaner knows that Jan van Riebeeck founded the first Dutch settlement in 1652, and that two hundred French Huguenots, fleeing religious persecution in their homeland, followed in 1688. Many Afrikaners believe also that the harsh rule of the Dutch East India Company at the Cape and the hard life on the frontier fostered a spirit of unity and independence within the pioneer settlement. So, according to their creation story, Afrikaners were Calvinists of Western European origin and a nation in their own right before the arrival of the English.[4]

(1963, pp. 46-70) demonstrates clearly that the main outlines of the sacred history have persevered with remarkable consistency.

[3] *'n Eeu van Onreg* ("A Century of Injustice") was written by Jacob de Villiers Roos and Jan Smuts on the eve of the Boer War and issued by Reitz as state secretary on behalf of the government of the South African Republic. It is the first original attempt to write an inspirational version of South African history with an appeal to all Afrikaners. S. J. du Toit, et al. (1895), is earlier but is no more than a translation of earlier sympathetic English histories (especially Cloete, 1856) with very occasional civil-religion editorial comment.

[4] The best brief account of Dutch colonial life before the coming of the British is de Kiewiet (1941). See also for racial attitudes, McCrone (1937, part 1), and, for the development of the frontier, van der Merwe (1938).

Many Afrikaner historians, following the civil faith, find the origins of Afrikaner national self-consciousness to be in the frontier society of the eighteenth century. The most carefully argued statement of this position is that of van Schoor (1963). He equates the objective preconditions for national unity (e.g., a common language, religion, interests, color consciousness), with national consciousness itself. Having shown the existence of the former to his satisfaction, he concludes the latter without citing examples as proof. F. A. van Jaarsveld (1961) marshals the evidence for a much later development of Afrikaner national consciousness. He supports this argu-

The subsequent history of this people, as interpreted by the civil religion, centers on the Great Trek.[5] The latter forms the national epic—formal proof of God's election of the Afrikaner people and His special destiny for them.

Certain events that occurred immediately after the British occupation are selected out as a prologue to the Great Trek.[6] The "liberal" policy of the British toward black Africans seemed particularly designed to provoke the Afrikaners. Under pressure from English missionaries, the government created a circuit court, known as the "Black Circuit" among Afrikaners, which was empowered to hear complaints of Hottentot servants against their masters. "It was not so much love for the native that underlay the apparent negrophilistic policy as hatred and contempt of the Boer" (Reitz, 1900, p. 92). The British even went so far as to employ natives "as police against us; they were provided with arms and ammunition and we deprived of ours to be used against us; they were incited to fight us, and, wherever it was possible, they murdered and plundered us.

"No wonder that in 1815 a number of Boers were driven into rebellion, a rebellion [in which] six of the Boers were half hung up in the most inhuman way in the compulsory presence of their wives and children. Their death was truly horrible, for the gallows broke down before the end came;

---

ment historiographically in van Jaarsveld (1959), where his first footnote is especially important for sources on the Great Trek. The manner in which the Great Trek achieved a central position in Afrikaner sacred history is found in his two pamphlets (van Jaarsveld, 1962 and 1963a).

[5] Walker (1934) remains the most readable and accurate account of the Great Trek. C. F. J. Muller (1961) raises many questions not discussed, but we await Muller's forthcoming history of the Great Trek for answers to these questions. Meanwhile, extracts from the letters of Daniel Lindley (Smith, E. W. 1949) shed light on the trekkers from an independent but sympathetic contemporary source. L. M. Thompson (1969a and 1969b) is a brilliant attempt to set the Great Trek in its wider South African context.

[6] C. F. J. Muller (1948) is the best discussion of the causes of the Great Trek. For conditions on the northern frontier at the time of the coming of the British, see van der Merwe (1937). For the eastern frontier, see Marais (1944). For Cape Dutch reactions to the British occupation, see J. du P. Scholtz (1939) on the language question and Hanekom (1951) on church accommodations.

but they were hoisted up in the agony of dying, and strangled
to death in the murderous tragedy of Slachter's Nek. . . .
[I]t was at Slachter's Nek that the first blood-stained beacon
was erected between Boer and Briton in South Africa" (Reitz,
1900, pp. 5-6). The episode is poignantly recalled in the first
Afrikaans history:

Weep Afrikaners!
—Here lies your flesh and blood!
—martyred in the most brutal fashion.
Wrong it was to rise up against their government:
yet they did it not without reason!
Wrong it was to take up weapons;
only because they were too weak!
They were guilty, says the earthly judge;
but what will the Heavenly Judge have to say?
. . . But come! It grows darker!
—If we sit here too long we too shall be regarded as conspira-
    tors!
—come, another day will dawn,
—then we shall perhaps see the grave in another light!
—come, let us go home with a quiet sigh!
[du Toit, S. J., et al., 1877, cited in van Jaarsveld, 1959, pp.
                                98-99, my translation]

   The anglicization policy instituted under Lord Charles
Somerset, governor at the Cape from 1814 to 1826, struck
at the heart of Afrikanerdom. He brought out Scottish
ministers to serve in Dutch Reformed churches and Englishmen to teach in country schools. All official posts were
reserved for the English-speaking; and after 1825 all official
documents were required to be written in English. "Petitions
in the language of the country and complaints about bitter
grievances were not even acknowledged. The Boers were
excluded from the juries because their knowledge of English
was too faulty, and their causes and actions had to be
determined by Englishmen with whom they had nothing in
common" (Reitz, 1900, p. 10).
   The emancipation of slaves throughout the British empire
in 1832 was not in itself a cause for increased resentment

among the Afrikaners. Rather it was Britain's failure to keep
her promise of full compensation which led to embittered
feelings. "[G]reyheads and widows who had lived in ease and
comfort went down poverty-stricken to the grave, and gradually the hard fact was borne upon us that there was no
such thing as Justice in England" (Reitz, 1900, p. 8).

The Kaffir War of 1834 proved conclusively that "there
was no security for life and property under the flag of a
government which openly elected to uphold wrong" (Reitz,
1900, p. 10). After the Boers had helped drive the Xhosa back
beyond the frontier, the conquered territory was restored by
the colonial secretary to the same native tribe. In addition,
Boer cattle which had been stolen by the Africans and later
recovered were not returned to their rightful owners, but
instead auctioned by the British to defray the costs of the
war.

Bowed down under twenty years of British oppression, the
Afrikaners at length rose up and went out of the Cape Colony
and sought "shelter in the unknown wilderness of the North.
. . . [O]ur people had to pursue their pilgrimage of martyrdom
throughout South Africa, until every portion of that unhappy
country ha[d] been painted red with blood, not so much of
men capable of resistance as with that of our murdered and
defenceless women and children" (Reitz, 1900, pp. 92-93).
They were followed by the British army, like that of Pharoah,
and everywhere were beset by the unbelieving black "Can-
aanites." Yet because God's people acted according to His
will, He delivered them out of the hands of their enemies
and gave them their freedom in the promised land.

As the wagons proceeded northward on this Great Trek,
savage barbarians under Moselikatse fell upon the vanguard
"without rhyme or reason," murdering men, women, and
children. The handful who survived drew themselves up into
a small *laager* on Vegkop ("Battle Hill"), and trusting in
God to defend them, they withstood a second attack of
barbarians in numbers of thousands fifteen days later. "God
stood by the people and they called upon God and beat off
the enemy." But the Matabele escaped with all their cattle,
which left the trekkers immobilized and with very limited

food supplies. Once again His people called upon the Lord and He succored them and sent reinforcements from the main company of trekkers, so that an expedition was mounted "to pursue and punish the enemy and to redeem ther past losses. God blessed them and they defeated the enemy" (du Plessis, J. S., n.d., p. 94).

The eyes of the emigrants then turned east in search of more fertile pasture and an outlet to the sea. They sent a commission under Piet Retief to purchase from the Zulu chief, Dingaan, the land which was later to be known as Natalia. As soon as Retief had paid for the land, however, the Zulus treacherously murdered him and his deputation and set forth to rout the other trekkers, who were spread out in camps in the foothills of the Drakensberg along the Blaauwkrantz and Bushman's River. "The earth swarmed with thousands of enemies. No human help was possible and even tiny children cried to the Lord and the voice of the people came up to God" (du Plessis, J. S., n.d., p. 104). "The grass was matted with the noble blood of women, girls, and tiny babes. The wagons were smashed and burned, the earth white with feathers from the bedding. Infants nursing at their mother's breast were pierced with tens of *assegaais*—so that both bodies were fixed together. Children were seized by the legs and their heads smashed against wagon wheels. Women's breasts were severed, their bodies mutilated and ravished. Vultures circled over the *laager* of yesterday; among the dead and the still-smoldering ashes wild animals prowled around—presently to gorge themselves on human flesh" (Preller, 1909, pp. 152-153).

"Those who survived immediately sent word to their brothers in the Colony and Free State. [Answering their call,] Andries Pretorius arrived with his brave band to unite with them and punish the enemy and subjugate him. There followed the memorable battle of Blood River on December 16, 1838, where the solemn oath was sworn to celebrate that day each year to the glory of the Lord if He would grant them victory. And God gave them victory over thousands of enemies, and therein was God's hand seen again. The people were without hope before the advent of Pretorius; they lifted up their hands and salvation came" (du Plessis, J. S., p. 94).

The Boers then settled down peacefully in Natal and established a republic. "The territory had been purchased with our money and baptized with our blood. But the republic was not permitted to remain long in peace. The Colonial Office was in pursuit" (Reitz, 1900, p. 13). Against strong Afrikaner protest, the British decided upon annexation and military occupation of Natal, so as to "crush the Boers. The Boer women, however, were not so easily to be deprived of their blood-bought freedom. [They] informed the British Commissioner that sooner than subject themselves to British domination, they would walk barefoot over the Drakensberg—to freedom or to death. And they were true to their word. . . ." (Reitz, 1900, p. 15). Together with their men, they endured to found the Republic of the Orange Free State and the Transvaal Republic.[7] There they could be free from British domination and deal with the black Africans as they saw fit. There they dwelt in an earthly paradise where "the hills lie like rams along streams which laugh and chatter. . ." (du Toit, J. D., 1962, 8:285).

But this pastoral bliss was not to be long-lived. In 1877, the British again used the pretext of Afrikaner treatment of black Africans to annex the Transvaal Republic as they had Natal. Although 6,800 of the 8,000 burghers signed a petition protesting the annexation, the British once more turnd a deaf ear. This time the Boers had no other recourse than force, and Paul Kruger emerged as their leader.[8]

The people came together at Paardekraal on December 16, 1880, to renew their covenant with the Lord. "Each one of us, without instructions from the leaders, picked up a stone and threw it upon [a pile]. . . .as a memorial between ourselves and the Lord. Thus was the vow of Blood River renewed. . . . You know the history of 1880 and 1881. . . . There can be no greater miracles and wonders than in the War of

---

[7] Walker (1934) has a good account of the rise and fall of the Natal Republic. See also the excellent summaries of early republican struggles in van Jaarsveld (1951) and L. M. Thompson (1969b).

[8] The most readable and reliable history of the 1870s and 1880s remains de Kiewiet (1937).

Freedom. . . . God's hand was so evident that even blind heathen and unblievers had to acknowledge that it was God's hand. . ." (du Plessis, J. S., p. 95). "Trusting in the Almighty God of righteousness and justice, we armed ourselves for an apparently hopeless struggle. . . . With God's all-powerful aid we gained the victory, and for a time at least it seemed as if our liberty was secure. At Bronkhorst Spruit, at Laing's Nek, at Ingogo, and at Majuba, God gave us victory although in each case the British outnumbered us and were more powerfully armed than ourselves" (Reitz, 1900, p. 32). So the Transvaal republic won back its freedom by armed force and the might of its God.

But even with this triumph, the Afrikaners did not see the end of their persecution. Imperialism returned a few years later armed with gold and allied with the cohorts of capitalism. Gold was discovered on the Rand in 1886, and the curmudgeons of the empire poured into Johannesburg.[9] Cecil Rhodes was the very incarnation of this imperialist capitalism. And it was he who in 1895 inspired the Jameson Raid into the Transvaal. "The world has not yet forgotten how [these imperial capitalist forces] attacked the South African Republic with an armed band in order to assist the Capitalist revolution of Johannesburg in overthrowing the Boer government; how this raid and this revolution were upset by the vigilance of the Boers; how Jameson and his filibusters were handed over to England to stand their trial—although the Boers had the power and the right to shoot them down as robbers; how the whole gang of Johannesburg capitalists pleaded guilty to treason and sedition; how . . . the Government [of the Republic] dealt most leniently with them. . ." (Reitz, 1900, pp. 46-47).

Afrikaners throughout South Africa rallied together with a renewed sense of unity. A Cape Dutch newspaper wrote, "The stab which was intended to paralyze Afrikanerdom once and for all in the Republics has sent an electric thrill direct to the national heart. Afrikanerdom has awakened to a sense of earnestness and consciousness which we have not observed

[9] The best histories of the events leading up to the Boer War are J. S. Marais (1961) and L. M. Thompson (1971).

since the heroic war for Liberty in 1881; . . . now the psychological moment has arrived; now our people have awakened all over South Africa; a new glow illuminates our hearts; let us now lay the foundation stone of a real united South Africa on the soil of a pure and all-comprehensive national sentiment" (Reitz, 1900, pp. 49-50).

The united cry which came up from Afrikaners in the Cape, the Free State, and the Transvaal made British jingos fear for England's supremacy in South Africa. But Sir Alfred Milner, newly appointed governor of the Cape Colony "would know very well how to evolve 'Constitutional means' in order to humiliate the South African Republic and to crush it into the dust" (Reitz, 1900, p. 52). He made unjust and impossible demands and backed them by force. He was as King Ahab to the Boers. "Naboth's title to his vineyard [had to] be cancelled. The easiest way of securing that object . . . was to prove that Naboth was a scoundrel and Ahab an angel" (Reitz, 1900, p. 91).

Negotiation failed in the face of continued British provocation, and the Boers declared war on October 11, 1899. After initial successes at Magersfontein, Stormberg, Colenso, and Spionkop, they were forced to retreat before the overwhelming numbers of British troops. By June 1900, both the Free State and the Transvaal had been declared British territory.[10] President Paul Kruger fled to Europe, but President Martinus Steyn of the Orange Free State remained behind in South Africa to travel about restoring courage and inspiration to the guerilla commandos, who were led by an array of heroic generals. Such were C. R. de Wet, Louis Botha, Koos de la Rey, C. F. Beyers, J. B. M. Hertzog, Jan Christiaan Smuts, and Jan Kemp.

Despite the brave resistance of these latter, however, the British persisted in their efforts to "wipe out the Boers. Women and children who were found on the farms were driven to the so-called concentration camps. . . . [Others who were] fearful of falling into the hands of the British, fled barefoot and lacerated through the veld . . . only to end up [as well]

---

[10] Le May (1965) offers a good brief account of the way in which the events of the Boer War affected Dutch-speaking South Africans.

at the murderous women's camps. Thousands of dwellings were burned down and everything on the farms was destroyed. Cattle were driven away or slaughtered in heaps. . . . Those were days of lamentation and bitterness. The suffering was indescribably great. . . . It was as though the people had been forsaken by God. . . . The moaning and weeping of sick mothers, the crying and pleading of little children dying of hunger in cold tents mounted up to heaven. But in vain" (Smith, J. A., 1917, pp. 133-134).

The sufferings of their families alone caused the Boers to give up the fight and surrender at Vereeniging. Over twenty-six thousand of their women and children had died in concentration camps. War-weary men returned to empty homes and devastated farms. But the peace treaty, despite its promises of compensation, was to prove an empty hope for restoration of their liberties. Lord Milner denied outright both its guarantees of education in Dutch and of economic aid.[11] In addition, the governor adopted a policy of strengthening the English population by importing British officials, teachers, artisans, and even unmarried women (Smith, J. A., 1917, p. 140).

At this time of greatest despair for the Afrikaner people, two of their most illustrious generals—Botha and Smuts—defected to the imperialist cause. When war was declared in Europe in 1914, they brought South Africa in on the side of Great Britain, mounting an attack on German South West Africa. Afrikaners were expected to join ranks with men who had been their bitter foes fifteen years earlier. Old feelings of enmity kindled rebellion under the leadership of Generals de Wet and Beyers and "renewed bloodshed not only between Boer and Briton but also between Boer and Boer,"[12] for Botha called out the Afrikaner citizen force to put down the uprising (Smith, J. A., 1917, p. 145). The rebellious Boers were easily

[11] Milner's administration is best summarized in L. M. Thompson (1960, chapter 1).

[12] The only historical monograph on the rebellion, G. D. Scholtz (1942), is somewhat misleading since it is based only on the evidence of General Beyers rather than including that of Generals de Wet and de la Rey as well. The Cape church reaction is well covered in Booyens (1969).

defeated, and one Jopie Fourie, who remained still faithful
to his People, was martyred before a firing squad on the orders
of General Smuts in spite of a deputation of Afrikaner clergy
to plead for mercy. With the theme of Afrikaner suffering
thus reaffirmed, the sacred period of Afrikaner history comes
to an end.

Civil Theology

The outlines of this sacred history remained essentially
unchanged throughout the period covered by this study.
However, the interpretations imputed to it varied consider-
ably. *A Century of Wrong* (Reitz, 1900), for instance, contained an introduction and conclusion by Jan Smuts which
were clearly informed by liberal doctrine. The interpretation
which I regard as typical, however, was developed by C. J.
Langenhoven after the Anglo-Boer War and became semi-of-
ficial at the end of the thirties. My major source in describing
and analyzing this interpretation are civil-religion speeches
published in the Afrikaans press between 1930 and 1940, and
the *Ossewa Gedenkboek* (1940). The review in *Die Burger*
said of this book on its first appearance: "In all reverence,
I would call it the New Testament of Afrikanerdom. Again
with the greatest reverence I would declare that it deserves
a place on the household altar beside the family Bible. For
if the Bible shaped the Afrikaner People, then the *Gedenkboek*
reveals that product in its deepest being..." (*Die Burger*,
March 30, 1940).

This mainstream civil-theological interpretation of the
sacred history was, of course, based on the past. One would
be mistaken, however, to assume that this theology was a
form of traditionalism, a wistful appeal to the republican past;
nor should it be understood as simply negative theology, a
diatribe against the English oppressors. Such interpretations
fail to take account of the concept of God which the civil
religion inherited from the Old Testament and from Calvin.

The Lord of Afrikanerdom is sovereign and intensely active,
busy at every turning point in the affairs of nations and men.
Like Assyria in the Book of Isaiah, the British empire was
not only the incarnation of evil; it was ultimately the foil

against which God revealed His magnitude and glory to His Afrikaner people. In similar fashion, although the Zulu army symbolized the black African threat to the Afrikaner's racial identity, in theological terms the Zulus became God's agents for uniting His people in holy covenant with Himself. The civil theology is thus rooted in the belief that God has chosen the Afrikaner people for a special destiny.

The most immediate question is how the Afrikaner sustained his belief in God's election through such a tale of woe. For, with the exception of the republican period which forms a pastoral interlude, the sacred history is made up of two cycles of suffering and death—the Great Trek and the Anglo-Boer War. The saga which began with the gallows at Slagtersnek ended with an execution in Pretoria; the flight from the British in the Cape and Natal was duplicated by defeat at the hands of the same enemy in 1902; the suffering and death of women and children at Blaauwkrantz forshadowed the agony of the concentration camps; and the martyrdom of Piet Retief was reflected in Paul Kruger's death in exile and the execution of Jopie Fourie. All seemed lost, for the victories of the heroes of the Trek period were cancelled out by the defeat of the Boer War generals. Indeed, the situation in 1915 appeared worse than that of 1815, for certain of the Boer War leaders seemed to have turned renegade. On the face of it, the whole history might have been interpreted as a fruitless, however heroic, waste of life and liberty.[13]

In the Christian tradition, however, suffering is not always seen as a sign of God's chastisement and rejection. God tests His innocent servants, and righteous suffering may be taken as assurance of God's favor. The Cross is, of course, the prototype of such innocent suffering, and Christians are called to bear their crosses in imitation of Christ. Calvin puts it well: "How much can it do to soften all the bitterness of the cross, that the more we are afflicted with adversities, the more surely our fellowship with Christ is confirmed. . . .[T]o suffer persecution for righteousness' sake is a singular comfort. For it ought to occur to us how much honor God bestows

[13] This appears to have been General Smuts' feeling immediately after the Boer War (Hancock, 1962, p. 120).

upon us in thus furnishing us with the special badge of his soldiery" (*Institutes*, III, 8:1 and 8:7). Oppression by British overlords and harassment by black hordes could thus be understood as an honor to be accepted and glorified for its own sake as the seal of God's election. In 1938, Henning Klopper testified that: "Disasters, adversity, privation, reversals, and suffering are some of the best means in God's hand to form a people.... These are the tests by fire which refine a people and determine its worth" (*Ossewa Gedenkboek*, 1940, p. 11).

However, the logic of Christian theodicy does not rest alone in the notion of suffering for righteousness' sake. The agony of the Cross is followed by the resurrection, with its implicit promise to the Christian of a life to come. Again, Calvin says: "Whenever we consider the resurrection, let Christ's image come before us. In the nature which he took from us he so completed the course of mortal life that now, having obtained immortality, he is the pledge of our coming resurrection" (*Institutes,* III, 25:3). In his *Institutes,* Calvin's chapter on "Bearing the Cross" is quite naturally followed by an eschatological "Meditation on the Future Life."

> The entire company of believers, so long as they dwell on earth, must be "as sheep destined for the slaughter," to be conformed to Christ their Head. . . . . If believers are troubled by the wickedness of men, bear their arrogant insults, are robbed through their greed, or harried by any other sort of inordinate desire on their part, they will without difficulty bear up under such evils. . . . For before them will be that day when the Lord will receive his faithful people into the peace of His Kingdom, "will wipe away every tear from their eyes" [quoting from Revelation 7:17 in *Institutes*, III, 9:6]

An eschatology sustained the Afrikaners, too, in their national suffering. Even as the resurrection followed Christ's passion, so the foundation of the republics resolved the sufferings of the Great Trek. The God who struck His people with such terrible misfortune in the death of Retief and the murders at Blaauwkrantz finally raised them up again in their own free states. The analogy with Christ's suffering and resurrection was explicitly developed by Langenhoven in a

popular epic poem published in 1921, where he spoke of the
trekker martyrs as "first of a new line . . . of an Afrikaner
nation, worthy to bear the crown won upon the Way of the
Cross by our fathers who died [at the hands of the Zulus]."
The via dolorosa of South Africa did not "run dead" on
"Dingaan's Golgotha" but passed over and beyond it into
God's future, which held a republican resurrection (Langenhoven, C. J., 1921, p. 115). Langenhoven, however, wrote in
the knowledge that the republican era had come to an end;
and implicit in his poem is the awareness that the sacred
history had closed with yet another suffering-and-death cycle
that remained unresolved. He thus subtly emphasized the
open-endedness of the Afrikaner civil theology, a theological
tension analogous to the Christian's anticipation of the final
coming of God's kingdom.

The republics, like Christ, had come and were yet to come.
Even as the resurrection was the promised first-fruits of the
final resurrection, so the Orange Free State and the South
African Republic were first-fruits of a republican second
coming. The miraculous republican outcome of the trekker's
sufferings symbolized God's pledge to bring His people together in a new and greater united republic. Klopper confessed
this faith in 1938: "We believe that the Afrikaner will do
it again under the guidance of God. He will arise from the
debris and ashes of his defeats, shake them off, overcome them
and finally become a powerful and victorious People. His sense
of freedom is too strong to be quenched or extinguished. It
burns in his heart and lives on there like the burning bramble
bush, unextinguishable, kept burning by God" (*Ossewa Gedenboek*, 1940, p. 11).

The promised future republic linked the past and the future,
ensuring a dynamic tension of crucial importance to Afrikanerdom in the 1930s and 1940s. Any appeal to the sacred
Afrikaner past was thus implicitly, and sometimes explicitly,
a reminder of the coming glory. This hope transformed the
sufferings of the present by an exalted anticipation which
sanctified them. Thus English-speaking prejudice and discrimination proved God's election and at the same time
ensured the separate existence of the Afrikaner consciousness.

Maintenance of this separation came to be a sacred duty. In the light of God's intention to create another republic, everything which emphasized Afrikaner uniqueness—their language, their Calvinist faith, their customs and conventions, their very dress—took on sacred significance.

Because of the divine election of Afrikanerdom, anything threatening Afrikaner separateness became demonic. The greatest evil remained British imperialism, whose threat began at Slagtersnek and continued throughout the sacred period and into the present. After the discovery of gold in 1886, imperialism became linked in the Afrikaner mind with capitalism. Capitalist interests, especially mining interests, were early epitomized in the gross cartoon figure, "Hoggenheimer," who was English-speaking, imperialist, and clearly Jewish. Beside this popular association between capitalism and Jewishness, British imperial refusal to make racial distinctions linked in Afrikaner minds the English threat with that of the black masses. Fear of the black man was ever-present in Afrikaner consciousness; but events in the sacred history, especially the battles of Vegkop and Blood River, implied that this threat could be met, by force if need be, if only the Afrikaner were master in his own land. The notion of "Englishness" thus evoked for the Afrikaner the three great evils which threatened his separate existence—imperialism, capitalism, and egalitarian liberalism.

Leaders of the civil faith were frequently attacked for anti-English racism. But this charge was countered by the positive assertion of the divine right of each nation to an independent existence. Both British and Afrikaner had an equal right to separate existence. It was essential, they argued, to distinguish between general anglophobia and anti-imperialism—and for that matter, between blatant anti-Semitism and anti-capitalism.

These same spokesmen for the civil religion, however, did not hesitate to depict imperialism by painting English jingos, to incarnate capitalism in the gross Hoggenheimer image. Did they really expect the ordinary Afrikaner to avoid anti-English or anti-Semitic conclusions, especially if his inclinations lay that way? From the standpoint of popular support, where a prejudice already existed leaders could not help but take advantage of it, since on the emotive level they perhaps shared this antipathy. If challenged on the grounds of prejudice, however, leaders could retain a clear conscience by falling back on their subtle intellectual distinctions.[14]

Although the ordinary Afrikaner did not require a fully ramified theological justification for his civil faith, his comprehension was sufficiently coherent on the conceptual and emotive level for him to respond with outrage to such civil-religious symbols as Slagtersnek, Blaauwkrantz or the concentration camps.[15] These symbols evoked multiple associations. One of the most despicable in the civil theology was that of "the Afrikaner in English service" (Thom, 1965, p. 102). Being a renegade, he was most heartily to be despised. On the other hand, he was an ambivalent figure, for he remained an Afrikaner and thus one of the elect. For the civil religion, such an Afrikaner raised difficulties similar to St. Paul's problem of the Jew who rejected Christianity:

> What advantage has the Jew? . . . Much in every way. To begin with, the Jews are entrusted with the oracles of God. What if some were unfaithful? Does their faithlessness nullify the faithfulness of God? By no means. Let God be true enough though every man be false. . . .[Romans 3:1-4][16]

In a similar way the Afrikaner turncoat was of the elect and yet not chosen—much despised and yet never wholly rejected. General Smuts, dubbed by *Die Burger* "Handyman of the Empire," became the prototype of such an Afrikaner. His support of imperialism was all the more bitter to the faithful

[14] Similar sophistry is also useful to modern South African leaders when stating the solution to the racial problem. An apparently enlightened doctrine of guardianship and separate development is easily accepted by the ordinary white South African as justifying continued white domination.

[15] The emotional response to the concentration camps is graphically described by D. J. Opperman: "As one sees stars and lights shiver in the depths of the waters of Table Bay at night, so images of concentration camps still move in a dark corner of this people" (Opperman, 1949, p. 21).

[16] The Revised Standard Version of the Bible is used throughout this book.

because he had fought so well for the Boers during the Anglo-Boer War.

On the other hand, the civil faith reserved a special place of pride for the figure of the Afrikaner woman. If the Afrikaner man was indeed the instrumental agent who worked out God's will in Afrikaner history, the woman provided a deep well of moral fortitude which complemented and even surpassed her husband's more practical exploits. In the struggle against the English oppressor, her strength of courage buoyed up the wavering will of her husband, urging him on to further feats.

> If we take note of all that the woman has meant in our People's history, [said Ds. J. D. Kestell in 1929],[17] then we cannot but recognize that undergirding it all lay a great moral principle. Her influence was consoling and uplifting. The sheer power of the life of our People had its roots in the pure life of the woman. Her influence kept the man from despair. [*Die Burger*, December 17, 1929]

She not only comforted and sustained her husband in times of crisis, it was because of her willingness to accompany her husband into the wilderness that the racial purity of Afrikanerdom had been preserved. It was to the woman that God had entrusted the task of bearing and raising Afrikaner children in the true civil faith. She held the future in trust on behalf of God and her People. Hers was the responsibility for inspiring the younger generation—the hope of Afrikanerdom—with deep love for their language and culture.

The Afrikaner woman in her faith and purity took on certain attributes of the Holy Virgin in Catholicism. She was a symbol of God's grace and intercession in the life of his People. Throughout the bitter Afrikaner struggle for freedom, she provided a haven of gentleness and renewal. The innocence and purity of Afrikaner women and children made the tales of their suffering, at the hands of Zulu and English alike, all the more atrocious. The suffering of these righteous, innocent victims not only enhanced the analogy to the Passion, the patience and enduring faith of the women in

---

[17] Ds. (*Dominee*) is the title of the pastor in a Dutch Reformed church. He may also be referred to as a *predikant* (preacher).

the concentration camps carried a further message for every Afrikaner. According to the Afrikaner eschatology, the coming republic would result from divine, not human action. Thus the role of the faithful Afrikaner during the 1930s demanded patient suffering and watchful waiting in anticipation of the republic which God Himself would call into being. Thus by example the Afrikaner woman taught one of the deepest truths of the civil religion.

Civil Ritual

The abstractions of the civil beliefs became personified for the ordinary Afrikaner in tales of heroes and martyrs and in emotion-laden symbols that graphically portrayed the most important themes. Constant repetition of the civil theological themes and images on innumerable ritual occasions made the emotional logic of the civil faith personal to ordinary men and women. Emile Durkheim observes that "moral remaking" of the individual "cannot be achieved except by the means of reunions, assemblies and meetings where the individuals, being closely united with one another, reaffirm in common their common sentiments. . ." (Durkheim, 1965, p. 465).

Such ritual reunions for Afrikaners were associated with certain holy gathering places—the sacred shrines of the civil religion. South African soil is scattered with monuments commemorating civil-religious themes—such as the Children's Monument and the Language Monument—and events, such as at Paardekraal and Blaauwkrantz and Blood River (van Tonder, 1961). The two most important of these holy places are undoubtedly the Vrouemonument ("National Women's Monument"), near Bloemfontein, and the Voortrekker Monument on a hill outside Pretoria.[18]

The Vrouemonument bears a plaque dedicating it to "the memory of the 26,370 women and children who died in the concentration camps and to the other women and children who perished as a result of the War of 1899-1902." Within a circular enclosure stands a sandstone obelisk. At its foot

[18] A Voortrekker is one who took part in the Great Trek.

is a statue by Anton van Wouw of a bareheaded woman holding a dying child. Another woman in Voortrekker garb stands beside her staring resolutely out across the Free State veld. On either side of this group are two bas-relief panels. On the left panel, under the caption "For freedom, *volk* and fatherland," we see women and children entering a concentration camp, herded together and clutching a few paltry possessions. On the right panel is depicted an emaciated child dying in a camp tent with his mother by his side, while the life of the camp carries on around them. The panel is headed, "If you do not despair, I shall not forsake you." Within the circular enclosure of the monument lie the graves of President Steyn (with his wife), General de Wet, and Ds. Kestell—the ideal Afrikaner statesman, warrior, and churchman, respectively—and the grave of Emily Hobhouse.[19] The monument was unveiled on December 16, 1913, but as yet no particular significance was attributed to the Great Trek. A decade was to pass before Totius (J. D. du Toit), Langenhoven and D. F. Malherbe were to push back the sacred history from its origins in Boer War suffering to the epic of the Great Trek, **and to illustrate the intimate theological connection between** them. The foundation stone of the Voortrekker Monument was not laid until December 1938.[20]

This monument is a vast granite temple visible for miles around. Broad steps lead through a bas-relief oxwagon *laager*

[19] The inclusion of an Englishwoman deserves some comment. Emily Hobhouse was an English liberal, a close friend of General Smuts; she struggled hard for the Boer cause, especially for the cause of Boer women during and after the war (see Hancock, 1962, for more detail). However, it is symptomatic that despite the prominence of her gravesite, no mention of her was made in any reported civil-religion speech during the 1930s and 1940s. Even speakers at the Vrouemonument itself chose to ignore her.

[20] The monument was not officially opened until 1949. However, Afrikaners were well acquainted with its architectural layout after 1938, at which time pictures and diagrams were given prominence in the Afrikaans press. At Helpmekaar High School in Johannesburg a scale model was erected in 1939 to inspire students and visitors until the monument itself was actually completed. After 1938, the hill upon which the foundations of the monument had been laid, Monumentkoppie, was undoubtedly the holiest of holies for Afrikanerdom.

to the main hall. Halfway up, the steps divide to make room
for a huge van Wouw statue of an austere pioneer woman
with her two children; this is flanked by four bas-relief
wildebeest representing the Zulu *impis* of Dingaan. The vast
domed hall at the top is empty save for a marble frieze on
the walls that depicts the events of the Trek, with the
covenant oath figuring prominently. In the center of the
sanctuary is a circular opening like a well reaching down
into the basement. In this lower vault lies a granite cenotaph,
the symbolic grave of Piet Retief and his fellow martyrs,
inscribed with the words: *"Ons vir jou, Suid-Afrika"* ("We
for you, South Africa"). This forms the altar of the civil
religion. Every year at noon on December 16, the sun shines
directly through an aperture in the roof of the monument
and into the depths below to illuminate the word *"Suid-Afrika"* inscribed upon the symbolic altar.

The Vrouemonument and the Voortrekker Monument are
thus holy ground and places of pilgrimage for faithful Afrikaners. But on each December 16, a public holiday, this
holiness pervades even the more mundane areas of the Afrikaner world. In all the large cities and in country towns and
villages, Afrikaners gather in the open to renew their covenant
with Almighty God. Inspired by fiery speeches from churchmen, academics, and politicians, they sing the sacred psalms
(notably Psalms 38, 46, 118, 130 and 146) and civil-religion
hymns (especially *"Die Stem van Suid-Afrika"*, now the
South African national anthem, and the anthems of the
former Boer Republics). Other holy days figure in the civil
religion—such as Kruger Day on October 10; van Riebeeck
Day on April 6; and in the 1930s, Culture Day, which is
now celebrated as Republic Day—but none are quite so
revered as December 16, Geloftedag, the Day of the Covenant.
On that day, sanctified ground extends beyond the great
monuments to every gathering place of Afrikanerdom; and
holy space and sacred time become one when the sun lights
upon the word *"Suid-Afrika."* The spirit of the day and its
meaning for Afrikanerdom is captured here in an editorial:

Ban December 16 from the life of the Afrikaans People, ban
all memories associated with that date . . . and you rob the

People of its national life. The religious sense of the People is the foundation upon which everything rests, but upon that foundation the People has built a spiritual structure, the cornerstone of which is the vow of Sarel Cilliers. It is this spiritual structure which differentiates the Afrikaans People from all others. When the Afrikaner celebrates the Day of the Covenant the peculiar relationship between Creator and People is articulated as on no other day of the year. . . . It teaches [the Afrikaner People] that nothing occurs without a purpose, that his own misfortunes are safe in a Higher Hand, that he can submit to its guidance, and that something good is always born of apparent defeat. . . . [W]ithout the inspiration which stems from [the celebration of Geloftedag] the Afrikaner would truly never have shown the battle-readiness he displays today. . . . The Day of the Covenant is indeed the day of inspiration for the People. It is the day upon which the heart-strings of the People are tuned in harmony with the great Divine Plan here on the southern point of Africa. [*Die Transvaler*, December 15, 1945]

This civil ritual provides the civil faith with positive content. It unites Afrikaners in their sense of unique identity and destiny, inspiring the faithful, converting the skeptical, and ever reminding them of their sacred separation from English and black African.

Certainly by 1938, the ordinary Afrikaner had made the main themes of the civil religion part of his own emotional identity. Most Afrikaners believed that they belonged to an elect People, most believed that at some time in the future, and sooner rather than later, God would give them another republic, but that this would come only through patience and faith. Indeed, for most of them, their identity as Afrikaners was crucial to their personal integration, overriding their loyalty to the wider South African state.

2

The Calvinist Origins
of the Civil Religion

The civil religion that came to fruition in the 1930s was first systematically expounded by Paul Kruger, who was a Voortrekker as well as president of the South African Republic from 1881 to 1900. In a series of speeches at Paardekraal he formulated a civil faith for the Transvaal Republic which was more strictly Calvinist than the pan-South-African civil religion described in the previous chapter.

Kruger's concepts of God and the world manifested strong influence of Reformation thought, especially the theology of John Calvin. Reformation theology grew out of the responses of sensitive men to the decay of medieval ideas and institutions. Of the great reformers, Martin Luther was the first to break completely from the traditional belief in salvation through works. Having denied the sacramental doctrine of reconciliation and penance, he left the individual exposed in all his sin to the wrath and righteousness of God. Justification could then be achieved only through faith in Christ (Erikson, 1958).

Calvin accepted the essentials of Luther's theology but placed greater emphasis on the sovereignty of God. Thus he stated: "Truly God claims, and would have us grant him, omnipotence—not the empty, idle and almost unconscious sort that the Sophists imagine, but a watchful, effective, active sort, engaged in ceaseless activity . . . directed toward individual and particular motions" (*Institutes*, I, 16:3). Indeed, so particular is God's providential rule, "that some mothers have full and abundant breasts, but other's are almost dry, as God wills to fill one more liberally, but another more meagerly" (*Institutes*, I, 16:3).

If God were so deliberately involved in each natural event, then His will must surely be supreme in matters of salvation. Calvin states boldly that "those whom God passes over, he condemns; and this he does for no other reason than that he wills to exclude them from the inheritance which he predestines for his own children" (*Institutes*, III, 23:1). Not that God is unjust, for He is by definition righteous, but His righteousness is simply beyond our ken (*Institutes*, III, 22:5; cf. Miller, 1964, pp. 51-52).

Such an arbitrary notion of God's righteousness does little to allay the believer's anxiety,[1] and Calvin shows that he is aware of this when he hastens to provide both subjective and objective assurances of election. The experience of God's call, he says, is the believer's guarantee of election. "If we desire to know whether God cares for our salvation, let us inquire whether he has entrusted us to Christ whom he has established as the sole savior of all his people" (*Institutes*, III, 24:6). The call which assures salvation is no ordinary call, but one that "bears with it the spirit of regeneration, the guarantee and seal of the inheritance to come with which our hearts are sealed unto the day of the Lord" (*Institutes*, III, 24:8). This spirit of regeneration is effective through Christ in God. So Calvin returns to Luther's Christ-mysticism for subjective assurance of salvation. But who are those who have been called in this way? Only God and the individual really know. Even for the individual himself, uncertainty may reappear. "Anxiety about our future state steals in," says Calvin, "for Christ shows that 'many are called but few are

[1] The great Puritan Calvinist Willian Perkins, "died crying out 'Mercy, Mercy,' which some standers by misinterpreted for despair" (quoted in Hill, 1964, p. 217, n. 5). The emphasis on anxiety in Calvinism was a major theme of Max Weber's analysis, and has been disputed by some scholars (see Little, 1969, p. 23 ff). However, whatever *theological* objections might be leveled against Weber's emphasis on predestination and anxiety, the *psychological* value of his position can hardly be denied.

chosen.' Indeed Paul himself also dissuades us from overas-surance: 'Let him,' he says,'who stands well, take heed lest he fall.' Again: You are grafted into the people of God? 'Be not proud but fear.' For God can cut you off again that he may engraft others" (*Institutes*, III, 24:6). Thus the Calvinist once more runs adrift on the arbitrary sovereignty of Calvin's God.

Although "we have a sufficiently clear and firm testimony that we have been inscribed in the book of life if we are in communion with Christ" (*Institutes*, III, 24:5), such subjective certainty seeks for overt objective indications. "Call and faith are of little account unless perseverance be added" (*Institutes*, III, 24:6). Although good works are never in themselves sufficient means of justification, the sober and orderly Christian life is an important sign of election (Wendel, 1963, pp. 276ff.) Calvin enjoins all believers to foster the virtues of "abstinence, sobriety, frugality, and moderation . . . [and to abominate] excess, pride, ostentation, and vanity . . ." (*Institutes*, III, 10:5).

Calvin has too poor an opinion of human nature to leave the Christian to persevere in isolation. He recommends mem-bership in a disciplined community as a guide and mainstay for the conscience. "Since . . . in our ignorance and sloth (to which I add fickleness of disposition) we need outward helps to beget and increase the faith within us, and advance it to its goal, God has also added these aids [the church, the sacraments, and the civil order] that he may provide for our weakness. . . So powerful is participation in the church that it keeps us in the society of God" (*Institutes*, IV, 1:1 and 1:3). Membership in a Christian community, like perse-verance, is thus necessary but not sufficient for salvation.[2] Sufficiency resides always in the will of a sovereign and, to human reason, arbitrary God.

Calvinism as a belief system thus emphasizes collective individualism. The individual's election is a matter between himself and God, but it remains both theologically and psychologically necessary that he voluntarily join a Christian

[2] Notice that for Calvin the Christian community included civil order.

community in which he is subject to strict disciplinary control.[3]

The Puritans of the seventeenth century expressed this collective individualism in slightly different, rather more contractual terms. The subjective assurance by which the individual, through Christ, was enabled to be convinced of his election—the "special call"—became for them "the covenant of Grace," an agreement between God and the individual by which his salvation was assured (Miller, 1961, chapter 13). The disciplined community of Christians also came to be expressed in terms of a voluntary covenant—the social covenant—by which the believing individual willingly submitted to an earthly authority, always remembering, of course, that both ruler and community were finally subject to God (Miller, 1961, chapter 14). Those in the community who did not believe were simply coerced for the sake of God's honor.

Such a covenant might include the sovereign state, as at Geneva and in New England, or the church within the state, as with the English congregationalists, or an army, such as Cromwell's New Order, or even a nation, as in the case of the Scots Covenanters. However, all such communities were expressly based upon a principle of voluntarism and were dependant on the member's faith. Unconditional inheritance of the covenant on grounds of birth was not known in the seventeenth century, although with their doctrine of the "halfway covenant" the New England Puritans came close to such "tribalism" (Morgan, 1966, chapter 7).

In developing his doctrine of predestination, however, Calvin embraced the Old Testament idea of an ethnic covenant between God and a chosen people. In the election of Israel, "one people is peculiarly chosen, while others are rejected," without any reference to merit (*Institutes*, III, 21:5). Such election, however, was not election to salvation for every member of the nation, for "where God has made a covenant of eternal life and calls any people to himself, a special mode of election is employed for a part of them, so that he does

---

[3] The separation of individualism from collectivism and the ensuing conflict between enthusiasm and discipline in revolutionary England is well developed in Haller (1963).

not with indiscriminate grace elect all; . . .to those with whom God makes a covenant, he does not at once give the spirit of regeneration that would enable them to persevere in the covenant to the very end. Rather, the outward call, without the workings of inner grace, which might have availed to keep them, is intermediate between the rejection of mankind and the election of a meager number of the godly" (*Institutes*, III, 21:7). Thus Calvin insisted on a distinction between the individual's "special call" to salvation and the "intermediate election" of an ethnic group called by God to fulfill His special purposes.

It was in terms of such a notion of "intermediate election" that President Paul Kruger applied the doctrine of the national covenant to the people of the South African Republic. It is clear that Kruger had intimate knowledge of "the working of inner grace," as we may see from a letter written by Andrew Murray in 1862 from the Transvaal: "Mr. Kruger says that when God gave him a new heart, it was as if he wanted to tell everyone about Jesus' love, as if he wanted the birds and trees and everything to help him praise his Saviour . . ." (du Plessis, J., 1919, p. 203). Perhaps because he stood so clearly in an individual "covenant of grace," Kruger was careful to distinguish in his speeches between the personal experience of salvation, solidly based on God's reconciling act in Christ, which he called the "inward call" (*inwendige roeping*), and God's "external calling" (*uitwendige roeping*) of the people of the Transvaal.[4] This latter call was proved by God's intervention in their history, a revelation "which God attests to His whole people in the Old Covenant as well as in our own time" (du Plessis, J. S., n.d., p. 89).

According to Kruger's understanding of the sacred history, God chose His People (*volk*) in the Cape Colony and brought them out into the wilderness. There He chastised them, "so that they would ask all help and strength from Him" for "it was necessary that the vine be pruned down to the stem so that it could bear good fruit." God then covenanted with the chastened People, and "the enemies were defeated and

[4] For Calvin's distinction between special and general calling see *Institutes* (III, 24:8).

the trekkers inhabited the land which God had given them in this rightful manner" (du Plessis, J. S., n.d., p. 103).

The covenant at Blood River was central to Kruger's civil theology, although he seems to have perceived its essential significance only after his participation in its renewal at **Paardekraal in 1880. Kruger then saw the cause of God's wrath—that his People had neglected their contractual** obligations in failing to celebrate Blood River for over thirty years. For this sin, He had visited them with the oppression of British occupation and had delivered them into the hands of the enemy until, with contrite hearts, they congregated at Paardekraal to renew their vow in humility before Him. Only then did He mercifully save them by His miraculous intervention. On the evidence of this experience, Kruger was able to affirm his faith that the People of the Transvaal Republic were, "a People of God in the external calling" or more simply, "God's People" (du Plessis, J. S., n.d., p. 89).

God's election of the People of the Transvaal, Kruger believed, in no way accorded with their merits. He had a twofold purpose in choosing them. First, He wanted to convince the unbelievers who denied His inherence in historical events that He does in fact "act in this way from generation to generation until He shall come on the clouds to judge and all eyes shall see Him, even those who have stood up and rebelled against Him in their natural state." Second, He used historical events to "break the [sinful] nature" of his People, bringing them to Him (du Plessis, J. S., n.d., p. 88). His election was thus His way of revealing Himself to mankind as well as a means of spiritual refinement for those whom He had called. Thus, according to Kruger, to be "chosen of the Lord" was more likely to incur God's judgment than prosperity. Unless his People served him in complete loyalty and obedience, He chastised them. "Just as firm as His promises are from generation to generation, so certain is the punishment also," said Kruger to his People (du Plessis, J. S., n.d., p. 91).

The miraculous outcome of the war of 1881 was more than final proof of God's election of the Transvaal people. It also established beyond doubt that God desired His chosen people to remain politically independent. "God made us free," said Kruge, "so that we may pay our vows and remain" (du Plessis, J. S., p. 99). The independence of the republic became a major tenet of Kruger's civil faith. God had covenanted with them and granted them independence in order that they might serve Him. Should they fail Him, He would chastise them and might even take their independence from them, but He would never utterly forsake them. In terms of the covenant, He would return them their independence once they had truly repented.

Kruger's civil theology thus amounted to a simple cycle of transgression, retribution, and reconciliation, well expressed in his favorite quotation from Psalm 89:

> If they violate my statutes
> and do not keep my commandments;
> Then I will punish their transgression with the rod
> and their iniquity with scourges;
> but I will not remove from him my steadfast love
> or be false to my faithfulness.
> I will not violate my covenant,
> or alter the word that went forth from my lips.
>
> [Psalm 89:31-34]

Certain questions spring immediately to mind. Of whom was Kruger speaking when he used the word "People"? Were the indigenous black inhabitants of the republic also among the People of God? And were English-speaking citizens of the Transvaal included or not?

The native Africans were certainly *not* among the "elect." The most definitive experiences and powerful traditions of the Boer people labeled them as "nations without the law" (van Jaarsveld, 1963, p. 7). The Transvaal civil religion grew out of the experiences of the war of 1881. Before that the different religious and political groups in the Transvaal were joined only by a fierce sense of racial superiority over the indigenous peoples. Such racial attitudes had come into being before the Great Trek and were in fact one of the major reasons for that migration.[5] The racial beliefs of people on

[5] For the origins of Afrikaner racial attitudes, McCrone (1937) remains the standard work. G. D. Scholtz (1969, pp. 215-219) shows

the eastern frontier prior to the Great Trek are epitomized by a magistrate's report from Uitenhage in 1805:

> It is difficult and often impossible to get the colonists to understand that the Hottentots ought to be protected by the laws no less than themselves, and that the judge may make no distinction between them and the Hottentots. According to the unfortunate notion prevalent here, a heathen is not actually human, but at the same time he cannot really be classed among the animals. He is therefore a sort of creature not known elsewhere. His word can in no wise be believed, and only by violent measures can he be brought to do good and shun evil. [Marais, 1944, p. 73, n. 61]

Such beliefs made no mention of racial separation but argued rather that the African peoples ought to be kept in perpetual subjugation, serving their white (Christian!) masters.[6]

The sons of Ham, argued the frontier farmers, were destined from earliest times to be hewers of wood and drawers of water. On the frontier, the desire for black African servants and for Bantu cattle, tended to override the discretion of the leaders, who usually preached a policy of justice and separation. Kruger himself appears to have abstained from many of the excesses of his countrymen. He insisted upon equality before the law, at least in theory (Smit, 1951, p. 55); and he was convinced that missionary evangelism was both necessary and desirable, going so far as to argue that christianized Africans might own land in white areas (Smit, 1951, pp. 58-59). In practice, however, he acceded to the popular view that no black man, heathen or Christian, could ever be a member of the Transvaal People.

---

that Winthrop Jordan is correct when he says, "So far as their response to Negroes is concerned, the cultural background of Dutchmen was not very different from Englishmen. They shared a similar commercial orientation and large portions of religious and intellectual heritage" (Jordan, 1969, p. 84). Jordan's excellent description of English impressions in the first chapter of his book is very relevant for understanding the Afrikaner's European background. For a most suggestive account of the European's reaction to "blackness" see van der Post, *The Dark Eye in Africa* (1955).

[6] It is ironical that both the opposition to Maynier on the eastern frontier and also the speedy collapse of the first Boer republic in Natal stemmed at least in part from a refusal on the part of ordinary Afrikaners to abide by the policy of apartheid.

Radical egalitarian liberalism was early combined with biblical example to further justify this Boer racism.[7] In a petition submitted to Landrost Honoratus Maynier in 1795, a group of frontier farmers complained that he, Maynier, had not adequately protected their property from black African thieves and furthermore that he had treated Hottentots as equal to white men. His intention, they argued, in a reference to the Dutch War of Independence, was "to place the Spanish yoke upon the People again." The petition closed with an avowal never again to obey illegitimate laws and to restore proper laws by means of "a general voice of the People" (Scholtz, G. D., 1969, pp. 314-315). Such distortion of revolutionary liberalism was possible only because of a prior assumption that membership in "the People" was restricted to persons with white skins. Radical egalitarian democracy was thus used to justify racial oppression in the name of the "sovereign will" of the majority of white individuals.

The notion of the voice of the People, in this narrow racial sense, eventually led to a system of government in the Transvaal Republic which, for white men, was liberal in the extreme. Thus, when Paul Kruger adhered tenaciously to radical democracy, he was following the tradition of his forebears. Ironically, the conservatives in the South African Republic were those who adhered most rigorously to the liberalism of the French Revolution. "The voice of the People," said Kruger, "is the voice of God." Even as the word of God received on Mount Sinai was normative for the children of Israel, so white public opinion in the republic was normative for these new children of the Lord (Smit, 1951, p. 15). The right of appeal from the legislature to the courts, so traditional to constitutional liberalism, was inimical to Kruger because it was in the legislature, the People's Council (*Volksraad*) itself, that the voice of God was to be heard. However, public opinion was sovereign even over the

[7] The route by which Rousseau's ideas reached the South African backveld is still the subject of much scholarly controversy (see Marais, 1944, chapter 7; and van Wijk, 1963). For alternative views see Wypkema (1939), who argues for the influence of the brief rule of the Batavian Republic at the Cape (1803-1806), and Beyers (1929) who believes that the influence was earlier.

People's Council, for the right of the public to review all legislation was written into the constitution. Most of the legislative action, in any event, resulted from petition by members of the public to the People's Council.[8] Within its racial limits, perhaps no other political system has so perfectly expressed Rousseau's notion of the "general will."[9]

Until the War of 1881, this combination of radical liberalism and racial discrimination met with no real theoretical challenge. Before 1877, Englishmen were included in "the People"; for example, English-speaking diggers in the alluvial mines at Lydenburg were given two seats on the People's Council (Engelbrecht, 1946, pp. 170-172). Furthermore, even after the influx of foreigners that accompanied the discovery of gold in 1886, Kruger showed that, in theory at least, he thought of "the People" as including all the white inhabitants of the republic. True to his Calvinist heritage, Kruger maintained in his speeches at Paardekraal celebrations that the "external calling" of the Transvaalers applied to all: "the old inhabitants of the land, foreigners, new immigrants, yea even murderers and thieves" (du Plessis, J. S., n.d., p. 89). Thus even sinners and English-speakers were included in the range of Kruger's civil religion.[10]

In practice, however, this inclusive notion of election came into conflict with Kruger's conviction that God had clearly shown in the 1881 war that He wished the republic to retain its independence. When under pressure, Kruger clearly stated

[8] Kleynhans (1966) deals specifically with the importance of petitions. Furthermore, this is the best discussion available of the government of the South African Republic.

[9] The Orange Free State had a far more rigid constitution. However, the influence of the Transvaal's radical ideas was not lacking there either—witness the attempts by President Steyn to alter the constitution in order to allow rule by plebiscite on important issues (see van Schoor and van Rooyen, 1960, pp. 139-140).

[10] Eternal salvation was another matter, of course. Any individual was excluded from that unless he was converted and had entered into communion with God through Christ, regardless of his status under the intermediate covenant. In his civil-religion speeches, Kruger could not forbear from making a personal appeal as well to those very sinners who were within the intermediate covenant, that they should turn to God through Christ for the sake of their eternal souls (du Plessis, J. S., n.d., p. 91).

that he placed independence before the rights of any individual or ethnic group. In his inaugural address of 1898, he said, "I shall particularly ensure that the independence of the land is not in the least endangered; not the least right which might undermine the independence of the land shall be given over, for I shall draw a judgment upon me if I hand over the independence. Indeed, God led us visibly so that the blindest heathen and the unbelieving creature must acknowledge that it was God's hand which gave us the independence" (du Plessis, J. S., p. 56; cf. Smit, 1951, pp. 68-69).

Thus "the People," who in theory included all the white inhabitants of the land, began to be limited in practice to "the old inhabitants of the land." Kruger's awareness that he had compromised on this issue goes far to explain his gradual loosening of voting restrictions and his eventual willingness to meet some of the most important of the British demands (Smit, 1951, pp. 76-82). In any case there was no ethnic pro-Afrikaner tendency in his restrictions on the vote, for they had applied to Cape Afrikaners as well as to English immigrants. Kruger's establishment of a Second People's Council[11] is further evidence that he preferred to give as much representation as possible to the immigrants—as long as the precious independence was not threatened, for to sacrifice that would have been to place himself and his People full in the path of God's wrath.

At the beginning of the Anglo-Boer War, Kruger believed that the republics were engaged in battle for the divinely appointed independence of the country; and he was sure that God would once again grant victory to His people. So certain was Kruger of the righteousness of the Boer cause that in a telegram to General Piet Joubert he stated that although the British might have thousands in the field to the hundreds of the Boers, "we have a supreme commander of heaven and earth, Jesus Christ" (Krüger, 1963, p. 244). He saw the British onslaught on the republics as an attack of the devil against the church of the Lord, "but God would

---

[11] This Second People's Council had rights curiously similar to those now enjoyed by the black African governments of the Bantustans. In other words, it was a local authority for a status group.

not allow His church to be destroyed" (Krüger, 1963, p. 248). As the battle turned against the Boer arms, Kruger's cables took on an apocalyptic note: "God will drive them [the Boer army] into the dust and thereafter will rescue them with miracles. They live at a time when power is given to the beast to persecute the church of Christ" (Krüger, 1961, p. 251). It thus seems that in the heat of the republican Armageddon, Kruger's careful distinction between the "internal calling" and the "external calling" began to dissolve.

It is well-nigh impossible to estimate the extent to which the ordinary Transvaaler understood and accepted Kruger's civil theology. It is true that during his presidency great crowds gathered to hear him speak at the official Paardekraal celebrations. The symbolic events of the sacred history were at least sufficiently well-known at the time of the Jameson Raid for English-speakers on the Rand to fear a rumor that the Transvaal government intended to import the historic Slagtersnek gallows to hang those who had actively supported the raid (Coetzee, A., 1937, p. 103).

During the Boer War, local commandos celebrated December 16 in the field. In 1900 at Nooitgedacht, "for the first time in many years, public confession was made of the People's sin; . . . about 2,000 persons recognized and acknowledged that the Boer People had been unfaithful to the true Covenant—they had not celebrated the Day in proper fashion during the years of peace" (Swart, 1961, pp. 37-38). Such public avowals of guilt were quite rare, however, since as we shall see, the majority of the Boers never doubted the righteousness of their cause.

The best indication of the extent to which the civil religion permeated the "collective consciousness" of those who fought until the bitter end remains the minutes of the debates at Vereniging (Kestell and van der Velden, 1912). From May 15 to May 17, 1902, elected representatives of the Boer commandos in the field met together to debate whether they should surrender.[12] Civil-religion themes permeated the arguments of many of these men. The strongest argument of those who wished to continue the struggle was that they were God's

[12] The negotiations are well discussed in Le May (1965).

elect and He would not go back on His covenant. "The war is a matter of faith," said General de Wet, ". . .Let us again renew our covenant with God. If we fix our eyes on the past . . . we have ground to continue in faith. The entire war has been a miracle, and without faith it would have been childish to commence the war" (Kestell and van der Velden, 1912, p. 91). Later he stressed the historical grounds of his faith: "What tangible grounds had we when we began? .. . It is still all Faith, and we know that a small people can by faith triumph over the most powerful enemy. . . . In the first war the South African Republic stood alone against the powerful England without any assistance. There were wavering ones then also—the so-called loyalists. It was then also a struggle in Faith only, and what was the result? They fought in Faith only and won. Is our Faith, then, going to be so much weaker than that of our forefathers? It is asked, "What about our families?" Certainly we must care for them, but only as far, and as well, as we can. More we cannot do." (Kestell and van der Velden, 1912, p. 166).

Almost to a man the Free Staters sided with de Wet. "What were our prospects when we started the war?" they asked in chorus, until this became virtually a litany for the civil faith. "Were there grouds then?" continued Cronje of Winburg "It was indeed believed that might was right, and trust was put in God. And God helped us. If we want grounds we must look back. . . I have always said that we must put our trust in God" (Kestell and van der Velden, 1912, p. 152). "We commenced the war with prayer and faith in God," argued Froneman of Ladybrand, "we have suffered but it was the Lord who allowed this war to come over us. We prayed that the war might be warded off, but God disposed otherwise. . . . If we accept these proposals our name as "Republicans' is lost forever and always" (Kestall and van der Velden, 1912, p. 154).

A few Transvaalers stood with their Free State brethren. "If once they were vanquished," argued General Kemp, "it was all over for the Afrikaner people, and all chance of a revival would be gone forever. Why should they not continue to place their trust in God? They had no right to distrust a God who had helped them hitherto" (Kestell and van der Veden, 1912, p. 70).

Most of those who favored surrender urged the importance of reason as opposed to faith. The deaths in the concentration camps, the devastation of the countryside, and the danger of an armed black uprising were weighty arguments indeed. Smut's final speech at Vereniging summarized the position of those who were for surrender: "We commenced the struggle, and continued it to this moment, because we wished to maintain our independence, and were prepared to sacrifice everything for it. But we may not sacrifice the Afrikaner people for that independence" (Hancock, 1962, p. 162). Viljoen stated the disagreement bluntly: "Those who are for peace have given facts and grounds for their opinion. The others speak only of faith" (Kestell and van der Velden, 1912, p. 155).

Some who favored surrender, however, attempted to meet the civil-religious faithful on their own ground. Schalk Burger, for instance, suggested that the defeat of the Boers was a result of their own sin.[13] "We were proud and despised the enemy and is it not perhaps God's will to humble us and cast down the pride in us by allowing us to be oppressed by the English people? The time will come when we shall again exist as a people" (Kestell and van der Velden, 1912, p. 77). Froneman of Ladybrand expressed shock at such arguments, ". . . our deliverance is from the Lord. It grieves me to observe a doubt among some of us whether God is indeed with us. . . . What has maintained us to this moment? It is the faith of those who in privacy prayed to God to ward off the war, and who, when they saw that it was not God's will . . . trusted in Him and fought bravely" (Kestell and van der Velden, 1912, p. 79).

Yet few even of those who were for surrender doubted the righteousness of the Boer cause. Most of them spoke simply of resignation to the will of God without attempting any

---

[13] Uys of Pretoria raised the same argument earlier (Kestell and van der Velden, 1912, p. 71). Notice the probable influence of the Nooitgedacht celebration of Covenant Day on the Transvaal delegates.

justification. "You speak of faith," said General de la Rey, "What is faith? Faith is: 'Lord, *thy* will be done—not *my* will to be the victor. I must kill my will, and I must act and think as He directs and leads me. That is what I understand by the faith in which God's children must live . . ." (Kestell and van der Velden, 1912, p. 158). General Botha was so extreme as to question the belief that God intended the continuance of republican independence, thus cutting at the very roots of Kruger's civil faith. "If the Lord God wills it," he said, "then, however bitter, we must come to terms, we cannot simply go blindly on and say that we trust in God. Miracles can happen, but it is not for me or you to say what God's will is with us, or that the Lord will allow us to retain our independence" (Kestell and van der Velden, 1912, p. 84).

Outright skepticism about the very possibility of a civil religion was expressed by only one of the delegates, General Hertzog:[14] "It grieves me that in every public meeting the question of religion is touched upon. It is continuously said that this or that is God's finger. Now, although I also have my beliefs, I say that neither you nor I know in the least what is the finger of God! God has given us a reason and a conscience, and if these lead us we need not follow anything else . . ." (Kestell and van der Velden, 1912, p. 175).

Defeat, of course, did not necessarily imply the denial of the whole civil religion. Kruger had already refined his civil theology to accommodate the theme of righteous suffering. As early as 1900, he was thinking of his People in terms of Christ's passion: "I believe that we must first undergo our Gethsemane and Golgotha before the day break of our liberation" (Krüger, 1963, p. 254). In exile after the war, he linked the idea of righteous suffering with the hope of a republican restoration based upon the prophecy of Joel.[15] In reply to a deeply despondent letter from General Smuts, he urged that the younger man read the book of Joel and continued,

[14] This is highly significant with regard to Hertzog's lifelong skepticism about civil religion, which eventually alienated some of his more ardent followers.

[15] Joel is the most apocalyptic of the prophets, emphasizing the Day of YHWH as a day of gloom, followed by a glorious restoration of Israel in which all nations bow down before her.

"God chastises heavily, but it is not punishment. It is only to purify the People. . . The Lord knows the time which He has set and at that time He shall come to lead and comfort His people" (Krüger, 1963, pp. 293-294). But although he clearly anticipated the return of the republics at the hand of God on some apocalyptic day set by Him, Kruger continued to limit his conception of the "People" to the white inhabitants of the conquered republics. This narrow notion of republican restoration that excluded the Cape Afrikaners did not die with the old President,[16] but was central to a conspiracy inspired by leaders such as General de Wet and de la Rey.[17]

When the First World War broke out in 1914, Botha and Smuts brought South Africa in on the side of Britain and prepared to campaign in German South West Africa. General de Wet called out his fellow conspirators to overthrow the Pretoria government in the name of the old republican independence.[18] They planned to cross into South West Africa

[16] At a Standerton Geloftedag celebration in 1910, for instance, General Brits expressed a crude ethnic version of the Transvaal civil religion, expressly excluding Cape Afrikaners:

He earnestly appealed to parents to prevent their children marrying any of the English race [People?]. They must not let the Colony [i.e., the Transvaal] become a bastard race, the same as Cape Colony. "If God had wanted us to be one race, he would not have made a distinction between English and Dutch." He further exhorted his hearers not to forget the fact that it was the English who had murdered 22,000 of their women and children during the late war. [*The Star*, December 17, 1910]

[17] General Kemp claimed that Smuts and Botha were originally in the plot too. For a discussion of the historians' controversy see the unpublished University of Cape Town honors thesis of Jan Kirstein. Personally, I see no reason to question Kemp's testimony on this point as long as we restrict the collusion of Botha and Smuts to the period before the victory of the Liberal party in England.

[18] General Beyers is traditionally included in the list of rebel leaders. However, G. D. Scholtz (1941) shows clearly that he did not see the rebellion as more than an "armed protest" in the style of the old Transvaal Republic. In a sense he was submitting an "armed petition" to Botha and Smuts, who were expected to attend to this "voice from the People." Beyers was forced to fight both because of the more violent attitude of de Wet and Colonel Saloman Maritz, and because of the steps taken by Botha and Smuts to curb the rebellion.

where, in the words of de Wet, "we are determined to arm ourselves to the teeth. From there the intention is to go directly to Pretoria, to raise our flag and declare independence" (van Schoor et al., 1964, p. 106). This step of rebellion was promptly quashed by Botha's Afrikaans-speaking commandos.

Although no further steps were ever taken to restore the independence of the two republics by force, republican supporters saw hope in Woodrow Wilson's promise that ethnic minorities would be given national self-determination. Somewhat reluctantly, General Hertzog led an unsuccessful delegation to the Paris peace talks in 1919,[19] which spelled the end of the old Kruger-styled republicanism of the north. Henceforth the civil religion would make a pan-Afrikaner appeal, so that when republicanism surfaced once more in the late 1920s and early 1930s, it became the rallying cry for nationalist Afrikaners throughout all of South Africa.

[19] For a most interesting and independent view of the delegation, see J. P. Verloren van Themaat, "Generaal Hertzog as juris en sy rol in ons staatsregtelike ontwikkeling" in *Hertzog Gedenboek* (1965, pp. 142-143).

3

The Afrikaans Language Movement and the Growth of Afrikaner Nationalism

Before the Boer War, Kruger's intense and narrow Transvaal republicanism had undercut early attempts to emphasize pan-Afrikaner unity. Nor would the loyalty which many Cape Afrikaners bore for the British empire countenance the extension of northern republicanism throughout all of South Africa.[1] Thus, if Afrikaners were to join forces and exercise majority rule in the new Union after 1910,[2] some theme other than republicanism would have to be exploited. What proved to be perhaps the major unifying factor was the Afrikaans language itself.

Dutch was the official language of the republics, and from 1882 it was permitted in the Cape parliament. However, in the republics as well as in the Cape colony, English threatened to replace Dutch as the language of commerce and higher education—indeed, of most cultured discourse. Even the Dutch Reformed church began to arrange English services. Hoogenhout's pre-Boer War doggerel verse, "Progress," puts it well:

[1] The best treatment of the pan-Afrikaner movement, which was based in the Cape, is Davenport (1965); cf. also J. A. Coetzee, (1941).

[2] Since the ratio of Afrikaans-speaking whites to English-speaking whites was about three to two, a united mobilization of Afrikaners would assure their supremacy.

English! English! All is English! English all you see and hear;
In our schools and in our churches, Mother Tongue is [foully]
    murdered.
Bastard is our People now; in this the clergy do comply;
Dutch in schools is a deception—nothing more than Dutch
    in name.
Those who refuse anglicization are derided and disdained:
Even in Transvaal and Free State, everywhere the self-same
    pain.
"It is *progress*," cry the loudmouths, "*Civilization* on the
    march!"
Out-of-date and very stupid are all of those who don't agree.[3]

[Opperman, 1967, p. 8; my translation]

General Hertzog, the great leader in the political struggle
for recognition of the Dutch language, himself corresponded
with his fiancée in English while he was a student (van den
Heever, 1944, pp. 36-37). At Stellenbosch, the major center
for higher education of Afrikaners, "the language used by
the students in debates, student journalism, and private
letters was generally English.... [Dr. D. F.] Malan[4] too used
English predominantly when writing, except in letters to his
parents" (Booyens, 1969, p. 47; cf. van Oostrum, 1936).

This use of English by educated Afrikaners could be explained in large part by the unrefined character of their home
language, which was not Dutch but the simplified Cape *patois*
which was to become Afrikaans. Before the Boer War, and
indeed for some time afterward, Afrikaans was regarded as
inappropriate for educated discourse, which meant that in
writing and public speaking the cultured Afrikaner had to
choose between two foreign languages, English or Dutch.

---

[3] *Engels! Engels! Alles Engels! Engels wat jy sien en hoor:*
In ons skole, in ons kerke word ons moedertaal vermoor.
Ag, hoe word ons volk verbaster; daartoe werk ons leraars saam:
Hollands nog in sekere skole—is bedrog, 'n blote naam!
Wie hom nie laat anglisere, word geskolde en gesmaad;
Tot in Vrystaat en Transvaal al, oweral dieselfde kwaad.
"Dis vooruitgang!" roep die skreeuers, "Dis beskawing wat nou kom!
Dié wat dit nie wil gelowe dié is ouderwets en dom.
[4] When in the text reference is made to Malan or Dr. Malan
it is this Dr. D. F. Malan who is meant.

Since English was spoken everywhere, whereas Dutch was heard regularly only in church and the classroom, he tended to use the former. Because Dutch remained a formal language for Afrikaners, their own particular dialect could be the only alternative to wholesale adoption of English.

For many years after the British occupation in 1806, Cape Afrikaners accepted the dominance of English. They tended to use English in town but simply to ignore it in the country-side (cf. Scholtz, 1939). This basic tolerance of English[5] was prejudiced by two events in particular, the Jameson Raid and the Boer War. The change in attitude is typified in a statement made by one of a large Swellendam family: "Before the [Boer] War our home language was English and we went to the Anglican church. The children born before the war were named Sydney, Lancelot, Henry, Gordon, May, Ethel-win, Gladys, Ursula, Kathleen: the post-war group, Wilhel-mina, Daniël, Aletta, Frederick" (Tomlinson, 1956, p. 4).

The Boer War renewed and strengthened ties of kinship between Cape Afrikaners and their brethren in the north. The suffering of those at the Cape was slight, however, compared to that of the republicans, whose defeat was ren-dered more bitter by the devastation left from the British anti-guerilla ravages. Yet out of this abysm of grief and anguish was born an Afrikaans lyric poetry of genuine literary merit (cf. Antonissen. 1965, chapter 8). Boer suffering and heroism was sung by a new breed of poets: Eugene Marais, Jan Celliers, Totius, and Louis Leipoldt. "The task of these writers was the spiritual transfiguration of the war," said van Wyk Louw, "so that it would become meaningful and not remain a brute material happening for us . . . so that [we] could again become men, with human values and evaluations" (van Wyk Louw, 1959, p. 10)[6]. Through the music of their own tongue, Afrikaner poets created beauty in the midst of suffering, and their poetry's cathartic renewal helped restore dignity and purpose to their people.

[5] It is not necessary for my purposes to detail the activities of the "Patriot" group, despite their intrinsic interest (cf. Nienaber and Nienaber, chapter 4).

[6] For an illuminating discussion of the role of understanding in handling suffering see Levi-Strauss (1963, chapter 10).

Jan Celliers was to become the poet laureate of the Afrikaner civil faith. He wrote of Jopie Fourie and President Steyn, Paul Kruger and General de Wet, concentration camps, ox wagons, constancy, struggle, freedom, and service to Afrikanerdom. In his first collection, *Die Vlakte* (published in 1908 by Volkstem Press, Pretoria), he drew upon his wartime experience to "catch up the pain of his People—the death-sigh of the women and children of his People. In his poems we hear enthusiasm for freedom: grief for those who have passed away; belief in purification and expiation, which sees flowers growing upon the graves of children who gave their tender lives for their country" (Pienaar, 1926, p. 233).

> Gold,
> blue,
> veld,
> sky;
> and one bird wheeling lonely, high-
> that's all.
>
> An exile come back
> from over the sea;
> a grave in the grass,
> a tear breaking free;
> that's all.[7]

[Grove and Harvey, 1962, p. 13; translation by Guy Butler]

Such poetry by objectifying the pain of suffering individuals made it more bearable. It also enabled those Afrikaners who had not been directly affected to partake in the national grief. By articulating and universalizing the Afrikaner fate, this

----

[7] *Dis die blond,*
dis die blou:
dis die veld,
dis die lug:
en 'n voël draai bowe in eensame vlug -
dis al.
Dis 'n balling gekom
oor die oseaan,
dis 'n graf in die gras,
dis 'n vallende traan -
dis al.

new Afrikaans literature helped to formulate a clear consciousness of national identity.

Totius' poem, "Forgive and Forget," was not only his most nationalistic but also his best known. It concludes his cycle of war poems, *By die Monument*[8], first published in 1908, and effectively summarizes the spirit of the whole.[9] Afrikaans-speaking children still learn and recite the poem in school:

"That you not forget the things which your eyes have seen"
(Deut. 4:9)

> A green and growing thorn-tree
> stood right against the track
> where long spans of oxen
> passed to the north and back.
>
> But one day as it grew there
> a wagon rode it down,
> the big wheels cut a pathway
> across the bright green crown.
>
> The wagon rolling onward
> was gone behind the hill;
> slowly the thorn came upright,
> slowly by its own will.
>
> Its loveliness was shattered,
> its young bark broken through;
> one place the sapling body
> was nearly cut in two.
>
> But slowly, surely upright
> the stricken tree has come,
> and healed its wounds by dropping
> the balm of its own gum.
>
> In course of time the hurt-marks
> fade where the wheels had lunged -

---

[8] This is true despite its omission from the first edition of the collection published in 1908. When it appeared in the second edition, its theme might have referred as well to Botha's conciliation policy.

[9] Pienaar referred to this poem cycle as "a wreath upon the graves of women and children" (Pienaar, 1926, p. 302).

only one place endures
that cannot be expunged.

The wounds grew healed and healthy,
with years that come and go,
but that one scar grew greater
and does not cease to grow.[10]

[Cope and Krige, 1968, p. 194; translation by Anthony Delius]

Totius achieves a distance from his subject quite absent from Celliers' more evocative verse. For Totius was a strict Calvinist—in fact a theologian, who saw the history of his People's suffering and their national recovery *sub specie aeternitas*. We live in a world of grief, he says, subject to God's sovereign will. Ever since the fall of man, the poet's only recourse is "to forge art out of suffering" (*"om die kunst te baren uit wee"*) (Cloete, T. T., 1963, p. 16, n. 3; cf. Genesis 3:16). In the poem, "The Thorn Trees at the Spring," Totius' symbolic thorn tree draws its strength from the eternal waters beneath the earth (Cloete, T. T., 1963, p. 205; but cf. pp. 77-78). Totius thus implies both the resignation and the hope in God's purpose, which echoes throughout the civil faith.

Eugene Marais' "Winternag," the first of the new poetry to be published (in 1904 in the journal *Land en Volk*), established without question the literary potential of the Afrikaner dialect. This poem was clearly but a fragment of something intended to be a much longer piece; here we have

[10] *Daar het 'n doringboompie vlak by die pad gestaan, waar lange ossespanne met sware vragte gaan.*

En eendag kom daarlanges 'n ossewa verby, wat met sy sware wiele dwars-oor die boompie ry.

Die ossewa verdwyn weer agter 'n heuweltop, en langsaam buig die boompie sy stammetjie weer op.

Sy skoonheid was geskonde sy bassies was geskeur;

op een plek was die stammetjie so amper middeldeur.

Maar tog het daardie boompie weer stadig reggekom, want oor sy wonde druppel die salf van eie gom.

Ook het die loop van jare die wonde weggewis - net een plek bly 'n teken wat onuitwisbaar is.

Die wonde word gesond weer as jare kom en gaan maar daardie merk word groter en groei maar aldeur aan.

[Opperman, 1967, pp. 44-45]

only the first lines of the meditations of a Boer War sentinel
on watch:

> O cold is the thin wind
>> and sere.
> And bright in the twilight
>> and bare,
> as wide as the mercy of God,
> lies the veld in starlight and shadow.
>> And high on the ridges
>> scattered in scorched earth,
> the grass ears are nodding
>> like beckoning hands.
> The tune of the east wind,
>> melancholy measure,
> sings the song of a maiden
> forlorn of her lover.
> In the fold of each grass
> shines a droplet of dew,
> and quickly it whitens
> to frost in the cold![11]

[Opperman, 1967, p. 25; my translation]

The work of Marais and Celliers, Totius and Leipoldt
proved that Afrikaans could be a language of true artistic
worth and beauty.[12] For many Afrikaners this poetry must
have come as startling illumination, awakening a realization

---

[11] *O koud is die windjie*
en skraal.
En blink in die dof-lig
en kaal,
so wyd as die Heer se genade,
lê die veld in sterlig en skade.
En hoog in die rande,
versprei in die brande,
is die grassaad aan roere

soos winkende hande.
O treurig die wysie
op die ooswind se maat,
soos die lied van 'n meisie
in haar liefde verlaat.
In elk' grashalm se vou
blink 'n druppel van dou,
en vinnig verbleek dit
tot ryp in die kou!

[12] I have not dealt in detail with Louis Leipoldt because, although
the human warmth of *Oom Gert vertel* (1911) superbly recreates
the humor and sentiment of the Boer in defeat, Leipoldt's very
humanity carried him beyond the severe austerities of the civil
religion. Thus, while he was perhaps the best of the early Afrikaner
poets, Leipoldt had least impact on the Afrikaans movement and
the civil faith.

of the lyricism and essential linguistic validity of the *patois* of home and hearth. Pienaar soon brought out a critical text of this poetry, to which he attached an unequivocally nationalist interpretation; and this book was thenceforth regularly prescribed in schools and universities. The general tone of Pienaar's work is well captured in the following extract from his discussion of Jan Celliers:

> Jan Celliers, as he already appears in his earliest collection, is a fine example of the Christian-patriot; a man of the deed, as he unwittingly portrays himself in *Trou* ["Loyal"], in vigorous powerful strokes as though chiselled in granite. If there is ever a poem which will become a classic in Afrikaans literature, then it is *Trou*; because there is no other poem from which equal inspiration flows, none in which the pulse-beat of the Afrikaner-heart beats more vigorously and purer than this. [Pienaar, 1926, pp. 246-247; first edition, 1921]

However, the emergence of a lyric poetry out of the sufferings of the Boer War would not in itself have sufficed to ensure the survival of Afrikaans. Events on the social and economic level were essential as well. Those few Afrikaners who moved to the cities before 1890 by and large spoke English in the home. Until the discovery of diamonds and gold, however, the white population of South Africa was overwhelmingly rural. These country people, who were seldom able to write a great deal more than their names, spoke Afrikaans. As a result of increasing rural poverty and the Boer War, however, Afrikaners from the *platteland* poured into the cities. The white urban population of South Africa grew from 36 percent in 1890, to 75 percent in 1946, but the most rapid increase took place between 1890 and 1904 (Welsh, 1971, p. 173). This urban influx left its scars on ordinary Afrikaners as much as did the Boer War, although the two causes were inevitably interrelated.

The leaders of the Afrikaans-speaking community feared that this rapid and widespread urbanization would bring anglicization of the entire Afrikaans-speaking white population. Individuals united to form voluntary associations in the Transvaal, Free State, and Cape in order to agitate for official recognition of Afrikaans.[13] Committed leaders of this language movement were found mostly among younger generation Dutch Reformed clergy, journalists, and students. These language enthusiasts sought to preserve their home language, but even more, they were desperately concerned with the survival of Afrikanerdom.

There was also the older, more conservative element, with spokesmen among established churchmen and university professors; this group argued for the greater literary worth of Dutch (especially as in the old Bible) and the importance of the Dutch cultural heritage. It was in response to this powerful rear-guard support for Dutch, that Dr. Malan delivered his apology for Afrikaans in 1908 before the Afrikaans Language Movement at Stellenbosch. Afrikaans was the only real, viable language for his People, he argued:

> A linguistic expert can no more create a living language than a chemist can create life in his laboratory.... A living powerful language is born from the soil of the People's heart [*volkshart*] and the People's history [*volksgeskiedenis*] and lives only in the mouth of the People [*volksmond*]. No People ever chooses its spoken language, or indeed, its written language, on the advice of experts. Peoples and languages are born together and die together. . . Give the young Afrikaner a written language which is easy and natural for him, and you will thereby have set up a bulwark against the anglicization of our People. . . Raise the Afrikaans language to a written language, make it the bearer of our culture, our history, our national ideals, and you will raise the People to a feeling of self-respect and to the calling to take a worthier place in world civilization. . . A healthy national feeling can only be rooted in ethnic [*volks*] art and science, ethnic customs and character, ethnic language and ethnic religion and, not least, in ethnic literature. [Pienaar, 1964, pp. 169, 175-176]

Thus from the outset the movement for Afrikaans was linked with Afrikaner nationalism. This language nationalism

[13] The most reliable account of the Afrikaans language movement is Nienaber and Nienaber (1941). See also de Waal (1932), Langenhoven (1932), and Tomlinson (1956).

was liberal,[14] emphasizing the importance of national ideals in the moral development of the individual and stressing the individual's right to speak his own language and cherish his own cultural traditions (Malan, D. F., 1911; Muller, Tobie, 1913).

It was on such liberal nationalist grounds that students at Stellenbosch united to oppose their professors on the language question. Their Afrikaans Language Movement gathered strong support under the leadership of the likes of Tobie Muller, N. J. van der Merwe, Gordon Tomlinson, B. B. Keet, and J. J. Smith. The importance of support for Afrikaans at Stellenbosch University and the various teachers' training colleges throughout South Africa cannot be overemphasized. These institutions were producing the elite for the rapidly urbanizing post-Boer-War Afrikaner community. Lawyer's offices, school rostrums, and Dutch Reformed pulpits were soon occupied by young men zealous for the cause of the Afrikaans language and the Afrikaner People.

These young enthusiasts wasted no time organizing on behalf of the new language nationalism. By 1918, the major Dutch teachers' organizations in the Cape and the Free State had declared themselves for Afrikaans and indeed had successfully pressed for its adoption in the junior grades at school. The Transvaal Onderwysers Vereniging ("Transvaal Teachers' Association," referred to as T. O.) was founded in Johannesburg in 1919 to provide a voice for Afrikaans-speaking teachers. In that same year, the conservative Cape synod of the Dutch Reformed church, following three years behind the synods of the ex-republics, granted Afrikaans equal rights with Dutch, and approved the translation of the Bible into Afrikaans. In 1925, Afrikaans replaced Dutch as the second official language, whose legal equality with English was written into the Constitution. "Truly it was of the Lord and wonderful to behold—too wonderful to believe our own experience," cried Langenhoven (Nienaber and Nienaber, 1941, p. 173).

[14] For an extended discussion of the political impact of this liberal language nationalism see chapter five of this book.

Until the Boer War, the rural way of life was implicit to Afrikanerdom. Widespread urbanization of Afrikaans-speakers following the war would eventually effect a new attitude toward the city. Meanwhile, rural prejudice towards the evil of cities combined with the fear of Englishness in the reverberating cry of "back to the land" (cf. *"Trekkerswee"* in du Toit, J. D., 1962, volume 8; and Welsh, 1971, pp. 182-183). As late as 1923, Dr. Malan was urging that urban Afrikaners be resettled in the *platteland (Die Burger,* July 12 and July 13, 1923).

A group of Afrikaners on the Rand, however, had by then discovered that the very speed and extent to which urbanization was proceeding meant that cities could be won over by Afrikaans and Afrikanerdom.[15] In the words of William Nicol:

> Ethnic feeling awakened along with the increase in our numbers. This was one of the most striking changes which came over us. Numerous households which still tried at the beginning of the [First World] War to be as English as possible found by the end that they had undergone a spiritual and national revival. . . .Persons who had earlier doubted the continued existence of Afrikanerdom as a separate People with its own outlook, mores and customs, persons who earlier had unconsciously behaved as though it were best to disappear into the other section of the nation, now realized that they had a unique past about which they could be proud and a unique future which they must seek and ensure for the sake of posterity. The most startling revelation of this change was their use of the Afrikaans language. In 1914, it was customary that the better Afrikaans families used English exclusively as home language and as a result their children were lost to us. . . . [By 1920 this had changed; Afrikaans was spoken in good homes;] it was preached in the Churches; and at meetings we worked joyously and easily with the new language. We were young again. [Nicol, 1942]

The establishment of solid Afrikaner blocs in the cities weakened the influence of the English language in the home. Furthermore, these Afrikaner ghettos were sufficiently numerous to warrant the establishment of urban Afrikaner

---

[15] This early acceptance of the positive potential of urbanization is one of the reasons that rural traditionalism never became a major theme of the civil faith.

schools and churches. These latter were to serve as channels for enthusiastic propagation of the new liberal nationalism.[16]

Among the organizations which came into being at this time to further nationalist aims awakened by the Afrikaans language movement was the Afrikaner Broederbond. This Afrikaner "Brothers' League," which went underground three years after its founding in 1919, continues even today to excite a great deal of attention in South Africa.[17] It was founded by the present Speaker of the House, Henning Klopper, who was later to initiate the Ossewatrek. The first meetings were held in William Nicol's parsonage. The explicit purpose of this society was to bring together "serious-minded young Afrikaners in Johannesburg and along the Reef" (du Plessis, Louis J., 1951, p. 9), in order:

a. To accomplish a healthy and progressive unity amongst all Afrikaners who actively seek the welfare of the Afrikaner.

b. To arouse Afrikaner national self-consciousness and to inspire love of the Afrikaans language, religion, traditions, country and People.

c. To further every concern of the Afrikaner nation.

Membership was restricted to "Afrikaans-speaking Protestants who accept South Africa as their fatherland, are of sound moral character and stand firm in the defence of their Afrikaner identity. (*Raad van Kerke Handelinge*, May 1951, p. 50).

The Bond was at first limited to only a small band of ardent Afrikaners on the Witwatersrand whose major activities aimed at securing acceptance of Afrikaans as equal to English in the social and economic life of the city. The Broers thus

[16] For example, see the early numbers of the Ermelo High School Annual Magazine housed in the South African Public Library in Cape Town.

[17] Scholars have argued that the Afrikaner rise to power may be entirely explained by the machinations of this secret society. Others insist that South African history between the wars would not have been substantially different if the Broederbond had never existed. No doubt the truth lies somewhere between these two extremes, and I shall endeavor in my analysis to give the Broederbond its due without overemphasizing its influence.

spoke Afrikaans in public and insisted on being served in Afrikaans in places of business. According to Louis du Plessis, the Bond really took root when "large numbers of teachers joined it," (du Plessis, Louis J., 1951, p. 9) including Ivan Lombard, who was to be general secretary for three decades, and a certain Greybe, the chairman of the Transvaal Onderwysers Vereniging (T. O.). The acquisition of teachers as members, of course, meant not only that the Bond was itself strengthened by enthusiastic new members, but also that these teachers would be highly influential in forming the minds of the succeeding generation.

Unlike the language movement at the Cape, Henning Klopper's Broederbond had strongly republican leanings as well. Hence, despite the original objective of the Broederbond to further Afrikaans, this "semi-religious organization" (du Plessis, Louis J., 1951, p. 9) was potentially a major agency for propagation of the full civil faith. The growth of this Broederbond and the general diffusion of the civil religion must be placed in its political and religious context, however. Let us hence turn to a close scrutiny of the theological milieu which both hampered and fostered the general acceptance of the Afrikaner civil beliefs.

4

Dutch Reformed Theology and the Afrikaner Civil Religion

A brief overview of Dutch church history during the nineteenth century will help in understanding Afrikaner theological developments.[1] After the Napoleonic Wars, the rationalism of the enlightenment, which had swept through all of Europe, rapidly replaced Calvinist orthodoxy in the teaching of theology in Dutch universities. Certain conservative Calvinists responded by breaking away from the established church. Thus in 1834, Henrick de Cock, risking severe reprisals from the state, led a secession from the Hervormde Kerk ("Reformed Church") to form the Christelike Afgescheide Gemeentes ("Separated Christian Congregations"). Another group broke away in 1840 to form the Gereformeerde Kerken onder het Kruis ("Reformed Churches Beneath the Cross"). Discontents from these two newer churches established in turn the Christelike Gereformeerde Kerk ("Christian Reformed Church") in 1869.

Secession was not the sole response to rationalist tendencies in the Hervormde Kerk, however. Certain movements within

[1] A useful chart summarizing the complicated church politics of Holland is to be found in van der Meiden (1968). A brief summary of Dutch church history is Impeta (1964). I am indebted to Coenraad Brand for these references. For the rest, my account is taken from various Afrikaans sources, especially Hanekom (1951).

the state church itself also opposed the liberal deism of the major theologians. Especially important was the peitistic Reveil, a revivalist movement in the Methodist tradition, which was more concerned with religious warmth than with doctrinal purity. According to Hanekom, the Reveil had "a subjective tendency with a propensity for expression of feeling, for conscious emphasis on the religious life rather than doctrine, and for tacit avoidance of the question of the church" (Hanekom, 1951, p. 23, n. 1). In Holland this movement was most popular in literary and intellectual circles, and numbered among its members the jurist Groen van Prinsterer, and the poet Nicolaas Beets.

Under the leadership of Groen van Prinsterer and later of Abraham Kuyper, a minister in the Hervormde Kerk, the movement took on a theological and ecclesiological guise and began to make powerful demands for doctrinal reform within the church itself. The Hervormdes refused to concede at all. Indeed, in the new inaugural oath required of all ordinands, the Synod of 1882 deliberately omitted any mention of scripture and confession. Having failed to reverse this decision, Kuyper and his followers left the church. The participants in this secession (known as the Doleantie, "Grieving") were soon absorbed by the Gereformeerde Kerken, which formed an ecclesiastical base for Kuyper's political platform.

Dutch Christian politics, both Catholic and Protestant, made educational policy their major thrust (cf. *Koers in die Krisis*, 2(1940): 377-390). Both Groen van Prinsterer and Kuyper fought persistently for the right to teach religious doctrine in schools. Groen van Prinsterer argued that the Dutch state should live up to its Christian character and provide a Christian directive to public schools. Even if the government refused to accept its Christian commitment, at least it should allow the Gereformeerdes and Roman Catholics to establish their own schools where their doctrine could be taught. In 1857, a law was finally enacted which did permit the construction of private religious schools if parents were prepared to meet the cost. At the same time, the state reaffirmed that public education must remain neutral, thus implicitly denying Groen van Prinsterer's contention that the state was essentially Christian in outlook.

Groen van Prinsterer accepted this official pronouncement, and in 1860 organized the Vereniging voor Christelijk Schoolonderwijs ("Union for Christian Education"), whose purpose was to establish Calvinist schools with parental support. The movement outlived Groen but limped along painfully until in 1888 a coalition of Gereformeerdes and Roman Catholics achieved power in the Dutch parliament. This new government granted subsidies to the independent schools. Although Kuyper became prime minister in 1901, it was not until twenty years later that parochial schools, Catholic and Reformed, finally obtained full support from the state.[2]

Quite as important to Afrikanerdom as this struggle for Christian schools in Holland was the theological rationale which Kuyper used to justify his political position.[3] Kuyper argued that Calvinism had resolved the medieval dualism between church and world by placing both equally under the sovereignty of God.

The state, according to Kuyper, is the institutional embodiment of God's sovereignty in the face of the threat of chaos which stems from human depravity. Kuyper expressed his "political faith" summarily in the following three theses. First, God is the creator and only sovereign power over nations. However, second, in the realm of politics, sin has broken down God's direct government and hence the exercise of authority in the state has been vested in man "as a mechanical remedy." Finally, man possesses power over his fellows only as a delegate of "the majesty of God" (Kuyper, 1899, p. 31). This Calvinist doctrine of the state stood, at least in Kuyper's opinion, directly opposed to both the popular sovereignty of radical liberalism and the state sovereignty of German absolutism.

As stated above, Kuyper's doctrine of the state conformed to orthodox Calvinism. However, he proceeded to develop a

[2] From that time dates the Dutch system of *verzuiling* ("vertical pluralism"), whereby Dutch society is segregated institutionally into three separate streams, Reformed, Catholic and Neutral. (See, for *verzuiling*, Moberg, 1961, pp. 333-337).

[3] The best brief account of Kuyper's position is given in his Stone Lectures (Kuyper, 1899). For a good summary, see the appendix in L. J. du Plessis (1941).

doctrine of common grace not mentioned in the *Institutes*.[4]
He distinguished between the particular grace of God, necessary for salvation, and God's common grace, which is built
into the structure of creation and which holds the cosmos
together despite man's sin. Not only nature, but human
society as well exists by virtue of God's common grace. "In
a Calvinistic sense we understand hereby, that the family,
the business, science, art, and so forth are all social spheres,
which do not owe their existence to the State, and which
do not derive the law of their life from the superiority of
the State, but obey a high authority within their own bosom
. . ." (Kuyper, 1899, p. 116).

Each sphere of social life thus exists independent of the
state and of the other spheres and is subject only to God.
"In this independent character a special *higher authority* is
of necessity involved and this highest authority we intention-
ally call *sovereignty of the individual social spheres*, in order
that it may be sharply and decidedly expressed that these
different developments of social life have *nothing above
themselves but God*, and that the State cannot intrude here,
and has nothing to command in their domain" (Kuyper, 1899,
p. 116).

The structure of these individual spheres was laid down
in their original creation, and their purpose and function is
thus defined by their very nature.

> "Whatever among men originates directly from creation is
> possessed of all the data for its development, in human nature
> as such. You see this at once in the family and in the connection
> of blood relations and other ties. From the duality of men
> and women marriage arises. From the original existence of *one*
> man and *one* woman monogamy comes forth. The children
> exist by reason of the innate power of reproduction. . . . In
> all this there is nothing mechanical. The development is
> spontaneous, just as that of the stem and the branches of
> a plant. True, sin here also has exerted its disturbing influence
> and has distorted much which was intended for a blessing,
> into a curse. But this fatal efficiency of sin has been stopped

[4] See Calvin (*Institutes*, II, 2:17, editor's notes 63) for references
to "common grace." Most of these in fact refer to "natural knowledge of moral law" rather than to the ordinances of creation, of
which we find no mention in Calvin.

by common grace. . . . The same may be said of the other spheres of life. . . When we admit therefore that sin, though arrested by "common grace" has caused many modifications of these several expressions of life, which originated only after paradise was lost, and will disappear again. . .we still maintain that the fundamental character of these expressions remains as it was originally. All together they form the life of creation, in accord with the ordinances of creation, and therefore are *organically* developed."[5] [Kuyper, 1899, pp. 117-118]

The character of government, on the other hand, is not organic but mechanical, for, since sin abolished the original order of God's perfect kingdom, an external order had to be imposed. The government "is not a natural head, which organically grew from the body of the people, but a *mechanical* head, which from without has been placed upon the trunk of the nation. . .[a] stick placed beside the plant to hold it up, since without it, by reason of its inherent weakness, it would fall to the ground" (Kuyper, 1899, p. 119). The true function of the state is thus to maintain order and mete out justice, although the inclination of the state is always to interfere in the organic sphere of social life. On this issue, said Kuyper, "Calvinism was the first to take its stand. For just in proportion as it honoured the authority of the magistrate, instituted by God, did it lift up that second sovereignty, which had been implanted by God in the social spheres, in accordance with the ordinances of creation. It demanded for both independence in their own sphere and regulation of the relation between both, not by the executive, but *under the law*" (Kuyper, 1899, pp. 120-121).

Kuyper distinguished between several different categories of "social sphere": the sovereignty of the individual; sovereignty in the corporate sphere, such as universities, guilds, associations, etc.; sovereignty in the domestic sphere of the family; and the communal autonomy of towns and villages

[5] Although his doctrine of *sowereiniteit in eie kring* may indeed avoid the Scylla of popular sovereignty as well as the Charybdis of German conservatism, it is perhaps apropos here to point out that in his doctrine of the "ordinance of creation" Kuyper sailed perilously close to the German shore! For a discussion of the importance of "ordinances of creation" in later (Nazi) German theology, see Janson (1967).

(Kuyper, 1899, pp.122-123). "In all these four spheres," said Kuyper, "the State-government cannot impose its laws, but must reverence the innate laws of life. God rules in these spheres, just as supremely and sovereignly through His chosen *virtuosi*, as He exercises dominion in the sphere of the State itself through His chosen magistrates" (Kuyper, 1899, p.124). The sovereignty of each individual, of the patriarch in every family, and the ruler of each social sphere is just as directly derived from God as the supremacy of state authority. "A people therefore which abandons to it the rights of science, is just as guilty before God as a nation which lays its hands upon the rights of the magistrates. And thus the struggle for liberty is not only declared permissible, but is made a duty for each individual in his own sphere" (Kuyper, 1899, p. 127). On these grounds Kuyper based his opposition to neutralism in education, for formal as well as informal instruction of children belongs to the sphere of the family. The state, by denying the right to teach doctrine in public schools, was hence challenging the authority of the parents to exercise one of their primary functions.

Kuyper's theology was to become dominant in the Dutch Reformed churches in South Africa. This did not occur, however, without intense opposition from an evangelistic strain of Scottish Calvinism. This revivalist theology had been preached in South Africa since the early 1800s, when Lord Charles Somerset imported Scottish ministers to anglicize the understaffed Reformed church at the Cape. One of the first and most eminent of the new *predikants* was the elder Andrew Murray, whose religious fervor was transcribed in his daughter's memories:

> The occasions on which he spoke to his children about their souls were few but well chosen, and his words never failed to make an impression. It was generally on a Sabbath evening after family worship when the child came for a good-night kiss. "Will you not, before you go to bed tonight, give yourself to Jesus?" Or on a birthday he would say, "This is your birthday: are you born again?" . . . As sacred as the memories of the Sunday evenings are those of the Friday evenings which our father regularly devoted to praying for a revival. He would shut himself up in the study, and read accounts of former

revivals in Scotland and other countries, and sometimes come out of his study with *Gillie's Collection* in his hand, to read us the story of the outpouring of the Spirit on the Kirk of Shotts or of the revivals in Kilsyth and Cambuslang. ... His children will never forget standing outside his study door, listening to the loud crying to God and pleading for an outpouring of the Holy Spirit. [Du Plessis, J., 1919, pp. 27-28]

The influence of this Andrew Murray on church life and theology in the Nederduits Gereformeerde Kerk ("Dutch Reformed Church") at the Cape can hardly be overemphasized. In that small church, five of his six sons were ordained and four of his five daughters married men who were to become influential ministers. His son, John Murray, was one of the two professors appointed in 1859 at the foundation of the Stellenbosch Seminary, which thereafter trained almost every minister who entered the service of the Nederduits Gereformeerde Kerk (henceforth referred to as the N.G.). Furthermore, another son, Andrew Murray the younger, was the dominating figure at N.G. Cape synods from 1860 until the Anglo-Boer War.

The Scottish influence on the N.G. was enhanced by overseas contact with the Dutch Reveil. On arrival in Utrecht for study in 1845, the young brothers John and Andrew Murray immediately joined an association called Sechor Dabar ("Remember the Word"), whose purpose was "to promote the study of the subjects required for the ministerial calling in the spirit of the Reveil" (du Plessis, J., 1919, p. 59). They were thus insulated from the rationalism and scepticism which prevailed at Utrecht. The influence of Sechor Dabar on the South African clergy was not limited to the Murrays, however. Among others who joined them as members were Nicholaas Hofmeyr and J. H. Neethling, both of whom later became important figures at Stellenbosch.

Nourished by Scottish Calvinism and the Dutch Reveil, the orthodox but evangelically enthusiastic movement in the Cape Reformed church reached its high point in the early 1860s with the Great Revival. Outbreaks of communal ecstasy occurred in village after village throughout the Cape province. With a new zeal for Christian witness, hundreds were returned to the fold of the N.G.

When the "blessing" came to Graaff-Reinet, one of the children who was away from home wrote of the elder Andrew Murray: "I can imagine Papa's joy. . . I think he must be saying with Simeon, 'Lord, now lettest Thou thy servant depart in peace, for mine eyes have seen Thy salvation.' " When this letter was read to Murray, the tears came to his eyes and he said, "It is just that" (du Plessis, J., 1919, p. 28).

The revival was all the more inspiring to orthodox leaders because the threat of liberalism was making powerful inroads at the Cape, both among lay people and clergy (cf. Hanekom, 1951, pp. 415-445; and Spoelstra, 1963, pp. 33-62). The orthodox "Murray" position nonetheless managed to retain a bare majority in synod and was hence able to organize effectively to combat modernist theology.

The root cause of the modernist heresy was the training received by aspirant clergymen in Holland, for by no means all of them joined Sechor Dabar. In order to exclude such heterodoxy from the ministry, the *colloquium doctum*, a pro forma examination required of all aspirant ministers before legitimation, was expanded into a searching inquiry into the theological soundness of all ministerial candidates. In addition, the theological seminary was established at Stellenbosch in 1859 to ensure orthodox training for ministers in the future. The first two professors of the seminary were John Murray and Nicolaas Hofmeyr, both of whom had been ardent members of Sechor Dabar. Very soon this institution was staffed by its own graduates, who were immunized against modernism before further study in Holland or Scotland. Thus, the N.G. in the Cape as well as in the republics was assured a continuous flow of evangelical Calvinist preachers (du Plessis, J., 1919, pp. 230-231).

The settlers in the Orange Free State remained largely N.G. in their church membership, but across the Vaal River, the Voortrekkers formed their own church, the Hervormde Kerk. Ostensibly they feared that any connection with the N.G.

at the Cape would lay them open to control by the British governor. Perhaps they also feared the policy of racial egalitarianism of the Cape church (Engelbrecht, S. P., 1951, p. 36). There seems little doubt, however, that Leiden-trained Dirk van der Hoff, the first Transvaal Hervormde minister, encouraged these suspicions because he had no desire to fall under the control of the orthodox Cape synod.

Even today, the Hervormde Kerk continues to be more liberal in theology (and more white supremacist) than either of the other Dutch Reformed churches in South Africa. Despite a few exceptions, the Hervormdes provided less overt support for Afrikaner nationalism during the 1930s and 1940s than did the others. The church went so far as to invite General Smuts, the prime minister, to its centenary celebrations in 1942,[6] a time when his imperial loyalties were most flagrant (*Eeufeestoesprake*, 1842-1942). This may in part be explained by the "Erastianism" which has tended to go hand in hand with Dutch theological liberalism since 1816. Certainly, since the Nationalist achievement of power in 1948, the Hervormdes have admitted the civil religion.

At the other extreme, the Gereformeerde Kerk has always been the most theologically conservative of the Dutch Reformed churches in South Africa. It broke from the Hervormdes in 1859,[7] largely because its founders objected to the singing of hymns in church.[8] The first minister, Ds. Dirk

[6] No mention was made of civil-religion themes in any of the speeches.

[7] The schism in the Transvaal church has been the subject of heated scholarly controversy. For the Hervormde position, see Engelbrecht (1951): for the Gereformeerde statement, see Jooste (1959): G. D. Scholtz (1956 and 1960) takes a strongly N.G. position. (Engelbrecht wrote a pamphlet attacking Scholtz's position on the schism, to which Scholtz replied with yet another pamphlet.) Perhaps the most reliable source is Gerdener (1934). At present, the Gerformeerdes number about eight percent of Afrikanerdom. Since a partially successful reunion with the N.G. in 1880, the Hervormde Kerk has claimed the allegiance of about seven percent of the Afrikaans-speaking white population.

[8] Jooste (1959, chapter 3) finds other, more theological, reasons for the break. These seem to be a reading-back from the Dutch *Afscheiding* ("Secession") into the South African material. They may, however, have weighed with the ministers, Postma and Van der Hoff, themselves.

Postma, of the Christelike Afgescheide Kerken in Holland, provided a focus for conservative secessions in the Transvaal, but also in the Free State and the Northern Cape. He rallied the *Dopper* ("conservative") element among the frontier farmers, and provided them with a strictly Calvinist locus for their conservatism. Soon they no longer had to rely on Holland for their ministers, since a Gereformeerde theological school, founded at Burgersdorp in 1869 and moved to Potchefstroom in 1905, was training clergy at home. Some of the latter, especially those destined to become lecturers at the seminary—which became in time a full university at Potchefstroom—still went to Holland to complete their training. Their Mecca was the Free University of Amsterdam, which Abraham Kuyper had founded in 1880 "on reformed principles." By the 1920s, a Potchefstroom school of thought which sought to extend Kuyper's doctrine of *sowereiniteit in eie kring* ("sovereignty in each particular sphere") was received with approval in Holland (cf. Boodt, 1939). Important representatives of this South African Kuyperianism were Professors H. G. Stoker in philosophy, J. D. du Toit (the poet Totius) in theology, J. A. du Plessis and L. J. du Plessis in political science, J. Chris Coetzee in education and A. J. H. van der Walt in history.

The Calvinist right became as a matter of course another opponent for the evangelical Murray tradition in the N.G. at the Cape. Weary from their struggle with liberalism, Murray adherents were forced to wheel and face a new series of attacks led by Ds. S. J. du Toit, a disciple of Abraham Kuyper, who accused them of Methodism, roundly declaring that they were outside the true Reformed tradition in church government, worship, and theology. He especially condemned centralized church government and practices such as prayer meetings, revivals, special revivalist preachers, and prayers to the Holy Spirit, as well as co-operation with non-Calvinist mission bodies. Between 1897 and 1911, various N.G. congregations staged their own Doleantie under the leadership of S. J. du Toit, founding the Gereformeerde Kerke onder die Kruis in Suid-Africa. By 1914, these congregations had been incorporated into the Gereformeerde Kerk (Oberholster, 1953).

The schism inspired by S. J. du Toit did not end the attack on the Murray-styled evangelical revivalism within the N.G. More and more of the N.G. ministerial candidates who pursued post graduate studies in Holland attended the Free University because, as Professor J. I. Marais of Stellenbosch observed in 1898, "He who wishes to study theology in the Netherlands will have to go to the Free University of Amsterdam. The new [Dutch] law on Higher Education no longer acknowledges Christian, let alone *Reformed* Theology" (Booyens, 1969, p. 72).

The Free University turned out Calvinists more rigid than their old Stellenbosch teachers. The infiltration of Kuyperian ideas into the N.G. culminated in the heresy trial and dismissal in 1928 of Professor Johan du Plessis of the Stellenbosch Seminary.[9] However, although the ousting of du Plessis was a victory for Kuyperian Calvinism within the seminary, it by no means signified a general "reform" of the N.G. Even at the time of du Plessis' dismissal, the Transvaal synod of the N.G. strongly condemned the action. Among those who publicly expressed their sympathy were such prominent Broederbond Afrikaners as Dr. D. F. Malan, Professors E. C. Pienaar, N. H. Brummer, D. F. du Toit Malherbe, T. J. Hugo, and others (*Die Volkstem*, March 30, 1930; and *Die Burger*, March 26, 1930). Rearguard support for the revivalist tradition remains strong even today among both ministers and lay people in country parishes throughout South Africa.

In 1935, a series of articles by a certain *Bekommerd* ("Worried") appeared in *Die Kerkbode*, journal of the N.G. (and later in a pamphlet, *Bekommerd*, 1935). They amounted to a trenchant attack by an old-style "Murray" man on the new Calvinism which he felt was infiltrating the church. In

[9] Du Plessis, who was Andrew Murray's biographer, was charged with teaching a non-Calvinist doctrine of scriptural inspiration, with accepting the results of "Higher Criticism" of the Bible, and with holding a kenotic doctrine of the incarnation. Professor J. D. du Toit of Potchefstroom was one of those who testified against him. Having been dismissed from his post as professor at Stellenbosch, du Plessis appealed to the civil courts, which ordered his reinstatement. However, he tactfully accepted an indefinite period of leave until his retirement. For details, cf. F. S. Malan (1933), Kotze (1932), and the published court hearings (*Kerksaak*, 1932).

his foreword, the editor stated that *Bekommerd* gave "the interpretation of Calvinism which has been taught by our Church during all its years in the land. This is what was taught by Professors Murray, Hofmeyr, Marais and [P. H. G.] de Vos, and preached by such men as Ds. J. H. Neethling and Dr. Andrew Murray." *Bekommerd's* first article summed up his position:

> There are among the followers of Calvinism, in our land and in our Church, TWO DIRECTIONS. The first is embodied in the (Narrow) Reformed [Gereformeerde] Church, the other in the N.G. . . . During the last ten or fifteen years . . . POWERFUL FORCES HAVE BEEN AT WORK TO ROB OUR N.G. CHURCH OF ITS OWN CHARACTER AND TO MAKE IT MORE AND MORE NARROWLY REFORMED (Gereformeerd). [*Bekommerd*, 1935, pp. 1-2].

Having stated his fear of neo-Calvinist subversion within the N.G., *Bekommerd* proclaimed the evangelical Calvinism of the old N.G. as the truly South African variety of Calvinism: "In my opinion the N.G. is above all characterized by its strongly Evangelistic tendency. . .whilst this is definitely not an outstanding characteristic of the (Narrow) Reformed. . . .The (Narrow) Reformed glorifies the Law; the N.G. glorifies the Gospel." (*Bekommerd*, 1935, p. 2).

The main thrust of his argument rejected Kuyperian neo-Calvinism as a form of sterile intellectualism, drained of the longing to "save souls," which he believed was central the the Christian gospel. He complained of the Gereformeerdes that they

> do not feel called to go much out of their way to save the millions who are lost because they do not know of a Savior. There is no need to become anxious about them. They believe that those who are chosen will be saved, and those who are not chosen—well, all the labor in the world will mean nothing but rather will only make their doom more dreadful. With us, on the other hand, it causes a shiver to run through our body and spurs us on to greater earnestness and more prayer and increased activity. We are called . . . to proclaim the Gospel to all creatures, amongst all peoples and nations and tongues. All who live *must* know that there is a Savior! For that we must offer ourselves up . . . [*Bekommerd*, 1935, pp. 21-22]

The publication of *Bekommerd's* articles in pamphlet form did elicit a reply from three of the new school of Stellenbosch professors, D. G. Malan, D. Lategan, and E. E. van Rooyen (Malan, D. G., et al., 1936), but their critique was petty and pedantic. Most of the new Calvinists in the N.G. simply ignored *Bekommerd* and carried on the positive work of organizing a series of "Calvinist" voluntary associations which would unite the three Dutch Reformed Churches on the basis of the new theology. Although many of these never really got off the ground,[10] the Federasie van Kalvinistiese Studenteverenigings, ("Federation of Calvinist Student Unions) succeeded in publishing a collection of articles from each of the three churches in a series called *Koers in die Krisis* ("Direction in the Crisis"), of which volume one appeared in 1935. One of the articles, *"Calvinisme en Sending"* ("Calvinism and Missions"), by P. J. S. de Klerk, confirms the accuracy of *Bekommerd's* attack. The mission of the church was not to save souls for its own sake, said de Klerk, but rather because this was one way to serve God.

> The Calvinist knows that the full number of the chosen ones must come in before Christ will come. Through missions he works for the coming of his Savior. He is not concerned with the Christianization of the world, but rather with filling up the number of the chosen... There must not be a methodist or individualistic hunger for a large number of converts.
> [*Koers in die Krisis,* 1(1935):122-126]

Indeed, the contributors to *Koers in die Krisis* would not have denied that they differed radically from *Bekommerd's* view of them. They would have insisted, however, that his position was not an alternative Calvinist one. They would have argued that *Bekommerd's* stance was rooted in an individualistic liberalism totally alien to the true spirit of Calvinism. For, like Kuyper, these Afrikaner neo-Calvinists believed that Calvinism was more than simple evangelism,

[10] For the failure of the Calvinistiese Bond, for example, see G. D. Scholtz (1944, pp. 66-70).

[11] *Koers in die Krisis* (1935, 1: 380-386) has a brief history of the Federasie. For an interesting review of the book from the traditional Murray standpoint, see A. H. Murray (*Die Vaderland*, September 27, 1935).

that it embodied its own unique *Weltanschauung*. In order to illuminate the essential differences between *Bekommerd* and those whom he attacks, one must do more than discuss missions. Let us look deeper into the philosophical basis of this new brand of South African Calvinism.

Bekommerd was correct in dubbing his opponents Kuyperian. Professor J. D. du Toit of Potchefstroom set forth in *Koers in de Krisis* (1(1935): 36-47) the three basic principles of Calvinism as follows: first, the Bible must be the sole intellectual and normative standard; second, the Calvinist believes in the absolute sovereignty of God as reflected in the principle of *sowereiniteit in eie kring*; and finally, the true Calvinist believes in the distinction between particular elective grace and common grace. This statement could have been made by Kuyper himself.

In the writings of Professor H. G. Stoker, however, South African neo-Calvinism moved beyond Kuyper in its systematic specification of the different types of "spheres" within which God's sovereignty is independently exercised. Stoker carefully distinguished between the sphere of the individual, the spheres of human social relationships (such as church, state, people, and family),[12] and the cultural spheres (such as morality, law, art, science, economy, and language). These spheres, although complete in themselves, naturally intersect on various planes (Stoker, 1941).

Each of these three categories of spheres has a special "destiny" (*bestemming*) in God's plan. Hence, one might speak of individual, social, or cultural "calling" (*roeping*), depending on the sphere in which it is discharged. However, for all the diversity of destinies and callings, all are ultimately interdependent because of their common subjection to God's will.

Stoker thus accepted and expanded Kuyper's metaphysical system, in which diversity of function is rooted in the structure of creation. Stoker wrote that God directs His creation in a threefold manner: first, directly through miraculous

[12] The social spheres, for Stoker, were either organic or mechanical and often a mixture of the two because of sin (Stoker, 1941, p. 71 and p. 147).

intervention (especially in the Incarnation); second, indirectly through allowing creation to develop according to the laws by which He structured it; and third, indirectly through using mankind as collaborator in His work of creation (Stoker, 1941, p. 222). This cultural collaboration of man is, however, strictly bound by the laws of the natural ordinances:

> Mankind subjugates the earth, dominates nature, defends order, and so on, in the name of God. [Thus] he created culture. In so doing he is bound by the laws of nature and by cultural norms. . . . To dominate nature and thereby form it into culture is the glorious task, the calling which God gives to mankind as individual and social being. . . . In his cultural creations man is bound by the laws of his own being and constitution, by the laws of nature and the norms of culture—all ordinances of God. [Stoker, 1941, pp. 222-224 and p. 247]

Culture is thus the handiwork of God, working through man. Cultural spheres exist apart from social relationships and have their own structural principles defined by their own unique destinies. However, because of the interdependence of all created spheres, cultural spheres bear an individual and social imprint:

> Men, as individual and social beings, have a uniqueness with which they stamp their cultural creations. Their individual and social (including national) characters are practical limitations imposed upon their culture. . . . German, English, French, Russian and Italian culture may differ in so far as the different Peoples have different structures and callings, but, as culture as such, they do not differ. Russian, German, Italian art, for example, remains *art*, even if it is the art of different Peoples. [Stoker, 1941, p. 248]

However, for all the independence of the cultural sphere, culture along with race, history, and fatherland, remained for Stoker one of the defining characteristics of a People (Stoker, 1941, pp. 146-147). For Stoker, the People (*volk*) was a separate social sphere with its own structure and purpose, grounded in the ordinances of God's creation. Here Stoker's Calvinism was able to accommodate the Afrikaner civil religion, indeed to undergird it, for the Afrikaner People, too, was sovereign in its own circle, acknowledging no other master than God, whose purpose was to be seen in its structure and calling, its historical destiny:

God willed the diversity of Peoples. Thus far He has preserved the identity of our People. Such preservation was not for naught, for God allows nothing to happen for naught. He might have allowed our People to be bastardized with the native tribes as happened with other Europeans. He did not allow it. He might have allowed us to be anglicized, like for example, the Dutch in America. . . He did not allow that either. He maintained the identity of our People, He has a future task for us, a calling laid away. On this I base my fullest conviction that our People will again win back their freedom as a People. This lesson of our history must always be kept before our eyes.

God disposes the misfortunes of the nations, but God also sends the opportunities, including those which overcome division in the ranks of our People. When He sent the Jameson Raid, our People once more became one, from the Cape to the Zambesi. If He wishes to make us one People again and to give us our freedom, He will create the necessary circumstances. If we get our free republic, then it will not be from the hand of man, but will be a gift of God. . . .

Humanly speaking, if we had had to predict what would happen to the Voortrekkers in 1838, if we had noticed the Black peril, the wilderness and barbarism of the interior, the danger of bastardization and anglicization, each of us would have prophesied that our little People were doomed to extinction. And yet that little People remains. Not because we Afrikaners are such tremendously good people, but because God, the Disposer of the lot of the nations, has a future task laid away for our People. Thus let us become conscious of our calling. . . [Stoker, 1941, pp. 250-251]

The length of this citation is justified by its relevance to our civil-religion theme. Notice the recurring motifs here: the coming republic, the insistence that freedom will come at the hand of God only, and the promise implicit in the sacred history.

We seem to have moved far from *Bekommerd's* critique of Kuyperian apathy towards evangelism. Yet, in fact, Stoker's notion of the People as a distinct and unique sphere of God's creation was essential to P. H. S. de Klerk's conception of missionary vocation:

Alongside the conversion of the individual goes the Christianizing of the People. Missions must also be directed to the People as a whole. . . Calvinism teaches that God gave each People its particular task. . . The missionary does not suppress the nationality of a People; he enlists it and raises it to a unique and native Christendom. Therefore the right method is to found native churches. Their own confession, their own hymns, and their own form of prayer must develop from within their own bosom. . . [*Koers in Die Krisis*, 1(1935): 126-127]

Such a theory of missions sounds very modern—certainly it might have served as a rebuke to *Bekommerd's* primitive zeal for "souls." On the other hand, we see that from his own theological standpoint, *Bekommerd's* criticism of the neo-Calvinists was well founded; the latter did indeed tend to intellectualize the evangelical "concern" for the salvation of individual souls. In a very real sense, *Bekommerd*, as a Murray man, and de Klerk, as a Kuyperian, were talking past each other because they started from fundamentally different metaphysical presuppositions.

The question of the relationship between the civil religion and Christian theology posed no real theoretical problem for Stoker and the South African Kuyperians. We have seen how easily Stoker was able to incorporate civil-religion themes into his version of Calvinism. The Murray-type evangelicals also had no real difficulty, for they simply made a radical distinction between church and national faith. Even when Murray and the Stellenbosch "old school" were most critical of the state, as during the Boer War, they appealed to common Christian values of Boer and British and not to the People's divine right to existence (du Plessis, J., 1919, pp. 424-426). Andrew Murray wrote in this vein to Dr. Malan in 1915, that "the church is surely a spiritual body specially created by the Lord with the purpose of uniting . . . all His members, drawn even from nations which may have hated and despised one another." The church stands above the state, he argued, reconciling political differences by educating her members in the love of God and brotherhood. The church must not interfere in practical politics, but must rather assist men in applying in their daily lives "the great principles of the Word of God" (du Plessis, J., 1919, pp. 431-432).

Between this liberal view of strict separation of church and state and Stoker's cosmic Calvinism lay a great gulf. Within that rift stood a large number of N.G. ministers who agreed with neither position. The most prominent representative of this middle position was Dr. D. F. Malan, although such eminent churchmen as William Nicol, J. R. Albertyn, P. K. Albertyn, J. D. Kestell, and A. F. Louw also figured amongst its proponents.

The rationale for this intermediate position was social rather than theological. It was a particular response to the plight of poor white Afrikaners who were suffering the early stages of industrialization. We have noted already that one of the aftermaths of the opening of the gold fields and the Boer War was an increasing influx of Afrikaners into the cities of South Africa and the creation of Afrikaner ghettos. The visibility of such slums prompted an increasing awareness among Afrikaner intellectuals, especially churchmen, that much of the white poverty in South Africa was in fact Afrikaner poverty.

It seemed natural that the N.G. in particular should commit itself to fight poverty among its own members. Many who had been trained at Stellenbosch to care for the soul of the individual in the Murray tradition, were drawn into caring for the bodily welfare of their congregations as well. This growing concern for Afrikaner material well-being as well as spiritual well-being coincided with the upsurge of Afrikaner national consciousness and the language movement, and quite naturally the N.G. came to be thought of as the "People's Church" (*volkskerk*). This assumption was fully articulated in theological terms only at a later date.[13]

This pragmatic and unsophisticated care of the N.G. for the welfare of the Afrikaner People had first begun in the former Boer republics. N.G. ministers had not only served as chaplains to the Boer commandos, but later, in response to the anglicization policies of Lord Milner, they had established schools for Christian National education in the Transvaal and Free State.[14] This intimate involvement of N.G.

[13] For the theological subtlety that is necessitated by the integration of the *volkskerk* notion with Murrayite ideals, see Hanekom (1951a). More naive are Kestell (1939) and Albertyn *My Eie Kerk* (n.d.).
[14] For an account of such activities on the part of the N.G. ministers on the Rand, see Nicol (1958, chapter 9).

clergy in local education was to continue and, in fact, gather momentum. Now the problems of anglicization and poverty were seen as two sides of the same coin, and education as a major solution to both. Christian charity was becoming Christian nationalist charity, for the N.G. was coming to see that without the Afrikaans-speaking community, their church could not survive. Thus those of the *volkskerk* persuasion began to argue that not only was education required, but specifically *Afrikaans* education.

Although the *volkskerk* men had been trained at Stellenbosch, and so stood firmly within the evangelistic Murray tradition, they specified the social implications of Murray's theology in nationalist terms. Andrew Murray was a great educationalist, but the schools which he founded were English-speaking for purely pragmatic reasons. English education worried the younger generation, however. In August, 1912, P. K. Albertyn wrote to his friend D. F. Malan about the Murray school in Graaff-Reinet that Miss Murray, the principal, was most "frightfully English in her opinions." In her thirty years there she had accomplished blessed Christian work, Albertyn acknowledged, but this was not enough. Her influence had "done an appalling amount to anglicize the staff and children"[15] (Booyens, 1969, p. 239).

In Johannesburg as well, William Nicol recalled that '[e]ducation between 1900 and 1920, being almost exclusively limited to the English language medium, robbed Afrikanerdom of many outstanding leaders; on the Rand it came down to the theft of an entire generation out of our People's life" (Nicol, 1958, p. 193). In an address to English-speaking churchmen in 1920, Nicol, who also was a younger generation Murrayite, affirmed that mother-tongue education was "not

[15] According to Professor Booyens who takes an unabashedly "Afrikaner" point of view, Afrikaner children in Graaff-Reinet were "threatened on three sides from: the wide-spread poverty which was dominant in the congregation: increasing neighborhood integration between White and non-White in certain sections of the town, and the English spirit which emerged from the local educational establishments" (Booyens, 1969, p. 257). Miss Murray was Andrew Murray's daughter. Her father had warned her about possible opposition from exclusivist Afrikaners (du Plessis, J., 1919, pp. 428-429).

in the first place an educational question, but a deep conviction that our children can only be preserved for our People through Afrikaans schools" (Nicol, 1958, p. 203).

In the face of what was believed to be a threat to the existence of Afrikanerdom, then, young graduates of Stellenbosch Seminary dismissed Kuyperianism, by dint of their training, but they readily adopted a *volkskerk* position, which accommodated the new language nationalism and lent dignity to the Afrikaner cause. While still a minister of the N.G., Dr. Malan iterated this new direction at the Stellenbosch student conference in 1911, without fear of synodical disapproval.

> We are Afrikaners and so ought we always to be, because any nationality, formed by God through history and environment, has in itself a right to existence... God wills differences between nation and nation. And He wills these because He has placed before each People a unique destiny, a unique calling, like that of any individual. And if I read the history of my own People, a history which shows me the birth and growth of a People despite itself, a People which became People without its own co-operation... then I cannot free myself from the impression that God desires our People's continued existence. And He desires this because He has a unique calling for our People with its own ethnic nature. My feeling of nationality thus rests finally upon a religious foundation. [D. F. Malan, 1911, p. 38]

The extent to which this civil-religion style of thought was generally accepted in the N.G. may be seen in the compromise statement drawn up by Dr. Malan for the minister's conference held to forestall schism in the N.G. during the rebellion in 1915. All the ministers of the N.G., both those who were for Botha and those who were against him, were able to agree with regard to the essential calling of the church:

> First, the church has a special calling with respect to the Dutch-speaking population, "with whose existence it is bound up in such an intimate manner" and it is thus the duty of the church "in itself to be nationalist, to watch over our particular national concerns," to teach the People to see the hand of God in their history and "to keep alive in the Afrikaner People the awareness of national calling and destiny, in which is laid up the spiritual, moral and material progress and strength of a People." Second, the church can only fulfill its

high calling if it keeps strictly outside the boundaries of party-politics, unless religious or moral principles are at stake or the concerns of the Kingdom of God are touched.[Booyens, 1959, p. 289, citing decision of minister's conference from *Die Kerkbode*, February 11, 1915]

This position, then, reflected a deep conviction that the N.G. ought to be a People's church, and yet at the same time that church and state must be kept separate. In order to accomodate these two ideals, churchmen began to make a practical distinction between party politics (*partypolitiek*) and People's politics (*volkspolitiek* or, often, *kultuurpolitiek*). Because the N.G. was a People's church, concerns such as Afrikaans-medium education, Afrikaner poverty, and the Afrikaner People's unity (*volkseenheid*) were relevant issues for the N.G. pastor. On the other hand, he could not directly tell his parishioners how to vote, unless he knew without doubt, and they agreed, that one political party represented the side of God and the People and the other was expressly opposed to Christian and Afrikaner ideals.

This distinction between *volkspolitiek* and *partypolitiek* enabled *volkskerk* adherents to enthusiastically adopt the full civil faith, as did the Kuyperians. However, the Kuyperian doctrine of God's sovereignty in all spheres of life made it possible for Gereformeerde ministers to take temporary leave of absence from the pulpit to serve God in parliament. N.G. clergy, such as D. F. Malan and N. J. van der Merwe, on the other hand, were obliged to resign from the ministry upon entering party politics. In either case, whether they remained ordained or had to resign, Afrikaner clergy—the elite of their *volk*—were to be among the most important leaders in the articulation and dissemination of their People's civil faith. On the other hand party political action in the first three decades of Union was led by secular party leaders, such as Smuts and Hertzog. These men, as we shall see, had their own political philosophies, which were not rooted in the civil faith.

5
Afrikaner Political Developments Before 1930

In 1902, General Smuts wrote that his ideal was

> a United South Africa in which there would be the greatest
> possible freedom, but from which the disturbing influence of
> Downing Street would finally be eliminated, ... not ... "Dutch"
> supremacy or predominance over English Afrikaners. ... Let
> us try so to arrange our politics, our administration and our
> legislation that a compact South African nationality may be
> built up with the best elements of both parts of the colonial
> population, so that when eventually we become politically
> independent (as we necessarily must in the course of time)
> we shall ... be united within and present a united front to
> the outside world. Then this war which we have gone through
> will remain for *all* South Africa as a memory and heritage
> and glory and not as a nightmare. [Hancock, 1968, p. 199]

President Steyn, General Hertzog, and even Dr. Malan would
have echoed these words, although they would have laid
greater stress on the danger of English predominance over
Dutch-speaking South Africans, rather than vice versa. They,
too, shared an ideal of an independent South Africa, united
and free of imperial control.

In an article dated 1891, sent to a Dutch student magazine,
Hertzog wrote that "the friction is not between Dutch-speaking colonists and the colonial Englishman, but between the
colonist in Africa and the Englishman 'at home' ... France,
Holland, Germany, England each had a share in the origin
of this People, and thus the name Afrikaner includes them

all, both Hollander and Englishman, who have learned to unite their concerns with those of the land which they have made their home" (van den Heever, 1944, pp. 45-46). In 1904, Dr. Malan wrote to a Dutch editor in the same vein, suggesting that "there was a broader basis upon which English and Afrikaners could work together—the love of South Africa as fatherland of both sectors and the defence of her concerns above those of all other countries" (Booyens, 1969, pp. 101-102).

This tradition of cooperation had strong precedent in South Africa despite the history of conflict. There were English-speaking colonists who had fought for the republics, and the Afrikaner Bond, the first political party at the Cape, was open to both English-speaking and Dutch-speaking South Africans who had South Africa's interests at heart. Nor was the talk of cooperation after the Anglo-Boer War simply rhetoric. In 1910, for instance, Hertzog and Steyn supported John X. Merriman, the English-speaking candidate for prime minister, against the Afrikaans-speaking Botha.

When Botha was appointed, however, Hertzog accepted a position in his cabinet, agreeing to work with him on the basis of a policy which would "secure the cooperation of all South Africans, of whatever race, and . . . eliminate racialism from all political and national questions" (Krüger, 1960, p. 48). On one point, however, both Hertzog and Steyn stood quite firm. Integration in a common citizenship must never threaten the separate existence and traditions of the Dutch-speaking group.

Unlike Smuts, who had learned his constitutional law at Cambridge, both Steyn and Hertzog were trained in law in Holland, where there was a strong tradition of federalist pluralism dating back to Althusius and the States-General of the Dutch Commonwealth.[1] During the framing of the South African constitution, Steyn and Hertzog had insisted that equal rights for Dutch and English be ensured. Fearful

---

[1] See Murray, A. H., (n.d.) for the Dutch background. A most informative article on Hertzog as a lawyer is J. P. Verloren van Themaat, "Generaal Hertzog as juris en sy rol in ons staatsregtelike ontwikkeling," *Hertzog Gedenkboek,* 1965. Hertzog's preoccupation with Roman-Dutch law is discussed on pp. 133-134.

that Botha's policy of reconciling the English would ultimately lead to the destruction of the Afrikaner People, they argued that the most stable white South African state would be a poly-ethnic one, in which patriotic loyalty to the common fatherland would be mediated through separate nationalisms.

Hertzog was soon speaking of two ethnic currents within a single civil state:

> "Community life in South Africa flows in two streams—the English-speaking stream and the Dutch-speaking stream, each stream with its own language, its own way of life, its own great men, heroic deeds and noble characters. That this is so is the result of history. No one is to be blamed for it and each has the right to prize, to protect and to defend what is his own. But it is our duty to ensure that we develop a higher community life, one in which despite retention of language and whatever else may go along with it, we arise as one People in spirit and feeling." [Van den Heever, 1944, p. 333]

Thus Hertzog insisted that the separate language and cultural traditions of the two white groups must be maintained. At the same time he seemed to envisage that the weight of political sentiment would gradually shift from emphasis on primordial attachments, which divide, to civic allegiance, which unites (Cilliers, 1940b, p. 19; cf. Geertz, 1963).

On this issue Botha and Smuts were directly opposed to Steyn and Hertzog. The former agreed that whites should rule, but within this exclusivism they favored what Akzin calls an "integrationist" pattern of political organization, "an official policy favoring equal rights of individuals, whatever their ethnic origin, but discouraging . . . any claim of non-dominant ethnic groups to group-rights" (Akzin, 1964, p. 88).[2] In Smuts' own words:

> "The whole meaning of Union in South Africa is this: We are going to create a nation—a nation which will be of a composite character, including Dutch, German, English and Jew, and whatever white nationality seeks refuge in this land—all can combine. All will be welcome." [Hancock, 1968, p. 36]

[2] The theoretical discussion in this chapter is deeply indebted to Akzin's incisive and informative little book (Akzin, 1964) as well as to Geertz (1963).

Smuts and Botha thus continued to hold that combination of white racism and egalitarian liberalism which had been earlier propounded by Paul Kruger.

In fact, it was on the point of loyalty to the common South African fatherland, rather than the two-stream policy, that Hertzog and Botha finally parted ways. In a key speech at Germiston in December 1911, General Hertzog mapped out his understanding of the South African political situaion. There are two streams of cultural life which are truly South African in sentiment, he said. The first is the old Dutch-speaking stream with its own national life and national spirit, which is only one part of the nation as a whole. This has been supplemented by descendants of the early English Colonists, who now acknowledge South Africa as their home. These two separate streams have been brought together in the South African party under General Botha. Hertzog spoke of members of both these streams as "Afrikaners."[3] There was yet a third class of persons, however, whom he refused to call Afrikaner. These individuals might be legal citizens and so have the franchise, but they did not share the national spirit. They were in South Africa for what they could get out of her, and they would happily shake the South African dust off their feet when it no longer profited them to remain (Krüger, 1960, pp. 61-62).

General Botha appears to have agreed, in private at least, with Hertzog's diagnosis of South Africa's political ills (van den Heever, 1944, p. 317). He, too, deplored the British jingoism of the opposition Unionist party.[4] Where Botha and Hertzog differed was on the method of treatment which ought to be followed. Botha believed that jingos should be conciliated until common life in a unified state should have its mellowing effect on their ardent imperialism. Hertzog, on the other hand, urged that they should be exposed for what they

[3] For another example of Hertzog's use of the term "Afrikaner," see van den Heever (1944, pp. 221-222), where the text of a Covenant Day address from this period is printed in full.

[4] At the time of the Union, the few Englishmen who favored closer imperial ties formed the Unionist party. Until the establishment of the National party in 1915, this was the only opposition in the South African parliament.

were and, if necessary, excluded from political life. In speaking to his constituents at Smithfield in 1912, he spelled this out explicitly:

> Only one person has the right to be "boss" in South Africa, namely the Afrikaner. . .The people have become conscious of themselves as a nation. They feel their own power, they have reached nation manhood and they feel that Afrikaners and not strangers should rule the country. [Krüger, 1960, pp. 62-65]

Most of the English-speaking Unionists, he continued, were not Afrikaners but foreign fortune seekers.

Hertzog's attack on the imperial sentiments of the English-speaking opposition caused an uproar in the English South African press. Botha wrote to Smuts from Pietermaritzburg in Natal: "The whole of Natal feels insulted by it—in newspapers, clubs, streets, houses, or wherever one goes. There is unprecedented excitement which, as you can understand, is doing us much, very much harm. . . . Whatever I say and do, I get only one answer: They are regarded as *uitlanders*" (Hancock, 1968, p. 335).

In his speech at de Wildt the following week, Hertzog cited this reaction in Natal as proof that they, in fact, were *uitlanders*. The leader of the opposition, Sir Thomas Smartt, had publicly announced that he differed from Hertzog on the imperial issue. He did indeed place the welfare of the empire before that of South Africa. If this were so, replied Hertzog, "then I was right when I said that Sir Thomas Smartt is not yet a true Afrikaner. Imperialism, in my view, is only good insofar as it is useful to South Africa. Where it conflicts with the interests of South Africa I oppose it unequivocally. I am prepared to stake my future as a politician on this doctrine. I am not one of those who talks always of conciliation and loyalty; these are idle words which deceive no one. I have always said that I do not know what this conciliation means . . ." (van den Heever, 1944, pp. 312-313).

He was lashing out here at Botha as well as at the Unionist "foreign adventurers," for "conciliation" had been Botha's watchword since the formation of the South African party. Hertzog had now rendered his seat in Botha's cabinet untenable. At the same time he had stated the political platform on which his career hereafter was to rest: the two-stream idea of white South African unity, and the policy of "South Africa first." Once out of the cabinet, he proceeded to establish his own political party, the National party.

The first "Program of Principles" of the National party, published in 1914, clearly bore Hertzog's stamp. The doctrine of the two streams was stated in article nine, which declared that "the foundation of our welfare rests on the unity of the European population of the Union. . . . [We] must be one People, but this unity need be no more than a social and spiritual unity, with complete retention of our many-sided ethnic riches stemming from language, history, religion, customs and morals" (van den Heever, 1944, pp. 354-355). These principles were institutionalized in the National party constitution, which stated on the one hand that the duty and calling of the state was the promotion of the prosperity and welfare of the People in matters spiritual, material, and national. On the other hand, it insisted that this new deal could only be attained by "conscientiously and impartially respect[ing] the rights and privileges of each section of the population [as] guaranteed by the [Union] Constitution" (van den Heever, 1944, p. 354).

The new National party accepted, as well, Hertzog's policy of placing South African interests before those of the empire. According to article three of the "Program of Principles," white South African unity could be attained only through "the cultivation of an intense conception of national auton-omy, [in which] the interests of the Union are emphatically placed above those of any other country or people" (van den Heever, 1944, p. 352). The exposition of this article was careful to distinguish "national autonomy" from national independence. By developing a theory of the divisibility of the Crown, Hertzog, even this early, defended himself from the threat of republican extremism. "Our ministers are indeed ministers of the Crown, because the King of Great Britain is our king," reads the exposition, "but we are not ministers of Great Britain or of the Empire. This is the meaning of responsible government . . ." (van den Heever, 1944, p. 352). This view of South Africa's relationship to Britain was to become very important later.

The most cogent and consistent theoretical statement of Hertzog's position is to be found in a lecture delivered to the Afrikaans Language Union at Stellenbosch in 1913 by the liberal nationalist Tobie Muller. This lecture, published as a pamphlet under the title *Die Geloofsbelydenis van 'n Nasionalist* ("A Nationalist's Confession of Faith") exerted profound influence in Afrikaner intellectual circles (Muller, Tobie, 1913).

Muller traced the beginnings of Afrikaner nationalism to the struggle of the early frontiersmen with the African wilderness and the gradual development of white racial consciousness during the years of expansion before the Great Trek. Thus far, however, these white men were conscious only of their unity against their tribal inferiors ("*al wat lager staan dan hulleself*"). "Against the natives," said Muller, "every white man was one, no matter whence he came." This was the meaning of the Day of the Covenant. Such racial consciousness was not true nationalism, however, "They had yet to learn the greater lesson, that they formed a self-conscious unity over against other whites—their equals." (Muller, Tobie, 1913, p. 7)

Recognition that the Dutch Afrikaner also filled a unique and autonomous place among the whites was born from conflict with England and the English. "So far," he said, "our national consciousness was largely negative; after the war it began to become more and more *positive*. Having learned in the school of suffering that we are neither Hottentots, nor Kaffirs, nor Englishmen, we finally discovered that we are *ourselves*" (Muller, Tobie, 1913, p. 9). This statement might have appeared to contradict the contemporary argument that Dutch and English Afrikaners ought to form one nation in the new Union. Not so, said Muller, for there ought to be no discrepancy between "Union consciousness" and the individual national consciousness of Dutch and English Afrikaners:

> The best way to cultivate a stronger Union consciousness is when Boer and Briton in South Africa each develop strongly

their own individual consciousness. . . . And let those, who speak so easily about the fusion of the two races remember that a fusion which would come into being through the concession by both races of their individual characteristics would be a curse for South Africa. It would mean that we should have in our country a colorless, flaccid uniformity, neither fish nor fowl, which would be a denial of the earlier history of both races. . . . Our state is named the Union, not the Uniformity of South Africa. And it will remain a morally strong and healthy unity only as long as the common South African spirit of union, in which both Boer and Briton must share, is always born out of the individual nationalisms which are unique to each of them. [Muller, Tobie, 1913, pp. 11-13]

Making no effort to renounce the imperial connection, he went on to say that "[t]he British Empire will become stronger the more independent nationalities are included in it" (Muller, Tobie, 1913, p. 13.

Having argued for separate ethnicities within a civic unity, in terms akin to General Hertzog's, Muller proceeded to list the factors essential to healthy national self-respect for the Dutch Afrikaner ethnic stream. These included the development of a distinct language to be used in school and church and a fostering of the traditions of the forefathers.

We are constantly urged to "Forgive and forget!". . . But this is actually a summons to the Dutch Afrikaner nation to commit suicide. *Forgive*—yes, that we have done; and that is our holy duty as a Christian people; *forget*—that we cannot and may not do! A People which loses its national memory also loses its personal identity and comes to naught. And while it is sinful for a Christian people not to forgive, it is equally sinful for it to forget how Providence guided its ways in the past, led it through dark days, and made it what it is. The blood of the forefathers does not cry out for revenge, but it does call us to defend the moral and religious principles for which they suffered. *Forgive, but do not forget*! this is the word which comes to us out of the past. [Muller, Tobie, 1913, p. 22]

Like President Kruger before him, Muller insisted that the Afrikaner's calling did not guarantee God's eternal favor, but rather imposed certain moral injunctions upon all Dutch Afrikaners. "Our task as a nation," he said, "is to build up our national character and culture in order to influence for the good other nations with whom we have come into contact. . . . Even if we have to die an early death, there is still no room for pessimism. Our business is to deepen our ethnic life; its length we leave in the hand of Providence" (Muller, Tobie, 1913, pp. 32-33).

In the absence of exclusivism and the emphasis on moral obligation, this early formulation of Afrikaner nationalism by Tobie Muller stands close in spirit to General Hertzog's. Hertzog's dual ethnicism never aimed at Dutch Afrikaner dominance. Throughout his public career he emphasized complete ethnic equality between English-seaking and Afrikaans-speaking South Africans. His moderation did not, of course, extend to the indigenous African peoples. In respect to the native inhabitants, the National party envisaged "the supremacy of the European population in a spirit of Christian trusteeship," which meant "providing the Native with the opportunity to develop according to this natural talent and aptitude" (Krüger, 1960, p. 71). We thus find in nationalist policy at its inception a glimmering of respect for the black African's own ethnic rights, firmly checked by the assertion of white superiority.

Despite the ideological consistency of Hertzog's party program, the National party was limited in its immediate impact on ordinary Afrikaners. However much intellectuals supported the new party, the average voter was still bound by his personal loyalties to wartime leaders. Although the Free State flocked to their General's banner, in the Transvaal even Beyers and de la Rey, who were later to rebel, remained true to Botha. In the Cape, too, where the Englishman H. E. S. Fremantle was elected first National party leader, support was limited to country towns on the Free State border and to a few staunch supporters of the Afrikaans language movement in Cape Town, such as W. A. Hofmeyer and J. H. H. de Waal. In fact, so feeble was the support for Hertzog's party that by August 1914, Oswald Pirow, his confidant, admitted that "Hertzog was ready to give up the struggle. If the People did not wish to be saved, he would not try further to impose his leadership upon them" (*Hertzog Gedenkboek*, 1965, p. 299).

Then, on September 4, 1914, the Union parliament voted to join Britain in the war with Germany. The small National party, advancing Hertgoz's slogan, "South Africa First," fought the declaration of war in parliament with vain determination. Botha's support in the Transvaal was broken, however, by his suppression of the 1915 Boer rebellion. Many Transvaalers, who had fought under the rebels Beyers and de la Rey during the Boer War, interpreted Botha's decision to call up the South African Citizen Force to quash the uprising as rank treachery to the Afrikaner cause. Hence the insurrection not only added a final martyr to the sacred history, in the person of Jopie Fourie, but it also secured Transvaal support for the National party. Although Hertzog and President Steyn counseled against rebellion, their neutral stance and pleas for clemency on behalf of the captured rebels were sufficient to satisfy many extremist Afrikaners. Public opinion in the Transvaal ran so high on both sides that the Transvaal synod of the N.G. refused to censure the rebellion, despite strong pressure from General Botha (Nicol, 1958, p. 219).

The reaction of Cape Afrikaners was very different from that of the Transvaalers, however. Newspapers which had taken an anti-government position at the outbreak of war changed sides as soon as word became public about the rebellion. In large and small country towns, spontaneous commandos sprang into being, eagerly volunteering their support for the government. In Graaff-Reinet, for instance, "roughly £1,500 was collected in cash and the newspapers published . . . pledges of guns, horses, saddles, bridles, goggles, Christmas puddings, and so on" (Booyens, 1969, p. 277). The Graaff-Reinet commando left for battle against fellow Afrikaners with fervent acclamation from a large crowd of locals assembled on the church green. Eleven Cape N.G. leaders at the same time published an "Open Letter" in which they "earnestly warned against the effort to free South Africa from the British Empire." This attempt was described as "an exceptionally dangerous and reckless undertaking, a faithless violation of the Treaty of Vereniging and a definite transgression before God" (Booyens, 1969, p. 275). We have already discussed the ministers' conference at which Malan's compromise statement was unanimously accepted in order to keep peace in the N.G. Despite this mutual agreement, several N.G. churches underwent schism in the Free State, as well as the N.G. congregation at Uitenhage n the Cape.

An address by the Wellington National party branch chairman on September 11, 1915, epitomizes the attitude of ordinary Cape nationalists to the insurrection. There was a large measure of ambivalence: "It is being contended that the National party approves of the rebellion. The party sympathizes with the rebels (our own flesh and blood) but strongly disapproves of the rebellion." With this cursory dismissal of the rebellion, the chairman then turned to a much more vital issue for the Cape party—the language question. "We as a Party," he said, "must demand with calmness and deliberation that to which we have a right and not allow that the right to use our language be merely hypothetical, but ensure that it really be used in practice" (Wellington National party branch, minutes, September 11, 1915).[5]

On October 2, the same local branch was addressed by Ds. Neethling, who had attended Jopie Fourie in his last hours. Neethling, speaking for the Transvaal National party, expressed far greater concern about civil-religion issues, focusing particularly on the recent martyrdom: "The wistful longing of Jopie Fourie [was] that his blood might awaken the Afrikaner People. He was one of the bravest men whom he [Neethling] had ever met—he refused to be blindfolded. He [Neethling again] is sure that the blood of the unforgettable Jopie Fourie was one of the foundation-stones of the National Party" (Wellington National party branch, minutes, October 2, 1915). Neethling's visit to this small local branch near Cape Town implies that he was touring the western Cape in an effort to convince Cape Nationalists of the civil-religion viewpoint.[6] If this is so, it is perhaps safe to conclude that

[5] National party local branch minute-books are few and far between. Those quoted in this study (mostly from the Cape National party) are at present held in the political archives at the University of the Orange Free State in Bloemfontein.

[6] As we shall see, the activities of the local organization of the Cape National party were often at variance with the public state-

a section of the leadership in the Cape National Party, almost certainly including W. A. Hofmeyr, was rather more sympathetic to republicanism than were the majority of lay Cape Nationalists.

It was the same W. A. Hofmeyr, who took the lead in persuading Dr. Malan to leave the pulpit in June 1915 in order to accept the post of editor of *Die Burger*, the new nationalist newspaper at the Cape. The growing popularity of *Die Burger* was important in establishing a solid National party base at the Cape.[7] It capitalized on the violence and destruction wrought by imperialist mobs in the streets of Cape Town during the war. It established the Helpmekaar ("Help One Another") movement to collect contributions for fines imposed by the courts on the rebels, and indeed succeeded in collecting more money for this cause than any other province.

Under Malan's editorship, *Die Burger* was not only a spokesman for Hertzogite opinion, but also an important innovator in matters of policy and principle. True to Malan's personal commitment, the ethnic particularity of the Afrikaner People was emphasized. At the same time, Botha became a scapegoat, criticized for his supposed pandering to imperial interests. "*Bymekaar bring wat bymekaar hoort*" ("bring together those who belong together") was Malan's editorial policy. Of course, Hertzog's cry for "South Africa First" was never denied, but Malan made little of the possibil-

---

ments of national leaders. The Cape party was far more the instrument of the will of men such as W. A. Hofmeyr, Dr. Malan, and the organizing secretary for the Cape, F. C. Erasmus, than it was ever controlled by Hertzog. Hertzog's personal appeal was stronger in the Free State and Transvaal, however.

[7] The circulation of this powerful mouthpiece of Hertzogism grew from 3,000 in 1915, to 7,000 in 1921. By 1921, an additional 4,000 copies of the biweekly country edition brought the total circulation to 11,000. Compared to the 20,000 circulation of the *Cape Argus* in 1920, this may seem slight, but one must bear in mind that the *Argus* appealed to an almost exclusively urban readership, that the readership per copy has always been greater for the Afrikaans newspapers, and that the *Argus* was not an unswerving supporter of the Botha party in the way in which Malan (and later A. L. Geyer) supported the National party. Circulation figures are culled from Scannell (1965, pp. 14-15).

ity of cooperation with English-speaking South Africans.

This difference in emphasis points up a source of contention in liberal Afrikaner nationalist philosophy which ultimately justified party schism. Hertzog divided the white population according to two different criteria: first, an ethnic criterion which distinguished between the Afrikaans-speaking and the English-speaking sections, and second, a civic criterion which distinguished between those whose primary loyalty was to the British empire and those who placed "South Africa First." There was a problem in classifying English-speaking South Africans who met the civic criterion but failed by definition on the ethnic one. Hertzog himself categorized members of this group as English-speaking Afrikaners (as distinguished from Dutch-speaking Afrikaners). This linguistic usage, along with hints that at some future time the two streams might combine, suggests the priority in his thinking of the civic sentiment. Tobie Muller, too, adopted Hertzog's inclusive use of the term Afrikaner, although Malan restricted the term to Afrikaans-speakers only. This distinction became crucial when English-speakers in large numbers seemed to qualify as Afrikaners under the principle of "South Africa First."[8]

Meanwhile, the National party capitalized on South Africa's participation in the First World War. In the election of 1915, the Nationalists increased their representation in parliament from seven to twenty-six members. Indeed, in the rural districts of the Cape, Free State, and Transvaal, they obtained more than half the votes. The policy of opposing imperialism was paying handsome dividends. The South African party's fifty-four seats, together with the support of

---

[8] Notice the difference was one of emphasis only—Malan, too, spoke of "the larger South African People" becoming "one, a spiritual unity, grounded in common love for a common fatherland." But he refused to apply the term *volkseenheid* to such unity, for that was "a unity which exists only in duality—two-in-oneness" (Malan, D. F., 1911, pp. 39-40). Notice that this use of two-in-oneness is linguistically similar to the three-in-oneness of the Christian Trinity. Notice, too, that during the 1930s many Afrikaners began to use the ethnic criterion exclusively, although Malan himself was never able totally to abandon occasional appeals to the English-speaking voter.

the forty Unionist members of parliament, made it possible, however, for Botha and Smuts to carry on the war unimpeded by the Nationalists' growing strength. Smuts, in fact, served overseas for several years as a member of the Imperial War Cabinet, which added cogency to Nationalist charges that he was simply the "Handyman of the Empire." When Smuts became prime minister in 1919, upon Botha's death, the position of the South African party was further weakened.

The political division of Afrikaans-speaking South Africa was a matter of deep concern to many ordinary Afrikaners, however, and grassroots pressure for reunion, usually organized by Afrikaner churchmen, was strong in the postwar years. In October 1919, two coordinating committees set up by the South African party and National party congresses, respectively, met to discuss the question of Afrikaner reunion. The major spokesman for the National party was W. A. Hofmeyr. Negotiations predictably broke down on the question of whether the reunited party would permit propaganda for an independent South African republic (van Rooyen, 1956, pp. 60-68). The major issue in the election of 1920 remained the British colonial tie. This time the National party won a plurality of seats, forty-four, against Smuts' South African party's forty-one, largely because of a strong swing to the Nationalists in the rural districts of the western and northern Cape and the northern and western Transvaal. Unionist representation was reduced to twenty-five, owing to the growing popularity of the Labour party in the cities. Although Smuts had been resoundingly beaten, he continued as prime minister with Unionist support.

Immediately after the election, Hertzog wrote to Smuts suggesting that they form a coalition. Hertzog was prepared to forego any immediate demands for secession, he said, but only on condition that Smuts.agree to allow free propaganda for a republic. Smuts rejected this proposal on the grounds that a new party on such terms would be an Afrikaner racial bloc, excluding English-speaking South Africans.

Nonetheless, popular pressure for reunion, led by the *volkskerk* element in the N.G., did not abate. A conference was called in Bloemfontein on September 22, 1920, which was declared a day of prayer throughout Afrikaner South Africa. The conference foundered once again on the question of republican propaganda. Five days later, Smuts called a special congress of the South African party to announce an agreement with Sir Thomas Smartt, leader of the Unionists. To many Afrikaners it must have seemed clear that Smuts' recalcitrance on the republican issue at the earlier conference was explained by a previous agreement with the Unionists, representatives of imperialist capitalism.[9] Although Smuts himself argued that his fusion with the Unionists spelled the end of a "jingo" party in South Africa, for those Afrikaners who believed in *volkseenheid* he had sold out to imperialism.[10]

Smuts called an election immediately, and the new South African party swept into parliament with seventy-nine seats against the Nationalists' forty-five. Smuts scored most of his gains in the cities, where his warnings on the danger of secession caused many English-speaking workers to desert the Labour party and flock to his banner. This victory was short-lived, however, and in 1924, a further election brought Hertzog's National party into power through a coalition with the Labourites.

In a letter to the editor of *Die Weste*, the Nationalist newspaper of Potchefstroom, one Piet Joubert explained this victory in purely civil-religion terms: "At the darkest moment [the time of the 1915 rebellion] God be thanked that there were men who again breathed in new life. The National party was born, and the powerful tree which grew so astonishingly fast that today it surpasses all others, owes its growth to the blood of Jopie Fourie and the suffering of his comrades, the heroes of that time" (*Die Weste*, July 20, 1926).

We have seen that the rebellion did indeed break Botha's support in the northern and western Transvaal, but Piet Joubert's explanation of the 1924 triumph was greatly oversimplified. Botha, until his death in 1919, was able to rally

[9] Van Rooyen says as much (1956, pp. 78-79).

[10] The 1920 annual report of the church council of Kuruman, which had sent its minister as a representative to the Bloemfontein conference, sadly noted that, "The breach in our People had a deleterious effect on both church and People" (Smit, A. P., 1966, p. 52).

Afrikaner sentiments in support of the integrationism of the South African party. At an official Covenant Day ceremony at Paardekraal in 1916, Botha pleaded for reunion of the Afrikaner People, a category in which he specifically included English-speaking South Africans. Throughout his life Botha received strong support in the Transvaal, especially in the east, and several leaders in the Transvaal N.G. were solid Botha men. Dominees Hermanus Bosman (a Murray protégé), Paul Nel, and J. W. G. Strasheim, for example, all spoke at the 1916 Paardekraal ceremony, echoing Botha's call for the unity of Afrikanerdom.

Smuts, the "Handyman of the Empire," provided a far more vulnerable target for the opposition than the essentially lovable Botha. In fact, Botha's greatest political liability was his continued liaison with Smuts. As early as 1915, Nationalists were labeling Smuts a supporter of Johannesburg capitalism and British imperialism (*Ons Vaderland*, September 14, 1915). A National party pamphlet, *Politieke Toespraak* ("Political Address"), published in early 1918, lamented the loss to Afrikanerdom of two great leaders:

> It is as clear as midday that Botha and Smuts and their clique are now in the same kraal with the Unionists, the millionaires, mine magnates and capitalists. . . When I think back in our history, to the Voortrekkers, their persecution, the first annexation of the Transvaal, the Boer War, the elections of 1907 and 1910, not to go into the the things mentioned in *A Century of Injustice*, which Jan Smuts himself wrote, then it is difficult to believe that the capitalists and their supporters have changed. No, I cannot believe that the Unionists have changed. [National Party, n.d., pp. 10-11][11]

The implication was quite clear—Smuts had changed.

Such charges could only be leveled by implication in 1918. But when Smuts rejected the reunion of Afrikanerdom in 1920 and turned instead to the Unionists, he proved beyond a doubt what the Nationalists had been saying for some years: he was a renegade from his People, who meant far less to him than did the wealthy, English-speaking capitalists of Johannesburg.

[11] The pamphlet is anonymous and not dated. The authors were probably Advocate F. W. Beyers and J. H. H. de Waal of the Cape party. The date, from internal evidence, was about January 1918.

To be sure, Smuts had flown in the face of Afrikaner church and People when he joined with the Unionists. However, he was thereby able to rally increased English-speaking support to his cause. As long as he could continue to unite the urban English-speakers with his own residual Afrikaner supporters, Smuts would remain at the helm. The weak link in his chain of support proved to be white urban working-class people on the Witwatersrand, and it is to this category of the population that we must now briefly turn.

After the discovery of gold in 1884, skilled artisans flocked into the Transvaal in droves. Most of them were British, and, true to their traditions, they established trade unions to represent their interests. In South Africa, however, unlike most countries, it has always been in interests of the white artisan class to support the status quo. From the beginning, industry was conducted on the principle of high pay for skilled white labor and miserably low wages for unskilled black African labor. As black African immigrants to the large cities became increasingly skilled, the temptation to employ them rather than expensive white labor proved time and again irresistible to South African mine owners. Almost all industrial agitation in South Africa may be interpreted as stemming from conflict between management and skilled labor on this point.

During the years immediately after the Boer War, the urban migration of poverty-stricken Afrikaners added a further complicating factor to this conflict between capital and a privileged white laboring elite. Since these new urban immigrants were unskilled (indeed, more so in many cases than their black fellow-townsmen), they were ineligible for union membership and were initially perceived as a further threat by English-speaking skilled artisans. During the recession of 1907, a decision by management to reduce white miners' wages by 15 percent sparked a strike. The newly arrived Afrikaners were only too happy to accept work for the lower wage, and the employment of these "scabs," in fact, defeated the strike. Many of the British miners were thus permanently replaced by Afrikaners.

Soon after this, unions were opened to Afrikaners, and their advent added a stiff dose of racial consciousness to the economic self-interest of English artisans. In the ensuing labor struggles of 1912 and 1913, the Afrikaners fought side by side with their English-speaking comrades; and Smuts, as Minister of Mines, was obliged to use force to restore order for industry. Another recession after the First World War gave rise to further disputes in the mines. In 1921, when there were nine black African workers in the mines to every white man, the total wages paid to blacks was scarcely more than half of the white total. Management again attempted to promote blacks to skilled jobs, and, in 1922, the inevitable strike ensued. A cry arose from the strikers, three-quarters of whom were Afrikaners, that white civilization was in danger. Forming commandos, they marched in the streets of Johannesburg. After some days of unrest, Smuts called out the Defence Force, and for nearly a week there was a civil war on the Rand, during which more than two hundred white South Africans lost their lives.

When it was all over, Smuts attempted to justify to parliament his delay in declaring martial law: "If we are continuously walking on the edge of a volcano, let the country see it, let us even at the risk, the very serious risk of revolution, delay the declaration of Martial Law and let [things] develop" (Hancock, 1968, p. 86). Smuts had prefaced these words with a statement of the genuine desire of the government for a peaceful resolution of the strike, but Hertzog snatched at the phrase, "let things develop," and used it so effectively that these words were to haunt Smuts throughout the remainder of his political career. "The Prime Minister's footsteps dripped with blood," said Hertzog, "his footsteps would go down in history in that manner" (Hancock, 1968, p. 88). Both the Nationalists and the Labour party began to belabor Smuts' liason with "Hoggenheimer," the gross figure created by the cartoonist Boonzaaier to depict Johannesburg financial interests.

In 1923, Hertzog and the Labourites formed a parliamentary pact. Dr. Malan was uneasy about this cooperation with English-speaking workers and agreed to the pact only on the condition that "the National party and the Labour party will not work together further than their respective principles allow, and that they ought also not to stand further apart than their common concerns and principles allow, or than the struggle for life and death of the People against capitalist-monopolistic domination demands" (van Rooyen, 1956, p. 106). Malan was thus careful to ensure that the pact was not a union but simply an agreement between two political parties, each of which would retain its own individual integrity. On one matter, however, the National party did temporize. They agreed that while no member of either party would be forbidden to speak on any subject he chose, if the pact came to power, no Nationalist member of parliament could use his vote to alter the constitutional relationship between South Africa and the British Crown.

With this stroke, Smuts' anti-republican attacks on the National party were at once rendered impotent. And when the pact did indeed sweep into power the following year, republicanism was not one of its rallying calls, although it was tacitly acknowledged that the party continued republican, in spite of the pact. The major voting swing was in the growing urban areas where the anti-capitalist and white-racist pact promised protection for "civilized labour" against both "Hoggenheimer" and the urban black African immigrants.

Once in power, Hertzog took immediate steps to buttress discriminatory industrial legislation and practices until it could be said that, "taken as a whole, industrial legislation was a protective barrier against the competition of men in a lower social and economic position, and against their encroachment upon spheres of employment and standards of living dedicated to white labour" (de Kiewiet, 1941, p. 276). In addition, his government took positive action against "poor whiteism" by reserving even manual work on the government-owned South African Railways for white men and by paying them "white wages." Since most poor whites were Afrikaners, the railways soon became a bastion of Afrikaner sentiment.

On the constitutional front, Hertzog sought to achieve imperial recognition of what he conceived to be South Africa's de facto "national autonomy" within the British empire. At the Imperial Conference of 1926, the famous Balfour Declaration, which was issued largely through the insistence of Hertzog, laid the foundation-stone of the British Commonwealth.[12] This document stated that the Dominions are "autonomous communities within the British empire, equal in status . . ." (van Rooyen, 1956, p. 293). This provided for South Africa a guarantee of that sovereign independence which the National party had asserted from the beginning, and Hertzog declared himself satisfied. At a reception in Paarl on his return from the conference, he asserted: "we are just as free as the English People, and he who seeks more freedom seeks the impossible. With respect to the empire, there ought to be no fear of schism because it is in our interest to remain within it. We should be stupid to withdraw . . ." (Scholtz, G. D., 1944, p. 82). Dr. Malan and Tielman Roos, Nationalist leaders in the Cape and Transvaal, respectively, agreed. At Paardekraal on December 16, the fiery republican P. G. W. Grobler announced that "we have obtained our freedom. It does not have the form that we thought it would have, but we have it all the same" (Scholtz, G. D., 1944, pp. 81-82).

There were a few in the ranks of the National party, however, who disagreed. Foremost among them was Dr. N. J. van der Merwe, Nationalist member of parliament for Winburg and formerly an N.G. minister with Kuyperian leanings, who was wont to speak eloquently of the calling of the Afrikaner People. As a child he had been interned in a Boer War concentration camp; and, when a student at Stellenbosch, he was the major organizer of the Language conference of 1911. By the mid-1920s, he was an enthusiastic member of the Afrikaner Broederbond.

In an article titled "Watchman, what of the night?" in *Die Volksblad*, the new Free State newspaper of the National party, van der Merwe took serious issue with Hertzog and his enthusiastic acceptance of the Balfour Declaration. His article reads like a sermon of the civil faith, based on a text from Isaiah 21:12, "The morning has come and it is still night":

[12] See, however, Hancock (1968, p. 200) for the preparatory work undertaken by Jan Smuts, and notice, too, that Hertzog had strong support, especially from Wilfred Laurier of Canada.

We [like the Edomites of old] have also often thought that the morning has finally dawned only to discover that it is still night. When the Voortrekkers crossed the Orange river, they thought: "Now we are free." Speedily they discovered that, in truth, dark shadows of the night still overhung them. After the battle of Blood river they hoped that the longed-for day of rest and peace and freedom had dawned. Shortly thereafter Natal was proclaimed English and "it was still night." The struggles in the Free State and Transvaal finally ended in the Sand river and Bloemfontein conventions. There was a declaration of independence and yet England as sovereign power turned back the rays of freedom which tried to break through and finally came the sour experience, "it is still night." After 1881 the call came again: "Watchman, what now? Had the day finally dawned?" This hope was confounded and the Three-Year War brought on an hour of darkness such as had never been seen before. Finally self-government came. It began to look like daybreak but consensus-politics under imperialist and capitalist influences brought on the dark hours of 1914. Who shall ever forget those days? The night was darker than ever. It is enough to mention the names of de la Rey, Beyers and Jopie Fourie. And now ten years later the National Government has come to power with the help of Labour. Surely, *this* time the Prophet has no right to say to us: "It is still night." General Hertzog goes to the Imperial Conference and returns with the assurance: "Day has dawned. We have our sovereign independence." And South Africa rejoices as though it already finds the golden rays of morning strengthening and inspiring. And yet! And yet! And yet! Is it truly the long-awaited day? Is this the beloved aspect of freedom for which in the past there flowed so many tears and so much blood? . . . I await the answer of the watchman. I take hold of myself in fear that upon saying "Morning has come," once more the somber words shall fall "But it is still night." (Scholtz, G. D., 1944, pp. 84-85).

Van der Merwe's doubts grew as Hertzog began to insist more and more belligerently, against growing republican opposition, that he had obtained the long-sought freedom. Smuts, too, continued to affirm that, however divisible the British Crown might now be in theory, in practice South African could never remain neutral in a European war because of the ties of loyalty which bound the Commonwealth together. Indeed, a series of newspaper articles dealing with this subject in *Die Weste* demonstrated the continued

strength of republican spirit, especially in the western Transvaal.[13] Finally, in May 1930, encouraged by correspondence
from Ds. L. P. Vorster of Krugersdorp, Dr. A. M. Moll of
Johannesburg, and L. J. du Plessis of the political science
department at Potchefstroom University, van der Merwe
formed a parliamentary Republican Union ("Republikeinse
Bond"), whose express purpose was to encourage republicanism within the National party (Scholtz, G. D., 1944, p. 99).
Three months later, van der Merwe officially publicized the
existence of this pressure group in an effort to extend its
activities beyond the confines of the parliamentary caucus.
In his speech on this occasion, he continued where his earlier
article on Isaiah 21:12 had left off. He had decided that it
was indeed still night. "If I am true to myself and if I look
into the future," said van der Merwe, "[then I must aver
that] the Great Trek to Freedom and Independence is not
yet over. . . .

> We must have a definite positive ideal to proclaim publicly.
> . . Our ideal is the Republic of South Africa. . . When I think
> of the struggle of the past, when I think of the thousands
> of sacrifices which today lie under the ground, of the women
> and children who died in the camps, of which I myself as a
> child was witness, when I think of more than one who died
> on the battlefield or even hung on the gallows, when I think
> of Steyn and de Wet, then I say: In truth, No! They did not
> die to see their posterity submit to the British Crown. . . . Then
> I hear a voice cry out from the bloodstained soil of my
> fatherland: "Trek on! Not far enough!" [Scholtz, G. D., 1944,
> pp. 193-195]

It was to some extent inevitable that, once securely in
power, General Hertzog, with his basically skeptical attitude
toward the civil religion, should come into conflict with its
true believers—even more so after the Balfour Declaration.
At the same time, the forces of the civil religion were becoming
organized by the Afrikaner Broederbond, both through the
growth of its membership and in its systematization of an

[13] See editorials in *Die Weste* (January 20 and August 14, 1928);
Die Burger (October 22, 1929); and also articles in *Die Weste* by
Dr. A. M. Moll of Johannesburg and Dr. H. J. Steyn of Bloemfontein. These were republished in pamphlet form (Moll, n.d. (a) and
(b); and Steyn, 1929).

Afrikaner ideology. New and stronger clashes would eventually ensue. It is hence to the Afrikaner Broederbond that we shall now turn.

6

The Afrikaner Broederbond and the Resurgence of the Civil Religion

In his little history of the Day of the Covenant, Marius Swart notes that December 16, Geloftedag, is "an excellent barometer of the national consciousness" (Swart, 1961, p. 70). If this is so, then the period from the formation of the Union until 1928 was a low one indeed for an exclusively Afrikaner ethnic consciousness. With the exception of the Smuts-Botha paper, *Die Volkstem*, little was made of December 16 in the Transvaal Afrikaans press, which on the other hand dwelt at interminable length on the political struggle.[1] From reports in *Die Burger*, it is clear that the day was seldom celebrated in the Cape at all.

In all four provinces important speakers at these celebrations, when they were held, tended to emphasize white unity in the face of the supposed threat from black South Africans, rather than Afrikaner uniqueness. General Hertzog's speech at Oudefontein on December 16, 1925, was typical:

> The European must keep to a standard of living which shall meet the demands of white civilization. Civilization and standards of living always go hand in hand. Thus a white cannot

---

[1] *Ons Vaderland*, however, did publish a cultural supplement called *Brandwag* ("Sentinel") which occasionally dealt with Afrikaner sacred history.

exist on a native wage-scale, because this means that he has
to give up his own standard of living and take on the standard
of living of the native. In short, the white man becomes a
white nigger [*wit kaffer*]. [*Volkstem*, December 17, 1925]

Die Burger, in its editorials on December 16 in both 1925
and 1927 classes the English settlers with the Afrikaner
Voortrekkers as fellow sufferers under imperial policy and
black depredation. At important Geloftedag celebrations, the
governor-general of South Africa, representing King George
V, not only attended but spoke at length in English. "God
Save the King" heralded his arrival at all such ceremonies.
(Cf. *Die Volkstem*, December 17, 1926; December 16, 1927;
December 17, 1928).

The irony is that in 1924, right in the middle of this low
period on the "Covenant Day barometer," the National party
under General Hertzog came to power. Is Marius Swart then
simply wrong? The difficulty would seem to lie in his omnibus
phrase, "national consciousness." In the South African context, the phrase may be used in at least two ways: either
in the sense of the civil religion—that is, a sophisticated
theological interpretation of God's acts in Afrikaner history
with an explicitly republican eschatology; or in the far more
inchoate sense of a generalized feeling of "Afrikanerness," with
emphasis on the common language.[2] The Day of the Covenant
celebrations were certainly a barometer of "national consciousness" in the former, civil-religion sense, while they were
less relevant in the latter, primal nationalist issue.

The previous chapter has attempted to show that Hertzog's
victory in 1924 was based on this primal "Afrikaner national
feeling" combined with fear of black competition and capitalism. Thus, in emphasizing "white unity," the Day of the
Covenant editorials and speeches at this time tended to reflect
political exigencies of the day rather than the "true" civil
theology. In fact, we have noted that as early as the Vereinig-
ing debates, Hertzog had made clear that an exclusive interpretation of the Afrikaner civil religion was essentially alien
to his liberal political thought as well as to his very personal

[2] Robert Bellah would refer to this as the civil "religious ground
bass" (Bellah, 1970, p. 126).

religious faith. Despite his scorn for public appeal to the Lord on behalf of Afrikanerism, Hertzog retained the support of the civil-religion enthusiasts before the Balfour Declaration because he seemed to be moving in the right direction. "Hertzog has his faults," said W. A. Hofmeyr in a 1916 address before the Cape local National party branch at Wellington (reported in the local minutes, August 5, 1916), "but he is a man of principle."

Whatever Hertzog felt about the civil religion, the Wellington local Nationalists were typical in making little distinction at this time between their political functions and organization of the Day of the Covenant celebrations. On November 27, 1915, the Wellington branch had a long discussion as to whether the annual Day of the Covenant celebration should be held indoors or outside. They decided to hold it outdoors, but should a change of plan be necessitated by weather, it would be held in the church. At no time did any of these Hertzogite discussants suggest consulting the South African party's Afrikaner adherents in the town, and the Wellington National party branch seemed quite able to answer for the N.G. church council. Thus no concern was shown, at least on the local level, for enforcing the principle of strict separation between party politics, church and civil religion.

Such casual disregard of these distinctions could not long continue once the implications of the split between Botha and Hertzog began to be felt at the grassroots. Until the establishment of the National party, the political unity of Afrikanerdom had not required conscious differentation between the spheres of political activity, church affairs, and the nascent civil religion. It was the exigency of Afrikaner political disagreements which forced upon intellectuals and churchmen the subtle distinction between *partypolitiek* and *kultuurpolitiek*, which allowed them to pursue the goal of Afrikaner *volkseenheid* and at the same time to eschew party-political squabbles.

Rival celebrations of Geloftedag at Paardekraal and Senekal in 1916, for example, clearly revealed the dangers inherent in party-political involvement. While Botha and a few loyal dominees urged English-Afrikaner national unity at Paardekraal, speakers at Senekal (including Dr. Malan, Tobie Muller, a Nationalist senator and two Nationalist members of parliament) dealt with such topics as "Are we a People?", "The Afrikaner Woman," and "The Place of Suffering in our People's History." Significantly, General Smuts took time out from his imperial activities overseas to send a congratulatory cable to Paardekraal, while the proceedings at Senekal included the reading of a brief telegram from General Hertzog. Both celebrations called forth angry protest from political opponents, who argued that party politics was being drawn into the civil ritual. It was partly because of such charges that interest in celebrating the day waned during the next decade (Swart, 1961, pp. 65-66).

Under the influence of the Afrikaner Broederbond, small local celebrations continued to be held on the Rand, however. These Geloftedag festivals in and around Johannesburg made an appeal to the new urban Afrikaner and were expressly intended to offset the attraction of the government-organized Paardekraal celebrations. The mere organization of these Day of the Covenant festivals was an early positive step toward the realization of the Broederbond's original intention, that is "the positive cultivation of reciprocal goodwill, friendship, brotherhood as binding factors in the struggle to bring together all Afrikaans-speaking Afrikaners who longed for the elevation of our People" (Erasmus, n.d., p. 11).

When the Bond went underground in 1922, with Ivan Lombard as organizing secretary, its influence began to extend far beyond the Rand. Its members, drawn from all parts of the country, became a new Afrikaner elite who felt themselves united in a civil-religious crusade for their People. Although the administrative center of the Bond remained in Johannesburg, its ideological leadership shifted to Potchefstroom, where Professor J. C. van Rooy became chairman. This was a very determinative factor in the direction that the Bond was to take, for Potchefstroom was the hotbed of Kuyperianism. Let us recall that Kuyperian doctrine preached the immutable exclusiveness of ethnic nationalities, and that all the various spheres of national life were subsumed within God's calling.

The major organizational unit for Bond activities was the local "division" or "cell" made up of between five and twenty members who met at least once a month to discuss "how the ethnic life of the Afrikaner might be enriched." Each cell was ideally composed of representatives of a variety of different occupations so that a cross-section of Afrikaner opinion might be expressed at the meetings. The Bond thus attempted to create a multiplicity of primary groups in which "ordinary persons" might interact creatively to bring about desired changes.

> The bond is based [said Lombard in 1944[3]] on the notion that if many people come together in a hall, they may listen to speeches and agree or disagree, but they cannot really deliberate with one another. The result is that the leaders can originate plans and carry them out, but not the ordinary members. . . The bond thus grew out of ordinary persons who wanted to help . . [*Die Burger*, December 28, 1944).

Precise data on the socioeconomic background of Bond members seems impossible to procure, but we know that in 1944, a third of the Broers were school teachers and almost a tenth were civil servants. The majority of the remaining percentage were wealthy farmers. We may safely assume that a relatively high proportion of Afrikaner academics, churchmen of the Kuyperian as well as of the *volkskerk* persuasion, and a number of rural attorneys were important leading members.[4] Since the *platteland* ("rural") elite consisted of the local magistrate and attorney, the doctor, the pastor, the school principal, and the wealthiest farmers, rural membership of the Bond was clearly drawn from the local "gentry." Among the new urban Afrikaners, the most rapid channels to social advancement lay in teaching or through the civil service, so here, too, the Broederbond membership was strik-

---

[3] For an English translation (somewhat paraphrased) of the 1944-1945 statements of van Rooy and Lombard, see Vatcher (1965, pp. 277-284).

[4] These estimates are taken from Lombard's statements, supplemented by the 1944 report of General Smuts' Intelligence Service (reprinted in Vatcher, 1965, pp. 256-276). Where possible, I have relied on the Bond's own statements, or statements authorized by the Bond. Hostile accounts have been considered only when they were not explicitly denied by Bond members.

ingly similar to pre-revolutionary English Puritanism, which was, in Michael Walzer's words, "the political religion of intellectuals (ministers) and gentlemen" (Walzer, 1965, p. 328).

We have seen that in his 1944 statement, Lombard strongly denied that the Broederbond was an elitist organization. Many of the Afrikaner elite were excluded from consideration, he said, because of a two-fold effort to keep the groups small and to represent all the different occupational groups. "This attempt meant that many important Afrikaners in high positions who [were] also held in high regard by Afrikanerdom [were not] approached to become members, while persons in inferior positions [did] indeed become members" (*Die Burger*, December 28, 1944). In fact, Lombard implied elsewhere that older persons in key positions were deliberately excluded from consideration:

> The standard used is the zeal and readiness of members to work for People's causes and regularly to make sacrifices, monetary or otherwise, without any expectation of reward. The tendency is rather to give preference to young men, so that they may have the opportunity to learn to perform useful service to the People. Older persons in key positions already have that opportunity. [*Die Volksblad*, December 14, 1944]

Clearly Lombard believed that these latter did not use their opportunity to best advantage.

However, despite this explicit policy of recruiting only zealous young men, by the time of Lombard's statement the Bond had been in existence for twenty-five years; and there seems no cause to doubt the 1944 report by Smuts' military intelligence that Bond members did indeed hold leading positions in the National party, Afrikaner businesses and trade unions, the civil service, the teaching profession, and the synods of the N.G. and Gereformeerde churches (Vatcher, 1965, pp. 264-272). If this was the case, then either the Bond was remarkably astute in selecting its promising young men, or membership in the Bond was itself useful for professional advancement. In fact, probably both factors applied. Since the Afrikaner elite was very small in the 1920s and the 1930s, young men with ambition and ability must have been widely known. On the other hand, as Lombard himself acknowledged, the true Broer gave preference "to Afrikaners and other well-disposed persons and firms in the economic, public, and professional life" (*Die Burger*, December 28, 1944). Undoubtedly the best proof that one was a "well-disposed Afrikaner" was his very membership in the Bond.[5]

The formal procedure for nomination of new Bond members was tightly controlled, with elaborate screening to ensure that only the truly faithful be offered the opportunity of joining. Before suggesting a prospective member, the proposer and seconder had to be quite sure that he met the following requirements:

1. Does he strive for the ideal of the eternal existence of a separate Afrikaner nation with its own language and culture?

2. Does he give preference to Afrikaners and other well-disposed persons and firms in economic, public, and professional life?

3. Does he uphold Afrikaans in his home and profession and in the wider society?

4. Is he of Protestant faith?

5. Are the proposer and seconder convinced that nothing in his person, character, or behavior precludes him from brotherhood?

6. Particularly, is he principled, faithful, and cautious enough to meet the demands of the Bond?

7. Is he financially sound?

8. Is he able and willing to take part actively, regularly, and faithfully in all the functions and activites of the Bond?

[Oelofse, 1964, pp. 11-12][6]

[5] Once the secret society had achieved its major ends, the original idealistic purposes became distorted. On his deathbed, Professor E. C. Pienaar, who had been an ardent Broer, and indeed chairman of the Bond in the early fifties, recalled that in the old days (the thirties and forties), the Bond had been an "idealistic movement to make Afrikaans and Afrikaners count in South African life," and lamented that it had deteriorated to a simple matter of "jobs for pals" (*baantjies vir boeties*).

[6] This pamphlet reported findings from an investigation into the Broederbond by an Hervormde church elder who was instructed

The names of prospective new members were mentioned at a cell meeting, fully discussed at a second, and voted on at a third. A single dissenting vote on the cell level automatically excluded an individual member from further consideration for one year. Once an individual was duly nominated by a local cell, his name would then be circulated for a three-month period to all Bond members, who discussed all nominees and submitted any objections in writing to the general secretary. If more than three members objected to a particular nominee, his name would be withdrawn. Finally, the executive council (elected by representatives of each cell at an annual general meeting) could exercise ultimate veto power. Only after having been approved by the executive council, would the prospective member be approached and asked to join. If the individual agreed, he was then introduced to his cell-brothers at a formal ceremony of initiation. This ceremony, often held by candlelight (Oelofse, 1964, p. 29), opened with a reading from scripture and with prayer. The objectives of the organization were read aloud, and the new member would swear to uphold them.[7] A reliable source outlines the major tenets of the initiation formula as follows:

1. The prospective member is informed that the Afrikaner Broederbond is born out of the deep conviction that the Afrikaner nation with its own character and task was called into being in this land by the hand of God, and is destined to continue to exist as long as God so wishes.

2. "You are expected to live and act in the firm conviction that the fate of nations is controlled by an Almighty, Divine hand, and to stand firm upon the Christian-his-

---

to ascertain whether the secret organization was exercising undue influence in church decisions. A few months before Oelofse's investigation, certain Broederbond documents had been published in the *Johannesburg Sunday Times*, and his report published these documents with the Broederbond imprimatur.

[7] The Smuts report speaks of a far more elaborate ritual of initiation, one involving blood and bodies (Vatcher, 1965, pp. 259-260). This Oelofse mentions, but only to deny it on the basis of the documents placed at his disposal and testimony of members. However, since each cell had the freedom to arrange its own *mise en scene*, dramatic initiation rites cannot be ruled out entirely.

torical tradition, founded upon the two tables of the Holy Law of God [the Ten Commandments], which is the inheritance of our Afrikaner nation."

3. "You are expected to strive for the realization of the ideals of the Bond, not only by cooperating in organized efforts, but also by your individual conduct in your own sphere of influence and work-circle, inspired and supported by your fellow-brothers and guided by the ideals of the Bond."

[Oelofse, 1964, pp. 28-29]

These formulae of initiation reveal close correspondence between the ruling principles of the Bond and the fully developed Afrikaner civil theology of the 1940s. Underlying both was a conviction that God had elected the Afrikaner People for a special calling, as proved by their history in "the Christian-historical tradition."

A fourth tenet to which the new initiate had to swear emphasized the necessity for secrecy about Bond activities, especially the names of fellow members. As Georg Simmel demonstrates at length, secrecy leads to exclusivism and group egoism (Wolff, 1950, pp. 362-376). When the group has been called into being in order to serve exclusivist ends, this tendency is, of course, all the more strengthened. By virtue of God's election of his People, every Afrikaner was part of an elite. But within this elite, members of the Broederbond were particularly chosen. Indeed, the careful procedure for selection to membership cannot but have enhanced the psychological sense of being called by God to serve Afrikanerdom in a special way.[8]

Once an individual was initiated into the Bond, he was expected to attend regular meetings at which were discussed matters of vital interest to the Afrikaner People, such as the

[8] Lombard went so far as to argue that the Broederbond served Afrikanerdom in much the same way that the parliamentary cabinet serves a democratic nation-state. Everything that the Bond did was for the benefit and advancement of the People, he said. It always served the interests of Afrikanerdom. Furthermore, even as the cabinet submits its decisions to parliament for approval, so the Broederbond turned to the People before it acted (Vatcher, 1965, pp. 280-281).

poverty of Afrikaners, mother-tongue education, the anglicization of Afrikanerdom, racial segregation, etc. Every proposal on such issues was considered, ideally at least, from a broad
spectrum of Afrikaner points of view, by virtue of cell-mem-
bership composition. Once a particular suggestion for furthering the Afrikaner cause had been approved by a local group,
it was submitted for debate to other local cells throughout
the land. Finally, the proposal would be brought before the
annual general meeting of the Bond. If it was ratified there,
the next stage was to "submit it to the People."

"The issue itself, with all its pros and cons, was not
submitted to the People in the name of the Broederbond,"
said Lombard, "because the Bond [did] not seek any credit
for itself. The proposals [were] normally left in the hands
of those persons who [had] shown the most concern for the
problem and [were] most informed about it." (*Die Volksblad*,
December 30, 1944). The usual way for these experts to bring
their case before the People was to call a Volkskongres
("People's Congress"), which would receive much publicity
in the Afrikaans press and which all interested Afrikaners
were urged to attend. Such Volkskongresse, often billed as
arising spontaneously from the bosom of the People, typically
led to the formulation of an independent association specifically dedicated to furthering the proposals which had originated in the secrecy of Broederbond discussion and been sealed
by the "People's" approval at the Volkskongres.

An important example of this modus operandi was the
formation in 1929 of the F.A.K. ("Federation of Afrikaner
Cultural Organizations"). This consequential organization
was created to meet certain ideological needs which other
local Afrikaner voluntary associations in the Transvaal had
earlier sought to fill in a more limited way. Private, church-
supported schools for "Christian National education," for
instance, had arisen after the Boer War to protect children
from anglicization through Lord Milner's government education.[9] Teachers at these schools saw themselves as guardians

---

[9] These Christian National schools were integrated into the state
educational system as soon as the Transvaal obtained responsible
government.

of the "true" language of the community as well as educationalists. These same teachers helped to establish young people's associations and debating societies.

> In these associations, oratory, acting and folk-singing were appropriated as weapons—not merely for education and entertainment, but in the elaboration of a new struggle with other methods. They were an incalculable and indispensable force, since they awakened an awareness of nationality in the youth and spurred them to protect their language and traditions. [Euvrard, 1956, pp. 23-24]

The Transvaal Teachers' Union (T.O.) provided an institutional base after 1919 for the involvement of educators in Afrikaner cultural affairs, for the T.O. took the position that the teacher, "in addition to his classwork [ought to] apply himself to the broader task of the education and service of the People" (Erasmus, n.d., p. 87). There were strong ties through common membership between the T.O. and the Broederbond.

As the Broederbond spread beyond the Transvaal, members began to establish new voluntary cultural associations for the furtherance of Christian National ideology. The Cape and the Orange Free State did not want for an intense associational life already.[10] "In even the smallest of villages," said G. D. Scholtz, "there [were] the debating society, the youth group, the women's association, the dramatic society, the agricultural cooperative, and so on" (Scholtz, G. D., 1944, p. 121). However, in contrast to organizations established before 1925, "the newer [Broederbond inspired] bodies accented assertion (*handhawing*) and positive proselytization. In the background of the struggle lurked the awareness that Afrikaans culture had not yet become something which the Afrikaner himself could claim through action and application" (F.A.K. Memorial Album, cited in Euvrard, 1956, p. 77). In the older, more liberal tradition, voluntary associations were established to meet certain limited ends, such as entertainment, charity, the moral education of young people, or informal speaking and reading of Afrikaans. But the old order,

[10] James Luther Adams, in his lectures at Harvard Divinity School, was wont to emphasize the extent to which Calvinism encourages the formation of voluntary associations.

"and old orders are always stubborn," had to be "attacked and transformed" (Euvrard, 1956, p. 77). The new bodies, or older ones transformed by Broederbond leadership, continued to emphasize earlier goals but placed them in the wider context of the awakening and assertion of the Afrikaner People.

In this process, the general meaning of the word 'culture" shifted from emphasis on the creative arts to a more technical and ethnic sense that limited "culture" to the civil-religious conception of traditional forms of Afrikaner life. *Die Republikein* spelled out this meaning of the word in an article on its children's page:

> Culture is the name given to the common spiritual possessions of a People. It is their birthright, left to them by their ancestors, their history and their tradition; a birthright, however, which is carefully preserved against foreign interference and just as carefully supplemented only to the extent that ethnic consciousness increases. [*Die Republikein*, November 22, 1935]

The use of the term "culture" defined in turn the boundaries of creative art by arguing that works of art ought to speak in Afrikaner, or Christian National, language and symbol.

The new ethnic conception of culture, although it was occasionally attacked,[11] was perhaps an inevitable accompaniment of the Broederbond belief that "the Afrikaner People was planted in our land by the hand of God, and is destined to continue to exist as a People with its own character and particular calling" (*Die Volksblad*, December 14, 1944). In the opinion of the Broederbond, the cause of Afrikaner culture was hampered by the coexistence of a plethora of cultural organizations with different goals and often conflicting ideologies. By 1929, according to Secretary Lombard,

> various [Broederbond] cells had become aware of the possibility of cultural chaos and of the need for some or other form of central guidance which, in the midst of the various goals of numerous associations, could help to build up the common factor, namely the Afrikaans language, art, and culture, and help all of them to defend it aggressively (*handhaaf*). The

---

[11] The Afrikaans poet, Elizabeth Eybers, called it "a thoroughly systematic exploitation of the herd instinct" (Antonissen, 1964, p. 197: cf. also *Besembos*, September 1930).

various forms which such a central organization might take were thoroughly thrashed out in Broederbond discussions. [*Volksblad*, December 30, 1944]

At the June 1929 annual general meeting of the Broederbond, it was decided to call a great congress of representatives from all Afrikaner cultural organizations. A summons went out, signed by Ivan M. Lombard, that called all Afrikaners to a Union-wide conference to be held in Bloemfontein on December 18, 1929. This announcement was followed by exhortations by other prominent Afrikaners, many in the language movement (e.g., *Die Volksblad*, October 7 and October 8, 1929), and as the date of the conference drew nearer, Afrikaans newspapers carried numerous letters to the editor urging every Afrikaner organization in the country to send representation to the gathering (e.g., *Die Burger*, November 25 and November 29; December 12, December 14, and December 16, 1929). Even the editorial in *Die Burger* on Covenant Day dealt with the coming conference:

> There is a task which the Dutch-Afrikaner has in common with his English-Afrikaner compatriots as bearer of white civilization, but there is also the special task which rests upon him in his own area, namely Dutch-Afrikaner culture. . . The remembrances and inspiration which the Dutch Afrikaner today obtains by looking back to the sufferings and struggles of the forefathers must pass over into deeds. . . .[*Die Burger*, December 16, 1929]

At the conference there was much "remembrance and inspiration." The opening address, by N. J. van der Merwe, set the general tone of the congress:

> The whole past of our People calls us to press on. . . [T]he spirit of the heroes of our People hovers over the Conference. I hear the voices of thousands who gave their lives for preservation of the Afrikaner cry out, "Say to this People that they must rise up and take possession of their inheritance. In God's name let them not rest now and accept a peace which will be more dangerous than the war which we went through." [*Die Burger*, December 19, 1929]

Professor Pienaar's speech at the congress aimed at integrating the old Cape language movement into the wider concern for Afrikaner culture.

[I]t must be obvious, [he said], that our call to maintain and assert [*handhaaf*] our language is not born out of racial hatred or from sentimental or chauvinistic considerations, but that we are here concerned with our highest and holiest ethnic concerns, for defence of language means in the nature of the case defence of the People, because it means the cultivation and confirmation of national consciousness, national pride, national calling, and national destiny. . . Providence would not have given us a language if we ought not to have had one, otherwise the whole world would have been populated with Britons. That is why we must safeguard [*handhaaf*] [our culture]. [*Die Burger*, December 19, 1929]

What the assembled gathering achieved was to elect a central executive and four provincial bodies which would be responsible for establishing the new cultural federation. The central executive consisted of Dr. N. J. van der Merwe, Professor E. C. Pienaar of Stellenbosch University, Dr. T. J. Hugo of Pretoria University and Mr. L. J. Erasmus of the T.O., all of whom were prominent Broers, and Mrs. E. G. Jansen, a fiery Afrikaner from Natal. The overwhelming majority of provincial executive members were likewise members of the Broederbond.

Scholtz could look back with pride in 1944 on the attainments of the Federasie van Afrikaner Kultuurorganisasies (F.A.K.):

It was the F.A.K. which was the first to urge that Afrikaans music examinations be set up; it was the F.A.K. which was the first to concern itself with the right of Afrikaans to equality on the radio; it was the F.A.K. which began to gather Afrikaans folksongs in a single volume; it was the F.A.K. which initiated the establishment of "Culture Days"; it was the F.A.K. which arranged Afrikaans art exhibitions and book weeks; it was the F.A.K. which first thought of the great centenary festivals of 1938; it was the F.A.K. which endeavored in all possible ways to awaken concern for the People's past in the Afrikaner; it was the F.A.K. which first strove for an Afrikaans national anthem. . . .[Scholtz, G. D., 1944, pp. 123-124]

Thus did the F.A.K. "safeguard." Its major function was a symbolic one, ensuring that all the diverse activities listed above were done in the name of a consistent rhetoric. This latter pattern of ideological justification was referred to by members as Christian Nationalism, which was in fact a Kuyperian interpretation of the civil religion.

The words "Christian National" originated in Holland where Groen van Prinsterer coined the term to refer to the necessary interdependence of culture and faith in Christian education. The Christian National movement was kindled in South Africa after the Boer War to ensure Christian education for young Transvaalers and Free Staters in their own language. However, the original emphasis had shifted somewhat under the assumptions of *volkskerk* theology. The movement was concerned with the continuance of the Christian faith among Afrikaners, but now it recognized that the Dutch Reformed churches could not exist without the Afrikaner People. Hence the separate ethnic characteristics of Afrikaners had to be preserved at all cost. As used by members of the Broederbond, this stress on the "national" as opposed to the "Christian" element was carried to its logical conclusion. No longer was the major concern directed to the continuance of the church per se, but rather to the interpretation of the history of this ethnic group in terms of God's sovereign will as shown forth in the ordinances of creation. What had started as a method of Christian education had thus become a theory of national election and henceforth ideological articulation of the civil religion was usually dubbed "Christian National."

It was largely owing to the part played by the F.A.K. that the Christian National interpretation of the sacred history soon became the most widely accepted version of the civil theology. The philosophical basis of this interpretation was clearly stated by van Rooy in a speech at Stellenbosch in 1944:

> In every People in the world is embodied a Divine Idea and the task of each People is to build upon that Idea and to perfect it. So God created the Afrikaner People with a unique language, a unique philosophy of life, and their own history and tradition in order that they might fulfill a particular calling and destiny here in the southern corner of Africa. We must stand guard on all that is peculiar to us and build upon it. We must believe that God has called us to be servants of his

righteousness in this place. We must walk the way of obedience
to faith. . . [*Die Burger*, October 11, 1944]

Notice here the insistence on the ethnic ordinances of creation, and more particularly the view that each People is
part of God's cosmic purpose, which was a typical stance
of Stoker and the Potchefstroom Kuyperians.

However, one cannot speak continuously of "calling" and
"destiny" without eventually articulating the specific content
of the ideal. Whither was the Afrikaner destiny and to what
end their call? The calling of the Afrikaner was to remain
true to his express particularity, "to continue with the struggle to maintain our language and culture," said van Rooy.
In order to realize the Divine Idea which was embodied in
Afrikanerdom, he continued, the People would have to achieve
a Christian republic. Afrikaner nationhood might have been
written in the ordinances of creation, but it could be developed
and perfected only in the republican eschaton. As van Rooy
stated, "the Christian republican state is the only constitutional form for the proper completion of our calling. Thus
we must proceed in this direction and steadfastly strive for
the realization of the republican idea" (*Die Burger*, Octber
11, 1944).

In 1933, eleven years before the speech cited above, the
Broederbond had decided to include the republican ideal in
its formal declaration of purpose. At its annual congress of
1932,[12] van Rooy had observed that the most pressing need
of the People, that of cultural assertion, had been effectively
met. The Broederbond thus felt satisfied to continue to hand
over "cultural work" to its "large child, the F.A.K." (Vatcher,
1965, p. 246). After cultural concerns came political exigencies,
according to van Rooy. Hence, the Bond's second avenue of

---

[12] Although references to this congress are culled from an anti-
Broederbond speech by General Hertzog in 1935, Broederbond
members who replied to his attack made no attempt to deny the
accuracy of his sources. In fact, van der Merwe, for one, implicitly
acknowledged the accuracy of Hertzog's documentation, but insisted on a different interpretation of the material (*Die Volksblad*,
November 16, 1935).

attack lay in the political sphere. This Chairman van Rooy acknowledged at the same Congress:

> I consider that the national culture and the welfare of the nation will not be able to flourish to the fullest extent if the People of South Africa do not politically break all foreign bonds. After the cultural and economic needs, the Broederbond will have to dedicate its attention to the political needs of our People. And this aim must include a completely independent, truly Afrikaans government for South Africa—a government which by its embodiment of our own personal head of state, bone of our bone, flesh of our flesh, will inspire us and bind us together to irresistible unity and power. [Vatcher, 1965, p. 246]

Now, article six of the Bond constitution states clearly that "party politics is excluded from the Bond . . . [Nevertheless, in] connection with the activities of the general divisional meetings [cells], the meeting may discuss any ethnic or historical point in order impartially to discover that which is best for the moral, intellectual, social, and political progress of our nation.[13] However, no speaker may advance as a propagandist for any existing political party or for party-politics as such" (*Die Volksblad*, January 2, 1945). Thus, although the Bond specifically excluded involvement in *partypolitiek* the "political progress of the People" in a broader and more general sense, was certainly a matter for discussion at meetings. This broader political commitment of the Bond was carefully outlined and specified at the 1933 congress in the following terms:[14]

> The bond expects that all Broers will seek the following sevenfold ideal in their political activities:
>
> 1. The elimination of everything that conflicts with the full international independence of South Africa.
>
> 2. Removal of the inferiority in the state-organization of the Afrikaans-speaking section and their language.
>
> 3. Segregation of all the colored races domiciled in South

[13] Notice again the assumption that the Broederbond is somehow uniquely equipped to speak for the People.

[14] I calculate this date from internal evidence in Hertzog's 1935 speech and should welcome correction if I am wrong.

Africa, while allowing their independent development under the guardianship of the whites.

4. Abolition of the exploitation by foreigners of the natural resources and population of South Africa. This shall include more intensive industrial development.

5. Rehabilitation of the farming community and the guarantee of a civilized standard of life through work for all white citizens.

6. The nationalization of finance and the planned coordination of economic policy.

7. The Afrikanerization of our public life and our education in a Christian Nationalist direction, while leaving free the internal development of all sections of the population insofar as this is not dangerous to the state.

[*Die Volksblad,* January 3, 1945]

Thus, although the Broederbond formally excluded *partypolitiek*, it allowed—indeed encouraged—*kultuurpolitiek*, which included civil-religion ideals such as the republic. Only in a republic, in fact, would Bond ideals, including mother-tongue education, Afrikanerization of public life, and racial separation, be realized (cf. du Plessis, et al., n.d.).

On January 16, 1934, van Rooy and Lombard sent out a circular letter to all members of the Bond which read:

Our test of Brotherhood and Afrikanerhood is not a party-political direction, [but we are] persons who strive for the ideal of the everlasting existence of a separate Afrikaans nation with its own culture. At the previous Bond Council, it was clearly expressed that what was expected of such persons was that they would have as their object Afrikanerization of South Africa in all its spheres of life. Brothers, your Executive Council cannot say to you: "Further party-political Fusion or Union or Reunion, or fight against it. . . but we can make a call on every Brother to choose in the sphere of party politics what, according to his fixed conviction, is most profitable for the object of the Bond and the Bond's ideal, as recorded above and as known to all of us. Let us keep the eye fixed on this—that the main object is . . . that Afrikanerdom shall reach its ultimate destiny of domination in South Africa. . . . Brother, our solution for South Africa's troubles is not that this or that party shall gain the upper hand, but that the Afrikaner

Broederbond shall rule South Africa. [Vatcher, 1965, pp. 146-147]

This final sentence, once made public, provided splendid ammunition for opponents of the Broederbond, who argued that it was a sinister political network whose ambition was to control all of South African life from a secret headquarters somewhere in Johannesburg (or was it Potchefstroom)? In fact, from the full context of van Rooy and Lombard's letter, it is clear that they did not seek political power for themselves, but rather that those who did hold political power in South Africa should be inspired by the ideals of the Afrikaner Broederbond. Although this subtle distinction might strike one as trifling, to those members of the Broederbond who were party politicans, on the one hand, or churchmen, on the other, it was crucial. In times of political crisis, the Bond might sail very close to the wind, but efforts were always made to adhere to the distinction between party politics and political ideals (*kultuurpolitiek*).

Once again we are reminded of the analogy to the English Puritans. Michael Walzer's portrait of early English Calvinists might well have been written with the Afrikaner Broers in mind:

> They were committed. . . to the literal reforming of human society, to the creation of a Holy Commonwealth in which conscientious activity would be encouraged and even required. The saints saw themselves as divine *instruments* and theirs was the politics of wreckers, architects, and builders—hard at work upon the political world. . . Because their work required cooperation, they organized to carry it through successfully and they joined forces with any man who might help them. . . They sought "brethren". . . The saint's personality . . . was marked above all by an uncompromising and sustained commitment to a political ideal (which other men called hypocrisy), and by a pattern of rigorous and systematic labor in pursuit of that ideal (which other men called meddlesomeness). [Walzer, 1965, p. 3]

In similar fashion the Brothers of the Bond were labeled racists because of their commitment to "the ideal of the everlasting existence of a separate Afrikaans nation with its own culture." Their mere acknowledgement of their calling to serve the Afrikanns-speaking People of South Africa elicited accusations from enemies, who accused them, at best, of presumption, and at worst of self-righteous arrogance. One critic, speaking for Smuts' liberal idea of civic integration, summed up his attack on the Bond by condemning it outright as

> an attempt by the Afrikaners to establish a national state within a state that to them, at any rate, is the antithesis of what they desire. This attempt must by its very character be both subversive and reactionary. It is subversive because it diverts the loyalty of its adherents from the "de facto" state and must, whether it does so consciously or not, ultimately aim at displacing that state.[15]

The arrogant purpose of the Bond amounted to more than an immoral platform, he argued. It was, in effect, a subversive and revolutionary effort to overthrow the South African state.

Within the overall process of Afrikaner achievement of political dominance in South Africa, however, one must beware of overrating the importance of the Afrikaner Broederbond. The role of the Brotherhood was crucial, both in organizing the rising Afrikaner elite, and in providing an interpretation of the civil theology which was tight enough to unite Afrikaners and yet loose enough to allow considerable difference of opinion on practical matters. But to overemphasize the contribution of the Broederbond is to denigarate the importance of the National party, whose role in the eventual triumph of Afrikanerdom was quite as important as that of the Bond. Neither may one assume that the party and the Broederbond, *partypolitiek* and *kultuurpolitiek*, always worked hand-in-glove. In spite of the fact that many members of the National party elite were Bond members, ideological radicals of the Brotherhood found much cause for irritation and impatience with the pragmatic maneuverings of the National party, as we shall have frequent occasion to note. Indeed, Afrikaner politics after 1930 was greatly complicated by the vagaries of the relationship between *partypolitiek* and *kultuurpolitiek*.

[15] This was set forth in *The Afrikaner-Broederbond* (pp. 24-25), a pamphlet written anonymously by "a well-known Afrikaner" and issued by the Campaign for Right and Justice, Exploration Buildings, Johannesburg, about 1945.

7

Samesmelting and Republicanism

The enthusiastic demand that Afrikaners "stand on guard" (*handhaaf*) for their culture grew out of deliberations in the Afrikaner Broederbond, but republicanism, as we have seen, had a history which went back into the preceding century. Thus when Jan Celliers, poet laureate of the civil religion, spoke on Geloftedag in 1925 he was not witnessing to membership in the Broederbond but to a deep republican sentiment which was traditional in the Transvaal:

> The Afrikaner will speak of the suffering and struggle of the Voortrekkers and the agonies of women and children in the Second War for Freedom [Boer War]. Today is the day to shed a tear upon their graves. We shall water the tree that the Voortrekkers planted until one day we may pluck the fruit. And I shall name that fruit, even though the Governor-General and others are here, for it is not political, but a universal human need. That fruit is our total sovereign independence. [*Die Burger*, December 18, 1925]

Total sovereign independence had indeed been realized, declared General Hertzog on his return from the Imperial Conference in 1926. He did not speak with the full concurrence of the National party, however.

The anti-Hertzog republican movement, which began to gather momentum after 1926, was rooted in a simple sentimental attachment to the past and made a special appeal to ordinary Afrikaners in the Transvaal and Orange Free

State. Its emotional force is poignantly expressed in a letter written by one F. Joubert-Pienaar to Hertzog's newspaper:

> Republicanism cannot be suppressed, smothered, or slaughtered. It was planted at Vegkop, Blood River, and Paardekraal in ground made fruitful by the blood and tears of the Boer, his wife and child; and the roots penetrated so deeply that the plant can never again be destroyed by anything. [An English officer during the Boer War arranged that the sacred pile of stones at Paardekraal be thrown into the sea] . . . so that that pile of stones might never again be a monument to the trust of a People in their God. But that Englishman could not know that the root which penetrated so deeply in the lives of Republicans would grow into a tree of such mighty aspect. . . . My stone and that of my wife lay there too, and I know the feeling that gripped us that day when the fierce covenant of brotherhood, of sacrifice and of religion was sworn with prayer and tears. . . . When we fought and died in the Wars of Freedom for our two Republics, was it to become "Free Britishers?" . . . Do you think that the 23,000 women and children who rest beneath that Monument in Bloemfontein gave their lives for that? Is that the reason that President Steyn and General de Wet lie there? Was that the reason that President Kruger had to die a fugitive in Europe? And where is the blood of Beyers, Jopie Fourie, and thousands of others? Oh please do not allow those bones to begin moving under the ground! [*Ons Vaderland*, February 10, 1931]

This was the ground bass of republican opposition to Hertzog, on which the intellectual leaders developed their philosophical justifications, two of which were relevant at this early stage.

One position stemmed from Hertzog's own liberal nationalism but pushed for more tangible fruits from the Balfour Declaration. Among its foremost representatives was Dr. A. M. Mol of Johannesburg, who prefaced his pamphlet *Die Onafhanklikheid van Suid-Afrika*, (*The Independence of South Africa*) with a series of quotations from John Stuart Mill, Edmund Burke, Montesquieu, Heinrich von Treitschke, Thomas Paine and the life of Cavour. He used the arguments of John Locke to sustain his republican position. He queried whether the Balfour Declaration could allow South Africa to remain neutral in an imperial war and whether South Africa was indeed independent if its governor-general was an

English peer, if South Africans continued to carry British passports, and if South Africa continued to rely economically on Britain. These were objections which Hertzog himself was able to recognize and which he tried to meet. First, at the Imperial Conference in 1930, he urged that the British parliament enact in the Statute of Westminister the principles of the Balfour Declaration. Second, he disposed the passing of the 1934 Status Acts by the South African parliament. These acts made South African citizenship a reality and entrenched in legislation the notion of the divisibility of the Crown. Liberal republicans who failed to be converted by Hertzog's accomplishments were increasingly forced to fall back on the argument of pure sentiment (cf. Steyn's letter in *Die Volksblad*, August 17, 1934),[1] or to cross over to the Kuyperian camp, whose objections to Hertzog's form of "sovereign independence" were couched in a language which he neither understood nor respected.

The major proponent of the Kuyperian variety of republicanism in the early years was the Potchefstroom political scientist, L. J. du Plessis. A firm believer in voluntarism, du Plessis worked indefatigably to found new associations for the furtherance of Kuyperian political ends. Since he usually ended up as secretary of these associations, he was in a position to issue manifesto after manifesto of his version of republicanism.

In an article expounding the draft program of his Kristelike Unie,[2] du Plessis conceded that South Africa was indeed all but an independent state. "However," he continued, "although we may acknowledge this fact, we confess as an irrefutable demand of our Christian National principle that we ought to be sovereignly independent. . . . Furthermore, sovereign independence in South Africa is necessarily associated with some or other form of *republicanism*." Although

[1] In a letter to *Die Volkstem* (April 8, 1931), J. Albert Coetzee confessed himself converted to the South African party by Hertzog's arguments.

[2] This was an utterly abortive association which attempted to inspire South African politics with the spirit of "Christian National" Calvinism (cf. *Die Weste*, June 81, 1928). For a useful recent study of the political thought of L. J. du Plessis, see Potgieter (1972).

it was part of the divine plan that Afrikaners should have experienced British rule in order "to develop a unity of law and order in South Africa," it was now time to throw off the British yoke. Only then may their "independent ethnic existence have the freedom to develop according to its own nature" (*Die Weste*, July 6, 1928). Hertzog might meet the criticisms of liberals like Moll and Visser, but the arguments of du Plessis lifted simple sentiment for the former republics onto a different plane. According to du Plessis, God's will was made manifest in Afrikaner history; and the duty of the true believer was to work and wait for the republican eschaton. It was du Plessis' version of republicanism which was accepted as part of the program of the Broederbond.

The Republican Union of N. J. van der Merwe was a combination of both of these varieties of Afrikaner republicanism—the liberal and the Christian National. As such, it was hamstrung from the start by disagreements between its members. However, it did drive General Hertzog to attack republicanism up and down the land, and thus helped to destroy his image as the personification of traditional, sentimental republicanism.[3]

General Hertzog not only estranged some of his republican support by assertions that South Africa had obtained sovereign independence under the British monarchy. He also argued that since "the great question of our freedom and independence" has been decided, there is "not the least reason" for the English-speaking and Afrikaans-speaking sectors of the white population not to "work together in all respects" (*Die Volkstem*, December 6, 1930). *Die Weste*, the small nationalist newspaper in the western Transvaal,[4] promptly retorted in a biting editorial entitled "Watchman, What of the Night?":

[3] See *Die Volkstem* (October 28, November 4, and December 27, 1929; January 16 and August 8, 1931: and October 10, 1932) *Die Weste* (December 28, 1929; January 9 and May 15, 1931), and *Die Burger* (December 24, 1929: July 3, November 11, December 6, December 14, and December 18, 1930: and October 12, 1932). See also *Ons Vaderland* (December 19 and December 26, 1930; and October 20, 1931).

[4] *Ons Vaderland*, the name of which changed in March 1932 to *Die Vaderland*, was the major Transvaal Nationalist newspaper:

General Hertzog now predicts a peace between nationalism and imperialism! Let us say at once that it is a false peace. . . . Are we Republicans going to resign ourselves to this? No! Never! The voice from our history calls out; "Ahead on the wagon-track burns a light!" We cannot outspan, we must trek on. Our ideal is not yet achieved, we must trek further (reprinted in *Die Volkstem*, December 6, 1930).

However, as long as they were free to make propaganda for a republic, the majority of the republicans, headed by N. J. van der Merwe, remained in the National party, for although Hertzog might not be their ideal, they preferred him to the alternative of Smuts as prime minister (cf. *Die Burger*, December 13, 1930; and February 21, 1931).

By 1931, Hertzog's National party, although still very much in power, was in a somewhat shaky position. When Britain devalued, Hertzog insisted on remaining on the gold standard as testimony to South Africa's sovereign independence in the economic sphere. As a result, South African farmers had great difficulty selling their produce overseas. Since the National party was predominantly the farmers' party, this spelled severe trouble for Hertzog. It seemed to many, to whom Smuts was anathema, that their only recourse lay in the formation of a party which would discard both old leaders.

Ever since 1928, there had been rumors and occasional reports of renewed efforts in the countryside to bring the two parties together again,[5] and by 1931, economic difficulties had caused this movement to reach a crescendo. As we have seen, Hertzog at first believed that union between English-speaking and Afrikaans-speaking white South Africans was but a matter of time (cf. *Die Burger*, December 11, 1930). However, as General Smuts and his lieutenants traveled the country urging devaluation in line with Britain, Hertzog began to temper his talk of cooperation with warnings of

---

it remained true to Hertzog. An attempt to found a rival weekly magazine, *Die Republikein*, folded after three experimental issues (the last two being dated March 18 and August 21, 1933).

[5] *Die Weste* (April 18 and June 15, 1928), *Die Volkstem* (November 18, 1929 and April 12, 1930) and *Ons Vaderland* (April 15 and July 18, 1930).

the imperialist threat. It seemed that exigencies posed by
the Great Depression would ruin the possibility of rapprochement between Smuts and Hertzog.

An editorial in *Die Weste* on April 19, 1932 encapsulated
the ambivalent attitude which renewed hostility between
Smuts and Hertzog evoked among ordinary Transvaal
country folk. It expressed the basic goodwill and longing for
reunion on the part of the Transvaal Afrikaners,[6] as well
as the grim determination of republican Nationalists not to
compromise on their principles:

> At the moment we live as Afrikaners peacefully together.
> Members of the National Party do not feel the least enmity
> to members of the South African Party. We live completely
> as brothers together; we sit together in the different churches
> to hear God's word proclaimed. We receive Communion to-
> gether at the same table. We come together on National feast
> days and at social gatherings; we help each other where there
> is poverty and suffering, at times of death and burials. We
> live completely happily, we visit together, drink tea and coffee
> together, we talk about problems, the world depression, some-
> times even discuss politics, but always in a brotherly fashion.
> Our children grow up together although their parents belong
> to different political parties; they maintain our language, our
> history and our traditions. They are together in the Voor-
> trekker movement, in the cadet corps and debating societies.
> We differ on one point only—the policies of the different parties.
> We should not mind chewing again on the bones of the Reunion
> Congress if there was the smallest chance that a solution might
> be found. But the political differences of both parties still
> remain. . . . The South African party still espouses the ideal
> of "Empire first" and the National party adheres to the ideal,
> "South Africa first and last." [*Die Weste*, April 19, 1932]

The party-political differences described in this editorial
belonged essentially to the Transvaal platteland. The Cape
and Free State rural communities, on the other hand, were
almost exclusively Nationalist. It is thus not surprising that
the strongest pressures for "reunion" came from the Transvaal, where Afrikaans-speaking rural communities were so
painfully divided along party-political lines.

---

[6] J. A. Coetzee (1931) provides good evidence for the strong
sentiment for *volkshereniging* ("ethnic reunion") in the Transvaal
during this period.

Tielman Roos, former head of the Transvaal National party,[7] was to be the successful catalyst for reconciliation between Smuts and Hertzog. On the Day of the Covenant, 1932, Judge Roos spoke at Lichtenburg urging reunion and devaluation. A few days later he formally announced his reentry into politics at a meeting in the Johannesburg Town Hall. He had at his side nine Transvaal Nationalist members of parliament, one Labourite, and the venerable liberal republican, Senator T. C. Visser (*Die Burger*, December 29, 1932). Roos' unanticipated intervention immediately forced South Africa off the gold standard. Equally important was the threat which Roos' Transvaal Nationalist support posed to Hertzog's tenure of power in parliament. Roos promptly opened negotiations with General Smuts and the South African party. These broke down within a matter of weeks, indeed by January 14, 1933, because Roos demanded the premiership. Although a large number of South African party members of parliament were at first prepared to "dump Smuts for Roos," Smuts with remarkable political acuity managed to hold his party together; and Roos faded from the picture. Confident that Roos had shot his bolt, Smuts prepared to make his move.

Instead of proposing the customary motion of no confidence when parliament opened on January 24, Smuts instead suggested coalition. He advocated a National government on the grounds that the country was worn weary by political strife. Hertzog, however, was not prepared to support such a motion without more consideration of the actual substance and consequences of the proposal.[8] Who would be prime minister? How long would the cooperation continue? Would bitterness not simply be worse when it was all over? What of differences of principle over the language question, agricultural policy, and so on? (*Hansard*, January 24, 1933)

---

[7] Hertzog had purportedly withdrawn Roos from party politics when he elevated him to the Supreme Court bench in 1929 (van den Heever, 1944, pp. 569-580).

[8] Paton states that Hertzog replied "with a bitterness of invective that the House had rarely heard equalled" (Paton, 1964, p. 193). No record of this appears in *Hansard*.

The National party unanimously rejected coalition on February first, as indeed they were obliged to do if Hertzog were to negotiate from a position of power. All the while Hertzog was deep in discussion with his cabinet on the subject of a National government. On January 31, Hertzog had proposed a coalition on his own terms to the National party parliamentary caucus. His reasons for cooperation were four-fold: first, he was convinced that the National party would lose the forthcoming election, especially if they rejected Smuts' proposal outright; second, failure to achieve coalition would necessarily force Smuts back upon the imperialist wing of his party, who would demand in return for their support the undoing of all that the Nationalists had struggled for a decade to realize; third, the economic situation of the country demanded a National government: and finally, the People had evinced a deep-felt longing for political accord (van den Heever, 1944, pp. 592-593; cf. *Die Burger*, March 6, 1933).

These were strong arguments in themselves, but in this case personal factors complicated the political maneuvers. Hertzog tended to approach his tasks with grave seriousness. Smuts once remarked that Hertzog was possessed of "a strange mind, without a spark of humour, that savingest of Christian virtues" (Hancock, 1968, p. 246). Needless to say, Hertzog was remarkably consistent in matters of principle. Indeed, his overriding concern was to ensure that his princi-ples be entrenched in legislation. Interpretation and practical application of the law interested him little. Earlier as attorney and then judge in the Free State, his work had suffered precisely because he showed more concern for turning up obscure points of Roman-Dutch law than in arguing or hearing a case on its merits. Throughout his political career he saw his real vocation as the passage of legislation which embodied his principles. Where there was doubt in interpreta-tion of a law, his most ready response was to draft more legislation. Thus did he buttress the legal loopholes of the Balfour Declaration with the Statute of Westminister and the South African Status Acts of 1934. Whether it was the Free State Education Act of 1907, the bilingualism clause in the South African Constitution, or the Status Acts of 1934, once his principles were satisfactorily embodied in legislation, Hertzog believed his immediate object achieved; and he would quite champ at the bit to move on to the next principle and its accompanying piece of legislation. This propensity to refuse all compromise on matters of principle was reflected in his apparent unawareness of the human problems involved in the application and interpretation of laws. It is hence unsurprising to learn that Hertzog was extremely impatient with criticism and opposition, which explains his virulent attacks on the republicans and the South African party opposition. It also accounts for his exasperation and outspoken censure of the compromise and negotiation which inevitably accompanies parliamentary government.

While he was beset by the innumerable difficulties of the Depression period, Hertzog read Oswald Spengler's *Decline of the West*, which confirmed in him the view that civilization was doomed because of the democratic party system. He was now convinced beyond any doubt, he said, that a democracy

> slowly and systematically organizes the entire People on the political plane for the systematic furtherance of private interest, the general concerns of state and People being omitted from consideration. . . . Thus I accept that the *demos*—the voting People of the twentieth century—are, in the nature of the case, unsuited to rule, and in the long run, must be unsuited to rule either directly, as in the Greek city-state, or indirectly by means of a representative responsible party-government, such as our own. The existing system of party-government will and must lead to decline and Caesarism. [*Die Burger*, September 10, 1932]

The only way now to avoid dictatorship, argued Hertzog, was "voluntary reform through which the individual interests of voter and party will be precluded from any direct say in the exercise of authority and the government of the country." Just how this form would be realized, and how it would differ from dictatorship, Hertzog did not say; but he seems to have had Hitler and Mussolini in mind, for he spoke enthusiastically of the importance of the youth of the People. The hope for a new purified state lay in the youthful-minded, uncorrupted element of the populace:

Fortunately in every People there always remains a healthy core of men and women for whom the interests of State and People are paramount. . . . Where these persons belong to a particular political party, that is a party which may rightly dub itself a People's party, it will be the only true party of the People, and has the right, when it assumes office, to act as representative of the power of the People and the authority of the state. [Die Burger, September 10, 1932]

It does not come as a surprise that, holding such views, Hertzog could not in all good conscience resist Smuts' coalition offer, especially since he had always defined the Afrikaner People as English-speakers and Afrikaans-speakers who alike accepted South Africa's sovereign independence (on Herzogite terms). Only through the formation of a "People's party" in South Africa lay the chance of survival for modern civilization, which, for Hertzog, meant "white civilization." Indeed the next item on Hertzog's legislative agenda was a definitive resolution of what he termed the black African problem. To accomplish this he needed a two-thirds majority of both houses of parliament, which would necessitate the votes of Smuts' South African party supporters (cf. *Die Burger*, December 17, 1929; *Die Volkstem*, December 17, 1929, and February 28, 1931).

Although a majority of the Nationalist caucus supported Hertzog on coalition, he met with stiff opposition from Dr. Malan, who had the support of the Cape members of parliament, as well as such Free Staters as van der Merwe and C. R. Swart. This powerful antagonism decided the caucus to request that Hertzog submit to them his terms for coalition before entering into negotiations with Smuts.

However, [said Hertzog in his diary] it became clear to me that, with the apparent division in the cabinet and the caucus, it is not advisable for me to give ear to the request of the caucus. The time has now come for me simply to act as leader; to give ear to my sense of what is desired in the interest of the party and so fulfill my duty. It was clear to me that by demanding a decision of the caucus, even of my Nationalist colleagues in the cabinet, I should give the impression of passing off on my fellow-ministers, or the caucus, my responsibility as leader to investigate that which might be in the interest of the party. [Van den Heever, 1944, pp. 593-594]

He thus decided to ignore the caucus and present his own statement of terms to Smuts.

These terms, announced in the press on February 15, 1933, consisted of seven points of principle, acknowledging which, Smuts could hope for cooperation from Hertzog. These seven principles reiterated maintenance of sovereign independence, as defined by the Statute of Westminister, and maintenance of equal language rights; stated certain economic priorities, especially for farmers and "civilized" labor; and spelled out Hertzog's position regarding black South Africa. He desired separate political representation for the different racial groups in South Africa, placing the needs of "white civilization" first, without denying the black African's right to development.

On all but this last issue, Smuts expressed himself in full agreement with Hertzog. After all, the remainder of the seven points went no further than the legislative *status quo* to which Smuts had never objected in principle. Besides, there was a basic difference of approach between Hertzog and Smuts that made it easy for them to agree on a basis of principle, but that might lead to friction when it came to practical application. Because of his continental training, as well as personal and temperamental rigidities, Hertzog held that once a law was written onto the books, it could be strictly applied in practice. Smuts, on the other hand, took the common-law position that legal princple was essentially meaningless until it had been interpreted by the courts. Since his common-law training caused Smuts to play down the importance of the legislative principles which Hertzog had so struggled to pass through parliament, he quite readily accepted all but Hertzog's final term for coalition. Smuts persuaded Hertzog to state in slightly more open terms the item dealing with black Africans, so that segregation was not so definitely prescribed. All the same, it was on this issue that negotiations almost foundered (van den Heever, 1944, pp. 596-599; for Smuts' position, cf. Paton, 1964, pp. 198-199).

Presented with the Hertzog-Smuts agreement as a *fait accompli*, Dr. Malan could hardly reject it out of hand if he were to survive politically; but his acceptance was set about with cautious qualifications. "For the present," he stated, "we shall accept the coalition, not because we approve it, or ever could do so, but simply because it has been forced upon our party as a *fait accompli*. We thus agree under protest. . . . We agree to support the new government only insofar as no National party principles are slighted or rejected. . ." (*Die Burger*, February 25, 1933). He refused a seat in the new coalition cabinet. Malan's Cape and Free State supporters thus went into the 1933 elections as members of the coalition but with very definite reservations (Scholtz, G. D., 1944, pp. 233-241; *Die Burger*, March 20, 1933).

As soon as the election, which the coalition won by an overwhelming majority, was over, an impending fusion of the two parties began to be rumored. On May 8, 1933, Hertzog spoke of the possibility of closer union; and on August 9, the Transvaal National party congress accepted a motion authorizing Hertzog to take steps toward union with the South African party. The Natal Nationalist congress followed suit on August 23. Even before this, party branches in the Transvaal countryside had begun to amalgamate on the local level. In view of the Transvaal nostalgia for reunion, this movement is hardly surprising.

In the Cape and the Free State, however, *Die Burger* and *Die Volksblad*—both published by the Malanite Nasionale Pers—mounted a vigorous campaign against closer union. Malan himself began writing a weekly column called "On the Watchtower,"[9] which publicized his criticism of fusion and made clear his own position.

Malan was certainly a better parliamentary infighter than either Hertzog or Smuts. He excelled in committee as a skilled and persistent negotiator. He would always take a firm position and then back it up with detailed argument until he had a definite majority opinion each step of the way. By this *modus operandi* he usually prevailed; but if not, he was prepared to go along with the will of the majority. In later years his enemies were wont to mock his concept of "leader-

---

[9] This column was also published in *Die Weste*, which provided circulation in the Transvaal, however small, for Malan's ideas. Malan was able to keep up this weekly effort, however, only until parliament reconvened in January 1934.

ship in council" (*leierskap-in-rade*), but this method of close deliberation in a small and carefully selected committee was an essential corollary to Malan's political style. One can well imagine how Hertzog's autocratic conception of leadership irked Malan. Hertzog's refusal to come back to the parliamentary caucus before deliberating with Smuts, as well as his high-handedness during the later fusion discussions must have offended Malan's sense of justice. It is significant that Malan's first substantive article in "On the Watchtower" dealt with "Democracy or Dictatorship":

> For some time now we have become accustomed to more or less vague allusions on the part of the South African party as well as Nationalist leaders that democracy is no longer virtuous and that dictatorship would really not be such a bad thing right now. Imperceptibly this influence has gone further and in our idea of leadership the establishment of the *fait accompli* has slowly begun to take the place of preliminary consultation with the organized will of the People. [*Die Burger*, July 15, 1933; cf. also the earlier speech in *Die Burger*, June 24, 1933]

Although the expertise with which Smuts managed to hold his party together despite inner divisions on principle won Malan's admiration, Hertzog's dictatorial management of the National party showed nothing of the same tact and skill. Said Malan of Hertzog:

> He was too inclined to seek out enemies in his own party, and he interpreted perfectly normal criticism as an attack on his leadership. Time and again he attacked his own party newspapers in public for no other reasons than that, for example, they pleaded for a South African as governor-general, or protested some or other infringement of our language rights, or even argued too strongly for the interests of the farmers. He attacked and estranged the republican group (who form the backbone of the party). . . . Although he might have expected disagreement about coalition and fusion, since shortly before he proposed it no one condemned it more strongly than General Hertzog himself, yet he clearly did not see differences on the matter as a party difficulty which ought to be solved with patience and tact. On the contrary, he regarded differences on the subject as a personal quarrel and an attack on his leadership. Time and again he asked the Nationalists . . . to choose between himself and another, even before the

party as such had been consulted or had had the chance to discuss the merits of the case with him. [*Die Burger*, September 2, 1933]

About this time Malan made some very strong statements on the practical necessity for a two-party system in a democratic state and came out strongly against dictatorship as a form of political regression. His emphasis on the "organized will of the People" stood clearly opposed to the radical concept of the "voice of the People" earlier expressed by Kruger and Steyn. Malan thus emerged as a firm supporter of British parliamentary democracy.[10] The continuance of the National party was essential, he maintained, not only to preserve a representative two-party system, but also to achieve its original purposes. In the first place, Malan did not agree that the passage of the Statute of Westminister signified full independence. The gap between legal enactment and practical application was a wide one, and Smuts' interpretation of the statute was certainly different from that of Hertzog. For Malan, legal enactment and administrative interpretation were equally crucial for the successful application of the new law, and he did not see how a fusion party could carry out the full implications of South Africa's legal independence. At the very least, he insisted, a new law must be enacted guaranteeing South Africa's right to secession and right of neutrality.

In the second place, Malan set out to defend the right of republicans to make propaganda within the new fusion party. This was utterly essential for the spiritual health of the party, he argued. Although for practical political reasons the principles of the National party extended beyond simple republicanism, it was wrong to deny membership to its advocates. Indeed, "without itself becoming a republican party, the National party anchored itself in the republican ideal just as Paul Kruger and [other Afrikaner heroes] did in their time," Malan reminded his readers (*Die Burger*, October 28, 1933). The entire sacred history was but an

[10] The Cape, where Malan was born and raised, had a strong and established Afrikaner parliamentary tradition.

account of the struggle between imperialism and republicanism. In fact, Malan suggested, in the long run a republic might
be the only way to end English-Afrikaner racial strife.[11]

Malan was inclining more and more toward the mainstream
interpretation of the civil religion. Not only was he reverting
to the republican ideal in arguing against the dangers inherent
in fusion, he was also using civil-religion logic to argue that
the secret of the National party's success up until then had
been their courage to lose. He quoted Langenhoven's famous
summary of the sacred history: "For a hundred years we were
always losing, but while we lost throughout those hundred
years we were winning." (*Die Burger*, July 22, 1933) From
his "Watchtower" column, Malan recalled the words of
Christ: "He who seeks to save his life shall lose it, but he
who loses his life for My sake shall find it. What does it
profit a man that he gain the whole world and lose his own
soul?" (*Die Burger*, July 22, 1933) In Malan's opinion, the
very soul of Afrikanerdom was now at stake. Hertzog had
compromised too much, thought Malan, in accepting the
"Hoggenheimer" element of the South African party (cf. *Die
Burger*, August 5, 1933). Time and again Malan had made
witness for his fervent political ideal, that of reunion (*hereniging*). By *hereniging* he meant "to bring together those who
belong together" (*om bymekaar te bring wat bymekaar hoort*).
But what union between the South African party—which
was a mixture of imperialists, capitalists, and a few true
Afrikaners—and the Nationalists spelled out was not *hereniging* but *samesmelting* ("fusion").

Malan expressed himself willing to negotiate with Smuts,
the individual, as a leader of the Afrikaner element in the
South African party; but he refused on principle to approve
any negotiations with Smuts as leader of the South African
party as a whole (*Die Burger*, December 2, 1933). Any political
party which was truly representative of Afrikaner *volkseenheid*, ("People's unity"), or genuine *hereniging*, must neces-

[11] On the day that Malan first confessed publicly to republicanism
(*Die Burger*, November 4, 1933), the Republican Union met in
Johannesburg to discuss fusion and decided, largely on Malan's
assurances, not to form a separate party (*Die Volksblad*, November
6, 1933).

sarily exclude the imperialist and capitalist wing of the South
African party. "*Hereniging*," Malan explained, "rests upon
the completely realistic view that the National party group
is an inner unity and that the South African party is not.
Further, that under these circumstances, an important group
of *Sappe* ("South African party men"), who in reality stand
closer to the Nationalists than to their own party associates,
would be prepared to join where they belong. If there is no
such group of *Sappe* who want *hereniging* just as we do,
then obviously nothing can be done [in the way of reunion]"
(*Die Burger*, December 2, 1933). Malan thus solved the
contradiction between Hertzog's policy of "South Africa first"
and the "two streams" by tending to equate genuine South
African civic sentiment with the Afrikaans-speaking stream,
whose loyalties could not fluctuate between England and
South Africa.[12] In his view, the only viable alternative to
a continuation of the existing two-party system would be
to cut the British connection entirely by establishing a
republic, thus forcing English-speaking South Africans to
choose between South Africa and England. "After that," said
Malan, "South Africa will have two equal languages, but we
shall be one People" (*Die Burger*, December 23, 1933).

A political party could not operate on a level separate from
the social and cultural realities of South African life, which
was what a fusion party would be attempting. Malan went
on to specify the extent to which ethnic distinctions permeated white society in South Africa. His account reads like a
success story (an indirect tribute to the effectiveness of the
Broederbond).

> . . . in place of the original one-stream idea that Afrikaans
> and English-speaking children ought not to be separated in
> school, we had first the introduction of parallel classes and
> thereafter, in the face of great opposition, parallel schools.
> Thus also our universities and colleges, without state encour-
> agement, as by an inherent force, followed suit. . . . Thus also
> the original common teachers' associations in all the provinces
> split, and although they are in friendly cooperation with one

[12] Malan was careful never to exclude altogether the possibility
of *hereniging* with certain genuinely South African English-speakers (*Die Burger*, September 30, 1933).

another, Afrikaans and English-speaking teachers remain separately organized. The same thing happened with the originally common Art and Cultural Associations (Eisteddfords) and with the Child Welfare Associations and the Scout-movement, which found its Afrikaans parallel in the Voortrekkers. And finally, the same developments took place in the religious and student-worlds, for example in the Christian Endeavor Society and the Students' Christian Association, and again recently in the general student union. If the history of the last thirty years teaches us anything, it is that the one-stream ideal of the *Samesmelter* is impracticable. It has been weighed by the Afrikaner, found too light, and definitely been rejected. . . . The two-stream development of the Afrikaner has largely freed him of his inferiority feelings; has given him back his self-respect and self-confidence; has awakened in him a new and living concern in areas where he was previously dead; and has been unbelievably successful in helping him ahead in political, social, and cultural spheres. [*Die Burger*, December 23, 1933]

Was the National party prepared to sacrifice all this?

There is a general tendency to point to Malan's new membership in the Broederbond to account for a supposed shift in his position during the first half of 1933.[13] But Malan's stand for *hereniging* versus *samesmelting* was articulated at least as early as his editorship of *Die Burger*; and in 1933 his major advisers—W. A. Hofmeyr, A. L. Geyer (editor of *Die Burger*), and F. C. Erasmus (Cape National party organizing secretary)—were not members of the Broederbond. What Malan was advocating was all quite in keeping with the course of his career thus far, and especially with his earlier activities in the language movement.

A final issue which weighed very heavily with Dr. Malan and the other anti-fusion Nationalists was Afrikaner poverty—the poor white problem. As dominee, Malan had been deeply involved in church work on behalf of the poor; and as editor of *Die Burger*, he mounted his own campaign on the subject in July 1923. The publication of the Carnegie Report on the poor white question in 1932, renewed the active concern of many other Afrikaner intellectuals, and in October

[13] This charge was first leveled by General Hertzog in his famous 1935 Smithfield speech attacking the Broederbond (cf. Vatcher, 1965, pp. 249-250).

1934, a Volkskongres was organized, which led visible evidence to the timeliness of the topic.[14] Afrikaner poverty was important in determining Malan's and N. J. van der Merwe's attitude toward *samesmelting*, since they were convinced that fusion, by including the financial interests of the Rand, would soon set off a process of party division—this time on class rather than ethnic lines.[15] Such a consequence, they both agreed, would tragically divide the Afrikaner People and forever destroy Afrikaner nationalism as an effective political force (cf. *Ons Vaderland*, December 10, 1932; and *Die Burger*, June 6, June 10 and June 24, 1933; January 12 and January 13, 1934).

Malan's opposition to *samesmelting* was shared by F. C. Erasmus, the young organizing secretary of the Cape National party. While amalgamation was proceeding on the local level in the Transvaal, in the Cape, Erasmus was busy keeping the National party intact. He wrote profusely and traveled tirelessly from one local branch to another, explaining, cajoling, and, if need be, putting pressure to keep the party loyal to Malan.[16] Long before the Transvaal party congress voted

[14] There was even a precedent for linking Afrikaner poverty to the civil religion. On Geloftedag in 1930 Professor J. F. Burger of the University of Cape Town spoke of the "Great Trek" to the cities:

> The Trekkers trekked out of the cities; today the problem is exactly the opposite. . . . The mighty task which lies before us today [is] to teach Afrikaners to retain their souls in the cities where they have settled: in the midst of foreign elements [they must be taught] to remain Afrikaners in heart and soul. . . . The Blood River of the Nineteenth Century was won with material weapons: the Blood River of the Twentieth Century will be won or lost with spiritual weapons. In 1938 there was one decisive battle: today the struggle goes on, continuous, undiminished and relentless. . . . [*Die Burger*, December 17, 1930]

[15] Malan dealt with the absence of class divisions during the period of the sacred history in the course of Geloftedag addresses reported in *Die Burger*, December 18, 1932 and December 17, 1933. Besides revealing Malan's preoccupation with social class, both these civil-religion sermons are classics of the genre.

[16] The collection of local National party minutes for this period in the political archives at Bloemfontein is very scant. In rural towns as far apart as Wellington and Victoria-West, however, one finds traces of Erasmus' presence, urging that delegates to the

for *samesmelting*, Erasmus was reported to have sent a confidential circular to all Cape members of parliament and other Nationalist leaders, urging: "What I should like very confidentially to request of you is that you will make a point of arranging that the district organizations in your constituency or area will send a representative to the [Cape] Congress [in October 1933] who will vote against *samesmelting*" (*Die Vaderland*, November 17, 1933).

When the Cape party congress met at Port Elizabeth on October 4, 1933, Malan spoke first, declaring himself in favor of *hereniging* but not *samesmelting*. Hertzog retorted with an attack on the republican movement and an appeal for permission to draw up a constitution which could then be put before the provincial congresses. His motion declared the desirability of *vereniging*[17] between the Nationalists and the South African party if agreement could be reached on a basis of principles acceptable to all four provincial congresses. Malan then made a counter motion opposing *samesmelting* on principle if it involved negotiating with the South African party as a whole. Neither Hertzog nor his Cape lieutenant, A. J. Fourie, were given a fair chance to argue their case because of rowdy heckling from Erasmus and some of the younger Cape members of parliament. These crude tactics did nothing to win the respect of the Cape local representatives (cf. *Die Burger*, November 23, 1933; and Wellington local party minutes, October 19, 1933). Although these representatives were apparently bound by prior decisions of their local committees, it seems from the only extant local minutes discussing these proceedings that there was much spontaneous sympathy for the general. A certain du Toit, chairman

---

Congress be bound by their committees to vote against *samesmelting* before departing for the congress. (National party local minutes: Victoria-West, February 9, 1934; Wellington, August 25, 1933: cf. Olifantshoek, local minutes, August 28, 1933).

[17] Because Malan so adamantly insisted upon reunion, or *hereniging*, (the bringing together of those who belonged together) as against *samesmelting* (the fusion of the two political parties, including the "Hoggenheimer" element), Hertzog attempted a compromise by speaking of union, or *vereniging*, meaning combination of the two parties on the basis of a commonly agreed set of principles.

of the Wellington local branch, reported back to his executive that he had voted according to his mandate from them although his personal sympathies lay with Hertzog (Wellington local party minutes, October 19, 1933). Beukes, the Victoria-West representative, was actually one of the thirty representatives who voted for Hertzog. For this he was censured by the branch secretary, who stated that "his first and dearest duty was to carry out the decision of his executive" and refused to reimburse him for the trip to Port Elizabeth (Victoria-West local party minutes, February 9, 1934). Certainly Hertzog had more local support than the vote of the congress—one hundred forty in favor of Malan to thirty—would indicate. Erasmus seems to have done his work well.

At the congress of the Free State National party a week later, Hertzog prevailed by casting his motion in terms of a vote of confidence in himself. Although N. J. van der Merwe had first proposed an intermediary motion—hoping, it seemed, for a rapprochement between Hertzog and Malan—he agreed in the end that Hertzog be allowed to submit his principles to the National party congresses. He decided to attack Hertzog's detailed proposals rather than flatly oppose *samesmelting* itself.

N. J. van der Merwe had earlier declared that he would accept *samesmelting* only if it were grounded in Christian National principles, maintained South Africa's complete political and economic freedom, ensured equality for Afrikaans-speaking persons, guaranteed protection of white civilization, and opposed capitalism so that poor urban Afrikaners and Afrikaner farmers should not be alienated (Scholtz, G. D., 1944, pp. 242-243). By the beginning of 1934, he had decided to wait no longer for Hertzog's announcement of principles, since the capitalists were clearly in command of the coalition; and on January 19, he joined with a group of younger Free State members of parliament in a Bloemfontein meeting which firmly insisted that the National party be preserved (Scholtz, G. D., 1944, pp. 264-265). This group was following the example of another, smaller band of Transvaal Nationalist republicans who on January 11 had declared themselves unequivocally opposed to *samesmelting* (Scholtz, G. D., 1944, pp. 265-267). Both Free State and Transvaal groups formed vigilance committees to await developments.

Just when schism began to seem inevitable, Malan reopened negotiations with Hertzog; and by February 15, Hertzog issued the text of an agreement reached with the Cape National party, in which Hertzog's goals were expressed in terms acceptable to Malan and his followers. His intention in *vereniging,* said Hertzog, was to bring together only those English-speaking and Afrikaans-speaking South Africans who belonged together. Furthermore, he promisd that the new party would permit open expression of republican propaganda. On the matter of the divisibility of the Crown, which involved the rights of neutrality and secession, Hertzog reaffirmed his belief that the Statute of Westminister guaranteed these rights and that to include them in an agreement between the parties would be to question the validity of what the law already guaranteed. As for the specific procedure under which fusion would take place, Hertzog and the Nationalist federal council would each draw up a basis of principles, and if there were any disagreements, the provincial congresses would have ultimate say. With the Cape party executive behind Hertzog, National party unity appeared to be restored (*Die Burger,* February 16, 1934).

Why did Malan make so determined a conciliatory effort at this stage? Pirow believed that he didn't want Hertzog to take credit for the Status Acts, which were shortly to come before parliament. But Dr. Malan's commitment to *volkseenheid* was certainly genuine. His farewell sermon on leaving the ministry had specified his future vocation as furthering *volkseenheid* (Pienaar, 1964, pp. 9-18). It is thus not inconsistent that he would make a last attempt to avert schism. In addition, we might surmise that after the Port Elizabeth party congress there was certain pressure from the grassroots to go along with Hertzog—at least until his principles for union were announced. Finally, Malan probably hoped that publication of his agreement with Hertzog would alienate the imperialist-capitalist ("Hoggenheimer") element in the South African party. After all, the agreement did immediately force Hertzog to state unequivocally in public his belief in the right to secession and neutrality and the right of party members to make republican propaganda.

Whatever his reasons, Malan definitely shifted his position when he ceased to oppose all negotiations which aimed at *samesmelting* or *vereniging*. Furthermore, the Malan-Hertzog agreement did succeed in letting loose the cat among the South African party pigeons. Smuts had his extremists, even as did Hertzog! Smuts agreed to republican propaganda only after Hertzog issued him an ultimatum (van den Heever, 1944, pp. 618-619). After several meetings with Hertzog, Smuts issued a letter to the press with his interpretation of the Statute of Westminister (*Die Volkstem*, February 19, 1934). Hertzog categorized his differences with Smuts as only theoretical and carried on with his plans for the Status Acts, which he felt would clear things up. Malan agreed with him at this point. In effect the Status Acts simply restated the provisions of the Statute of Westminister in terms of South African constitutional law. In his speech supporting the bills, General Smuts as much as admitted the divisibility of the Crown and the rights of secession and neutrality, while he at the same time reassured his listeners that these rights need never be exercised (Krüger, 1960, p. 179). On May 9, 1934, Malan made a famous speech in the Cape at Mooreesburg, in which he praised Hertzog for the newly passed acts. These were, he declared, a victory for nationalism. On the same date, Smuts was telling the Rotary Club in Cape Town that the Status Acts made South Africa's ties with the empire tighter than ever before, since no legal bonds now existed, but only ties of affection. Smuts seemed able to make even the Status Acts innocuous to his imperialist supporters.

Although Malan declared himself ready to continue with the coalition as presently constituted, he could not envisage a fusion party—especially after Smuts' Rotary speech. (*Die Burger*, May 25, 1934) After all his painstaking effort, Hertzog felt that Malan was now letting him down. Their essential differences emerge with stark clarity from an interview with Malan recorded in Hertzog's diary entry for May 8, 1934:

> I asked him if he meant that not enough was done in the House by myself and other members of the government during the [Status] debate to make declarations which would drive

off undesirable members of the S.A.P. from the new party. His answer was: yes! I then indicated to him that I had expressed myself very clearly in the correspondence with the Cape executive that the *principles* of the new party alone would decide its membership. He assured me that they [the Cape people] were not complaining that anything I had said or done was in conflict with my assurances, but the feeling was . . . that now persons would join who were not meant to be in the party! [Van den Heever, 1944, p. 630]

Malan's position was explicit. Regardless of principles, any new party must exclude the "Hoggenheimer" element of the South African party. Malan definitely feared that Smuts would hold his party together no matter what; and if such were the case, Malan would not be part of the new party.

Malan was now in an acutely embarrassing position, since he had but recently declared his commitment to principles which he now realized would not suffice to achieve his aims. His speech at Paarl on May 24 mirrored his predicament (*Die Burger*, May 25, 1934). When the federal council of the National party met on June 20 to discuss Hertzog's proposed principles, the prime minister's majority on the council refused to accept any amendments. This was all that Malan and his followers required to cry *"fait accompli"* and withdraw. The Malan minority on the federal council consisted of the entire Cape delegation, van der Merwe of the Free State and Mrs. E. G. Jansen of Natal (Scholtz, G. D., 1944, pp. 286-287).

This time there could be no return. At a conference called by the Transvaal vigilance committee on July 4, 1934, the young Transvaal member of parliament J. G. Strydom announced that the "National Party must be maintained on a purified foundation" (*Die Burger*, July 5, 1934). From that time on, the followers of Malan were known as the "purified" (Gesuiwerde) National party. Speaker after speaker who arose to address the Transvaal meeting on July 4 insisted that the National party could continue only on the basis of "the republican ideal." *Die Weste* rejoiced with a great joy, for it seemed that at last the National party would become the republican party of its dreams (*Die Weste*, July 6, 1934). At this time the Afrikaner Broederbond voted to include a republic in its ideals; and *Die Weste* was replaced by a new

Nationalist newspaper in the Transvaal called *Die Republikein*, which published its first issue on September 14, 1934.

The victory was not so decisive as such rejoicing might have given cause to believe. The reason that the republicans were so strong in the Transvaal Purified National party was precisely because the party was so pathetically weak after an overwhelming majority of Nationalists had followed Hertzog into the new United party.[18] Those who remained were the elite on the Rand—teachers, lawyers, and doctors—and the Kuyperians of Potchefstroom. Purified nationalism in the Transvaal was thus precious little more than the Broederbond writ large. However, despite their numerical weakness, the Transvaal Gesuiwerdes had one trump card. They could elect all five Transvaal reprsentatives to the federal council of the National party, in which each province was equally represented. Thus, their influence in the council was out of all proportion to their actual numbers.

Since the Cape National party had stayed out of *samesmelting* en bloc, it had not lost its more conservative elements. The price of its wider political base was a less extreme policy. Consequent clashes between the Cape men and the Transvaalers resulted in a delay of two years before the federal council was able to agree on a program of principles.

At the first federal council meeting of the Gesuiwerdes on November 7 and November 8, 1934, the major topic of discussion was the form that the republicanism of the purified party should take. A number of Cape representatives wished to go no further than Hertzog himself had gone, to welcome non-republicans into the party and at the same time to allow republican propaganda. On the other hand, certain Transvaal republicans wanted to declare a republic as soon as a bare majority should be obtained in parliament.[19] The middle position was espoused by Malan, N. J. van der Merwe, and

[18] See the letter of C. J. H. de Wet in *Die Weste*, (February 22, 1935); see also the earlier analysis of the Transvaal situation in *Die Volksblad* (January 5, 1934).

[19] For an analysis from the point of view of Transvaal republicanism see *Die Republikein* (March 8, 1935). According to *Die Republikein*, certain of the Transvaal republicans rejected any talk of a majority at all, speaking rather of "an heroic act of power." These were inspired by Hitler's success in Germany.

W. A. Hofmeyr, who favored an outspokenly republican National party, but insisted that only constitutional means should be used. A bare majority would not suffice: there would have to be a decisive People's movement supporting it (*Die Burger*, November 8, 1934; and *Die Vaderland*, September 28, 1934). It is hardly surprising that the meeting adjourned without resolving these differences (Scholtz, G. D., 1944, pp. 298ff).

Out of this meeting, however, came a written "Program of Action," which contained a positive stand on economic issues, favoring the white agricultural and laboring classes. It proposed the formation of a national department of social welfare to cope with the poor white problem; it argued for territorial, political, and industrial segregation between white and black South Africans; it urged that bilingualism be a necessary requirement for advancement in the civil service: and it declared the party to be firmly in favor of separate-language schools for English and Afrikaans students in the large population centers. Under the rubric of "national independence" the program went little farther than Hertzog, except to state that South Africa would remain neutral in the event of war unless her shores were actually threatened. The word "republic" was conspicuously absent from the full text (*Die Volksblad*, November 24, 1934).

Publication of this program called forth immediate and varied responses. *Die Volkstem*, Pretoria's mouthpiece for General Smuts, crowed with delight that "Malan had disavowed the republic" (November 28, 1934). *Die Republikein*, on the other hand, deplored the fact that a "Program of Action" had been issued before there was agreement on principles, for action could be consistent and systematic only if it stemmed from "previously formulated principles." This editorial left no doubt that the foremost principle of the purified party should be republicanism, the "birthright of our People" (*Die Republikein*, November 30, 1934). A special congress of the Free State National party gathered on December 7, 1934 to declare itself "decisively in favor of the Christian-republican ideal" and "purposefully to struggle for the realization of that ideal" (*Die Burger*, December 7, 1934).

At the Transvaal party congress on April 4, 1935, Strydom proposed that an even more explicitly republican article be included in the new "Program of Principles" (*Die Volksblad*, April 17, 1935).

When the "Program of Principles" was finally issued, it stated "that the republican form of government, separate from the British Crown, is best suited to the traditions, circumstances and aspirations of the People of South Africa." The party would "protect and strive for the republican ideal," although no one would be refused membership in the party if he were not an avowed republican. The party further acknowledged that a republic could be created "only on the broad basis of the will of the People and with the faithful observance of the language rights of both sections of the white population ... as a result of a special and decisive mandate from the People" (*Die Burger*, July 9, 1935).

"The Gesuiwerdes disavow the Republic," rejoiced *Die Volkstem* (July 12, 1935) once again. *Die Republikein* was seriously distressed that the party had conceded so much —especially in granting membership to non-republicans and in specifying the rights of English-speakers. In its editorial, the paper stated unequivocally the ideal:

> The National party stands today again purely for the dominion of Afrikanerdom, which Milner ... destroyed. The National party will save the Afrikaner People and lift it up. . . . The National party must now keep its goal clearly before its eyes, for upon it rests the great task of forming a new state—a republic in which the Afrikaner can again look up with pride to its own president and its own flag, and with inspiration sing its own national anthem; a republic in which the Afrikaner may again take first place and in which he may develop freely with his language, traditions and ideals according to his own form and institutions; a republic which, like the earlier two republics, will make an end to party struggles and the division of our People; a republic which shall care for the interests of our People and purposively protect us against British imperialism and foreign parasitism ... [*Die Republikein*, July 12, 1935].

This opinion was more extreme than many Transvaal Nationalists and most Cape and Free State men thought desirable. Their intention was not to form a party to end all parties. Nonetheless, there was strong pressure from the Transvaal and Free State party congresses to alter the clause which permitted non-republicans to become party members. At a meeting of the federal council on February 22 and February, 1936 (Scholtz, G. D., 1944, pp. 304-305), the Cape delegation was outvoted and the clause was indeed dropped. Also, instead of the party's undertaking to "protect and strive for the republican ideal," the program now read that it would "protect the republican ideal and strive to bring about a republic in South Africa" (*Die Burger*, March 13, 1936). Although Strydom declared himself satisfied, still a number of Transvaal republicans resigned from the party in protest. The most important of these breakaway groups was that led by Dr. Steyn Vorster, F. C. K. Jacobz and Muller van der Ahee.[20] They were important ideologically because they represented an avowedly National Socialist view of the state, speaking for a "unitary state" (*Eenheidstaat*) as opposed to parliamentarism (*Die Republikein*, July 3, 1936). They were important practically because they controlled *Die Republikein*, which announced that it would henceforth remain independent of party-political affiliation.

The major objection of *Die Republikein* to the National party "Program of Principles" was that a republic could be declared only "on the broad basis of the will of the People" and not by a bare majority in parliament. To this Malan and Strydom replied that if the National party came to power before a majority of the population favored the republic, a premature republic would mean political suicide for both party and republic in the next election (*Die Republikein*, July 3 and July 24, 1936). *Die Republikein* responded that because of their attachment to the party system, Malan and Strydom had missed the whole point. When the National party came to power, the republic which it created should do away with the whole parliamentary system. There would be no reason to fear the next election, for in the new republican unitary state those who might vote to abandon the republic would

[20] This was the group whom Malan condemned in several speeches aimed specifically against advocates of a violent solution in South Africa (Scholtz, G. D., 1944, pp. 302-303).

have no voting rights; in a Christian National state, the English and the Jews ("parasites" and "*uitlanders*") would have to prove their worth to the nation and their faith in the People before they could exercise democratic rights.

N. G. S. van der Walt, at this time a student in Potchefstroom and later reporter on *Die Volksblad*, expressed, in his personal diary, the general frame of mind that lay behind the opinions of this group:

> We shall never get a free republic in the true meaning of the word with constitutional methods. Armed force is essential, in the first place to command the respect of the English element so that they will be willing to be assimilated by the Afrikaner; in the second place to weld the Afrikaners together again; and in the third place because I do not believe in the bloodless way; a sacrifice must consist of blood.
>
> The Afrikaans People today is not battle-weary . . . but they are tired of the method of struggle, namely the talk method. . . . By this I do not mean that we must launch a violent revolution but the People must be prepared for an uprising when the time comes—for there is time for all things, also for violence—and the time shall come when the World War breaks out, for then our blood will have to be spilled, and rather for freedom than for British imperialism . . . .
>
> If a part of the People threatens the national existence by trying to fuse the People with another, larger People, then it is not only the right but also the duty of the other section to reject that part and to fight for the national existence. In other words, in this case revolution is justified if there is no other way out. But is there for us? . . . The only other "purposeful" method is the so-called "constitutional path." Along this path we were theoretically as regards numbers closer to the possibility of a republic in 1924 (twelve years ago) than we are today. . . . [Van der Walt diary, entries for January 24 and January 28, 1936]

At this time, van der Walt's acknowledged leader was Professor C. J. H. de Wet, who upon leaving the National party in 1936, started his own Christian-Republican movement. In *Die Republikein*, van der Walt volunteered the support of his fellow student republicans to Professor de Wet,[21] and

[21] When van der Walt's student republican committee approached L. J. du Plessis on May 27, 1936 in an effort to obtain his support for de Wet's Christian Republicanism, du Plessis, for all his republi-

concluded by saying, "Let us as young Afrikaners stand together to take the straightest and shortest way to our ideal, even as Hitler came out openly for that which he struggled, thereby winning the trust of his whole People." (*Die Republikein*, May 15, 1936; cf. van der Walt diary, entries for May 23 and June 18, 1936).

De Wet's movement was not the only one of its kind. On January 22, 1937, *Die Republikein* announced the formation of a National Republican Unity Front under the leadership of S. P. E. Jacobz, the expressed purpose of which was to establish in South Africa an independent state on a Christian National basis, in which there would be no place for the evils of the "present British-Jewish imperialist capitalist system" (*Die Republikein*, January 23, 1937).

Neither of the above movements seems to have gained any widespread acceptance among Afrikaners except in the western and northern Transvaal. In 1938, *Die Republikein* went out of publication, and the various extremist groups on the republican fringe of Afrikaner life went underground. However, it is important to note that they continued to exist, their members zealous for republican independence along National Socialist lines and acting as a yeast in the ranks of Afrikanerdom, only to surface after the declaration of war in 1939.

Meanwhile, after the breakaway of *Die Republikein* in 1936, Cape Nationalists pressed on with plans to finance a new Transvaal Nationalist daily newspaper, one of whose major functions would be to tone down Transvaal republicanism (*Die Burger*, November 22, 1935; cf. van Jaarsveld, F. A., and

---

can zeal, was not prepared to reject the National party out of hand, partly because he saw C. J. H. de Wet as an "inconvincible schismatic," but also because he believed that republicanism alone would be insufficient to reach a national majority (van der Walt, N. G. S., diary entry, May 28, 1936). Du Plessis seems to have been quite right about de Wet, whose rather wavering theoretical line is traced in a pamphlet issued in 1945 by Die Sentrale Propaganda-komitee vir 'n Christelik-Republikeinse Politiek in Suid-Afrika, entitled *Die Stryd vir 'n Christelike-Republikeinse Politiek in Suid-Afrika.* De Wet's comments on the *Ossewabrandwag* are especially revealing since they appear to be based on deliberate misunderstanding.

Scholtz, G. D., 1966, p. 7). For those more moderate Gesuiwerdes who held sacred the Christian National ideals of the civil religion, the readiness of Cape Nationalists to declare themselves firmly for a republic was in itself highly encouraging (cf. Scholtz, G. D., 1944, p. 304). Relations between Cape and Transvaal would never be easy, but at least there was now in existence a South African National party which stood unequivocally for such Christian National ideals as separate mother-tongue education for both white groups, strict segregation between black and white, concern for poor whites, and above all, the republic. Henceforth the destinies of the National party and the civil religion would be inextricably bound together.

8

Organization and Ideology

Developments on the Cultural Front, 1930-1938

General Hertzog believed that his legislation provided a framework within which Afrikaner cultural development could take place. The encouragement and implementation of this development, however, was now in the hands of private citizens and voluntary associations; it was not the business of government, according to Hertzog. He looked with sympathy on the work of the F.A.K., the Voortrekker movement, and indeed the Broederbond itself before 1930. However, the inclination of these organizations towards the Christian National civil religion with its accompanying narrowness and cultural exclusivism, caused the general to have second thoughts about the whole Afrikaner "cultural movement," for it was becoming increasingly apparent to him that many of the leaders were convinced republicans who refused to treat the constitution of South Africa as a political question distinct from their cultural commitments.

Within the Broederbond, also, there were those who felt that the essentially symbolic activities of the F.A.K. overlooked its most essential purpose—to stand on guard for the Afrikaans language in every sphere of daily life. We have seen that the Afrikaner Broederbond began as a movement to implement the bilingualism clause of the South Africa Act, especially on the English-speaking Rand. The decision of the Broederbond to go underground, its ideological shift to Potchefstroom, and its attempt to reach out particularly to

Afrikaner elite throughout the country was considered by L. J. Erasmus and certain other members of the T.O. (Transvaal Teachers' Union) in Johannesburg as a departure from this earlier intention. Accordingly, in the spring of 1930, this group organized a new movement, the Handhawersbond ("Union of Militant Defenders"). It was at first composed largely of Afrikaans-speaking schoolteachers on the Rand (*Die Weste*, September 2, 1932; also Erasmus, L. J., n.d., pp. 87-88), and throughout its brief existence, teachers continued to hold most of the positions of leadership. Their avowed intent was to "insist on equal language rights, to which we are legally entitled but of which we see precious little in practice." In practice this meant that the good Handhawer "[spoke] only pure Afrikaans in our shops and other business and [undertook] to speak only pure Afrikaans among ourselves and everywhere else" (*Die Burger*, November 14, 1930).

Like the 1922 strikers, the Handhawersbond was organized along the lines of the commando system developed by Boer War guerillas. Mr. J. P. Bosman of Bellevue East, Johannesburg, in a letter to *Die Burger* (November 14, 1930), explained: "Our Bond is organized on the lines of the army: At the head of the movement stands a Commandant General and under him generals, commandants, field cornets and ordinary soldiers. (Women are not omitted.) Our discipline is extremely strict, and orders of the war council are immediately carried out." The slogan of the movement was "*opsaal*" ("saddle up"), and its motto and salute was a clenched fist. Members wore a button inscribed with this symbol. The clenched-fist button was "not a symbol of struggle against the English," however, Bosman insisted.

> [T]he mature English fellow citizen ... respects us if we struggle for principles. No Englishman respects anybody who is ashamed of his nation. If our button is a symbol of struggle, then it is a struggle against ourselves, we who are not always true to our language and People. It is a struggle against those Afrikaners who wish to be Englishmen, whom Celliers calls a "bastard generation"; those Afrikaners who would sacrifice all for the sake of "peace." [*Die Handhawer*, August 1931].

So strong grew the Handhawersbond on the Rand that in 1931 and 1932, it was able to organize Culture Day celebrations which drew up to 6,000 Afrikaners,[1] according to reports in *Die Burger* and *Die Vaderland.* More important however were the day-to-day activities of the organization. By adhering to strictly practical aims it was able to retain the support of Hertzog's *Die Vaderland* and Smuts' *Die Volkstem* as well as the F.A.K.

At the 1932 annual Congress of the Handhawersbond, L. J. Erasmus was unanimously re-elected commandant general; and generals of the various units reported good progress in their respective areas. The representative of Rand Central division reported general success in obtaining service in Afrikaans in shops and business offices; more jobs for Afrikaners were thus opening up. The East Rand division was happy with its efforts to promote the use of Afrikaans in magistrates' offices and in the post office. The town council at Benoni had been forced to issue translations of municipal announcements, and similar campaigns were meeting with success in Boksburg. In Roodepoort, the town council was now recognizing equal language rights, and an Afrikaner had been elected mayor for the first time in twenty-five years. The new hospital had two foundation stones, one for each language, and all superscriptions on hospital stationary were in both languages—with Afrikaans first! The Roodepoort division had also stepped forth to protect an Afrikaner worker from an English-speaking station master, who was now in the process of learning the country's "other language." For the platteland, the representative from Waterberg South reported that a new school committee had been elected on which Afrikaners were, for once, fairly represented. The report from the Alluvial Diggings indicated that English-speakers were being inspired to learn Afrikaans: indeed, a certain government official who had flatly refused to serve anyone who spoke Afrikaans had been replaced as a result of Hand-

[1] At the foundation of the F.A.K., this organization decided that May 31, Union Day, which annually reaffirmed the civic unity of white South Africa, should rather be celebrated by culture-conscious Afrikaners as Culture Day, an occasion for feting primordial Afrikaner culture at gatherings throughout the land, and, incidentally, a day for making cash collections for the activities of the F.A.K.

hawer efforts (*Die Volkstem*, June 20 and *Die Vaderland*, June 22, 1932.

Thus did the Handhawersbond "stand on guard" in a much more pragmatic manner than did the F.A.K. However, since this movement was almost entirely based on the Rand and it never developed a strong and consistent ideology, it was particularly vulnerable to the wave of conciliatory sentiment which swept over the Transvaal during the period of *samesmelting*. Although Afrikaans-speaking teachers on the Rand generally stood to their guns during this period, popular support for the Handhawersbond waned until only a few Handhawerverenigings ("Handhawer Associations") remained, without any central organization.[2]

Like the Handhawersbond, the F.A.K. also blossomed between 1930 and 1933, corresponding with a general renewed interest among Afrikaners in their sacred history. At both the Paardekraal and the Magersfontein Boer War battlefields, bones of fallen Afrikaner soldiers were disinterred and reburied with holy ceremony and inspiring speeches by such prominent leaders as N. J. van der Merwe and C. J. H. de Wet.[3] The Day of the Covenant was publicly celebrated at more and more places, extending even into areas in the Cape where the day had previously been ignored.

However, the debates about *samesmelting* thát divided Afrikanerdom in 1933 also marred the celebrations of Geloftedag (e.g., *Die Burger*, December 16 and December 18, 1933; and *Die Weste*, December 8, 1933). *Die Volkstem* reported that at the Wonderboom celebration near Pretoria, for instance, Ds. P. J. de Klerk of the Gereformeerde Kerk condemned *samesmelting* as "an opportunistic politics which was unknown to our fathers." Using the example of King Ahaz

[2] See *Die Vaderland* (December 21, 1934) and *Die Republikein* (October 4, 1935). An attempt to found a farmers' Handhawersbond never got underway. (They did issue a constitution; the Johannesburg Public Library has a copy and it is discussed in *Die Weste*, July 28, 1933.) As an example of waning enthusiasm, we may note that the Ermelo High School annual magazine that had been filled with civil-religious fervor from 1919 to 1930 simply went out of print between 1930 and 1939.

[3] See *Die Burger* (October 5, 1930; April 7 and April 8, 1931), *Die Weste* (April 10, 1931) and *Die Vaderland* (January 1, 1934).

in Isaiah (chapter 7 and 8), de Klerk warned against entering coalitions with foreign rulers:

> There prevails today in the life of our People an Ahaz spirit
> . . . Isaiah also despaired of the future of his People. Then
> he ranged himself on the side of the small circle of the faithful
> among them. In isolation he sought strength. Even if it be
> a small group, if they stand in firm conviction of faith, then
> they are the core from which a new ethnic life will blossom.
> God desires unity among our People, but a unity of those who
> belong together and are bound together by the bond of faith.
> [*Die Volkstem*, December 18, 1933]

Not only Gereformeerdes but many N.G. ministers as well felt deeply troubled by the threat of *samesmelting*. In 1933, nine Free State N.G. dominees, including the venerable J. D. Kestell, made a public declaration in which they proclaimed their "warm appreciation for and accord with the [strongly Malanite] course which *Die Volksblad* had maintained in our political world, especially in the present time of *storm en drang*. . . . So far as we can judge, *Die Volksblad* has honestly interpreted the soul-conviction and national aspirations of the Afrikaner and has sounded a pure note in the cause of right and righteousness" (*Die Volksblad*, September 16, 1933). The sentiments of the Kuyperian and *volkskerk* elements in the Dutch Reformed churches were certainly clear on the issue of *samesmelting*. However, once *samesmelting* was a *fait accompli*, most ministers chose to remain silent on political issues for fear of dividing their congregations. The F.A.K., to, endeavored to take a position which set it above the struggles of party politics.

Malan, however, continued to be outspoken on the inseparability of nationalism and culture since they shared the common goal of a free and independent ethnic existence for Afrikanerdom. Nationalism operated in the political and economic spheres, he believed, whereas culture emphasized the spiritual and intellectual side (*Die Burger*, December 16, 1933). N. J. van der Merwe, who continued his chairmanship of the F.A.K. despite his role as Gesuiwerde member of parliament, likewise insisted on ethnic unity, declaring that "despite disruption and discord there is a common ground where we as Afrikaners can sit around the same fire." Furthermore, he went on to state, "I believe the F.A.K. is more than a mere organization or organization of organizations. I believe that it is a revelation of a living national organism, a self-conscious ethnic soul which ensures unity in strife" (*Die Burger*, December 20, 1934). This appeal can hardly have endeared the F.A.K. to members of the new United party, with its ideal of a wider civic unity.[4] In fact, like the Hand-hawersbond, the F.A.K. lost support during the early *sames-melting* period, although it was able to weather the "anti-cultural storm" more successfully because of its broader backing and weight from the Broederbond, which had remained almost, if not quite exclusively, true to the purified Nationalists.

Although the activities of Afrikaner teachers in such organizations as the Broederbond were seriously hampered by lack of public support, enthusiasts continued to inculcate the civil religion in schools. Teachers of history and Afrikaans language and literature were especially prone to teach an inspirational version of the Afrikaner national struggle to their pupils. From the ranks of such teachers came leaders of the Voortrekker movement, which was founded in 1929 to provide Afrikaner children with their own ethnic scout association.[5] The annual magazine for 1936 of the Wellington Teachers' Training College provides insight into the struggles of those who attempted to replace the Boy Scouts with "a national movement, born from our People, and thus fitting to our ethnic soul. . . ." It drew a curious analogy between Jesus' destiny and the progress of the Voortrekker movement:

> When Jesus was born, His own countrymen tried to kill Him, and thus was he persecuted throughout His whole life. What else can we then expect? The puny child [the Voortrekker movement] was promptly beset from all sides and was it not for the pure Afrikaner soul which was also transmitted to our

[4] In fact Hertzog reversed the argument, claiming that the National party purified was no more than "a cultural gang" (*Die Volksblad*, October 28, 1936).

[5] The Voortrekker movement, an Afrikaans version of the Boy Scouts and Girl Guides was founded by N. J. van der Merwe because the Scout movement refused to do away with "God Save the King" and the Union Jack in its Afrikaans section.

younger generation, would have died an early death. . . . Dr.
van der Merwe, our chief leader is indeed a politician but I
am convinced that when he dons that veld-green uniform he
leaves politics behind in his suit pockets. . . . Dear colleagues,
do you wish to make a success of your calling? Then learn
to know your students outside the school and try to enter
into their ways of thought. The Voortrekker movement provides you the golden opportunity. [Wellington Teachers'
Training College, annual magazine, 1936]

One must not overemphasize the success which such civil-
religion inspired teachers attained during the thirties, however. Other annual school magazines, for instance, contain
surprisingly few student essays on civil-religion themes. Either students were simply not sufficiently inspired to write
on such subjects, or schools deliberately chose not to publish
them.[6] Since teachers were banned from participation in
political activities, in the Free State at least, it is possible
that "cultural" essays were deemed unsuitable for publication.[7] Divisions in the ranks of Afrikanerdom might well have
provided reason for avoiding contentious essay topics. However, since in the following decade school annuals were filled
with civil-religion essays, popular sentiment in favor of *samesmelting* and against the purified Nationalist view of
culture during the 1930s must have been quite strong. In
the 1936 issue of the Heilbron High School magazine, A. B.
du Toit sadly noted that even here, at the very scene of
Vegkop, only one student, a girl, had recognized the importance of October 16, on the centenary of that battle.

However, numerous teachers must have kept aloft the
banner of *kultuurpolitiek* in the schools, for General Hertzog

[6] School magazines for the 1930s are hard to come by. Of the
eleven that I could find in the South African Public Library in
Cape Town only two (for Wolmaranstad and Heilbron schools)
published student essays on civil-religion themes during the 1930s.
An editorial in *Die Republikein* (December 4, 1936) deplored the
fact that, although professors, ministers of the churches, teachers,
and students remained true to Afrikaner culture despite harassment
from the government, ordinary Afrikaners were somewhat luke-
warm in their support of Geloftedag celebrations.

[7] For a brief discussion of the problem of the headmaster in such
matters see Nel, (n.d., pp. 30-31).

made note in his famous 1935 speech attacking the Broederbond, that:

> When I was at Oudtschoorn recently at a Circle Conference
> of the United Party and the Conference had gone into Com-
> mittee, there were unexpected complaints by a number of
> persons about the excessive participation of teachers in politics
> and finally a very serious appeal was made to me by a
> prominent woman delegate. These were her words: "In God's
> name, General, we mothers make a call on you to do everything
> in your power to prevent our children in school being so put
> up against their parents. You have no idea how bad it is."
> This charge of improper influence exercised by teachers on
> children in the school benches had already come to my ears
> more than once here in the Free State. . . . [Vatcher, 1965,
> p. 254]

Furthermore the very moderate Union secretary of education, Professor M. C. Botha, felt obliged to reprove teachers
for their political bias in his annual report for 1936:

> Seen in the right light, the task of the teacher is too elevated
> for party politics; his ideal ought to be the education of the
> whole community. . . . We find here [in South Africa] a mixture
> of races, languages, beliefs and colors, and unfortunately these
> questions often form the basic principles upon which political
> parties are grounded. The teacher must serve the whole nation
> and not a particular party. He must thus be a man of broad
> insights; he must hold a humanistic view concerning national
> events. . . . [*Die Burger*, January 12, 1937]

In an editorial on this report, *Die Burger* declared itself fully
in agreement with Professor Botha—as well it might, for the
question was not one of whether or not the teacher should
serve the nation, but rather how he chose to define the
"nation." Even before *samesmelting*, *Die Burger* in an editorial entitled "*Nasie-bou*" ("Nation Building"), which dealt with
the necessity for greater consciousness of art and literature
among Afrikaners, stated that "our teachers must not be mere
educationalists, but nation builders" (*Die Burger*, September
13, 1932; cf. *Die Weste*, September 2, 1932). And this in the
context of the spiritual raising of the Afrikaner People!

However, this article from *Die Burger* cannot be valued
as much more than a straw in the wind. The major thrust
toward defining Afrikanerdom as the only truly South African

"nation" came from a source other than the liberal nationalism of the Malanite Nasionale Pers.[8] Young Afrikaner intellectuals were coming home after doctoral study in Europe
inspired with the ideals of neo-Fichtean nationalism.[9] Foremost among these was Dr. Nic Diederichs (later minister of
finance in Vorster's cabinet), who returned from studies in
Munich, Cologne, Berlin, and Leiden to take up the
chair in political philosophy at the University College of
the Orange Free State in Bloemfontein. Other leaders of this
new Afrikaner ideological development included Dr. Piet J.
Meyer (later Broederbond chairman in the Verwoerd era),
who became a paid official of the F.A.K. upon his return from
Germany; Dr. H. F. Verwoerd (later prime minister), professor
of sociology at Stellenbosch and later editor of *Die Trans-
valer*; Dr. Geoff. Cronje, professor of sociology at Pretoria
University; Dr. J. de W. Keyter, professor of sociology at
Bloemfontein; Dr. Albert Hertzog, son of the prime minister,
Pretoria advocate, and freelance Afrikaner organizer; and Dr.
T. J. Hugo, professor of political science at Pretoria. Among
the students who were most keenly attracted by neo-Fichtean
ideology may be mentioned P. C. Coetzee, D. G. Malan, Anton
Rupert (later a South African business tycoon), and F. S.
Steyn.

Evidence for the content of this new social philosophy is
plentiful, since its academic proponents were active in addressing Afrikaner cultural associations and were given full
coverage in the Nasionale Pers publications, especially *Die*

---

[8] Nasionale Pers, under the control of D. F. Malan, W. A. Hofmeyr
and A. L. Geyer was founded in 1915 in order to publish *Die Burger*.
By 1938, however, *Die Oosterlig* in Port Elizabeth and *Die Volksblad* in Bloemfontein were being published by Nasionale Pers with
a measure of control from Cape Town.

[9] The prime source for neo-Fichtean nationalism is of course
Johann Fichte's *Addresses to the German Nation*. However I use
the term in a slightly broader context to refer to "nationalism"
as described by Elie Kedourie (1960). What I call neo-Fichteanism
thus includes the views of such German romantics as J. D. Herder
and F. E. D. Schleiermacher as well as Fichte himself. Kedourie
feels that all nationalism fits the Fichtean mold. I respectfully beg
to differ, since in my opinion much of the modern discussion of
nationalism has failed to distinguish between, at least, liberal and
neo-Fichtean nationalism.

Volksblad and *Die Oosterlig*. The monthly journal of the
A.N.S. (Afrikaner Nastionale Studentebond) provided its
neo-Fichtean editorial board, consisting of both faculty and
students, with another stage for propaganda; and during the
war years Keyter, Diederichs, Cronje, and Piet J. Meyer edited
a series of small tracts for the times called *Die Tweede Trek
Reeks* ("Second Trek Series"). In fact, so abundant is the
documentary evidence on neo-Fichtean nationalism that one
is tempted to overlook the fact that this ideology was highly
controversial even among students,—especially at Stellenbosch where there was active opposition.[10] It was never widely
accepted in its pure form by the Afrikaans-speaking public.
Yet, at the same time, student and faculty supporters of the
A.N.S. rapidly became prominent in the Afrikaner Broederbond, whose Kuyperian Christian Nationalism was easily able
to accommodate a modified neo-Fichteanism.

The A.N.S. originated in 1933, when, under the leadership
of Piet J. Meyer, at that time a student at Bloemfontein,
student governments of the Afrikaans universities broke away
from the liberal National Union of South African Students
because of disagreement over the admission of black African
students to the union. By 1935, the organization had established branches at all the Afrikaans universities and at many
of the teachers' training colleges in the Transvaal, Free State,
and Cape. In the same year it published a manifesto declaring
its intention to "stand on guard" (*handhaaf*) for the national
struggle of a separate Afrikaans nation with its own separate
calling. It sought to inspire students to national service and
national cooperation on the basis of "the Protestant-Christian

[10] For the struggle at Stellenbosch see *Koers* (June 1934) and
also the editorial attacking the A.N.S. in *Die Stellenbosse Student,*
(August 1937) and its results (cf. *Die Oosterlig*, August 27, 1937).
See also *Die Stellenbosse Student* (October 1937), which contains
a carefully worded and moderate critique of the A.N.S. by A. J.
van der Velden and J. F. Holleman as well as the flippant reply
of the A.N.S. chairman, J. S. Gericke, who manages to deride them
without in any way meeting their arguments. That *Die Stellenbosse
Student* eventually fell into line with the A.N.S. is clear from the
editorial of April 1938, which commences "Stellenbosch is first and
last intended as a People's University . . . Stellenbosch stands for
the Afrikaans 'idea.'"

and Cultural-National principles of our Nation" (*Wapenskou*, November 1935). The new movement was early brought under the wing of Professors Diederichs and Cronje. In May 1934, Diederichs had appeared before the synod of the Free State N.G. in Bloemfontein and obtained its full support for the A.N.S.

Its philosophical basis was elaborated in a pamphlet by Diederichs entitled *Nationalisme as Lewensbeskouing en sy verhouding tot Internasionalisme* ("Nationalism as a *Weltanschauung* and its Relation to Internationalism") and published by *Nasionale Pers* in 1935. Diederichs argued here that in contrast to the materialism of internationalism, nationalism emphasizes man's spiritual (*geestelike*) nature as his defining characteristic:

> [Man] is a spiritual being [*geesteswese*] who indeed carries in himself the natural, but who yet is distinguished from all mere natural beings because he can rise above the natural and repair to the sphere of the spirit, becoming the creator of art, science, philosophy, culture, etc. [Diederichs, 1935, p. 14]

However, not only is man a dual being, but the realms of spirit and nature struggle within him for mastery. Man's calling is thus to carry the ideal into the real world and to reconcile the natural and the spiritual.

> [T]he destiny of man as a spiritual being is in the first place to be warrior and bearer of spiritual values, to place himself in the service of the eternal and immortal in and above himself, and to make the world more beautiful, better, holier and richer in spiritual and cultural goods. This is the true calling of man as man. [Diederichs, 1935, p. 15]

Mankind is more than individual men; indeed the individual is an abstraction which did not exist for Diederichs. Since man is by nature a social being, he is never fully man except within a human community. Moreover, according to Diederichs, man is called not only to be a member of a community, but specifically and above all, to belong to a *national* community.

> Without the uplifting, ennobling and enriching influence of this highest inclusive unity which we call a nation, [he argued] mankind cannot reach the fullest heights of his human exis-

tence. Only through his consecration to, his love for and his service to the nation can man come to the versatile and harmonious development of his human existence. Only in the nation as the most total, most inclusive human community can man realize himself to the full. The nation is the fulfillment of the individual life. [Diederichs, 1935, pp. 17-18]

Having thus defined human nature as spiritual (*geestelik*) and national, Diederichs proceeded to argue that man must be understood as an active and purposeful being:

The natural side of human life has the character of factual existence in the sense that it is given to man, and he possesses it without any instrumentality on his part. The situation is completely different in the spiritual side of our life. The spiritual possessions [*besit*] of a man are not given to him; he must conquer them. . . . The fully spiritual man is not what others or events have made him, but is rather what he has become in and through himself. His true possessions are not those which have been brought to him from without, but those which he has appropriated for himself through his own association and sacrifice. For human nature is not a mere fact, but a task, a calling, an idea. Mankind *is* never completely himself . . . he must always conquer himself to remain himself, more and more overcome himself in order to become that which he is not yet, but which he ought to be. Human nature means to live like a man, and life is a process, a becoming, a deed. [Diederichs, 1935, pp. 18-19]

Corresponding to his idealist view of mankind, Diederichs defined the nation in spiritual terms. Such factors as love for a common fatherland, common racial descent, or common political convictions might be present in any given nation, but are not necessarily present. The real unity of the nation rests upon a single, spiritual, defining characteristic, a common culture. Diederichs defined "culture" as the possession of certain values and principles and the struggle to realize those principles. Thus even as the individual was defined both in terms of his static nature and the dynamic process of his coming into being, so the nation was defined in both static and dynamic terms. In static terms or as defined subjectively, the nation is a community of feeling. But objectivity is dynamic and is attained only in the process of coming into being, in a unity of commitment to a common calling. A nation thus involves a unique cultural principle and a community of commitment to the active realization of this principle in every sphere of life.

> A nation is one because its members feel united in their common attitudes to the same values. Furthermore, their unity is no rigid, static unity but a living, moving, growing unity, a unity of direction and struggle. . . . Like any other spiritual being, a nation must continually struggle to remain itself. . . .The cultural history of a nation is the process along which this self-realization takes place. . . . But nations are not historical entities in the sense that history created their unity. Their unity is supra-temporal and grounded in the common ideal world of values. [Diederichs, 1935, pp. 36-41]

In fact, Diederichs posited the nation as the essential and necessary unit of social analysis. Individuals have existence only insofar as they are taken up into the national whole (Diederichs, 1935, p. 24). The notion of universal humanity, on the other hand, is also an abstraction, too vague and general to have any meaning unless by humanity one understands "the spiritual community of the various nations." The nation is thus the only true reality; true individuals and true humanity exist only in and through the nation.

On the basis of this social metaphysics, Diederichs was unequivocally opposed to any doctrine of human equality. There are grades of human nature, he argued, "and one man is more human than another to the extent that the spiritual powers within him are the more expressed and developed. . . . The only equality which must be accepted is the equality of opportunity for each to bring that which is within him to full expression" (Diederichs, 1935, p. 20). Such growth to full humanity, Diederichs argued, is possible only when the individual perceives himself as a member of the nation. Freedom does not mean exemption from every possible limitation, but rather the possibility of realizing oneself in service to the nation:

> Freedom is not simply a task which must be fulfilled, but seen from the angle of the nation, freedom is also a *duty*. . . . The highest freedom, which alone truly deserves the name of freedom, is inner spiritual freedom, freedom in service of supra-personal, eternally binding ideal values. [Diederichs, 1935, pp. 53-54]

Finally, Diederichs argued that nations are desirable and indeed necessary because there is a final goal to which all God's creation is striving:

> In realization of this goal, there rests upon everything which exists, every nation and each man, an allotted task and duty. But above all on each particular nation there rests a special task to do its part in the final divine goal of the cosmos both through being itself and through the fulfillment of its apportioned calling as a nation. [Diederichs, 1935, p. 50]

The very diversity of the nations was created by God himself for both aesthetic and teleological reasons. From the aesthetic point of view, said Diederichs:

> God willed that there should be nations so that through them the richness and beauty of His creation might be heightened. Just as He ruled that no deadly uniformity should prevail in nature, but that it should demonstrate a richness and variety of plants and animals, sounds and colors, forms and figures, so in the human sphere as well He ruled that there should exist a multiplicity and diversity of nations, languages and cultures. [Diederichs, 1935, pp. 23-24]

More important however, God created nations to execute His will:

> God does not work only through men, but also through nations. To each nation to which He entrusted a special calling He laid up a special task which would have to be fulfilled as part of His providential plan with creation.... An effort to obliterate national differences thus means more than collision with God's natural law. It also means an effort to shirk a divinely established duty or task. [Diederichs, 1935, pp. 23-24]

Nationalism was thus necessarily religious. Diederichs stated this clearly in the conclusion of his study. "To work for the realization of the national calling," he said, "is to work for the realization of God's plan. Service to the nation is thus service to God" (Diederichs, 1935, p. 63).

It was precisely because he seemed to deify the nation that Kuyperians like Stoker and du Plessis found it necessary to disagree with Diederichs. In a long critical review in *Die Volksblad* Stoker cautioned that:

> [Although] explicitly, the writer is not guilty of idolization of the nation, [yet] indirectly his analysis of nationalism houses the danger of deification of the nation precisely because in

my opinion, he wrongly perceives the relation of the individual to his nation. Diederichs rightly sets God above the nation. But he goes too far when in the manner in which he does it, he sets the nation above the individual. Because above me as an individual is not my nation but God and God alone. ... By placing my nation above me and God above the nation, he attributes to the nation at least in part that which belongs to God alone, and in so doing he deifies the nation. ... Nation and individual both stand under the ordinances of God and not the one beneath the other, however dependent they may be upon each other. ... [*Die Volksblad*, April 25, 1936]

The transcendent sovereignty of Calvin's God clashed directly with neo-Fichtean nationalism. The nation might be an ordinance of God's creation, but this gives it no priority over the other spheres, Stoker reminded his readers, for each sphere retains its own sovereignty and is directly responsible to God alone.

On similar grounds, Stoker also rejected Diederichs' idealism. Although man is both natural and spiritual according to Diederichs, the spiritual is the essentially human aspect of his being. Defined in cultural terms, the nation is pure spirit on one level. On the other hand, culture itself has both a natural and a spiritual aspect. The natural was the static subjective realm of feeling; the truly spiritual was the objective dynamic of development. He rejected race as in any way a defining characteristic of the nation, for race is feral and earthly for Diederichs—definitely inferior to culture. "In my opinion," said Stoker, "the spiritual (*geestelike*) is also earthly, also of [creation] and definitely not 'divine.' God must be distinguished from the spiritual and valuable in [his creation]; this spiritual is just as ... 'earthly' or bound to creation as dust and blood" (*Die Volksblad*, April 25, 1936).[11] Stoker thus included race as a necessary aspect of the nation, although he insisted that he did not wish to exclude the possibility of intermarriage, and the incorporation of individuals from other groups.[12]

[11] For a rather weak attempt to meet Stoker's major objections, see Meyer (1941, p. 33 and pp. 122-125).

[12] In a similarly critical though slightly less damning review in *Koers* (August 1935), L. J. du Plessis took Diederichs to task for his emphasis on the "spiritual" as opposed this time to the "politi-

Whatever objections Broederbond Kuyperians might have to Diederichs' metaphysical presuppositions, the practical implications for Afrikanerdom were agreeable to them:

> We are not a "section," [said Diederichs in a Cape Town speech] we are a nation. . . . We are a separate nation with anchors and roots in this country and this country alone. If there is a "section" in this country, then we may in all honesty say that our English fellow-citizens. . . . are no nation in the true sense of the word, but a section of a nation overseas. [Insisting that he was not speaking politics, Diederichs continued:] When one struggles for a distinct and separate Afrikaner nation, then one has to do with something higher and more eternal than any politics. One struggles for the spiritual liberation of Afrikanerdom. . . . The enemy of Afrikanerdom has seen its weak point, he has realized that nothing can so rapidly divide and shatter our nation as politics. [*Die Burger*, April 12, 1936; cf. Cronje's editorial in *Wapenskou*, June 1937]

Despite the apparent similarities between Diederichs' practical position as here set forth and Broederbond Christian Nationalism, their theoretical differences ranged wider than Stoker's objection to deification of the nation. The official ideology of the Broederbond is neatly summarized in a 1935 pamphlet article by L. J. du Plessis, in which the latter called for "Afrikanerism" characterized as "self-maintenance and self-development of the Afrikaans nation as an independent member of the great world community of Peoples" (du Plessis, L. J., Hugo and Labuschagne, n.d., p. 1). Such an ideal, du Plessis believed, could be achieved only by the Afrikanerization of South Africa. This meant in practice

> that there should be Afrikaners; that they should be ineradicably strong through unity; that they should outwardly establish and maintain their own nature (that is culture); that they should live out this nature (that is independence); that they should be unimpeded from without (that is freedom); that in view of this they should have control over the soil and riches of South Africa (that is solvency and domination); and that they finally in unity, with their own culture independently realized, freely and as owners should bring forth by their own power their own Afrikaans constitutional organization as

---

cal" in his definition of the nation. Diederichs' position, said du Plessis, was typical of the A.N.S.

armor and shield for their Afrikanerization of South Africa.
[Du Plessis, L. J., et al., n.d., p. 3]

The position of du Plessis here set forth differed on several
scores from that of Diederichs.[13] In the first place, du Plessis
used the terms "People" (*volk*) and "Nation" (*nasie*) inter-
changeably, whereas Diederichs scrupulously avoided the
term *volk*,[14] most probably because as a philosopher he wished
to avoid identification with the unacademic "Volkish Movement" (cf. Mosse, 1964; and Neumann, 1966, pp. 98-129), that
had recently triumphed in German National Socialism and
was based on anti-Semitic racism, which Diederichs specifically denied. Second, in place of Diederichs' "spiritual" conception of freedom, du Plessis strongly emphasized constitutional independence. Finally, where Diederichs advocated
Afrikaner separatism, du Plessis still argued for a form of
Afrikaner evangelism. Indeed, in a speech before the A.N.S.
in September 1934, du Plessis urged that "we must keep the
gate open" for "the other section;" indeed, he argued that
"we can take them up if they make South Africa their
Fatherland, use the Afrikaner language, make the South
African view of life their own and take on the South African
religion . . . even Jews could be incorporated if they met
these requirements" (*Die Republikein*, September 14, 1934).

By 1941, Diederichs had modified his position in order to
accommodate Stoker's insistence on the essential importance
of the individual and of race in defining the nation, as well
as du Plessis' notion of freedom as both political and spiritual
reality (Coetzee, Diederichs and Meyer, 1941, pp. 127-128).
By 1941 he had also adopted with seeming comfort the use
of the term *volk*.[15] On the other hand, the explicit separatism
which Diederichs advocated was sustained by the political
"purification" during the 1930s and the reaction to the

[13] There can be no doubt, however, of Diederichs' membership
in the Broederbond. He is at present South African minister of
finance.

[14] For a good discussion of the various uses of the terms *volk*,
nasie, and *bevolking* during the 1930s see Malherbe (1942, chapter
2).

[15] Diederichs' terminology seems to have changed at the time of
the 1938 Ossewatrek (cf. *Ossewa Gedenkboek*, 1940, pp. 54-57).

declaration of war in 1939, by which time the entire Broederbond had chosen to postpone the Afrikanerization of the
English to the distant future (cf. Malherbe, 1942).

Both Kuyperians and such neo-Fichteans as Diederichs and
Cronje laid great emphasis on the "calling" of Afrikanerdom.
Although they all believed that Afrikanerdom was called to
serve God in some unique way, and although public mention
of the calling aroused great enthusiasm in Afrikaner audiences, speakers and writers seldom attempted to specify the
precise content of the Afrikaner calling.

In a book called *Die Afrikaner* (1941), Dr. P. J. Meyer
made a bold effort to do as much, but only ended up in a
circular argument:

> The People as a faith-unit [*geloofseenheid*] fulfills its own
> calling on the one hand by realizing the value-whole [*waarde-
> geheel*] and on the other the life-order [*lewensordening*] or-
> dained by its faith. . . . The People is at the same time a
> social [*lewens*] and a cultural community. In the realization
> of its unique life-form the People creates its culture and in
> the creation of its culture it realizes its own life-form. These
> are the two sides of the fulfillment of its unique calling as
> given in its faith. . . . The ethnic calling which is contained
> in the ethnic faith is the most important and primary commu-
> nity-forming and culture-creating factor in the coming-into-
> being of the People. The realization of the sense and being
> of Peoplehood is the fulfillment of the ethnic calling which
> finds its most complete precipitation in the ethnic language.
> The fulfillment of a People's calling is a dual process, namely
> community formation and cultural creation out of the spiritual
> constitution of the People over against its actuality. [Meyer,
> 1941, pp. 55-57]

What Meyer was saying here seems to follow Diederichs'
argument that a nation both is and is coming-into-being.
Despite his lack of clarity, Meyer did deal more specifically
than Diederichs with historical factors, which he believed to
be normative for the vocation of Afrikanerdom. Most important for the Afrikaner "life-order" were the patriarchal family,
the republican constitutional form, and a system of wardship
over the South African natives; most important for the
cultural "value-whole" was a sense of subordination to an
absolute and sovereign God as found in Calvinism, general

economic welfare, Christian National education, and uniquely ethnic arts and science (Meyer, 1941, p. 39).

What was needed, Meyer indicated, was the re-creation of South African society in a uniquely Afrikaans-Calvinist spirit, in other words its Afrikanerization. Miscellaneous efforts to defend the Afrikaans language or to create Afrikaans art or an Afrikaans scientific system would inevitably fail if they operated within the existing atomistic South African social order. The symbols of the Afrikaner cultural "value-whole" had to become the organizing principles of an organic Afrikaner community. Such ideals as the coming of a republic were thus relative to the deeper need for Afrikaner unity,[16] the recognition that every Afrikaner was bound by his organic membership in his People to make a unique and ethnic contribution to the creation plan of God.

In the final analysis the argument remains circular. Afrikaners are Afrikaners because of God's calling and God's calling means that they should be exclusively Afrikaner. But this is precisely why mention of the "calling" met with such acclaim in public addresses. Although by definition the concept of calling involved service and subordination to God, it also implicitly spelled election and superiority over other men. One fears that for the ordinary Afrikaner Diederichs' "objective" sense of commitment, the dynamic element in the neo-Fichtean system, was too often subordinate to the static, "subjective" feeling of belonging, which was the secondary aspect of nationhood for Diederichs.[17]

The A.N.S. version of neo-Fichtean nationalism remained relatively independent of the doctrines of Adolph Hitler's National Socialism. Diederichs' stress on the "spiritual" definition of the nation, together with his express denial of the importance of both common biological descent and a common fatherland, implied a desire to avoid identification with the

[16] See Meyer (1941, p. 56) for his discussion of the ultimate relativity of history (curiously at odds with his professed Calvinism).

[17] Nepgen (1938) argues that the doctrine of predestination may lead to extraordinary perseverance but that it may also lead to resignation to one's fate and an extraordinary inactivity. Equally, I should argue, the doctrine of election may lead to a humble, fearful fulfillment of one's calling, but it may also lead to plain arrogance.

Blut und Boden ("Blood and Soil") school. Furthermore, throughout the thirties Diederichs showed no inclination to anti-Semitism.

Such an enlightened silence on the subject of the Jews is the more surprising because during the later thirties, when small numbers of German Jewish refugees began to enter South Africa, strong grassroots pressure urged a ban on Jewish immigration. Afrikaner opinion on the "Jewish question" was largely informed by the activities of one Louis Weichardt. In 1933 Weichardt organized a movement known as the Greyshirts that sought through democratic processes to obtain power. He planned thereafter to rule by dictatorship like Hitler in Germany.[18] Although the Greyshirts made slight political impact, since Weichardt's aspirations to dictatorship found little support, rural Afrikaners clearly responded to his typically Nazi anti-Semitism.

The 1930s brought many tribulations to the Afrikaner platteland, and farmers sought a locus for their frustrations. The years of the Great Depression saw several severe droughts, and the countryside continued to depopulate as the earlier subsistence economy adjusted more fully to a money economy. Jews in the rural towns, who tended to be small retailers, were also struggling to weather the depression and were targets for antipathy as the most visible agents of the industrial economy, with its emphasis on profit, production, and credit with interest.

Whatever its reasons, the upsurge of anti-Semitism was a definite source of embarrassment to Dr. Malan. During the 1920s, Jews in the Cape rural towns had often supported the National party; and in 1930, Malan could reciprocate in parliament:

> I think the people of South Africa generally, belonging to all parties and sections, desire to give to the Jewish people in this country full equality in every respect, every opportunity which every other section enjoys, full participation in our national life, and I am glad to say that we are still in that position today in South Africa to appreciate and appreciate

[18] For Weichardt's policy see *Die Volkstem* (January 2, 1934) and correspondence between the Greyshirts and the National party published in *Die Burger* (November 3, 1937).

very highly what the Jews have done for South Africa. [*Hansard*, February 10, 1930]

As early as 1934, Malan attacked the Greyshirts in George, declaiming that not all Jews are parasites and not all parasites are Jews (*Die Burger*, July 9, 1934; cf. *Die Burger*, October 30, 1934). As late as June 1936, he stated in parliament that "in this country we cannot discriminate against the Jewish race or any other race. All who are white in this country deserve to stand on an equal footing politically and otherwise" (*Hansard*, June 16, 1936).

In the same year, however, the number of Jewish immigrants from Nazi Germany increased dramatically; and Greyshirt demonstrations began to attract sizeable crowds. Political implications were clear. In November a group of Stellenboch professors and other prominent Cape Nationalists, including Professors A. C. Cilliers, Con de Villiers, H. F. Verwoerd, J. Basson, and Dr. T. E. Donges (a liberal Cape Nationalist who later became a minister in Malan's first cabinet) addressed large anti-Semitic protest meetings at Stellenbosch, Paarl, Caledon, and Malmesbury, all prosperous farming communities in the western Cape (*Die Burger*, November 5, November 9, and November 30, 1936). This professorial opposition was echoed by Professor Cronje in an editorial in *Wapenskou*:

> If the "anti-Jewish" movement in our country now becomes stronger by the day and is destined to play a large role in the political life of South Africa, nobody ought to be surprised, least of all the Jews themselves. They were simply looking for trouble by loading off on our shoulders that element which Germany no longer wanted . . . flotsam from the national life of another country. . . .[*Wapenskou*, November 1936]

Malan bowed to the pressure and spoke in parliament on January 12, 1937, supporting a National party proposal that all Jewish immigration be stopped and that Jews be refused entry to certain occupations in South Africa. The United party defeated this proposal, accepting instead a watered-down version which required that all immigrants be screened by a special selection board before entry. In 1939, Eric Louw (later to be foreign minister in Malan's cabinet) moved another version of the anti-Semitic Immigration Bill as a private measure. Although this proposal was defeated, Louis Weichardt was sufficiently convinced of Louw's and the National party's sincerity to join the party and urge his followers to do likewise (*Die Oosterlig*, January 20, 1939).

Dr. Verwoerd's part in the 1936 agitation at the Cape was, in fact, his last act before leaving for Johannesburg to edit the new Transvaal Nationalist newspaper. His article in the first issue of *Die Transvaler* (October 1, 1937) argued that since Jews were unassimilable and yet dominant in business and the professions, a quota system ought to be instituted which would prevent further Jewish entry into businesses and the professions until the racial balance had been restored. Verwoerd's article was no more than an elaboration of the 1937 Nationalist proposal in parliament, and the argument was reiterated by N. J. van der Merwe at the Free State party congress (*Die Volksblad*, October 13, 1937), and later by Strydom at a meeting in Johannesburg (*Die Oosterlig*, November 19, 1937).

Although I do not intend here to exonerate individual Nationalists from charges of anti-Semitism,[19] it does seem that the anti-Semitism which emerged at this stage resulted from grassroots pressure rather than from initiative by the leaders. In 1937, for example, the National party congresses in the Transvaal, Free State, and Natal excluded Jews from party membership—but only in the teeth of strong opposition from Malan's wing of the party.[20] In the 1938 campaign, anti-Semitism was a very muted theme of the Nationalist platform (cf. Hepple, 1967, pp. 224-225), but one is left with the impression that rural members of the Cape party would have welcomed more.

It is important to note that most of whatever attention the Jews received in South Africa during the 1930s was restricted to party-political circles, where speakers were open

[19] Hepple (1967) makes an interesting case against Verwoerd, although he overlooks the extent to which Verwoerd, as editor of *Die Transvaler*, was a mouthpiece for his party.
[20] See the arguments of C. W. M. Toit in *Die Vaderland* (October 10, 1937). The Cape Party never excluded Jewish members.

to public pressure. Members of the Broederbond, except insofar as they were involved in party politics, seldom gave expression to anti-Semitic opinions despite the temptation of the "Hoggenheimer" image. The problem in South Africa, most of them argued, extended beyond the Jews to include just about all English-speaking South Africans—Jewish and non-Jewish alike. In Germany it was impossible to be fully National Socialist without violent anti-Semitism; but for Afrikaners, Christian Nationalism excluded non-Calvinists as well as non-Christians (and, of course, all non-whites). Hence, insofar as Afrikaner intellectuals were anti-Semitic, they were elaborating a personal prejudice and not an integral aspect of the Christian National ideology.

Be that as it may, for intellectuals in the A.N.S., their foremost task and calling was to work for the return of all stray Afrikaners to the national fold. Unlike Malan, who was seeking the same goal on a political level, they chose to operate within the realm of *kultuurpolitiek.*

Two major divisions hindered Afrikaner *volkseenheid*, argued Diederichs in speech after speech—vertical political differences and urban migration, which divided the nation horizontally. Both these dislocations in the Afrikaner organism could be healed only by a higher adherence to "culture":

> There are matters upon which Afrikaners can clasp hands across the chasm of division, bitterness and fragmentation. Political programs disappear but culture continues to exist. We ought not to sacrifice our nation for a political party; we must stand together as a separate Afrikaner nation....
>
> If the worker is drawn away from our nation, then we might as well write Ichabod on the door of our temple. The worker has always supplemented the higher classes; the working classes are the spring from which the nation draws. Today there is a determined struggle underway which is aimed at the working classes, the foundation of our People. There are forces at work in the bosom of the People which seek to unite our workers with the proletariat of other lands. . . . The headquarters of this movement is in Moscow.... In South Africa we believe that the Afrikaner worker is still the best and most reliable Afrikaner. He must be drawn into his nation in order to be a genuine man. There must be no division or schism between class and class. May the day break here as

is the case in Italy and Germany, where the worker may comfort himself with the thought: "What I do here I do as a worker, but I do it in service of my nation." [*Die Oosterlig*, November 8, 1937][21]

Diederichs thus continued to preach his version of nationalism, but increasingly and with typical vigor and clarity he began to speak and write against communism. By 1935, neo-Fichtean nationalists seemed to believe that if there were not a concerted drive to bring city-dwellers back into the organic unity of the nation, communism would gather in the poor urban Afrikaners. This threat was indeed imminent, warned Dr. J. de W, Keyter:

In the cities black and white live together. There is no chance of moral development. Where is our religion and our love for the nation? We reject our own people and they shy from our religion. . . . The people are easily exploited. They have but one ideal, bread alone is necessary for life, they know not religion and ethnic feeling. They have no sense of duty. The feeling of dependence [on charity] has overcome them. . . . Youth is by nature interested in politics. They would rather follow heroes but we are driving our young people to communism. . . . The chase for profit, irresponsibility towards our neighbors and preference for native-labor is driving our young people away from us. . . . [*Die Vaderland*, September 24, 1935]

No systematic attack on class problems was launched until 1936. At the beginning of that year, Piet Meyer returned from Amsterdam having completed his doctoral studies and became assistant secretary of the F.A.K. (cf. *Wapenskou*, November 1935). His impact on the ideological direction of the organization was immediate. In May he issued, in the name of the F.A.K., two lengthy statements proposing cultural unity as the solution to the two most serious threats to Afrikaner *volkseenheid* as perceived by him and his fellows: the conciliatory party politics of the United party and the divisive effects of "communist-inspired" class conflict.[22] In

[21] The Nazi influence in this attitude to class conflict is obvious. It was explicitly acknowledged in a speech by H. G. Schultze at the 1934 A.N.S. congress (*Die Burger*, October 6, 1934).

[22] Characteristically wordy, these circulars were published in full in *Die Republikein* (May 1 and May 8, 1936). See also Cronje's editorial in *Wapenskou* (March 1936).

July 1936, after the annual meetings of the Broederbond and the F.A.K., he formed a Nasionale Kultuurraad ("National Cultural Council"). According to Meyer, the new Raad was designed to unite all organizations of the Afrikaner People under a single direction:

> Not only would the Afrikaans churches, the women's associations, teachers' organizations, cultural associations, youth organizations and so on be included, but provision would also be made for the establishment of political and legal study circles and the organization of Afrikaans workers and officials into Afrikaans-Christian personnel and labor unions. Finally, farmer and homecraft associations would also be represented on the great national council. [*Die Volksblad*, July 2 and July 3, 1936]

In practice, what Meyer was proposing was that the F.A.K. together with the Afrikaans churches become involved in organizing urban Afrikaner workers into "Christian National" labor unions in order to reintegrate them into the organic unity of the *volk.*

On October 4, 1936, Meyer and Diederichs along with Albert Hertzog and an Afrikaner banker named Frikkie de Wet met in Johannesburg to found an organization which would provide financial backing for the Christian-National Afrikaner trade unions. They called this organization the Nasionale Raad van Trustees ("National Council of Trustees"). Among those eminent Afrikaners who agreed to serve on this council were Mrs. M. T. Steyn, widow of the late president, along with Totius, J. D. Kestell, J. C. van Rooy, and Ivan Lombard—the last two chairman and secretary, respectively, of the Broederbond— and Ds. J. R. Albertyn, Poor-Relief Secretary of the Transvaal N.G. Two thousand pounds was given by Mrs. Jannie Marais in order that full time union organizers could be appointed (Naude, 1969, pp. 36-62).

There was only one precedent for the formation of "cultural" trade unions in South Africa. In March 1935, a few enthusiastic Broederbonders who were also railway employees founded a union for railwaymen called the Spoorbond. Their goals included the defense of the Afrikaans language and the encouragement of a Christian spirit in addition to better working conditions and higher wages. They made no distinction between different classes of railway workers, but appealed to all to unite in a single organization.[23] By 1938, a majority of the employees of the South African Railways had joined the Spoorbond. Then the United party broke the movement by requiring separate union representation for different skilled trades. However, at the time that Meyer, Diederichs, and Albert Hertzog founded the National Council of Trustees, the rapidly growing Spoorbond must have served as an inspiring example.

Since the whole South African economy revolves around gold production, the National Council of Trustees decided that their first major task was to organize the mine workers. Not only were a majority of white miners Afrikaans-speaking but there was general dissatisfaction within the existing Mine Workers' Union over its corruption and ineffectiveness (Sachs, 1953, pp. 169ff.). If the mine workers, the aristocrats of labor, could be organized along Christian National lines, other industrial employees would follow suit.

On November 24, 1936, Meyer and Albert Hertzog officially established the Afrikanerbond van Mynwerkers. Faas de Wet, himself a mine worker, was appointed part-time chief organizer. One of those who was part of the movement from the beginning described the task of enlightening and organizing the mine workers as "thankless work."

> Most of them had to be convinced of the necessity of joining a trade union and those who belonged to the [existing] Mine Workers' Union had to be persuaded to leave it. From one end of the Rand to the other the young men had to work night after night, from Nigel and Springs to Krugersdorp and Randfontein, at the shaft heads and in homes. And the time in which such work could be done was short—during the brief hours between the time when the worker returned from the afternoon shift and the time when he crawled early into bed. There were 52 mines with 189 shafts spread over a distance of 80 miles across the Rand. Thence Dr. Hertzog and his fellows had to hasten every evening, winding between endless mine heaps and through thickly populated areas. It was an enormous task. . . ." [Naude, 1969, pp. 27-28]

[23] A good brief account of the founding of the Spoorbond is the speech by P. J. de Kok at the foundation meeting of the Afrikanerbond van Mynwerkers reported in *Die Volksblad* (November 27, 1936). See also *Die Burger* (May 8, 1937) and *Die Transvaler* (October 8, 1937).

Within five months, however, they had met with sufficient
success for the Mine Workers' Union to see the new Afrikanerbond as an outright threat requiring quick, bold remedy.
On April first, M.W.U. members on the Simmer and Jack
mine came out on strike against the Afrikanerbond; and
within nine days their organizing secretary, Charlie Harris,
had wrapped up a "closed shop" agreement between the union
and the Chamber of Mines. This spelled doom for Albert
Hertzog's Afrikanerbond. Meanwhile, mine workers were
given until June first to join Harris' M.W.U.

Protests streamed in from the Afrikaans-speaking countryside, encouraged by a circular letter sent by Meyer, as
secretary of the F.A.K., to all member organizations (*Die
Burger*, April 11, 1937; and *Die Vaderland*, May 25, 1937).
The synod of the Free State N.G. joined the dissenting cry
and publicized its strong disapproval of all efforts to prevent
the Afrikaners in the cities from organizing themselves in
trade unions which contemplated the promotion of their
religious and cultural concerns (*Die Volksblad*, editorial,
April 23, 1937). Despite this opposition, the government
refused to intervene, and so placed its sanction on the closed
shop.

In spite of the dissolution of the Afrikanerbond van Mynwerkers, Dr. Albert Hertzog was still at work behind the
scenes. He was now busy organizing a reform movement
within the M.W.U. in an effort to unseat Harris from the
inside. However, as Mrs. Marais' gift was expended, Albert
Hertzog had to resort to the country roads in a campaign
for funds. So, in company with Ivan Lombard, he traveled
throughout the Cape countryside addressing small gatherings
of influential locals arranged by the Broederbond, appealing
for contributions to the Afrikaner struggle on the Rand.

> It was his task to explain the perilous situation of the Afrikaner
> worker to these people. . . . He honestly and forthrightly told
> them that the Afrikaner People could be saved only if these
> workers could be won back and anchored again in the values
> and ideals of the Afrikaner People. . . . For the first time it
> penetrated to the rural Afrikaner that these were his People.
> . . . The Afrikaner in the countryside began to open his heart
> and his hand to his brethren on the Rand. All were prepared
> to help and willing to give. . . . [Naude, 1969, p. 99]

In 1939, his opponent, Harris, was able to muster enough support in the M.W.U. general meeting (probably by dubious means) to do away with union elections, thus blockading all operations of the reform movement, so he thought. But he had reckoned without "the Hand which guides the fates of men and nations" (Naude, 1969, p. 126), for on June 15, 1939, before the new constitution could be ratified, he was assassinated by a young Afrikaans-speaking mine worker. Whether or not the Divine Hand had itself been prompted in this matter (Sachs, 1953, p. 170), the courts were unable to find evidence of conspiracy. New elections were called, and the reformers seemed on the brink of victory. Then war broke out in Europe, and all union activity was frozen for the sake of optimum production.

Albert Hertzog and his movement would have to wait six long years before they could begin to agitate once again for change, and meanwhile, the reform organization had to be kept alive. Financial support from the Broederbond and the F.A.K. slowly dwindled until, after 1944, the Raad van Trustees was entirely relying on its own resources. Most fortunately for the reformers, Albert Hertzog's uncle, Pieter Neethling, bequeathed them a large fortune, which, together with help from Piet Meyer and from Verwoerd and *Die Transvaler*, kept the reform organization more than just alive. By 1945, it could justly claim to be the true union within the M.W.U., with a stronghold at each mine head.

However, the story of the salvation of the mine workers by organization along Christian National lines has led us ahead of the most important of all the events in the 1930s for the civil religion. Even Albert Hertzog's expertise might have proven useless without the immense popular enthusiasm which accompanied the centenary celebrations of the Great Trek in the summer of 1938. In fact, by the end of 1937, Piet Meyer's grandiose scheme for aligning the ranks of the Afrikaner People through the F.A.K. had come to naught, and in the elections of the next year most Afrikaners voted for General Hertzog's United party.[24] Despite parliamentary

[24] In the election of 1938 the National party won only 27 seats to 111 for the United party. The Dominion party won 8 seats, Labor won 3, and the Socialists one.

gains in the Free State, the National party looked to have a long, hard pull ahead; and civil-religion enthusiasts seemed restricted to the intellectual and professional elite. For Christian Nationalism, however, the end of 1938 marked the turn of the tide as Afrikanerdom awoke to regain the "Path of South Africa."

9

The Centenary of Geloftedag
Highpoint of the Civil Faith

As we have seen, Piet Meyer's neo-Fichtean efforts to involve the F.A.K. in trade unionism were far from universally accepted in Afrikaner circles. The new Cape Afrikaans evening paper, *Die Suiderstem*, which supported the United party, roundly declared that the new Kultuurraad was a strategem to introduce Nazism into South Africa (*Die Vaderland*, July 12, 1937). Hertzog's *Die Vaderland* in Johannesburg had warned for some years about the dangers of dragging the "holy things" of Afrikanerdom through the political mud (*Die Vaderland*, July 12, 1937),[1] and it now condemned the involvement of the F.A.K. in trade unionism as a betrayal of its true purpose (cf. *Die Vaderland*, January 24, 1936; October 20, 1936; and July 13, 1937). In fact, the paper took issue with the Christian National definition of culture; cultural advance came through creative individuals, said an editorial, not through class or ethnic organization (*Die Vaderland*, July 6, 1937). More than that, it declared, the F.A.K. had become the political dummy (*fopspeen*) of the purified National party. If there were to be a general cultural organization, it would have to bridge political divisions and not simply represent one section of the Afrikaner People (*Die Vaderland*, May 27, 1938).

To this last attack, Verwoerd retorted:

[1] See also General Hertzog's outburst against Father Kestell and D. F. Malherbe at the 1935 United party congress: "They poison the holiest things of the People" (*Die Volksblad*, September 11, 1935).

The F.A.K. is an organization which has always set itself
outside the party-political struggle. If Afrikaner assertion in
the cultural sphere aims at somewhat the same goal as the
National party in the political sphere, that is no reason for
the United party press to ascribe party-political motives to
this Afrikaner movement. [*Die Transvaler*, May 29, 1938]

In effect then, Verwoerd was deploring *Die Vaderland's*
unwillingness to maintain the distinction between *partypolitiek* and *kultuurpolitiek*.

Not only was the United party unhappy about Meyer's
new venture, but *Die Burger*, too, was initially perturbed.
"Does it fall within the work-terrain of the F.A.K. to make
propaganda for one or another economic system, whether for
the capitalist system under which we live, or for a communist
or fascist system, or for any other?" the paper asked in a
concerned editorial. "We doubt that the author of the F.A.K.
press appeal [for a *kultuurraad*] can indeed be the executive
council of the F.A.K." (*Die Burger*, April 24, 1937) When
Die Burger did eventually accept the formation of the Kultuurraad one suspects that it was with a certain reluctance
(cf. *Die Burger*, July 8, 1937).

In addition, one of the strongest cultural associations, The
Afrikaans Language and Cultural Union of the South African
Railways and Harbors (A.T.K.V.), which represented the
cultural interests of over 18,000 Afrikaner railway workers
throughout South Africa, refused to have any part in the
new direction which the F.A.K. was taking (*Die Vaderland*,
July 23, 1937). Ironically enough, it was this movement, rather
than Meyer's new Kultuurraad, which was to play the major
role in a resurgence of popular adherence to the Afrikaner
civil religion. Founded in October 1930 by the same Henning
Klopper who had founded the Broederbond in 1918, the
A.T.K.V. rapidly increased in membership, performing on the
railways similar functions on behalf of Afrikaans and Afrikaners to those of the Handhawersbond on the Rand. Unlike
the Spoorbond, it maintained a strictly non-political policy
(*Die Burger*, September 30, 1933).

In 1936, the Cape N.G. synod acknowledged the A.T.K.V.
as a "mighty factor in the development of a purely Afrikaans

movement in one of the most important state departments in our country, which has as its purpose the social, cultural and religious elevation of our railwaymen upon a Christian foundation" (*Die Volksblad*, November 20, 1936). The synod promised all possible cooperation with the movement. At the congress of the A.T.K.V. in 1937, Henning Klopper spoke of it not only as "a luminary and a source of inspiration of our People," but as a spontaneous altruistic effort "born from the soul of the People. In the cause which we serve we do not seek . . . our own self-interest. We serve South Africa and we shall work as long as God gives us the zeal and the faith" (*Die Burger*, April 6, 1937).

An opponent of Henning Klopper who knew him well called him "an idealist of the first magnitude and a man who never touches alcohol and tobacco; [a] deamer who hopes to see the day when Afrikaans will be the only official language in South Africa and the *Vierkleur* [the flag of the old Transvaal republic] the only flag" (du Plessis, Louis J., 1951, p. 3). From the days of his youth, Klopper had dreamed of retracing the footsteps of the Voortrekkers in a pilgrimage across South Africa. By 1927, he already entertained ideas of how the centenary of the 1838 Blood River vow might be worthily celebrated. By 1933, he was suggesting to meetings and congresses his youthful vision of an oxwagon procession. When at the 1937 A.T.K.V. congress he proposed the building of a stinkwood oxwagon for a centenary trek to Pretoria, his proposal was received with well-prepared acclaim. At first the wagon was to depart from the A.T.K.V. center at Hartenbos (near Mossel Bay), but Klopper persevered for the complete realization of his ideal. Hence the trek was rescheduled to start in Cape Town and travel the whole "Path of South Africa" first moving east to the old frontier and then north to Pretoria. By the beginning of 1938, a second centenary wagon had been outfitted for the route which Klopper had painstakingly worked out as a symbolic replication of the Great Trek. The Dutch Reformed minister in each town and hamlet along the proposed way was asked to appoint a committee for arranging the reception of the wagons and for obtaining ox-teams from local farmers for the next lap of the journey. All these preparations were no doubt facilitated by Klopper's Broederbond contacts in rectories and rural schools throughout the land.

There was not great popular enthusiasm for the trek to begin with, but interest was contagious. Indeed, as time for the departure from Cape Town drew nigh, towns which were not included on the initial route wrote to request that they, too, might be visited by the wagons. Eventually nine wagons were assembled in order to meet all such requests, and the projected routes wound through even the most remote villages across the length and breadth of the land. Two great festivals were planned for December 16, 1938, one at the site of the Battle of Blood River, and the other in Pretoria where the cornerstone of the new Voortrekker Monument was to be laid. Two wagons would attend the Blood River festival, and the others would proceed to Pretoria, leaving one behind for the Cape Town celebration.[2]

The wagons were baptised at historically significant points en route and given names appropriate to the major themes of the sacred history. Five wagons were named after legendary Trek heroes: "Piet Retief," the martyr; "Andries Pretorius," the victor of Blood River; "Louis Trichardt," the first trekker; "Hendrik Potgieter," the early Transvaal leader; and, of course, "Sarel Cilliers," author of the covenant vow. The other four wagons, celebrating the importance of women and children in the sacred saga, were named: "Vrou en Moeder" (wife and mother); "Dirkie Uys," after a fourteen-year-old lad who chose to be martyred alongside his father rather than flee from the Zulus; and "Johanna van der Merwe" and "Magrieta Prinsloo," after two little girls who survived the Blaauwkrantz massacre largely because their mothers had hidden the children beneath their own bodies, thus taking upon themselves the spear-thrusts.

On August 8, 1938, the first two wagons, the "Piet Retief" and the "Andries Pretorius," set out from the foot of van Riebeeck's statue in Cape Town on their long journey north-

---

[2] For details on the organization of the Ossewatrek see *Ossewa Gedenkboek* (1940, pp. 38-48).

ward. Large crowds which gathered to see them off were addressed by Henning Klopper:

> On this solemn occasion, at this spot where almost three centuries ago Jan van Riebeeck stepped ashore, it is fitting, in view of the great ethnic deed [*volksdaad*] which we now begin to celebrate, that we should remember the vow of Sarel Cilliers:
>
> > "Brothers and fellow-countrymen, we stand here before the Holy God of Heaven and Earth to make a vow that, if He will be with us and protect us and give the foe into our hands, we shall ever celebrate the day and date as a Day of Thanksgiving like the Sabbath in His honor. We shall enjoin our children that they must take part with us in this, for a remembrance even for our posterity. For the honor of God shall herein be glorified, and to Him shall be given the fame and the honor of the victory."
>
> This is the spirit in which we trek.
>
> We place our trek in the service of the People of South Africa, so that we may celebrate this festival as suits a worthy and grateful posterity. We bring praise to those who won for us a land and a future and we give honor to the Almighty, in the firm belief that He will make us a powerful People before His countenance.
>
> We ask the entire Afrikanerdom to take part in the festival celebration in this spirit. We long that nothing shall hinder the Afrikaner People as a whole from taking part. This movement is born from the People; may the People carry it in their hearts all the way to Pretoria and Blood River.
>
> Let us build up a monument for Afrikaner hearts. May this simple trek bind together in love those Afrikaner hearts which do not yet beat together. We dedicate these wagons to our People and to our God. [*Ossewa Gedenkboek*, 1940, pp. 112-113]

The need for Afrikaner unity (*volkseenheid*) was in fact the major theme of the speeches made at hundreds of towns and villages along the path of the wagons. The message was to some extent tailored to its audiences, so that in the Eastern Transvaal—still a Smuts stronghold—and in Natal, English-speakers were carefully not excluded from the People. Usually, however, the term *volkseenheid* had a specifically Afrikaner reference. In the western Free State, where the 1938 elections had been fought with bitterness and some violence, common celebrations around the oxwagons had a noticeably soothing effect. Indeed, the symbolic trek brought into focus the long-felt disgust of ordinary Afrikaners with the divisions and squabbles of party politics. At last the appeal of the F.A.K. to an Afrikaner unity which transcended political factions was given concrete form. The memory of this "oxwagon unity" would constitute a potent political force during the next decade.

While the Broederbond elite had long preached the civil theology and celebrated the rituals of the civil faith, the Ossewatrek ("Oxwagon Trek") made Afrikaner civil religion an integral part of the consciousness of thousands of ordinary Afrikaners. Every Afrikaner I interviewed, of whatever political persuasion, recalled the events and activities of the 1938 centenary with deeply personal intensity. The sacred history was constituted and actualized as a general context of meaning for all Afrikanerdom in spontaneous liturgical re-enactment during the 1938 celebrations. Passionate enthusiasm seized Afrikaans-speaking South Africa.[3] Men grew beards and women donned Voortrekker dress; street after street in hamlet after hamlet was renamed after one or another Trek hero; babies were baptized in the shade of the wagons—one was christened "Eufeesia" (best translated "Centennalia")— and young couples were married in full trekker regalia on the village green before the wagons. With tearful eyes old men and women climbed onto the wagons—"Lord, now lettest thou thy servant depart in peace," said one old man—and the younger ones jostled with one another in their efforts to rub grease from the wagon-axles onto their handkerchiefs. Monuments were raised up and the wagons were pulled through freshly laid concrete so that the imprint of their tracks could be preserved forever. In Bloemfontein, when the English-speaking town council refused to change the name of Maitland Street to Voortrekker Street, the organizing committee rejected the oxen proffered by the town and a procession of women in Voortrekker garb dragged the "Vrou en Moeder" through the streets.

[3] The French, too, have a sacred history, the central event of which is the Revolution of 1789. For a sensitive account of moments since 1789 which may be interpreted as liturgical re-enactments of that crucial event see Zolberg (1972).

At night folks would gather around the campfires of the trekkers in their hundreds and thousands to sing traditional Afrikaans *liedjies* ("folksongs") and the old Dutch psalms, to watch scenes from the Voortrek enacted in pantomime, and to thrill to inspired sermons culled from the depths of the civil faith. "The groan of the oxwagon has penetrated to the marrow and bone of every true Afrikaner," said Ds. Bruwer of Citrusdal. "We erect memorial stones and consider the gallows at Slagtersnek, which symbolize for us a triumphal arch; we consider the Golgotha of Dingaan and the cairns at Weenen, Blood River, and Paardekraal. Here, too, now we have built an altar. May it mean for us renewed dedication to *volk* and fatherland" (*Ossewa Gedenkboek*, 1940, p. 483).

Wreaths were laid on the graves of all the Afrikaner heroes, from the victims of Slagtersnek to Jopie Fourie. Holy ground was thus resanctified by the visit of the wagons. "The national grain of wheat had first to die before it could bear fruit," said Henning Klopper at Vegkop: "They gave their lives for freedom—for what do we give our lives?" Dr. J. F. J. van Rensburg, administrator of the Free State, sketched the via dolorosa of the Voortrekkers and pointed to the guidepost of their faith. "Even death could not check them," he said, "and rightly so, because without graves there is no resurrection" (*Ossewa Gedenkboek*, 1940, p. 456). At the gravesite of Sarel Cilliers, Henning Klopper spoke of the holy covenant: "On the way which we have so far trekked, by all the graves, beacons, monuments and more, there was no place so mysterious and moving as the grave of Sarel Cilliers. That grave brought us into the milieu of the man who stood between our destruction and the might of God." Sarel Cilliers, he went on to say, erected the beacon of the first covenant between God and the People. That covenant-altar was sealed at Blood River. God kept his part of the covenant, but Afrikanerdom had failed to keep her part. The People had sinned, and Klopper's message was: "Return to the God who will honor us. . . . The continued existence of our People is a miracle. Our People is like the thornbush at Horeb—it burns and burns but is never consumed. Our People were frequently in deep grief and divided, but always became united again" (*Ossewa Gedenkboek*, 1940, p. 458).

As the wagons approached their destinations, so the call for unity reached a crescendo on the note of republican independence. The colors of the old republics were everywhere displayed, and republicanism became more and more the expressed goal. On December 3, 1938, at Pietersburg, Professor J. C. van Rooy, chairman of the Broederbond and normally a very cautious man,[4] was moved to say:

> We must gather as a consolidated People at the feast in Pretoria. If we stand together as Afrikaners, the leaders and enemies who would keep us divided will be unable to prevent us. We shall go there as one People despite the leaders and others who divide us, and we shall throw off all the ties which hinder our march to freedom. Why should not the privilege of freedom, which is granted to all the countries of the world, also be granted to us? [*Ossewa Gedenkboek*, 1940, p. 669]

In his diary, N. G. S. van der Walt reported:

> Last week I was in Johannesburg for important matters. Grobbelaar (of the Bondswag) came to fetch me for a meeting of four movements to decide about the freedom of our nation on December 16. From three in the afternoon to two the next morning, we discussed continuously The outcome is that we shall be ready should difficulties arise. We shall not ourselves lead a *coup d'etat*, but will make every effort to get the People thinking in that direction. [Van der Walt, N. G. S., diary, November 13, 1938]

Thus did the fringe movements make ready to profit from any fortuitous disruption. However, the wakeful watching was not restricted to the right-wing fringe of Afrikanerdom. According to Piet Cillié,[5] in the very editorial offices of *Die Burger* there was a sense of expectancy. Had the eschatological moment promised by the civil theology at last arrived? "Tomorrow," said the editorial in *Die Oosterlig*, (December 15, 1938) "a new day will dawn for the Afrikaner People; the dayspring of the fulfillment of its ideal; of victory in its freedom-struggle."

The slowly mounting tension as the oxwagons gradually, laboriously moved closer to Pretoria and Blood River was whipped to fever pitch by a torch marathon organized by

[4] For a measure of van Rooy's moderation see his article in *Koers* (August 1935).

[5] He is at present editor-in-chief of *Die Burger*.

N. J. van der Merwe's Voortrekker movement. Torches, symbolizing the light of both freedom and "white civilization," were handed from one group of runners to the next along the Path of South Africa, in order that, fourteen days after the departure from Cape Town, they should arrive on the eve of Geloftedag in Pretoria and Blood River together with the oxwagons.

In Bloemfontein on December 12, the arrival of the torches on their way north aroused an enthusiasm that knew no bounds. Traffic was at a standstill, and everyone pushed forward to touch a torch or place a handkerchief in the flame. Old Father Kestell haranged the assembled on the significance of the torches:

> We have received a fire from God, that fire is our nationhood. It is wonderful to think that this nationhood is from God—a burning torch which is not extinguished. It has been kept burning all the way from the statue of van Riebeeck to here. By the mercy of God it has burned until now. It must be kept burning. We must assure that it continues to burn in the future. To the gift of our nationhood is bound the virtues of righteousness, of goodness, sincerity and piety—the torch must be kept burning. [*Die Volksblad*, December 12, 1938]

On arrival in Pretoria, the holy torches were met by three thousand Voortrekkers, each with a torch of his own. They marched in company over the hill to the monument site. At their head strode the robust figure of N. J. van der Merwe. A huge bonfire had been prepared at the scene, and as each Voortrekker filed past it, he hurled his torch onto the conflagration. Flames shot heavenward—a signal for other fires to be lit on the hilltops all about Pretoria, so that the city should stand encircled with fire. Elsa Joubert, one of the three thousand scouts, who was then sixteen, described the scene:[6]

> The hearts of the three thousand Voortrekkers, each of whom in his own town had formed a link in the chain of the Torch Marathon, beat faster when they saw the light of the torch coming towards them over the hills in the dusk. . . .
>
> The hill is on fire; on fire with Afrikaner fire; on fire with the enthusiasm of Young South Africa! You are nothing—your

---

[6] *Die Burger* ran a competition in January 1939 which elicited many descriptions of "my most memorable moment in the Ossewatrek."

People is all. One light in the dusk is puny and small. But three thousand flames. Three thousand! And more! There's hope for your future, South Africa!

The mightly procession brings the torches to the festival ground where thousands await them. A matchless, unprecedented enthusiasm in the darkness of the night. Numerous prayers of thanks for the torches rise up, many a quiet tear is wiped away. The torches get their "Welcome home."

Behind them, like a blazing snake in the night, the belt of fire coils down the hillside. On the festival grounds the two torches set alight a huge joyous fire. Around it march the three thousand Voortrekkers and each throws his small puny torch upon it—to form one great mightly Afrikaner fire.

The logs crackle as they burn. And as they crackle so they exult—"The torches set us alight. Now we again set you alight, O youth of our South Africa! Alight to build. To build with Unity, Freedom, Justice and Love. Come along—there's work"

The torches are now led to their resting place in the Voortrekker *laager* protected day and night by an honor-guard of four Voortrekkers. One torch is then doused. And the other? It continues to burn, first at the University of Pretoria and then in the Voortrekker Monument.

Until when, you ask? Until the flame is no longer needed; until it has achieved its goal.

Is that the end, you say? No! answers Young South Africa—the beginning. [*Die Burger*, February 27, 1939]

December 16, 1938, dawned warm and fair. *Die Burger* calculated that about one-tenth of all Afrikanerdom (over 100,000 persons) had gathered in Pretoria for the festivities. Three women descendants of Retief, Pretorius, and Potgieter laid the foundation stone of the Voortrekker Monument. (Hertzog had been asked to do it, but backed down when Malan and the purified Nationalists impugned his motives, crying politics.) The crowds were entertained with numerous speeches, they sang the sacred anthems, and Father Kestell was present to bless the assembled multitude. But no more than that! There was no announcement of a republic, not even agitation to be judiciously redirected by N. G. S. van der Walt and his friends. When the great day was over, it could well have been just another celebration of the sabbath. Hertzog was still prime minister, and South Africa was still

part of the British Commonwealth. It seemed all over but
the shouting.

On the symbolic level, however, the Ossewatrek had
brought indelible changes. With the exception of one disruption at Kopjes in the western Free State (where L. J. du
Plessis had been shouted down for preaching politics) and
the celebration at Blood River (where Afrikaners objected
to Minister C. F. Clarkson's addressing them in English) there
had been remarkably little disruption at meetings around
the wagons. Afrikaners had learned in their worship at the
oxwagon altars how very much they had in common as
Afrikaners. Party-political differences were made to seem
insignificant.

The eschatological disappointment of the Day of the Covenant, 1938, did not greatly dismay Afrikanerdom's cultural
leaders. The coming of the republic had never been explicitly
promised; and despite the general air of expectancy, the
leaders of the People could not in all fairness expect General
Hertzog to call out a republic on the spot. The "spiritual"
emphasis of Diederich's neo-Fichteanism permitted those of
the Broederbond, at least, to readily retreat to the notion
of a "spiritual" republic. E. C. Pienaar epitomized this thinking in a speech about the Ossewatrek delivered at Bellville
in April 1939.

> A free, sovereign, and independent ethnic existence—that was
> the life-long ideal of Piet Retief, Paul Kruger, Marthinus Steyn
> and Christiaan de Wet. That was the ideal for which since
> the days of the Great Trek two wars of freedom have been
> fought in South Africa, the ideal for which tens of thousands
> of women and children have been brought to sacrifice, the
> ideal for which in the armed protest of 1914 Afrikaner blood
> flowed at Afrikaner hands.
>
> When one speaks of our People's ideal of freedom, one fact
> must not be lost from sight. That is that the highest form
> of freedom does not necessarily lie in constitutional indepen-
> dence.
>
> Certainly an independent ethnic existence would further the
> realization of the freedom ideal, but it is not absolutely
> essential, because even under political domination a People
> may be spiritually free, whilst a fully constitutionally indepen-
> dent People may be spiritually enslaved. . . .

Thus we do not need to wait until some day South Africa is an independent republic in order to participate fully in this spiritual [*geestelike*] freedom. On the contrary, the sooner Afrikanerdom as a homogeneous ethnic group achieves its spiritual-cultural independence, so much the sooner will its constitutional independence follow. . . .

As Afrikanerdom we would be free . . . to live out fully our own national calling and destiny on the Path of South Africa, whether within or outside the British constitutional connection. [*Die Burger*, April 3, 1939]

Pienaar, the foremost Cape Broederbonder of his day, thus believed that any disappointment stemming from the failure of an immediate republican eschaton was far outweighed by the achievements of Afrikaner unity inspired by the Ossewa-trek. In fact, the behavior of the two Afrikaner political parties revealed that they, too, were under powerful pressure of deeply felt popular concern for Afrikaner *volkseenheid*.[7]

Ever since *samesmelting*, the United party had declared itself to be the true party of *volkseenheid*, with Malan and his followers characterized as schismatics. General Hertzog, when he spoke of *volkseenheid*, referred to a union of all the "national elements in South African life" (that is, those who were prepared to put South Africa first) into a single great *volksparty* within a *volksstaat*, which for him meant neither an Afrikaner party nor state, but a citizen's party, leading to a truly unitary state. When the National party referred to *volkseenheid*, however, they spoke of consolidation into a single political party of all those who had inherited a common Afrikaner culture and who believed in the Afri-kaner civil religion (cf. *Die Burger*, November 21, 1938; and *Die Transvaler*, December 29, 1938). Both Hertzog and the National party were thus each very clear on the meaning of *volkseenheid*, and they differed irreconcilably with one another. For those who gathered around the oxwagons, however, such matters of doctrine seemed but arid dogmatism; what was important was that Afrikaners from both political parties *felt* unity because they had a common civil religion.

Such diffuse sentiment for *volkseenheid* actually favored

[7] January 1939 saw a lengthy editorial battle between *Die Burger* and *Die Suiderstem* on the subject of *volkseenheid*.

the United party.[8] Hertzog had always insisted that the United party welcomed all Afrikaners. What matter that he also included English-speaking South Africans? The primary concern was to get all Afrikaners together again, and it was the National party that was always making distinctions between different varieties of Afrikaner. Had Hertzog been prepared to state publicly that, in a united "citizens' party," the majority Afrikaner element would have the power, he might have carried many waverers with him, even if he had insisted that the formal rights of English-speaking South Africans could not be touched. However, whether for fear of losing their English-speaking support, or simply as a matter of principle, neither Smuts nor Hertzog were prepared to state openly such a conclusion (obvious though it was), so that the initiative finally passed to the National party.

The grassroots pressure was considerable. On December 27, 1938, van der Merwe wrote to Malan: "As you know many expectations have been aroused in the People that something must be done after the *Eeufees* ("Centenary festival") to bring together those who belong together. I am continually receiving letters and personal visits in connection with this matter" (Scholtz, G. D., 1944, p. 383). In the first month of 1939, a pamphlet appeared in which Professor A. C. Cilliers of Stellenbosch proposed the formation of a new party on the basis of Ossewatrek sentiment. This new party would be one which was specifically "Afrikaner" in spirit, drawing together all those who belonged together. However, the issue of the republic would be played down to accomodate some members of the United party, since "there is no possibility that at the moment a large majority of the white population will vote for a change in the constitution" (Cilliers, A. C., 1939, p. 15). The rights of English-speaking South Africans would be unconditionally guaranteed, and they would be readily accepted into the party if they were one in spirit with Afrikaners. Cilliers established a pressure group of Stellen-

---

[8] See, for example, the lengthy correspondence of *Die Burger* and *Die Suiderstem* with Ds. P. J. J. Boshoff in November 1938, which definitely ended in a moral victory for *Die Suiderstem*, regardless of the logic of *Die Burger's* position.

bosch academics, including E. C. Pienaar, to work for the new party.[9] *Die Suiderstem* (January 23, 1939) accepted the spirit of his proposals.

Although Malan, van der Merwe and W. A. Hofmeyr met with the Stellenbosch group on February 27, their discussion got nowhere because Malan would not hear of a new party. In rejecting the Cilliers-Pienaar group, the National party in fact demonstrated its independence of the Broederbond,[10] since the Stellenbosch group had van Rooy's support, and Cilliers, on the strength of his efforts, was offered membership in the Broederbond, which he nonetheless declined.

The next development came from the staunch Nationalist wing of the Broederbond in the form of an open letter from Dr. Albert Hertzog and "friends" to his father, the general, urging reunification of Afrikanerdom on the basis of "white civilization," Afrikaner national consciousness, and the ideal of complete independence (*Die Burger*, January 20, 1939).[11] This proposal was welcomed by the National party, and Dr. Malan at once conferred his sanction. General Hertzog, on the other hand, rejected it out of hand:

> From the principles given by you as a basis for cooperation, it is clear that the Afrikaans-speaking section of Afrikanerdom would be the only section of the population who would count as a People, and that the English-speaking section of Afrikanerdom would not count as part of the Afrikaner People. . . . I assure you that under no circumstances will I ever lend my political cooperation to persons who are not prepared to

[9] For a full account of the Stellenbosch group's efforts on behalf of *volkseenheid*, see Cilliers, A. C., (1940a).

[10] The only Nationalist newspaper which published favorable comment on the Stellenbosch proposals was *Die Volksblad* (March 13, 1939), whose editor, A. J. R. van Rhijn, was a solid Broer, and whose editorial columns were increasingly coming to represent the views of the Kuyperian wing of the Broederbond. Despite certain points of agreement with the neo-Fichtean wing of the Broederbond, Broer Verwoerd of *Die Transvaler*, on the other hand was definitely a strong National party man whose sympathies lay with Strydom's insistent republicanism. One may thus distinguish a "party wing" of the Broederbond, which stood for the National party right down the line despite variance with Broederbond leadership.

[11] Was this merely a power play on the part of Albert Hertzog to obtain more say in Broederbond affairs, as certain of my informants implied? Perhaps more than they were aware, they were

acknowledge and accept the principle of complete equality and complete justice between the English and Afrikaans sections of our People as laid down in the program of principles of the United party. [*Die Burger*, January 30, 1939]

This statement finally and definitively put the United party on the defensive over the issue of *volkseenheid*.

Thus ended the efforts for Afrikaner political unity on the basis of oxwagon sentiment. However, popular sentiment persisted, as did general Broederbond disgust with party politics. So strong was the latter, especially among Kuyperians, that van der Merwe felt moved to publish an article defending party politics. He wrote:

One of the objections which we continually hear brought against party politics is that it interferes with our *volkseenheid*. Get rid of politics and then, as is frequently said, our People will be one again. That may be true, but even unity might be too costly. There are principles which are more important than *volkseenheid*. . . . The only genuine sort of *volkseenheid* which has viability and carries promise for the future is that which finds its binding force in unity of principles resting upon the word of God. This unity we shall not find by listlessly standing aside and giving vent to our feelings by crying anathema on party principles. We can only advance by undertaking anew the struggle for principles, by testing ourselves against the word of God, and setting forth our Christian National principles undiluted against the unchristian and unnational tendencies of our time. [*Koers*, August 1939]

The experience of the Ossewatrek, however, had moved many, both within the Broederbond and outside it, to feel that the foremost Christian National principle was precisely that *volkseenheid* which van der Merwe seemed so readily prepared to sacrifice again for old party principles. In the Free State, such feeling gave rise to support for the Ossewabrandwag ("Oxwagon Sentinel," referred to as O.B.)

---

reading the events of 1939 in light of Hertzog's breakaway in 1969 from the National party. Anyway, according to J. H. P. Serfontein (1970, p. 25) the "friends" who joined Albert Hertzog in his plea to his father were not "Broers," but "Junior Broers," and the junior Broederbond was dissolved in 1942 because a separate organization led by Albert Hertzog was seen as a threat to the authority of the Broederbond proper.

The formation of the O.B. was publicly announced on February 6, 1939 by its founder, Colonel J. C. C. Laas, in *Die Volksblad*. According to Laas, enthusiasm was boundless; even before the official establishment of the organization, people had rallied together, quite literally in thousands. Since Laas was both a farmer and a part-time soldier engaged in organizing rifle units throughout the whole Free State, he stood in a good position to make widespread propaganda for his new organization. Indeed, he reported that in certain districts the Active Citizen Force (militia) had joined as one man. Van Rensburg wrote of Laas that: "He was happiest when tearing about in a motorcar and flinging sparks about in otherwise somnolent ranks; often rather lacking in a sense of responsibility, and ever addicted to a faint but unmistakable air of secrecy in all his acts. . . ." (van Rensburg, 1956, p. 156).

The goals of the O.B., as pronounced by Laas, were innocently idealistic on face value. They were:

1. The perpetuation of the oxwagon spirit in South Africa.

2. The maintenance [*handhawing*], extension, and realization [*uitlewing*] of the traditions and principles of the Boer nation.

3. The protection and furtherance of the religious, cultural, and material concerns of the Afrikaner.

4. The cultivation of love for fatherland and national pride.

5. The incorporation [*inskakeling*] and combination [*samesnoering*] of all Afrikaners, men as well as women, who endorse these principles and ideals and are willing effectively to strive for them.

[*Die Volksblad*, February 6, 1939]

What this list of principles failed to mention was that the "traditions and principles of the Boer nation" included the struggle for a republic, and that "effective struggle" included "the disciplining of the Afrikaner People." What Laas also omitted in his initial announcement was that among the 'traditional activities" of the Boer nation to be fostered was rifle shooting—with Defence Department ammunition! One of the earliest and most faithful members was the ubiquitous N. G. S. van der Walt, who recorded in his diary concerning the first meeting:

> Last Saturday, February 4, we founded the O.B. It could become a beautiful and great movement if it is properly supported and managed. I was appointed by Colonel Laas as secretary. Interest appears to be great throughout the land. . . .Last night I gave a talk before the Handhawersbond [Bloemfontein was one of the few centers where this organization remained active—in a radically republican form] about practical nationalism for South Africa . . . very well received . . . Naturally, I dealt with Boer domination in South Africa. [Van der Walt, N. G. S., diary, February 12, 1939]

If the leadership of the O.B. was in any way like its first secretary, we ought not to be surprised that the movement aroused the suspicion of the Hertzog government. As early as April 1939, Laas had been dismissed from the Active Citizen Force; and all citizen soldiers had been forbidden to join the O.B. (*Die Volksblad*, April 13, 1939). By August even the National party leadership in the Free State began to display some anxiety about possible rivalry. N. J. van der Merwe voiced his uneasiness in a speech reported by *Die Volksblad* (August 16, 1939; cf. *Die Transvaler*, February 15, 1939).

Laas, however, proved to be an incompetent administrator and an extraordinarily arbitrary leader, causing rapid turnover in local O.B. leadership (cf. *Die Vaderland*, June 2, 1939). After five months, only four of the fourteen original members of the O.B. Grootraad ("Grand Council") remained: Laas himself, Ds. C. R. Kotze, Ds. D. G. van der Merwe and the ever-faithful N. G. S. van der Walt. However, despite Laas' incompetent leadership, the movement continued to grow, fed by Ossewatrek enthusiasm and the general disenchantment with party-political wrangles. A. J. H. van der Walt gives a stirring picture of the O.B.'s appeal:

> Here was a movement which had an appeal not only to the "cultured people" but to all members of the *volk*—rich and poor, learned and ignorant. The military organizational form; the camps where Afrikaners, long estranged from one another could again find and value each other; the parades and military

exercises [*driloefeninge*], which spectacularly demonstrated
the value of open enforcement of discipline: the activation
of the *volk* in everyday life; these were all of great importance.
Above all, however, the ideal of a united front, in which all
nationally conscious members of the *volk* could work and
struggle on a basis of equality for the Voortrekker ideals, and
above all for their freedom ideal, offered an irresistible attraction. [Van der Walt, A. J. H., 1944, p. 21]

It is impossible to speculate how effectively this semi-mili-
tary "cultural" organization might have been able to bridge
the party-political rift in Afrikanerdom. Quite possibly, if only
because of the organizational poverty of the leadership and
the opposition of established organized elites, the O.B. might
have come to naught. In fact, however, the declaration of
war in September 1939 changed the complexion of Afrikaner
politics overnight. Hertzog proposed in parliament that South
Africa remain neutral, and he was outvoted by a majority
of thirteen. He promptly resigned to be succeeded by that
"Handyman of the Empire," Jan Smuts. The reaction of the
majority of Afrikaners was perhaps most outspokenly summarized in an editorial in *Besembos*, the student journal at
Potchefstroom University:

Parliament made an unjust decision. Indeed it was decided
that South Africa must wage war against a People which is
fighting for its right to life, against a People with which the
Afrikaner nation has had no other relationship than one of
friendship. In fact the matter is less simple than that, the
decision is even more unjust, if we regard it in the light of
our history. We are not merely obliged by a bare majority
to wage war against a friendly nation, but we have to support
England in this matter. We have to support our only foreign
enemy!
For no nation other than England has ever threatened our
existence. England not only threatened us, but also over-
whelmed us on the principle that might is right! In this violent
act of power against our nation, however, England acknowledged no limits. When she discovered that she could not
terminate the matter as quickly as she wished, she proceeded
to methods of barbarism and tried to massacre Afrikaner
mothers and children—notice *massacre*! The numerous concentration camp churchyards continue to testify to the brutality to which a civilized nation like England can proceed in
order to reach her goal. And even if England today talks sweet,

even if she appears as champion of small nations, we know better. The Vrouemonument continually cries out for vengeance! That injustice was perpetrated against our nation, that brutality which cries out to heaven. The mark is too deeply branded into our heart; it is too close to our heart ever to forget. . . .

We as students are therefore decided to shed no drop of blood in the interest of the British empire as a result of an unjust decision. For from injustice no salvation can be born, but only shame and debasement for our People. Thus we now say early and openly that we shall passively resist any attempt to call us up for compulsory war service. . . . [*Besembos*, September, 1939]

The many Afrikaners who held such views could obviously not honestly volunteer to fight "Smuts' war." On the other hand, as one of my informants said, "The English were signing up all around us, war was in the air, people felt compelled to take *some* action, and the militarily constituted O.B. seemed a good substitute." No doubt, too, those who joined the O.B. in such numbers to parade in uniform with their fellow Afrikaners,[12] believed that a German victory might soon provide them with an opportunity to take decisive action on behalf of "oxwagon ideals." That Smuts feared an uprising is indicated by his early ban on private ownership of firearms for the duration of the war. Afrikaners dutifully complied, handing in their rifles at appointed collection points. Yet they continued to parade in anticipation of the German victory, which seemed more and more imminent.

Meantime, on the party-political front, the declaration of war had led to a major realignment. After the parliamentary vote, Malan and Hertzog declared their intention of reuniting all of Afrikanerdom into a great political party. "A miracle has occurred," announced *Die Oosterlig* in an excited editorial:

Afrikanerdom is reunited. We cannot yet comprehend the deeper significance of these words. They are too overwhelming. In the anxious hour of crisis, the miracle occurred. Out of the darkness which has dominated the past historical week, a united Afrikaner people has emerged to view; never again

[12] Membership soon exceeded 200,000 (*Die Volksblad*, August 24, 1940).

will it allow imperialism to divide it and take from it its freedom
. . . The new day of Afrikaner unity for which we have all
so eagerly longed and pleaded has dawned. The final complete
freedom of Afrikanerdom and South Africa is assured. In the
spirit of the centenary year, Afrikanerdom now proceeds united
along the Path of South Africa. Perhaps the victory is nearer
than we realize. [*Die Oosterlig*, September 8, 1939]

The executive of the Broederbond, which had been struggling so hard and so unavailingly since the Ossewatrek for
reconciliation between the parties, now hastily arranged a
great open public meeting at the site of the Voortrekker
Monument. According to *Die Transvaler*, attendance was
more than seventy thousand. The main speech was delivered
by J. C. van Rooy, who welcomed Malan and Hertzog and
emphasized the miraculous unification which had transpired.
"Such unity as we are today experiencing is unique in the
history of our People," he said. "This happening stands out
above all past [sacred] happenings. We thank you all for this,
but above all we thank God. It is a miracle and yet it is
a divine reality" (*Die Transvaler*, September 11, 1939).

The poet Totius read aloud a declaration calling for a
renewal of the covenant in the following words:

> In this solemn hour in which the air about us quivers with
> emotion, in which the raiment of praise replaces an anxious
> spirit, in which a holy fire spatters its sparks from soul to
> soul, we stand where less than a year ago we stood bound
> together as a nation. Now, however, we have not only a *wish*
> in our heart, but the very *deed* of *volkseenheid* before our
> eyes. In this hour, in which we acknowledge and confess with
> inexpressible gratitude that God alone is the Awakener of our
> nation, we wish to declare that the God of our fathers gave
> us righteous decrees and trustworthy laws, but we must also
> acknowledge that we as a People have departed from them
> with the result that we have one and all not only neglected
> our high ethnic calling but also quarreled with one another.
> . . . We wish with this declaration to reveal our desire and
> seal our longing constructively . . . to serve our People. We
> grasp one anothers' hand on the Path of South Africa, never
> again to let go. This we declare solemnly by raising our hands.
> [Cilliers, A. C., 1940a, p. 3]

The assembled People conferred their amen by raising their
hands in their thousands.

Dr. Malan appealed to the shades of the sacred past, and then he too thanked God:

> In spirit I see the figures of Piet Retief, Andries Pretorius, Sarel Cilliers, Hendrik Potgieter and the host of Voortrekkers behind them, and it is as though I hear them saying: "Even when you were divided we loved you, but now that you are one, our love for you is doubled. Children seek out the path, hold to it, and proceed upon it.

> Our People is again one and the fact that this has happened is no less than a divine miracle. Last year Afrikanerdom gathered here in its tens of thousands and there was in your heart the desire and the expectation that the reunion of the People should happen then and there. When it did not occur ways were initiated to realize it through negotiation. It was the desire and longing of man that union should come.

> God also desired it, but at His own time and in his own manner, so that no person here today could say that he had done it or that it was the work of this one or that one. There is but One to whom the honor is due—God alone. [*Die Transvaler*, September 11, 1939]

To many Afrikaners beside Dr. Malan it must have seemed that the hour was at hand, the eschaton promised by the civil theology was in the process of realization. The editor of *Die Oosterlig* (September 11, 1939) compared the gathering at the monument to similar covenant-takings before Blood River and at Paardekraal. God in His good time had once more united His People; the republic could not now be far off.

To the experienced observer, however, there were ominous signs that the old party-political discord and disagreements had not been dissolved, even by such a mighty act of God. When Hertzog's time came to speak at the monument meeting, he reaffirmed his old stance: "The vote in parliament said nothing of the unity of heart which English and Afrikaans-speakers felt in their hearts. That unity is there and will increase until the entire Afrikanerdom becomes one" (*Die Transvaler*, September 11, 1939). The unity which Hertzog was celebrating at this exclusively Afrikaner gathering would necessarily include English-speaking South Africans. Verwoerd did not miss that point, and in his editorial (*Die*

Transvaler, September 11, 1939), he re-insisted that reunion could be effected only on the basis of "Voortrekker principles." These he carefully spelled out as the unity of *Afrikaans-speaking Afrikaners* (his italics) in their quest for the imminent republic. Party principles had not changed, and there would be no easy return for the old general and his faithful followers to the National party, although in the enthusiasm of the moment, it certainly appeared that the promise of the Ossewatrek had been finally realized in the political sphere.

10

The Ossewatrek and the Afrikaner Economic Movement

Volkseenheid was not the only rallying cry of the Ossewa-trek. The economic privation of urban Afrikaners was a favorite minor theme of oxwagon sermons. Urban poverty was easily linked to the major aim of *volkseenheid*, since class divisions seemed a definite obstacle to such unity. Afrikaners were streaming to the cities to find jobs in industry. In the period between 1932 and 1936, the number of employees in manufacturing rose 47 percent for white males and 52 percent for white females (Simons and Simons, 1969, p. 508). Most of these new white workers were Afrikaners. During the same period, non-white industrial workers increased 68 percent for males and 35 percent for females. Most of these new workers, Afrikaners and African, were unskilled and met with opposition from the craft unions similar to that which mine workers had experienced at an earlier stage. According to the Simons:

> Communists and other radicals who did not share the artisans' prejudices recognized the trend and made it their business to form industrial unions for workers of all races and both sexes who performed much the same kind of work in the new secondary industries.... Insofar as the new unions supple-mented rather than competed with the craft unions, conserva-tive and radical leaders could work together without much friction.... Industrial unions laid a firmer basis than any yet

provided for a non-racial class movement. The organizers, who came from all racial groups and both sections of the white population, introduced a new spirit of radicalism, which spread across the colour line. [Simons and Simons, 1969, p. 509]

What did this spell for the "Afrikaner woman," that hero and martyr of the sacred history? She was now often working in factories side by side with non-white workers and was being successfully organized into non-racial unions.

Meanwhile the neo-Fichteans looked on with growing desperation. The ideology of the civil religion would somehow, somewhere have to mobilize support within the urban life. Until now, rural Afrikaners had tended to regard the cities as dens of iniquity, and the most commonly proposed solution to urban poverty was that workers be returned to the country. However, the traditionalist and rural appeal of such literary works as Totius' narrative poem "Trekkerswee" had been opposed from the beginning by the Broederbond. Throughout the twenties and thirties the Broederbond had, in fact, provided a bridge connecting the elite of the platteland and cities. However, no successful ideological rapprochment between the traditional, republican rural areas and the transient, materialist urban world had been devised until the Ossewatrek.

The problem was less one of inventing a radically new ideology, for the neo-Fichtean concepts were quite adequate on the intellectual level, but rather of integrating the symbols of the civil faith into the problems of urban industrial life, with its more fluid and open class and racial structures. At the Blood River centennial celebrations on December 16, Dr. Malan, in one of the most important and skillful speeches of his career, succeeded in developing the theme of the "second Great Trek" in a manner which set the urban migration of Afrikanerdom firmly in the context of the civil religion.

He began by first reminding his fellow Afrikaners that here, at Blood River, and on this particular day, they stood at a crucial intersection of sacred time and holy space:

Here at Blood River you stand on holy ground. Here was made the great decision about the future of South Africa, about Christian civilization in our land, and about the continued existence and responsible power of the white race. . . . [But also] you stand here upon the boundary of two centuries. Behind you, you rest your eyes upon the year 1838 as upon a high, outstanding mountain-top, dominating everything in the blue distance. Before you, upon the yet untrodden Path of South Africa, lies the year 2038, equally far off and hazy. Behind you lie the tracks of the Voortrekker wagons, deeply and ineradicably etched upon the wide, outstretched plains and across the grinning dragon-tooth mountain ranges of our country's history. [Pienaar, S. W., 1964, p. 121]

In 1838, said Malan, the destiny of white civilization was played out in South Africa against the blacks at Blood River in a momentous encounter where, thanks to Voortrekker sacrifices and God's grace, Afrikanerdom prevailed. But the Afrikaner People are today on a trek to a new frontier, which is the city, the new Blood River, where fellow Afrikaners perish daily on a new battlefield—the labor market.

The Trekkers heard the voice of South Africa. They received their task from God's hand. They gave their answer. They made their sacrifices. There is still a white race. There is a new People. There is a unique language. There is an imperishable drive to freedom. There is an irrecusable ethnic destiny. . . . Their task is completed. . . . The struggle with weapons has passed. . . . Your Blood Rver is not here. Your Blood River lies in the city.

I scarcely need tell you that Afrikanerdom is on trek again. . . . It is not a trek away from the centers of civilization, as it was one hundred years ago, but a trek back—back from the country to the city. . . . In that new Blood River, black and white meet together in much closer contact and a much more binding struggle than when one hundred years ago the circle of white tented wagons protected the *laager*, and muzzleloader clashed with *assegaai*. Today black and white jostle together in the same labor market. [Pienaar, S. W., 1964, pp. 122-123]

The new Afrikaner trekker finds the urban battleground without geographical or economic defenses. He finds on the one hand "protected jobs and higher wages for skilled- non-whites equal with whites," on the other hand he is faced with "free competition between white and colored and black," which drives wages so low that, as was conceded by the Commission of 1934, "they are in no position to live respectably' (Pienaar, S. W., 1964, pp. 126-127).

So the struggle rages on mercilessly, day after day and year after year, still growing in extent and deadliness.

Where he too must stand in the breach for his People, the Afrikaner of the new Great Trek meets the non-white beside his Blood River, partly or completely unarmed, without the defenses of river bank or entrenchment, defenseless upon the open plain of economic equalization. [Pienaar, S. W., 1964, p. 127]

The freedom sought by Afrikanerdom means more than a republic, he cried. It means the right to preserve the rule of the white race.

The groaning of the oxwagon evokes clearly again the stars which held your forefathers on course through the darkest night. Their star of freedom shines brighter on your path as well.

But you know now that freedom meant more for them than simply the freedom to rule themselves and to live out their nationhood fully.

Their freedom was also, and above all, the freedom to preserve themselves as a white race. As you could never otherwise have realized, you realize today their task to make South Africa a white man's land is ten times more your task. [Pienaar, S. W., 1964, p. 128]

What good is the appeal for *volkseenheid* if that unity is without direction? White civilization is at stake. Afrikanerdom must act.

This centenary year has awakened the People from its sleep of death. Over South Afria's plains, Danskraal and Blood River again trumpet their message that to win you must above all look up and that with the resurrection of Afrikanerdom's old idealism will also arise new hope, new love of fatherland, new will power and new unity.

You want that new unity, and God be praised that you still want it. But have you ever asked yourself seriously: For what?.

Do you want unity merely to saunter forward aimlessly hand in hand, or do you want it in order purposefully and determinedly to solve great and pressing problems of your People along the Path of South Africa? [Pienaar, S. W., 1964, p. 129]

Afrikanerdom has reached a turning point, even at this moment. The People must now awaken to an awareness of their past as spiritual sustenance and direction for the future.

Even as the Great Trek was both the intervention of God and a purposeful communal effort, so the Second Trek can rely on divine help if Afrikaners are willing to mobilize their forces in order to buttress their beseiged brethren in the city. Hence, the city is the modern Blood River, the outcome of which will determine the path of tomorrow's nation.

> There is a power which is strong enough to lead us to our destination along that Path of South Africa—the power Above, which creates nations and fixes their lot. . . . [This is also] the power which can go out, and was intended to go out from that sixty percent of South Africa's white population who are flesh and blood of the exhausted trekker struggling in the city. Unite that power purposefully in a mighty salvation-deed [*reddingsdaad*] and then the future of Afrikanerdom will be assured and white civilization will be saved. [Pienaar, S. W., 1964, p. 129]

Thus did Malan marshall the symbols of the civil faith and reinterpret them in a new and urban context, attempting thereby to direct the emotional energies aroused by the Ossewatrek into a mighty People's movement, a *reddings-daad* on behalf of the Afrikaner urban poor. Malan had delivered much the same message six weeks before at a great National party United Congress on November 8, 1938, (Pienaar, S. W., 1964, pp. 110-120). The urban problem had been extensively elaborated even earlier by Diederichs, Meyer, Cronje, and Albert Hertzog, among others, but never before Malan's speech on December 16, 1938, had analysis of Afrikaner urban poverty been so skillfully blended with so many of the racial and ethnic themes of the civil faith. Although he never mentioned the term "class," Malan clearly viewed class consciousness as the fearful alternative to a return of poor Afrikaners to the true Afrikaner fold.

The "salvation-deed" (*reddingsdaad*) of which Malan spoke referred back to earlier events during the Ossewatrek. At the very outset of the ceremonial trek, J. H. Conradie, administrator of the Cape, had spoken of a second Great Trek to the cities and urged that a mighty campaign be mounted against the People's poverty (*Ossewa Gedenkboek*, 1940, pp. 115-119). His words were often echoed on the route north, especially in the southwestern Cape where there seems to have been a closely knit community of elite opinion centered on parliament.[1] The call for a great Afrikaner *reddingsdaad* on behalf of the city-dwelling Afrikaner was renewed by the A.N.S. neo-Fichteans, led by Diederichs, when the wagons reached Bloemfontein (*Die Vaderland*, October 10, 1938).[2]

In the context of the neo-Fichtean speeches, Father Kestell made a moving appeal to the Bloemfontein audience to contribute money to a great new fund, the Reddingsdaad.

> Now is the time of the great salvation-deed. I said yesterday that our People must rescue itself and now here begins our salvation-deed. I say that the moment has arrived. For a moment this is holy ground. Will you not try to realize that what you now do is of God, shot through with that great thought: I am now going to act to save my People? and for me it is dedicated to God. If that thought passes through your being, then it will be enough. [*Fees by die Waens*, 1939, pp. 49-50]

The multitude marched forward to place their contributions in the six chests provided and over £450 was collected. From there the chests were borne northward on the wagons, and the festival celebrants in every town and village in the Free State and the Transvaal were likewise given the opportunity of adding their contributions.

Whereas the earlier elaborate economic schemes of Piet Meyer had made little appeal to the popular imagination, the Ossewatrek demonstrated that Afrikaners could indeed be mobilized behind an interpretation of the civil religion which bridged the gap between town and country. The intent of the Reddingsdaad, at least on the part of the Broederbonders who administered it, was styled to do more than alleviate urban poverty in the fashion of Victorian charity. Rather it sought to change the whole fabric of urban industri-

---

[1] An appeal for a reddingsdaad was made by N. J. van der Merwe in Cape Town; W. A. Joubert at Paarl; H. A. Rust at Philadelphia; Senator C. A. van Niekerk at Worcester; T. J. Kotze at Robertson; and S. P. le Roux, M. P., at De Rust (*Ossewa Gedenkboek*, 1940, pp. 122, 131, 144, 157-158, 163, 229-231.

[2] Speakers included Ds. P. du Toit, former poor-relief secretary of the Transvaal N.G. and a close friend of Albert Hertzog; Geoff Cronje; Diederichs himself; and T. J. Hugo.

al life. Cronje elucidated to his listeners at Bloemfontein the general direction of the new movement:

> The Boer culture must be carried into the English cosmopolitan life of the city. . . . It is an appalling struggle and more than one Boer has already been demolished in this difficult transition period in our ethnic life. But our hope is that the organized Afrikaner action in the city will day by day become more purposeful and more irresistable. . . . We must not allow the urbanization of the Afrikaner to divide our People. We must not allow the city Afrikaner to become a different kind of Afrikaner from his fellow on the farm. [*Fees by Die Waens*, 1939, p. 40]

What was to be done with the large Reddingsdaad fund which had already been collected? Inevitably, a Broederbond committee had already thrashed out a plan of action to be initiated by an F.A.K. economic volkskongres. The latter was convened in October 1939[3] to present the Broederbond's three-fold plan of attack on the problem. They would establish an Economic Institute of the F.A.K. to coordinate activities on the three fronts. The first prong of the attack on the urban dilemma was to maintain support for Albert Hertzog's efforts to organize the mine workers. The second thrust incorporated Professor L. J. du Plessis' scheme for People's capitalism (*volkskapitalisme*) which he had outlined as early as 1934 in *Koers* (August 1934), although it had elicited little public attention then. He saw the origin of Afrikaner poverty not in capitalism as such, but in the control of the capitalist system by non-Afrikaners.[4] What the Afrikaner had therefore to do was not to overthrow capitalism but to seize his rightful share of the fruits thereof:

> The purpose of our economic struggle is thus national, even Christian National, as against the personal and sectional. As organized Afrikanerdom we wish consciously to take part in the economic development of our land, naturally in order to ensure our own existence, but above all to restore our People

---

[3] For a full discussion of the 1939 economic congress with summaries of the speeches, see du Plessis, E. P. (1964, chapter 7).

[4] At the congress, Professor du Plessis' scheme was echoed in turn by C. G. W. Schuman, T. E. Donges, M. S. Louw, H. F. Verwoerd, and G. E. N. Ross, each of whom offered his own individual variation.

to Prosperity and so enable it to fulfill its God-given calling.
. . . [In the past] we accepted as inevitable that the masses
who were unable to adjust [to capitalism] quickly or well
enough should drop to poor-whiteism. Sympathetically we
belittled them and separated ourselves from them, or at best
offered them "alms" in a philanthropic manner. . . . Meantime
this process of adjustment was destroying our People by
denationalization of its economic leaders and proletar-
ianization of its producing masses. But in the awakening of
self-consciousness the People has become aware of this also,
and the new ethnic movement is intended to prevent the
further destruction of the Afrikaner People in an effort to
adjust to a foreign capitalist system, and intends rather to
mobilize the People to conquer this system and to transform
it so that it fits our ethnic nature. [Du Plessis, E. P., 1964,
p. 104]

Capitalism had thus to be transformed from its base in liberal
individualism to an ethnic system which would work to the
good of the Afrikaner People as a nation. This was to be
achieved by Afrikaner control of both production and con-
sumption. Afrikaner capital should thus be organized to
support Afrikaner enterprise, both by investment in Afrikaner
business and by purchase of Afrikaner goods. For this purpose
M. S. Louw proposed the establishment of a specifically
Afrikaner investment house, and H. F. Verwoerd urged the
formation of Afrikaner consumers' cooperatives.

Fifty percent of the Reddingsdaad fund was to be invested
in the new Afrikaner investment house, Federale Volksbeleg-
gings, and the remainder was to be placed under the control
of the Economic Institute of the F.A.K., an appointed body
whose executive was made up entirely of members of the
Broederbond. Of this amount, ten percent was to be devoted
to miscellaneous expenditures—mostly grants to Afrikaner
church and women's poor-relief organizations. The remainder
would be invested in Afrikaner business. Although about
twenty percent of this sum was invested in the large Afrikaner
insurance companies, SANLAM and SANTAM, and in
Volkskas (the Afrikaans bank, founded by the Broederbond
in 1934) in the absence of other large Afrikaner companies
the rest was used to support retailers with short-term loans
(Diederichs, n.d.). Such loans were granted only after due

"investigation" by the Broers of the Economic Institute. Although by 1950, Afrikaners still numbered only about ten percent of all businessmen in South Africa, the Reddingsdaad fund did give the Broederbond a remarkable measure of control in Afrikaner business life. Director's lists of Afrikaner companies read extraordinarily like the membership rolls of the Broederbond.

What touched ordinary Afrikaners most closely, however, was the third prong of the Broederbond advance into the economic sphere. The economic congress also determined to establish the Reddingsdaadbond (R.D.B.) a "great ethnic organization, Christian National in principle," whose purpose was "to knit together all Afrikaners in order to further their cultural and, above all, their economic interests" (*Die Volksblad*, April 24, 1941). Dr. Diederichs gave up his professorship to become leader of the R.D.B. He embellished it with his own zeal and and rhetoric. The R.D.B., he said, must be seen not as an organization or association but as a "deed"—a deed which unites all Afrikaners, which frees them from economic bondage, a sacrificial deed, and above all, a deed of faith.

> Our People has need of such a salvation deed (*reddingsdaad*), And if Father Kestell were alive today, he would surely have cried out again to the whole People, saying: Come Afrikaners across the length and breadth of our land, come in your thousands, your tens of thousands, your hundreds of thousands. Come from near and come from far. Come you rich and come you poor, you learned and you unlettered, you from the farms and you from the cities. Come Afrikaners, children of the same nation, one and all you must come. For we are busy with a great work; we are building a temple. Come, let us build together. Come let us do great deeds. Deeds of sacrifice which unite, deeds of sacrifice which are fed by a great faith. Come, let us stand together for a great deed which shall unite and liberate. Come, let us stand together in an immovable sacrificial deed; let us stand together one and all in a great mighty resounding Reddingsdaad. [*Die Transvaler*, November 20, 1942]

The R.D.B. was financed from subscriptions (sixpence per month), and by 1946, the membership was more than 65,000. Local R.D.B. branches gathered throughout the year for properly Afrikaner recreations like folk dancing and *boeresport*. However, the movement was meant to be more than simply inspirational for the civil religion. Its major intention was to teach Afrikaners that trade and commerce were not at odds with the civil faith and Afrikaner *volkseenheid*. To this end, Afrikaners were provided with loans for the study of trades and business and were proffered advice on investments,[5] and efforts were made to organize the buying power of Afrikaners into cooperative unions. Afrikaners were urged to save in Afrikaans savings banks, and membership in the R.D.B. automatically brought a small amount of life insurance and burial insurance for those who joined (*Die Volksblad*, May 24, 1941).

The entire Broederbond attack on urban poverty was focused through a narrow ethnic lens. Despite the undoubted poverty of the white urban migrants, the major burden of industrialization in South Africa was borne not by these whites but by the mass of black men who were moving into the cities along with them. In 1935, the average annual cash earnings of whites in the mines was eleven times that of non-whites. In manufacturing and construction, the ratio of earnings was five to one. The fact that by 1950, the ratio had increased to fifteen to one in the mines perhaps reflects the success of Hertzog's reform movement; but in industry the ratio remained a fairly constant five to one, increasing to six to one during recessions (Houghton, 1967, p. 256). Malan's polemics of the "Afrikaner of the new Great Trek" meeting "the non-white beside his Blood River, partly or completely unarmed" bear no weight against such statistics. In fact, the new Afrikaner urban migrant was extremely well armed with the tradition of racial wage inequalities, backed by General Hertzog's "civilized labor" legislation, and with the vote, that was of course denied to the black man.

Economic advances through the Reddingsdaad were therefore slight for the ordinary Afrikaner, although it certainly helped enrich those Broederbonders who organized it. The economic "great leap forward" for the Afrikaner came after

[5] The R.D.B. was the instrument by which the Economic Institute circulated its loans to small businesses.

the victory of the National party in 1948, when political power reinforced the economic movement.[6] However, the Reddings-daad did have two important results. First, it gave the Afrikaner elite such experience in commerce that they would be able to make valuable economic use of their new-found political power once the National party came to power. Second, the symbolic effect of the Reddingsdaadbond, impos-sible though it is to measure, must have been considerable. For example, certain intellectual leaders of the Afrikaner civil faith began to shift from the old attack on "Hoggenheimer" to praise of the new "People's Capitalism," without in any way casting off their traditional civil religion, and to urge that Afrikaners cultivate the virtues of an urban industrial society: to invest, to strike, to spend, to borrow, and to lend at interest. Despite its rural origins, the Afrikaner civil religion adapted surprisingly easily to urban industrial life. Perhaps, as Marxists would argue, this was because the Afrikaner proletariat was part of a racial oligarchy. However, relative to his English-speaking white fellow countrymen, the Afri-kaner remained economically inferior (Afrikaners' average annual income was two-thirds that of English-speaking South Africans during this period); and the new interpretation of the civil religion had always to present ethnic interest against the English as well as racial domination of the black African.

[6] For a convincing statement of the argument that the economic successes of Afrikanerdom have been based upon the acquisition of political power, see Bunting (1969, Chapter 14).

11

The Second World War

The Failure of *Volkseenheid*

Despite the tremendous enthusiasm for *volkseenheid* on the basis of civil-religion principles, political differences remained, as General Hertzog's speech at the great Monumentkoppie oath-taking had again underscored. Although a parliamentary coalition was patched up for the session of 1940, thanks partly to the intercession of van Rooy and the Broederbond (*Die Vaderland*, April 1, 1942), Dr. Malan's hopes of reaching a *modus vivendi* with Hertzog were thwarted by Swart in the Free State,[1] and by Strydom, with backing from Verwoerd and *Die Transvaler*, in the north. These firebrands insisted on an Afrikaner republic by a bare majority,[2] and their political machinations proved more than the old general could stomach. Following a stormy Free State National party congress in November 1940, he resigned from the party and withdrew from the field, snorting his disgust at the deviousness of party politics and professional politicians (cf. Roberts and Trollip, 1947, chapter two).

But Hertzog's "Man Friday," N. C. Havenga, went on to head the Afrikaner party, which was founded in May 1941

[1] N. J. van der Merwe had died unexpectedly in August 1940, leaving the Free State leadership of the Gesuiwerdes within the new H.N.P. to C. R. Swart. Swart was not only less moderate than van der Merwe: he and General Hertzog also shared a hearty personal dislike for one another.

[2] In the end Verwoerd had his way. During his premiership, South Africa became a republic by a bare majority in a national referendum—limited to whites, of course.

as heir to Hertzog's pluralistic tradition of two-stream liberal nationalism (cf. Cilliers, 1941; and *Die Vaderland*, May 28, 1941). The general himself, however, making an *ex cathedra* statement in the press, rejected "the democratic-parliamentary form of government," urging that South Africans identify with the new "world-revolution," the "drive for reformation and creation of a new world order" (*Die Vaderland*, October 23, 1941). National Socialism, he argued, was the wave of the future. Hertzog's determination to abstain from party politics, despite attempts to woo him back, was intimately wedded to his commitment to National Socialism. His argument against the one formed the *raison d'être* of the other.

> Under no circumstances [he said] will I ever again take part in a political system which is calculated to do no more than further and conciliate the ambition, avarice, and thirst for power of individuals and groups, at the expense of national interests. [*Die Vaderland*, October 23, 1941]

He was prepared to assist the cause of Afrikanerdom, he announced on a later occasion, but only "free from the mudhole of party politics."

> Afrikanerdom has two blood-foes, the insatiable effort—old as the initiation of British domination in South Africa—to subordinate the freedom of Afrikanerdom in South Africa to the power of the British empire ... [and] the ambitious party peddler from among the People themselves, who seeks only honor and personal interests within his own party. The domination and exploitation of the political party by self-seekers is today the most searing scandal in the life of South African party politics. [*Die Vaderland*, February 25, 1942]

Hertzog's advocacy of National Socialism was more than simply the aberration of a bitter and disappointed man, for we have seen that this dissatisfaction with party politics was longstanding. He had long since read and absorbed Spengler, and *samesmelting* was in fact an effort to establish a truly "national party" in South Africa. The declaration of war and the political maneuvering which followed the reunion at Monumentkoppie bore only final proof for him of the inequities of the whole democratic system. If democratic processes allowed the imperialism of anglicized politicians and the ethnicism of Afrikaner political professionals to destroy that civic sentiment he had tried so hard to realize in *samesmelting*, then better that the party system be replaced by a National Socialist dictatorship. In abandoning democracy, however, Hertzog was not denying his ideal of a unified white nationalism in South Africa. One of the major sources of his conflict with Swart and Strydom was his trenchant insistence that the new order, whether republican or not, recognize equally the political and cultural rights of English-speaking as well as Afrikaans-speaking South Africans who "placed South Africa first." In this sense, right up to his death in November, 1942, Hertzog refused to budge from the principles which had inspired him throughout his career.

The National Socialist successor to Hertzog was Oswald Pirow, strongly militarist by inclination and never much of an advocate for democracy. As early as 1934, he had declared himself for a republic and dictatorship. At the same time, he eschewed in Hertzogite fashion any ethnic classification of the Afrikaner People, declaring that "our People" included "all those who make South Africa their home, regardless of their European origins or their home language" (*Die Republikein*, October 19, 1934). In 1940, Pirow announced himself in favor of a "New Order" which would consist of a strongly centralized white South African state in which home language would be unimportant. Its appeal was explicitly white, middle class, anti-communist, and racist—rather that ethnic (Pirow, 1940).

Pirow formed a "New Order study group" within Malan's Re-united National party (H.N.P.) to make propaganda for this ideal. At first, Pirow's ideas received favorable response from the more fascist and racist wing of the National party. Eric Louw and Otto du Plessis approved,[3] and C. W. M. du Toit actually joined the group.[4] However it soon emerged

---

[3] Otto du Plessis, editor of *Die Oosterlig*, and soon to be enlightenment secretary of the National party, produced a pamphlet soon after the fall of France, entitled, *Die Nuwe Suid-Afrika: Die Rewolusie van die Twintigste Eeu* ("The New South Africa: The Revolution of the Twentieth Century").

[4] C. W. M. du Toit, a Gerformeerde minister who had obtained leave of absence from the pulpit to serve God as a member of parliament, was the brother of Totius.

that the New Order was more than an ideological propaganda machine, as it began to constitute a veritable Hertzogite circle within the new H.N.P.

The possibility that the New Order group would now form a power base for Pirow in the Transvaal H.N.P. brought Strydom and Verwoerd out in full cry against National Socialism, especially that Pirowite form of National Socialism which chose to ignore the ethnic distinctions between English and Afrikaner. "The foremost question," insisted Strydom, "is the protection and maintenance of the Afrikaner or Boer nation as such, that is, as an independent and separate entity with its own language and culture and everything else which is unique to nationhood." True, a republic was needed, he said, but a genuinely Afrikaner republic—not an imitation of Italy or Germany or Portugal. "This republic which our party proposes will not be something imported from other lands. No! it will be cast in an Afrikaner mold, shaped to our past and traditions and taking into account the needs of our nation" (*Die Transvaler*, March 15, 1941). Malan was somewhat more conciliatory, claiming that National Socialism might be all very well for Germany, but that the Afrikaner republican tradition was democratic. At the same time, he continued, "about 80 to 85 percent of the 'New Order' is contained in the program of the party," so that Pirow's proposals ought not to be seen as too violently opposed to those of the party (*Die Burger*, March 25, 1941).

Rivalry between Pirow and Strydom was more acute since it was personal as well as ideological. One or the other would have to assume effective leadership of the Transvaal National party, and Strydom was determined that it should not be Pirow. Strydom had the support of *Die Transvaler* and did not hesitate to use symbols of the civil religion to bolster his position. Although the old United party machinery was split, the Gesuiwerdes, with their strong grassroots appeal, stood solid behind Strydom. Also in Strydom's favor, the Union congress of the H.N.P., in June 1941, had condemned any group-formation within the party. The dice were thus heavily loaded against Pirow. Strydom adherents waited with bated breath for the Transvaal National party congress in August 1941 when, it was generally felt, Pirow would receive his come-uppance. He did in fact receive a sound moral defeat there, but was saved from suspension from the party by Malan's moderate stance. This did not prevent the expulsion of Pirow and his parliamentary followers from the H.N.P. caucus during the next session of parliament, however, which effectively ended his political career. Any further influence he could exert was mediated through the fascist New Order periodical, *Die Anti-Kommunis*, which holds interest for students of Afrikaner National Socialism but had little political impact during its publication.

The defeat of Pirow did not mean the end of National Socialist commitment within Afrikanerdom. The continual wrangling in the ranks of the H.N.P. combined with wartime stresses to attract more and more Afrikaners to the ranks of the O.B.[5] In November 1940, Colonel Laas had resigned as commandant general under pressure from those who could no longer abide his administrative ineptitude; and in his place was elected Dr. J. F. J. van Rensburg, administrator of the Free State, who resigned from that position to take up his new duties. He was a Germanophile, a protege of Pirow and General Hertzog, and a firm admirer of Hitler. He defined his own ideological position with artless naiveté in an autobiography: "I could only call myself a race-conscious Afrikaner with tendencies which many people today would regard as fascistic" (van Rensburg, 1956, p. 135). Under his leadership, the O.B. tended to follow a rather wavering National Socialist direction while he moved decisively to tighten up on discipline and to bring the organization under his personal control. He saw himself as a man of action, rather than a "cultural fire-eater," and gravitated to an elitist action group within the Transvaal O.B. known as the Stormjaers (S.J.s), who publicized their objection to the war by blowing up vital installations and sabotaging government buildings. Van Rensburg said of the S.J.s in his autobiography that, "I immediately felt at home with this crowd. . . . We clicked at once. I wish to state here, thankfully, that never in my

[5] In February 1941, Malan announced in parliament that the O.B. had between 300,000 and 400,000 members (*Hansard*, 1940-1941, column 2195, cited in Stultz, 1974).

life have I stood so closely and so wholeheartedly to any
body of men as I did to the S.J.s in the years 1941 to 1945"
(Van Rensburg, 1956, p. 185).

After the war was over, under the pseudonym S. J. de Jongh,
van Rensburg wrote an Afrikaans novel about the activities
of the Stormjaers,[6] *Sonder Gewere* (*"Without Guns"*). A
strong current of opposition to the publication of this book
within the O.B. was illustrated by an anecdote in N. G. S.
van der Walt's diary which provides telling insight into van
Rensburg's character.

> Strong objections to the commandant general's book. It is clear
> to me that the man has lost all foundation. Like a reckless
> fatalist he lunges forward, without logic and without reflection.
> This was obvious from his reply to my objection that people
> would not respect these deeds of violence unless backed by
> a higher motive. He pointed to the sinking of the Ark Royal
> and said that even the English would value the courage of
> the German crew. I replied that the comparison did not apply.
> "Yes, I know," was his answer. I continued in spite of his
> rejection of logic, saying that anyone had respect for honorable
> execution of war duties, but many of our activities were of
> themselves most dishonorable and to glorify them without
> justification would be to release a turbulence of which we
> ourselves would be the sacrifices. "We shall repress it, let them
> try and we shall shoot them" he burst out in foolish irrespon-
> sibility. I walked out. [Van der Walt, N. G. S., diary, November
> 4, 1945]

In 1941, however, this criticism was far in the future, and
the O.B. was ready and willing to be the vehicle for van
Rensburg's boyish sense of high adventure. Besides the militant commitment to the cause of Afrikanerdom which van
Rensburg managed to convey, the nub of the O.B.'s attraction
was its acceptance of all republican Afrikaners regardless of
their ideological disposition. It thus stood close to the *volkseenheid* position of the Broederbond leadership, symbolized
by Chairman J. C. van Rooy's officiating at van Rensburg's
swearing-in ceremony on the slopes of Mount Majuba, the
site of the great Boer victory over Britain on February 28
in the war of 1881 (*Die Oosterlig*, January 3, 1941).

[6] See also J. J. Haywood, *Dr. J. F. J. van Rensburg en die
Stormjaers*, a party pamphlet attacking van Rensburg for his close
ties with the Stormjaers.

Broederbond efforts to organize *volkseenheid* were not restricted merely to the O.B., however. The idea that all the forces of organized Afrikanerdom should be united in a People's front (*volksorganisasie*) not only lay behind Piet Meyer's plans for the reorganization of the F.A.K. during the 1930s, but had been given new impetus by the Ossewatrek as well as at Monumentkoppie. At the unveiling of the Piet Retief monument in Coega on Covenant Day, 1939, Dr. Malan elaborated the issue of *volksorganisasie*:

> One consideration, which more and more intrudes upon thinking Afrikaners is that Afrikaner unity will finally be realized only as a result of intensive Afrikaner *volksorganisasie*. . .
> [*Die Burger*, December 18, 1939]

The Voortrekkers had to fall back upon their own strength, and that strength was enough to save South Africa for the white race and for civilization.

> But who shall deny that that strength would have been squandered in numerous isolated deeds of despair, however heroic this might have been, if Piet Retief, and later Andries Pretorius, had not properly organized those ethnic forces [*volkskragte*] into a political and ecclesiastical, and, where necessary, a military community. . . . *Volksorganisasie*! Without that in the background, the best efforts of individual Afrikaners or of Afrikaner groups to protect their interests, to recover economically, to live out their Afrikanerhood fully in all spheres, are to a large degree fruitless, and to a large measure a waste of money and strength. It might indicate life, but life does not necessarily mean resurrection. [*Die Burger*, December 18, 1939]

There follows a paragraph which very clearly linked the political party with the efforts of cultural leaders on all fronts.

> The problem of Afrikaner *volkseenheid* is a political one. That it always was, and always must be as long as our true and undivided South African love of fatherland is challenged and as long as South Africa has not yet realized her destiny as a free, independent nation, free of all foreign ties and loyalties. [*Die Burger*, December 18, 1939]

For Malan the *volkswil* had thus to be expressed through the agency of the party, but he argued for intimate cooperation with other ethnic organizations.

Ever since Monumentkoppie, a group of Broederbonders under the chairmanship of L. J. du Plessis had been meeting regularly to hammer out a republican constitution which could stand as a basis for Afrikaner unity. Members of of that "committee for unity of principle and leadership" included Diederichs, Meyer and Verwoerd. In August 1940, L. J. du Plessis issued a statement to the Afrikaans press in which he called for organized Afrikaner action on the basis of Calvinist principles, racial segregation, and a free and independent republican ideal.[7] At this time he condemned any tendency to totalitarianism as interference with the Calvinist principle of *sowereiniteit in eie kring* (*Die Volksblad*, August 6, 1940).

However, it was already clear that the relationship between the party and the O.B. was going to pose difficult problems. In April 1940, the Transvaal O.B. (probably the Stormjaer element), published a draft republican constitution, which was definitely National Socialist in spirit. According to *Die Suiderstem*, this draft expressed principles such as

citizenship for the elect alone, Afrikaans as official language with English as second (non-official) language, a president with *unlimited powers*, a People's Council [*Volksraad*] virtually without legislative powers, . . . strong emergency measures including control of key industries and the press, as well as control and purification of the civil service, the defense force and municipal councils. "Immediate action" would be taken to break the British connection, to ban the British flag and national anthem, along with "British so-called democratic institutions and concepts." The Jewish question, the poor-white question and the question of the coloureds would be settled without delay. The pre-conditions for citizenship in this republic would be so set up that "pure white descent and service to the Afrikaans ethnic calling and incorporation into organic ethnic life would be a first requirement." [Reprinted in *Die Volkstem*, October 5, 1940]

According to a statement by J. D. Jerling, this O.B. republican pamphlet was shown to Dr. Malan in September 1940.

---

[7] Verwoerd reviewed du Plessis' statement favorably in an editorial in *Die Transvaler* (August 6, 1940).

Dr. Malan said that the O.B. must proceed slowly, said Jerling, and first wait until the British connection had been broken. Jerling replied that this would not be honest with the People and General Kemp agreed wholeheartedly. . . . Ds. Kotze added that when you have broken the British connection, you still have to cope with the Briton, and when Malan further stated that sleeping dogs would be awakened by the pamphlet, Ds. Kotze replied that there are no dogs still asleep. [*Die Vaderland*, September 17, 1941]

Malan must have felt that the O.B. was moving into his sphere and, moreover, more resolutely than he was prepared to do. Some entente between the National party and the O.B. would clearly have to be reached to avoid abortion of plans for the projected *volksorganisasie*. At the 1940 congress of the H.N.P., Malan announced an agreement between the party and the O.B. intended to offset the impending conflict. The party would work on the party-political front, and the O.B. on non-political terrain. Malan received the assurances of the O.B. Grand Council:

a. That the major goal and struggle of the O.B. was the propagation and realization of Voortrekker principles and ideals, including the religious, moral and economic uplift of our People.

b. That, among other ideals, the O.B. accepts the freedom ideal of the Voortrekkers, namely, the establishment of a free, independent Christian National republic, and also wishes to help realize the deep desire of the centenary year, namely the establishment and furtherance of a firm, purposeful and enduring Afrikaner *volkseenheid*. . . .

[*Die Burger*, October 31, 1940]

In February 1941, Dr. Verwoerd felt free to speak publicly of the "triune power of the Afrikaner People," referring to the R.D.B., the O.B. and the National party (*Die Transvaler*, February 25, 1941); and in May, du Plessis was sufficiently confident of closer cooperation to propose that the "leadership corps" of Afrikanerdom be closely linked "above all through mediation of the O.B. because it is the most extensive (although as yet unproven) unity of organization of Afrikanerdom" (*Die Volksblad*, May 2, 1941). When delegates assembled for the Union congress of the H.N.P. in Pretoria on June 3, 1941, they were treated to a speech from Dr. Malan which accepted the nucleus idea of *volkseenheid*, but emphasized that the major institutionalization of its goals was the party and not the O.B. "We are no party-political organization in the normal sense of the word," he said.

> As Reunited National party or *Volksparty*, we embody two basic ideas without which the Afrikaner People could never have been.
>
> The one is the National idea and the other is the idea of our restored Afrikaner *volkseenheid*. We it is who took over the idea of a unique South African nationhood from the hands of our heroic forefathers. . . .
>
> We are the fulfillment—so far as it was fulfilled—of the deep desire of the centenary year for *volkseenheid*, the embodiment of the deed of September 4, 1939, and of the solemn vow on Monumentkoppie. We are no ordinary party political organization. We occupy a central position in Afrikaner ethnic life. [Pienaar, 1964, pp. 37-38]

Thus did Malan attempt to steal the civil religion thunder of the O.B. Any cooperation between the party and the O.B. would have to recognize the priority of the former according to Malan's terms. By claiming to be "more than an ordinary political party," Malan might have been held to be transgressing the previous agreement with the O.B. He went even farther, however. Although the *volksparty* notion was implicit in what Malan said, there were other National Socialist currents in Afrikaner life which he confessed were most disturbing. He referred to some of them:

> The idea which has been accepted by some that the party . . . is no longer necessary. . . . With some this is still merely a feeling . . . With others it has developed into a campaign.
>
> They know that we have the party to thank for our national consciousness, our language rights, our Afrikaans national newspapers, the extension of our freedom, our republican purpose and struggle, our united ethnic will for the maintenance of white civilization, our white labor policy and hundreds of other important matters. . . . The party is the mother, but as a result of various heretical concepts they are now prepared

218 *The Rise of Afrikanerdom*

to commit matricide, and that at a time when in the face
of the crisis on the political front we need the party more
than ever before. . . .

Our new ethnic organizations are all necessary and signs of
life and growth, but they must all stand upon their own roots
and draw their strength from the Afrikaans mother earth which
has been prepared by our party in years of struggle and
sacrifice. . . . (Pienaar, S. W., 1964, pp. 38-39)

Malan's speech was greeted with wild enthusiasm by the
delegates, who not only voted to establish the leadership of
the party in party-political matters, but went as far as to
declare Malan *volksleier* ("leader of the People") as well as
the party leader.

Furthermore, du Plessis' Broederbond *Eenheidskomitee*
("Unity Committee") issued a "Declaration on Behalf of
Volksorganisasies", signed by Ivan Lombard for the F.A.K.;
by J. F. J. van Rensburg for the O.B.; by L. J. du Plessis
for the Economic Institute of the F.A.K.; by Nic Diederichs
for the R.D.B.; and, in their individual capacities, by Ds. J.
P. van der Spuy, chairman of the Council of Dutch Reformed
churches; Ds. I. D. Kruger, chairman of the interchurch
commission of the Dutch churches; and Ds. D. F. Erasmus,
of the Calvinist Union. Each signatory promised support in
his own respective terrain to any political party whose principles coincided with his own. Their statement of principles,
although lengthy, I quote in full because it provides in
reasonable compass a summary of the Christian National
ideology which was acceptable to both party and O.B. groups
within the Broederbond, as well as representing a compromise
between the social metaphysics of the Kuyperians on the
one hand and Diederichs and the A.N.S. on the other. The
declaration reads with regard to principles:

The state must be genuinely free and republican and Christian
National. It must acknowledge as basic the eternal legal
principles of the Word of God, the clear direction of the
development of our ethnic history, and the necessary application of this past to modern circumstances.

The constitutional system must not be cast in a foreign mold.
It must break away from all which is false or damaging to
the People in democracy as it is here known, and must make

possible a powerful government built upon the concepts of People's government of the South African republics, with necessary application in an industrial state for furthering the interests of the People. No inroads may be made upon the freedom of conscience and independence of the social spheres which are grounded in creation unless state policy as laid down is being undermined.

Far-reaching social and economic reforms must be undertaken. Exploitation of Afrikanerdom by any financial power must be ended. The riches of the land must be powerfully developed in service to the People and in order to ensure a worthwhile living standard for every member of the People. The backward position of Afrikaners in various professions must be eliminated. Education must rest upon a Christian National foundation, and the maintenance of mother-tongue education must be ensured. The Afrikaner, as the original exploiter of the land, must be confirmed in his citizenship, and protected against domination by any who will not extend their fullest loyalty to the country. His rights must receive absolute protection and be guarded at all times. The state must undertake the fullest measure of responsibility for the health of the People. ... Strongest emphasis must be laid upon the purposive disciplining of the People. The leaders must be able to expect complete obedience and faith from Afrikanerdom as long as they manage the state or other activities of ethnic concern in accordance with the way shown by Afrikanerdom itself and flowing from its history. [*Die Transvaler*, June 13, 1941]

The guiding principles of this Broederbond Christian Nationalism were thus the sacred history of Afrikanerdom and the Word of God. Hence the emphasis on the coming republic and on mother-tongue education. On the face of it, *sowereiniteit in eie kring* was assured, although on the condition that it not undermine state policy.[8] The principles of economic and social action are the areas in which the declaration comes closest to National Socialism. In fact, if one may be permitted a theological analogy, the *kerygma* ("gospel") was firmly rooted in the Kuyperian version of the civil religion, but the *didache* ("ethical prescriptions") were National Socialist, or at least neo-Fichtean.

---

[8] It is difficult to imagine that Kuyperians especially Stoker, can have felt easy about this reservation. Certainly Kuyper himself would have rejected it out of hand.

Appended to the Declaration was a draft republican constitution (*Die Burger*, January 23, 1942), that was similar to
the one issued by the Transvaal O.B. in 1940, except that
legislative power was vested in the Volksraad rather than
the presidency. Dr. Malan publicly accepted the declaration
as evidencing approval by the *volksorganisasies* of National
party policy, but he rejected any idea of a common policy
council as being an infringement of party autonomy: and
he suggested that although the draft constitution was acceptable in principle, the time was not yet ripe for publication.
In fact, he consistently maintained that the first step must
be to achieve the republic and that constitutional matters
could be decided after that.

There can be little doubt that Malan's hesitation concerning publication was also influenced by liberal nationalist
reservations. Malan's social philosophy, and also his *volkskerk*
theology, had always been more liberal than that of most
of his fellow Broers from the north. He rejected the ultimate
implications of their, and for that matter his own, ethnicism.
Thus, when the draft constitution was finally authorized for
publication, Malan was careful to say that it was published
for discussion rather than as policy. Furthermore, the edition
of *Die Burger* which carried the text of the constitution also
featured an editorial which was strongly critical of the draft
on two counts. First, the draft stated with regard to citizens'
rights that "recognition would only be given to such subjects
from whom it can be expected that they will act in an
ethnically constructive manner, whatever their status might
have been in the past." This was tantamount to restriction
of the franchise observed *Die Burger's* editorial, and furthermore, with what criteria would the worth of a citizen be
measured?

> Without further analyzing this obscure sentence, we may ask:
> Who decides what is "ethnically constructive?" And who will
> "expect" of the subjects that they display such characteristics?
> Citizens' rights in a free state cannot be granted and revoked
> according to a vague measure which can be so arbitrarily
> interpreted as to ensure the rights of no individual. Rights
> of citizenship may only be granted according to legally estab-
> lished rules and requirements. [*Die Burger*, January 23, 1942]

Second, the draft stated that Afrikaans would be the "only official language," with English as "a second or additional official language" which could enjoy equal rights "everywhere and whenever such use is judged by the state to be in the best interests of the state and its inhabitants."[9] *Die Burger* appealed to "a Nationalist principle which is as old as the Party itself":

> That is the principle that out of the two sections a united nation must be built up which will be bound by a common love of fatherland and national pride. . . . No person in his right senses can hope that that unity will ever be obtained in a republic if the language and culture of one of the two sections is slighted. [*Die Burger*, January 27, 1942; cf. also *Die Burger*, April 10, 1942]

Verwoerd of *Die Transvaler*, on the other hand, accepted the draft constitution without exception (*Die Transvaler*, January 23 and January 26, 1942). If we may assume, as I think we may, that *Die Burger* spoke for Malan, then one may place Malan in the liberal nationalist camp along with Havenga, whereas Verwoerd stood much closer to the neo-Fichteans. Within the echelons of the party, however, such ideological disagreements were firmly subordinated to the needs of the organization. On the issue of party unity, Malan and Verwoerd stood shoulder to shoulder. Verwoerd's editorials attacking Pirow's National Socialist New Order might at times evidence a certain hysteria, an exorcism of the devil within as well as outside, perhaps; but in the end ideological matters were not allowed to interfere one jot with his loyalty to the party machine.

Thus a split between the party and the O.B. was inevitable, not so much because of ideological differences, which tended to cut across organizational lines, but rather because peaceful coexistence of two movements, each claiming the total allegiance of the Afrikaner People, was a practical impossibility.[10] The complicated details of the split between the party and

[9] This clause is remarkably close to the current (1969) policy of Albert Hertzog's new Re-Constituted National party.

[10] Strydom was quite open about the nature of the problem in a speech at Potchefstroom reported in *Die Transvaler* (September 22, 1941).

the O.B. have been well covered by Michael Roberts and A.
E. G. Trollip (1947). We need only say that by August 27,
1941, Dr. Malan had made up his mind that the O.B. must
be broken.[11] On that day he made a speech at Stellenbosch
accusing the O.B. of sabotaging the party and the *volkseenheid* which had been obtained at the Union congress of the
party two months before (*Die Burger*, August 28, 1941). Malan
was well aware of the risks involved; he compared his decision
to fight the O.B. to the two other most important decisions
in his life—to leave the pulpit and to reject *samesmelting*—but
he insisted that in the face of van Rensburg's "aggression
and sabotage" there was no alternative. In fact, he was driving
home what he had said two months before—that the party would brook no rival as *the* People's Front. Verwoerd,
supporting the party, turned his anti-Nazi vitriol onto the
O.B. as well as onto Pirow. Although van Rensburg and the
S.J.s undoubtedly had National Socialist tendencies, the
majority of O.B. members had joined because of Ossewatrek
enthusiasm and disgust with party-political machinations.
Malan was now reorganizing the party to permit meaningful
action for ordinary members (*Die Burger*, June 26 and June
27, 1941), and O.B. adherents increasingly began to fall back
to the party.

Accusations of National Socialism were self-fulfilling, so
that O.B. publications did indeed incline more and more
toward a Nazi tone. Van Rensburg had repeatedly insisted
that the O.B. was a People's movement—not an ideological
cage—and that all republican Afrikaners were welcome to
join. However, the organization's newspaper, *Die O.B.*, edited
by N. G. S. van der Walt, and O.B. pamphlets, especially
one entitled *Die O. B.: Vanwaar en Waarheen* (1942a),
tended to belie such ideological openness. While the O.B.
insisted that it remained loyal to "Christian National ideas"
(O.B. 1942a, p. 23), it did so in keeping with a social philosophy
based on the "organic unity of Afrikanerdom" rooted in the
family (O.B., 1942a, pp. 24-30; cf. also O.B, 1942b) and the

[11] See especially Roberts and Trollip (1947, chapter four). For
contemporary statements, see the pamphlets, *Ons Party en die O.B.*,
issued by the party, and L. J. du Plessis' *Afrikanervolkseenheid*
pamphlet, which favors the O.B.

soil of the fatherland (O.B., 1942a, pp. 31-34). This social metaphysics distinguished between natural estates (*stande*) which divided the People by functions, and social classes, artificial constructs of atomistic liberalism. The new state (*gesagstaat*) was to be based on the authority of the People as an organic whole rather than as a congeries of isolated individuals (O.B., 1942a, pp. 50-54). "The *O.B.*," declared van Rensburg, "emphasizes blood rather than votes" (*Die O.B.*, July 1, 1942). Finally, the pamphlet identified the O.B. with the revolution of the twentieth century, arguing:

> The revolution of the twentieth century, carried by the *volks-beweging* ("People's movement") is the coming together of national and social undercurrents of the previous century. The national stream is the emphasis on the particularity and the permanence of the People. The social stream is directed to the strengthening of all strata and parts of the People as organic unity in which the individual finds his natural place and task. This tendency, incorporated into a movement, is the *volksbeweging*, which drives towards the formation of a unique state, a state with increased authority for the maintenance of the independence and assurance of the fullest and most far-reaching power of the unique People. The principle of leadership [*leierskap*] and corporative state regulation of the professional estates [*beroepstande*], is the means by which the *volksbeweging* brings this talk to fruition. [O.B., 1942a, p. 13]

A People who at that time most fully realized these ideals, concluded the pamphlet, was Nazi Germany. Indeed, van Rensburg on one occasion went so far as to state that "only a German victory could bring the republic" (*Die Vaderland*, August 1, 1944).

Along with this National Socialist policy (cf. Neumann, 1966, pp. 41-129), the O.B. developed the first genuinely new reinterpretation of the sacred history since the fall of Kruger's republic. The old emphasis on suffering and resurrection at God's hand seemed somehow inadequate to contain the new militant *volksbeweging* ideology. Whereas the party continued to emphasize the theme of suffering—"Our newly formed *volkseenheid* must be confirmed upon the Way of South Africa, upon which way stands Slagtersnek, Blood River and the Second War of Freedom, upon which way many tears have flowed. . . ." (Strydom, quoted in *Die Transvaler*,

September 18, 1939)—the O.B., under the leadership of van Rensburg, began to retell the whole of the sacred saga as a series of heroic uprisings against British rule. Slagtersnek as well as the Great Trek were both interpreted as acts of rebellion rather than as acts of redemptive suffering. The central episode in the People's history became, for the O.B., the crowning glory of Majuba. When the triumph at Majuba was negated by the forces of imperialist capitalism, the Boer People had no option but to rise up once more and struggle against the gigantic foe. The exploits of the Boer guerillas were exalted far above the afflictions of women and children in the concentration camps. The O.B. was born as direct heir to General de Wet's rebellious forces during the First World War. But the greatest hero of all was Jopie Fourie, not because he suffered as a misguided innocent, but because his Afrikaner heroism justified the lawlessness of his actions. The example of Jopie Fourie was applauded in a speech in December 1942 at his grave by Professor Cronje.

> We have come to declare that we as Afrikaners would remain true to the ideal for which Jopie Fourie struggled and died, namely the freedom and self-determination of the Boer nation. That ideal is not only our goal but also our measure. All which will further the realization of our freedom-ideal is right and good; everything which stands in the way of the realization of that ideal is wrong and bad. So judged Jopie Fourie. So do we judge. [*Die Vaderland*, December 23, 1942]

The great ritual days for the O.B. were the anniversaries of Paardekraal and, above all, Majuba—rather than Blaauwkrantz and Blood River.[12] Indeed, the O.B. purchased the farm encompassing Mount Majuba and, thereafter, at that site celebrated February 28 as the holiest day.

As one might expect, the disappointment in Broederbond circles over the split between the O.B. and the National party was sad and bitter. Van Rooy prevailed upon Totius to make a further declaration calling for *volkseenheid* (*Die Volksblad*,

---

[12] See *Die Vaderland* (February 28, 1942) *Die O.B.* (March 4 and March 11, 1942; January 20, 1943; February 2, 1944; December 10, 1944) and *Die O.B. Byvoegsel* (Supplement February 18, March 3, and March 31, 1948. See also the review of *Sonder Gewere* in *Die O.B.* (September 25, 1946).

September 16, 1941); du Plessis begged, albeit unsuccessfully, for a *volkskongres* (*Die Burger*, September 20 and September 22, 1941); and van Rooy was ultimately willing to lend advice to a new grassroots *volkseenheid* movement which, however, never really got off the ground (*Die Vaderland*, March 26 and April 20, 1942; *Die Volksblad*, April 29, 1941). Both the R.D.B. and the F.A.K. withdrew from du Plessis' *Eenheidskomitee*, and the ideal of a Christian National republic established upon Afrikaner *volkseenheid* foundered once again upon the rocks of Afrikaner division (*Die Volksblad*, January 31, 1942).

The final report of du Plessis as chairman of the *Eenheidskomitee* (*Die Vaderland*, October 8, 1941) had definitely favored the O.B. against the party; and in the winter of 1942, he himself followed H. G. Stoker and several leading neo-Fichteans, including Cronje and Meyer, into the O.B. He lamented that Afrikanerdom had not yet been able to achieve a viable united front in the form of a fully ethnic party:

> The party consistently refuses to enlarge itself to ethnic leadership, which can happen only through the organic incorporation of many faceted non-parliamentary forces as well as of *all* republican parliamentary forces. . . . [*Koers*, August 1941]

The only hope lay not in the party machine but in the promise of the O.B.

> Now the O.B. begins to show signs that it is prepared to build itself out to be the political *volksbeweging* of Afrikanerdom. What has hindered it thus far was above all . . . the determined opposition from the side of the party. . . . If the party continues in its attitude, then the inevitable conclusion will be that either its leadership or its very constitution [*wese*] is so narrow that the first requirement of the *volksbeweging* will be the total destruction of the party system which divides the People. [*Koers*, August 1942; cf. also *Die Vaderland*, August 22, 1942]

Du Plessis' decision to join the O.B., where he at once became head of the policy council, did not imply his uncritical acceptance of National Socialism. He joined because he believed that the O.B. was moving on the crest of the wave of the future—the revolution of the twentieth century—and he wished to assure Calvinist influence in the coming revolution.

By February 1941, du Plessis had completed a study entitled *Die Moderne Stat* (1941), a masterful account of the development of Western political thought. It was this analysis which provided the basis for his predictions about future trends. Western civilization, he concluded, was moving toward "nomocratic democracy," which he defined as follows:

> While the medieval Christian state was essentially nomocratic, that is, incorporated in natural law [*regsgebonde*], I believe the modern state to be basically democratic, that is, representative and national. But modern democracy has been falsified by liberalism to depravity and impotence because it has diluted and mechanized the Christian state's foundation from organic law to free coluntary contract. [Du Plessis, L. J., 1942]

The nomocratic tendency, however, has surfaced once more to impose but a one-sided, sectional unity. From this originates the tyranny of Bolshevism or Nazism, instead of law established in the "full [multiple] divinely limited reality."

> Calvinism, which is determinative for our ethnic existence, can and will bring the necessary correction in our case by eliminating all despotism and tyranny in principle, because it has a concept of natural and positive law [*wets - en regsbegrip*] which is supra-arbitrary and liberating and all-inclusive because it is anchored in God and the fullness of creation itself. Indeed, only Calvinism acknowledges the scripturally revealed law of God as universally determinative of all reality and of every aspect of human life and also acknowledges a divine economy [*wetmatigheid*] which is revealed in nature and history and is necessarily determined by the destiny and nature of every sphere of human association. [Du Plessis, L. J., 1942]

By defining Calvinism as normatively imposed order,[13] du Plessis was thus able to argue a position which came very close to the National Socialism of the O.B. Hence, too, the irony of du Plessis' Calvinist authorship of such articles as "Revolution, National Socialism and Calvinism" (*Wapenskou*, June 1943) and "The Present Origins of the *Volksbeweging*" (*Wapenskou*, September 1942).

The virtue of du Plessis' decision to join the O.B. was enhanced by support from the philosopher H. G. Stoker, who

[13] For complementary discussions of Calvinism from this point of view, see Walzer (1965, chapter two) and Little (1969, chapter three).

universalized du Plessis' political ideas by articulating a distinction between "Calvinist statics" and "Calvinist dynamics," along lines very similar to Diederichs' neo-Fichteanism. "Calvinism (with regard to its basic principles)," he said, "is not only a firm *weltanschauung*, but it is also (with regard to its development) a world movement" (*Koers*, December 1942). Moreover, Calvinism always takes root in a unique, national, spatial, and temporal form. Stoker proceeded to compare Dutch and Afrikaner Calvinism. Whereas Dutch Calvinists found their strength by establishing separate Calvinist (he meant Kuyperian) institutions—schools, press, party, voluntary associations, economic organizations, and so on—Afrikaner Calvinists (Kuyperians) had found strength

> not in detachment but in cooperation with others who were Christian in a broader sense and wished to be National in a particular sense. This cooperation was realized amongst the F.A.K., the R.D.B., the Broederbond, the O.B., the A.N.S., the Youth movement, the Voortrekker movement, the Handhawersbond, the Federation of Women, the Racial institute, the Education institute....and so on. [*Koers*, December 1942]

The Calvinist Union and the Federation of Calvinist Student Unions were not "antithetical to the other ethnic organizations" but stood separate "with an eye to pure leadership in principles and propagation of principle...."

> The Afrikaner Calvinist can only seek and find power in cooperation with other Christian ethnic fellows because our existence as a People was threatened in various ways by imperialists, Jews, coloureds, natives, Indians, Afrikaner renegades and so on.... This was further necessary because only a small section of our People was deliberately and purposively Calvinist, whereas the largest section of our People in all its organizations and outside, was only intuitively and inadvertently Calvinist ... and purposeful Calvinists could not make contact with inadvertent Calvinists without cooperation. [*Koers*, December 1942]

Stoker justified his involvement in the O.B. *volksbeweging* not only through the pragmatic need for cooperation of all Christian National Afrikaners in their common struggle. He offered full metaphysical justification, as well, for choosing the O.B. over the party. Three basic metaphysical truths undergirded Calvinism, he argued. First, that God was abso-

lute sovereign: second, that God willed the diversity of
creation; and, third, that God determined the interdependence of this diversity. The first two of these truths had been
emphasized by Dutch Calvinism because of the historical
situation in Holland. In Afrikaner South Africa, however,
"God has, through the history of our People, bound us by
directing our attention to the third of these basic principles,
the interdependence of diversity." This verity is demonstrated
in the principles of segregation and guardianship which exist
between the races, as well as by the ethnic organizations
through which Afrikaners have grappled with the problems
of interdependence between "People and State, People and
culture, People and language, People and the woman, People
and race, People and education, People and science, and so
on" (*Koers*, December 1942).

With the same logic, Stoker discussed the philosophical
reasons behind the schism between the O.B. and the party.
At the root of their division lay the propensity of the H.N.P.
to be controlled by its liberal structure. Instead of being
guided by the spirit of its principles, the H.N.P. was compelled
by its constitutional structure to view other fellow republicans as competitors. Because the H.N.P. was not broad-mind-
ed enough to acknowledge that the state of the future would
have no party system, quarreling erupted within the People—
regardless of who emerged as leaders of the respective organizations. Such differences led to estrangement between the
H.N.P. and the O.B., the Afrikaner party and the New Order,
and defeated any chance of *volkseenheid* in principle as well
as in practice. Although Stoker was not unaware of the
shortcomings of the O.B., he believed that "since the O.B.
properly starts from the principle of cooperation between all
republicans and not from the liberal doctrine of separation
of terrains . . . the O.B. offers better opportunity to the
Calvinist to work out the principle of interdependence more
fundamentally than in the H.N.P." (*Koers*, December 1942,
p. 981; cf. du Plessis in *Koers*, June 1944; cf. also Stoker's
speech in *Die Vaderland*, November 19, 1941).

There were, however, other Kuyperian Calvinists, notably
Professor Stephanus du Toit of Potchefstroom and Ds. P.

J. S. de Klerk[14] who argued for the party on precisely the grounds that Stoker himself had used against Diederichs in 1935. The "revolution of the twentieth century" elevated the community or the proletariat or the People to the status of idols. The new order, said du Toit, emphasizes not only worthy aspects, such as "social righteousness, racial purity and the meaning of family, but also the propulsion of blood and blind passions, the religion of blood and race, *Wille zur Macht* militarism" (*Koers*, August 1944). Logic does not lead, rather "the instincts control." He agreed that "Calvinism ought always to be dynamic as well as static, in other words, always relevant," but Calvinism "also carries immutable and eternal principles, and in our time we have more need of the latter than the preaching of the demands of the times" (*Koers*, August 1944). Stoker and du Plessis would have echoed du Toit's call to stand on "immutable and eternal principles," but the question was whether one attempted to purify the revolutionary movement in line with his Kuyperian objectives or condemned the "new order" outright and sought to implement his higher calling outside the profaned tilth. Stoker and du Plessis set out to serve as a Calvinist yeast within the new *volksbeweging*, whereas du Toit saw that movement in a demonic light. "If we speak of reformation," he said, "it must be clearly understood that the work of Satan is not subject to reform" (*Koers*, August 1944). The objections of de Klerk were more orthodox. The idea of the *volksbeweging*, he said, led to weakening of the boundaries which separated the inviolable sovereign spheres of Kuyper's theology (*Koers*, October 1942). In other words, Stoker's talk of "interdependence" was rank heresy.

Fortunately, there is no need for us to further debate these positions. Du Toit even today believes in the rightfulness of his attack on the movement. Stoker continues to insist that the O.B. was not National Socialist in essence, although he readily admits that certain members were undoubtedly Nazi. Indeed, many of the articles in *Die O.B.* were distinctly

[14] For du Toit, see *Koers* (August 1942 and August 1944), and for de Klerk, see *Koers* (October 1942) and *Die Volksblad* (February 12, 1944).

National Socialist in tone, especially the *Dienslaerstukke* column. Piet Meyer, by this time propaganda chief of the O.B., was directly responsible for this column. Since the beginning of the war, Meyer's neo-Fichteanism had rapidly moved toward Afrikaner National Socialism, shifting from his earlier idealism to speak of an organic basis of unity for the Afrikaner People which was now seen to be rooted in race and family.[15] At the same time, he incorporated certain Kuyperian notions which stood rather at odds to the National Socialism of his system as a whole. Kuyper's idea of sovereignty in each sphere, for example, became for Meyer totalitarianism in each sphere.

> The totalitarianism of the *volksbeweging*, which is subordinate to the Word of God, means on the one hand the struggle toward an organic community on the part of the estates of the People [*volksstande*] which are integrated into the *volksbeweging*, and on the other hand it means the independent existence alongside the People of other organic human entities like the individual, the family and the church. [Meyer, 1942b, p. 12]

Despite the total commitment which each of the spheres demanded, Meyer seemed to envisage no divided loyalties. Complete immersion in the cause of the People would alone realize the highest potential of each individual in every sphere.

The first duty of the *volk*, and thus of the

> *volksbeweging*, is to save and sustain the members of the People for that People to form and direct them into a national and social unity on the basis of existing organic ties in order to create the necessary pre-conditions and possibilities for each member to achieve his highest individual development within the ethnic bonds and in service to the ethnic whole, and in this way to further the fulfillment of the divinely imposed calling of the individual. [Meyer, 1942b, p. 13]

Only if the organic unit broke down would resistence to the "leadership principle" be justified (Meyer, 1942b, p. 23).

In fact, family and work soon became for Meyer the only two relevant spheres, directly subordinate to the organic ethnic unity.

---

[15] Meyer's views during the war years were set forth in a series of pamphlets, the most important being Meyer (1942a, 1942b, 1943) and *Die Stryd van die Afrikanerwerker* (n.d.), as well as the column *Dienslaerstukke* which appeared each week in *Die O.B.*

> Within the organic life of the People may be distinguished two core associations [*Kernverbande*], namely, the family, which is linked to a house, and the work-circle [*arbeidskring*] which is linked to a work-place. . . .
>
> The People as family-unity is an organic unity of blood, language, culture, genesis, tradition, and destiny, a unity of inner spiritual community, the bearer of its own political regulation of authority and organization.
>
> The People as work-unity is a creative and productive unity of work-force (spiritual, psychic and physical), which is the bearer of the welfare and spiritual-material regulation of interests of the ethnic life as a whole. [*Meyer*, 1943, p. 7]

The sphere of the family was the organic root of nationalism; the work-circle was the basis of socialism. Insofar as both spheres could be integrated into the organic unity of the People, the *volksbeweging* was National Socialist in organization and essence. This distinction between family and work-circle corresponded in some measure to his earlier differentiation between the cultural and economic spheres within which he expected the F.A.K. to operate, and Meyer's abortive plans for the reorganization of the F.A.K., were transferred almost wholesale to the new *volksbeweging*. However, the new system remained organic rather than idealist in expression.

After the 1943 elections, when it became increasingly clear that Hitler was losing the war, van Rensburg was particularly receptive to Meyer's dreams for the People. Although he continued to preach fire and brimstone and to support the unconstitutional exercises of the Stormjaers, van Rensburg seemed to realize that these exploits would produce little real political effect. He not only began to toy with the idea of a parliamentary front for the O.B., but also to adopt Meyer's suggestion that the O.B. involve itself in action on the economic front. In November 1943, he came forth with a new venture for the O.B., a Labor Front to work under the leadership of Piet Meyer. The new organization, according to van Rensburg, was intended to cement urban and platteland Afrikaners, through the O.B., into an effective bastion against communism and other insidious foes.[16]

---

[16] See the Kommandant General's Annual Report for 1944 in the O.B. archives. See also *Wapenskou* (September 1944), which

The *purpose* of this Front is to bind the urban white worker—the conclusive power factor in the future—and his rural compatriot closer together by means of the *Volksbeweging* in order by so doing to oppose influences like communism which are dividing the People and at the same time to increase the striking power of the O.B. The *method* is, together with ideological cultivation of the workers, to win the trust and devotion of the worker by offering him O.B. support without asking him to leave or weaken his trade-unions or other organizations. [O.B. Kommandant General's Annual Report, 1944]

A year later, Meyer issued an O.B. pamphlet, *Die Stryd van die Afrikanerwerker* ("The Struggle of the Afrikaner Worker"), in which he deplored the lack of cooperation between nationalist forces, which opposed imperialism, and socialist elements which had opposed capitalism (Meyer, n.d.). So lucid and objective was this account of labor struggles in South Africa that the pamphlet was hailed by *The Guardian*, the Communist Party newspaper, and roundly condemned by Eric Louw as evidence of a Communist leaning in the O.B. (*Die Vaderland*, November 17, 1944). Meyer's account was, however, biased in favor of Afrikaner ideals (especially racism) and forms of organization (particularly the commando system) for labor. He concluded his tract by calling for a form of Afrikaner socialism from which all traces of internationalism would be removed and which would stand firmly on the pillars of white racism and the O.B. commando organization.

In the course of his treatise, Meyer spoke favorably of Albert Hertzog's *Raad van Trustees*, but his assumption was that Hertzog had failed (Meyer, n.d., p. 83). Although we possess insufficient evidence to accurately assess the respective roles of Albert Hertzog's Raad van Trustees Reform Organization and Piet Meyer's O.B. Labor Front in the Afrikaner mine workers' movement, it is most likely that their efforts were largely complementary, with considerable overlap.[17] This

is entirely devoted to the Labor Front. *Wapenskou*, the journal of the A.N.S., was by this time virtually the theoretical journal of the entire O.B.

[17] It is indeed possible that Hertzog's Reform Organization was moribund until interfused with Piet Meyer's O.B. Labor Front. A

conjecture is supported by an entry in N. G. S. van der Walt's diary for August 20, 1946, where he states that van Rensburg had informed him that in the mine workers' elections then in progress, "fourteen of the twenty-one mine worker representatives so far elected were O.B.s, . . . the leadership stems from an O.B., one Nel, . . [and if] the other eleven who have to be chosen are from the Reform group, that will mean a Reformers majority with an O.B. majority among them."

Outside the Labor Front, there was no sphere of Afrikaner life, however sacred, which was not rent by the ideological and institutional struggles of the war years. Nonetheless, forces were at work which would rally Afrikanerdom behind a decisive party offensive.

---

third group, under the leadership of Verwoerd, was apparently also active among the mine workers (van der Walt, N. G. S., diary, February 20, 1946).

12

1948: The Civil Religion and Political Victory

Ever since the Ossewatrek and Monumentkoppie, there had been genuine renewed interest in the sacred history among ordinary Afrikaners. School annual magazines, which had theretofore largely ignored the richness of such essay material as the Great Trek, the Boer War, and the like, suddenly burgeoned with civil-religion themes. Not only were school journals and newspaper letters to the editor inspired by revelations of the civil faith, but local dominees writing in their parish magazines came out in strong support of the R.D.B.[1]

Neither were protests against the war and declarations for the republic uncommon or without sizable popular backing during 1940 and early 1941. Voluntary associations proliferated on the local level and witnessed zealous activity. During May 1941 for instance, just prior to the great *Volkseenheid* congress of the H.N.P., *Die Burger* alone reported some twenty-three local party gatherings, eleven local gatherings of the R.D.B., fourteen meetings of cultural societies, twelve O.B. meetings, and two local gatherings of the junior branch of the party. The welter of Afrikaner sentiment on the local level was certainly concommitant with the spring tide of Afrikaner national unity on the leadership level. Afrikaner voters who had followed Hertzog out of the United party

[1] See, for instance, the congregational magazines for Zeerust (January, April, and July 1940) and Dordrecht (October 1939).

seemed now happily at home in Malan's new H.N.P. Neither the H.N.P.'s censure of Hertzog's parliamentary colleagues nor the establishment of the Afrikaner party harmed the H.N.P.'s grassroots appeal.[2] No doubt acceptance of Malan's leadership was facilitated by the *Volkseenheid* congress of the H.N.P. in May 1941, when Malan was dubbed *volksleier* with full backing from L. J. du Plessis' Broederbond committee, the O.B., the R.D.B., and three very prominent Dutch Reformed churchmen. The civil-religion fervor generated at Monumentkoppie seemed about to be realized in the H.N.P. as a great *volksorganisasie*.

If an election had been held in May 1941, Smuts' United party would have been hard pressed to beat the H.N.P.[3] When an election came two years later, however, the H.N.P. was trounced by Smuts' pro-war coalition (the United party, the Labour party and the Dominion party).[4] What had happened to the united Afrikaner opposition to the war? First, of course, by 1943, it was becoming clear that the Allies were on the road to victory. Opposition to Smuts' war was less effective when it seemed that South Africa was on the winning side and the enemy included not only the Germans, but also the yellow-skinned Japanese. As important as the course of the war, however, was the shock that had been dealt Afrikanerdom by the struggle between the National party and the O.B. Unlike the breakaway of the Afrikaner party under Havenga and of ex-Hertzogite M.P.s in Pirow's New Order, the party schism with the O.B. made a deep mark on local support. The party campaign against the O.B. set off reverberations which reached farther and deeper even than the tensions generated by *samesmelting* in 1934. Local National party branches, except for those in the western Free State,

[2] Most Hertzogite members of parliament followed Pirow into the New Order.

[3] Careful but firm support for this conclusion is to be found in Newell Stultz' recent work (Stultz, 1974).

[4] The United party won 89 seats in 1943, the National party won 43, Labor won 9, and the Dominion party won 7: and there were two pro-war Independents, making a total of 107 parliamentary votes for the war and 43 which Malan could muster against it. In 1939, the vote on war was 80 for and 57 against. Smuts' majority in parliament had thus rocketed from 13 in 1939 to 66 in 1943.

tended in 1934 to decide one way or the other on the basis of geographical area or personal loyalties. Increased ideological mobilization of Afrikaners after the civil-religion events of 1938 and 1939, however, meant that party-O.B. differences would be felt right down to the grassroots. The Wellington H.N.P. local secretary summed up the small-town story throughout South Africa:

> During the past nine or ten years our party seems to have been going through a sort of fiery furnace. The first shock was the coalition of 1933, but for our branch this was not such a terrible shock, because we lost only a few members at that time. Now, however, during the past year, we have again experienced a setback, namely the problems with the O.B. From the point of view of our branch this was surely the most serious trouble with which we have ever had to cope since our establishment; we may almost say that it truly shook our branch to its foundations. [Annual report, Minutes of National party local branch, Wellington, June 1942]

The major thrust of the H.N.P. attack in 1943 was aimed at the O.B., the New Order, and the Afrikaner party as "wreckers of Afrikanerdom," rather than at Smuts—which could hardly have helped garner ex-Hertzogite or *volkseenheid* votes. Stultz (1974) provides figures which suggest that "only one out of four Afrikaners who had voted for the United party voted against Smuts in 1943" (Stultz, 1974). Not all the others voted for the Smuts' war coalition, however; abstentions were notably higher in 1943 than in either 1938 or 1948. Van Rensburg had urged O.B.s to vote only for candidates who were pro-republican and did not openly attack the O.B. Many Afrikaners seem to have followed his advice, especially in the Transvaal.

However, although Nationalist leaders and press repeatedly and consistently refused to cooperate with the O.B., evidence suggests that local branches showed more forbearance. Wellington, for example, noted with pride that

> though we regret it, and will receive with open arms again those who left the party, nevertheless we rejoice that here locally there has developed no bitterness. From the side of the party we have tried to give no offence to those who think differently; the branch executive as well as all members have

not tried to persuade O.B. members to resign. Rather we took
the line that each individual must decide for himself which
way he will take.[5] [Annual report, Minutes of National party
local branch, Wellington, June 1942]

Despite the wrangle with the O.B., Erasmus' old Gesuiwerde
party machine in the Cape survived relatively intact.[6] Free
State support for the H.N.P. in 1943 suggests that there, too,
the party ably weathered the storm. In the Transvaal, on
the other hand, the H.N.P. had to start essentially from
scratch after 1943. Here the party would have to make a
stronger appeal to urban voters on the Rand. Most important,
if the Allies won the war, the "British-Jewish parliamentary
system" could not simply be disregarded—even van Rensburg
realized that—and the H.N.P. was now the sole remaining
viable organization to represent Afrikaner *volkseenheid* on
the political front. The problem was less one of converting
convinced Smuts men to Afrikaner nationalism than of
mobilizing disillusioned Afrikaners who had not voted in
1943.[7]

Political laymen tend to emphasize the importance of
bread-and-butter issues and of electoral manifestos as the
decisive factors in influencing election results. While not
denying the validity of these elements, they can apply only
when the balance of convinced party members is sufficiently

[5] The local O.B., he said, had not been quite so open-minded.

[6] The Leliedal local branch, for example, seemed to speak not
only for the H.N.P. but also for the O.B. On October 17, 1941,
it decided not to hold an O.B. meeting about the H.N.P. attack
on the organizaion and took a vote of fullest confidence in National
party principles and in Dr. Malan. However, it then proceeded as
an O.B. meeting, and decided to write to O.B. headquarters demanding that van Rensburg and the Grand Council resign immediately!

[7] A measure of the attempt to mobilize Afrikaner votes after
1943 can be seen in political activity on the municipal level. In
both Bloemfontein and Pretoria, Afrikaners organized to dominate
elections to the municipal government. In March 1944, the first
four Afrikaners were elected to the Bloemfontein city council (*Die
Volksblad*, March 24, 1944). C. T. M. Wilcocks, the candidate who
received most votes, "in the first instance expressed his thanks to
the Higher Hand for His help in freeing the Afrikanerdom of
Bloemfontein from the servitude of so many years" (for further

equal for the marginal or floating voter to become crucial. In the South African elections of 1938 and 1943, there was clearly no such balance. For the H.N.P. to obtain victory in 1948, it had first to achieve a breadth of support which would render it a viable alternative to the Smuts regime. It would have to ensure its identity as *the* party of Afrikaner *volkseenheid*, and then, having laid a firm foundation, mount an election campaign sufficiently compelling to swing the uncommitted vote to its cause.[8]

The first steps toward *volkseenheid* in support of the party were made by softening the party's extremist image. Several tacks were employed. Most important, the republican issue was played down,[9] and in 1947, the party entered a coalition with Havenga's Afrikaner party. In addition the H.N.P. focused on three pressing issues on which the Dutch Reformed churches and the Broederbond with its affiliated organizations seemed to be fully agreed—mother-tongue education, the communist peril, and, inevitably, apartheid.[10] Each of these three issues was interpreted in the light of Christian National ideology.

---

developments in Bloemfontein see *Die Volksblad*, May 24, 1946). In Pretoria, in face of bitter opposition from *Die Volkstem* (February 2, October 24, and October 27, 1944), the Afrikaner group, under leadership of that expert underground organizer, Albert Hertzog, managed to achieve a majority on the city council in October 1944, (*Die Transvaler*, February 26, and October 27, 1944; *Die Vaderland*, October 20 and October 26, 1944).

[8] Stultz (1974) provides a far more sophisticated analysis of these South African elections, making fine distinctions which are unnecessary for my purposes here, but which ultimately support my argument on this point.

[9] See, for example, the articles by E. G. Jansen in *Die Burger* (January 5 and January 6, 1944), and editorial comment on these by the major Afrikaans newspapers.

[10] Having arrived at this conclusion after a close perusal of pre-election Afrikaner sources, I was interested to discover that the issues which I select for mention are precisely those which were emphasized in a post-1948 election exhortation in the F.A.K. journal, *Inspan* (June 1948). This editorial expresses the hope that the new government will take immediate action on three crucial issues, *viz.*, the principle of mother-tongue education, communism, and the color question.

Mother-Tongue Education

We have seen that one of the most important wellheads of the Afrikaner civil faith was the fight for official recognition of Afrikaans and for its equality with English in everyday life. The struggle for Afrikaans united republicans and non-republicans, Cape Afrikaners and Transvaalers, liberals and neo-Fichteans. Whenever republicanism became impolitic, Afrikaners fell back upon their language as the most important foundation for *volkseenheid*. It is hence not surprising that the Broederbond, licking its wounds after the party-O.B. split, seized upon the language issue in order to salvage whatever *volkseenheid* still remained in Afrikanerdom. This time the language issue was centered less upon the use of Afrikaans in public life and more upon education. This was partly the result of political exigency, but also because "language" was now perceived as one of the taproots of the separate ethnic consciousness of Afrikaner culture. The writer D. F. Malherbe was hence able to speak of the word as living creative power of the national soul:

> Language is more than a means of expressing thoughts, feelings and evaluations, language is potentially creative power. . . . The basis of all education in and through the mother-tongue is hidden in the growth of the child's soul, the strengthening of his potential to think, and to think with feeling, along with controlled use of the word as he learns to know it in the natural sphere of home and environment, the word rooted in the nature of conceptual and emotional associations. . . .
>
> Thus the conscious mastering of the mother-tongue at school is an extension of natural activity, a broadening from day to day of the soul experience of the child, an entrance into the fuller experience of his human nature. . . . Thus mother-tongue education is the only way to a healthy development, that is a development which answers to the God-given law of the life of the soul. Whoever meddles with this law, whether parent, or teacher, or state, transgresses against the holiness of human nature and thereby against the ordinance of God. [*Koers in die Krisis*, III: 243-245]

Once the divine, inalienable right of mother-tongue education was recognized, education in single-medium Afrikaans schools rapidly came to mean more than purely pedagogical expedience. Mother-tongue education was above all the guarantee of Afrikanerdom, and Afrikaans schools held its future life in trust.

> If we Afrikaners are insistent upon being acknowledged as a nation, it is necessary to stress that the school must carry over the culture of the nation, *pure*, from one generation to the next. Political and cultural circumstances here make it necessary that cultural transference, which goes its way unhindered amongst the great nations, must be postulated as a goal of the education of the Afrikaner nation. [Nel, n.d., p. 13; cf. Steyn, n.d.]

"Cultural transference" necessarily placed heavy stress on the sacred history. Next to the Afrikaans language and literature, history carried the key to the Afrikaner heritage. Such history could not be taught in a mixed-language school:

> If a People would continue to exist as a People, it must know and honor earlier generations. We must preserve historical continuity. Pry us loose as a People from our past, from our history in which we see God's guiding hand, and we are lost.

> Can we honor our forefathers if we do not know their history? Is consciously national history today taught in our schools? May I as a teacher tell the children of the years of struggle against the British empire? May I tell them of the suppression of our language and cultural rights in the Cape Province despite all the cheap English promises . . .; of the liberal kaffir-politics and all the murders on the eastern frontier, where the Afrikaner was denied the right to defend his life and possessions; may I tell of the implications of Slagtersnek; of the hypocritical pursuit of a group of Boer families fleeing into the interior although they persecuted no innocent kaffir tribes; may I tell of the imperialism which wished to paint the map of South Africa red, and indeed did so, but red with the blood of innocent Afrikaners; of the greedy snatch at the gold and diamonds of the republics; of the low deeds of aggression practiced against us; of the base war waged not against the soldiers in the field, not against Christiaan de Wet and his comrades, but against women and children in the concentration camps; may I tell of the rebellion, of Jopie Fourie? . . . But enough. If I say these things it is politics, racial hatred, intolerance. . . .

> Our children may not be educated to be nationally conscious. But why not? No other free land in the world fails to use its schools for this purpose. . . . Our children sit in dual-medium schools which means that if you tell the one section its history,

you hurt the other. Thus we paper over the cracks neatly, else we are race haters. [L. du Toit in *Wapenskou*, June 1941]

The arguments for mother-tongue education in single-medium schools must thus to be understood against the assumptions of neo-Fichtean social metaphysics and the sacred history. What was at stake was not simply instruction in the mother-tongue, but also socialization into the Christian National ideology. The social nature of personal development was quite expectedly interpreted in ethnic terms:

> The person must interact with his environment, he must actively form and revise it according to his life's demands if he would exist and develop in a healthy manner. Thus education originates along with the development of a community; thus a person grows and changes along with the growth and changes of his community. *Thus genuine education is always in its deepest being national*, the utterance of the inner soul-force of the ethnic community from which it is born. [J. de W. Keyter in *Wapenskou*, September 1941]

The logical jump from "community" and "environment" to "nation" required no justification, for it is presupposed in the Christian National ideology. On this matter, then, all Broederbonders were agreed—any attack on separate Afrikaans schools was an attack on the Afrikaner civil faith. The two means by and through which God revealed himself to nations were language and history. Hence, to deprive a child of his ethnic language and history would not only constitute an injustice but wanton disobedience to the will of God.

> God gave but one language to the Afrikaans Christian parent in which his child could and should be educated, namely, his mother-tongue—the same language which is used in the churches and which must be used first and most in the school of the Afrikaans child as the exclusive medium of education. In education there are two subjects which . . . cannot be sufficiently emphasized, *language* and *history*; *language* because God used *human* language to reveal Himself in Holy Scripture and because a man can best honor and praise God and serve his fellow-man and himself by means of his language; and *history*—because God used and still uses human history to reveal His decisions with regard to mankind and His world and also because man serves and glorifies His God by means of his history. It was God Himself who made the national languages and groups and their history. Thus every effort to

estrange the child from his language and history is dishonoring God and an injustice to the child of the People. [Ds. H. C. J. Fleming in *Inspan*, October 1943]

Thus when in 1943, the United party sought to further bilingualism and South African civic unity by imposing dual-medium education upon exclusively single-language state schools, the F.A.K. convened a Volkskongres (*Die Burger*, December 15, 1943); and the N.G. church sent a deputation to confer with General Smuts on the subject (*Kerkbode*, September 8, 1943). Mother-tongue education was the principal platform of both parties in the 1943 provincial elections. Despite the abundant propaganda from the Nationalist press[11] and a much publicized pamphlet by E. G. Malherbe,[12] that sustained in an ostensibly objective argument the claim for bilingualism and dual-medium education, the election appeared to arouse little popular interest (*Die Transvaler*, November 4, 1943). In view of this apathetic response of lay members of both parties, the entire issue seemed a rather specious one. It did, however, provide a ground of consensus on which all members of the Broederbond—in fact the majority of Afrikaner intellectuals, whether from church, party, or cultural organizations—could come together. The F.A.K. Volkskongres was attended by representatives of National party branches as well as by churchmen and cultural organizers (*Die Transvaler*, November 11, 1943). So, although the bilingual school was a political non-issue from the point

[11] See the pamphlets of H. F. Verwoerd, *Red die Afrikaansmediumskole*, and of N. J. le Roux, *Enkel-of Dubbel-Mediumskool*, as well as numerous *Die Transvaler* editorials on the subject in 1943.

[12] Entitled *The Bilingual School*, this pamphlet was criticized by two Stellenbosch professors at a meeting in Cape Town reported in *Die Transvaler* (November 25, 1943). The pamphlet, which was based on analysis of 1938 survey data, reached an unsurprising conclusion which, however, horrified Malherbe. He found that students at single-medium schools tended to be in favor of educational separation, whereas those who attended dual-medium schools tended to favor bilingualism. Such conclusions were, of course, equally repugnant to Christian Nationalists, who were driven by these results only to greater efforts on behalf of single-medium education.

of view of vote-gathering, it marked the beginnings of renewed cooperation between party men and cultural leaders. The National party was gradually being restored to its vaunted position as *volksorganisasie.*

Early in 1944, the administration of Natal closed the lowest class in the Pietermaritzburg Afrikaans-medium school and stated that the children would be transferred to an English-medium school, where they would receive instruction in Afrikaans. As we have seen, this was at root more than a question of language: and a committee of Afrikaner parents, encouraged by two of the local Dutch Reformed ministers, refused to abide by the administrative dictum. Once more a deputation of churchmen and parents visited General Smuts (*Kerkbode*, February 9, 1944), and again the F.A.K. stepped in with support (*Inspan*, February 1944). The National party debated the matter at some length in parliament, which thus further improved its image as *volksorganisasie* (*Die Volkstem*, March 8, 1944; and *Die Transvaler*, March 13, 1944). When all their efforts proved unavailing, the F.A.K. and Afrikaans parents established a separate Christian National School in Pietermaritzburg and mounted a full-scale campaign for funds in anticipation that similar crises might arise elsewhere.

Surely enough, the provincial council of the Transvaal passed a plan gradually to introduce instruction in the second medium into English and Afrikaans schools. Despite an impassioned outcry from the F.A.K. (*Die Transvaler*, May 30, 1945), and a series of bitter editorials from Verwoerd (for example, "The Soul of the Child" and "Keep the Children for the People," *Die Transvaler*, August 14, 1945; January 16 and May 4, 1946), there seems to have been little other objection. On the contrary, *Die Vaderland* (January 16, 1945) said that it welcomed any measure which introduced Afrikaans instruction into English schools; and William Nicol, moderator of the Transvaal N.G., advised that the church take no action to establish separate schools (*Die Vaderland*, July 24, 1944). To the editor of Smuts' *Die Volkstem* (July 21, 1944), this recommendation by Nicol, a prominent Broer, smacked of inconsistency. Indeed, as moderator at the Transvaal N.G. synod the week before, Nicol had "advised young

244 The Rise of Afrikanerdom

Afrikaans-speakers not to marry English-speakers"[13] (*Die Burger*, July 17, 1944). Why then this apparent moderation on the introduction of certain English-medium classes into Afrikaans schools?

In fact, it was on the question of separate Christian National schools, rather than on the mother-tongue education issue, that Nicol disagreed with the official F.A.K. position. In the first place, he argued, the establishment of a plethora of Christian National schools was impractical and would not be supported by the People. Second, it seemed to him that the People should put political pressure on state schools, which served both sections of the white population, rather than attempt to establish untenable alternatives. Although there was general agreement in Broederbond circles on the "national" side of Christian National education, the "Christian" aspect raised contention between the *volkskerk* element, of whom Nicol was a prominent member, and the Kuyperians. The latter felt that the school should be self-supporting and under the sovereign sphere of the parents rather than the state. State interference in education, which disregarded the boundaries between spheres of sovereignty, was hence deplored (cf. *Koers*, October and December, 1936). The *volkskerk* element, on the other hand, pushed for the Christianization of the state schools as they stood. The issue of separate schools had for some time been a major source of conflict between the N.G. and the Gereformeerdes,[14] and it must have seemed to Nicol that such a Gereformeerde as van Rooy, in urging independent Christian National schools, was proselytizing for his denomination under the guise of mother-tongue education. Not only van Rooy's speeches at this time, but those of his cohorts as well, especially Dr. Eben

[13] When this statement caused an uproar in the English-speaking press, the synod supported its moderator unanimously. In fact, the first public use of the term "apartheid," by Ds. C. R. Kotze in Bloemfontein on December 15, 1941, referred to the necessity for separation between "the Boer People" and "the English," not between black and white. The progeny of "mixed marriages" between Afrikaners and Englishmen, opined the revered gentlemen, were "monstrosities" (*Die Volksblad*, December 16, 1941).

[14] A. K. Bot surveyed the dispute in *Koers* (August 1936).

Greyling and G. de Vos Hugo, lent credence to this suspicion (cf. *Die Burger*, May 19, 1944). Nonetheless, this disagreement between *volkskerk* and Kuyperian churchmen cut across earlier divisions between party and O.B., thus helping to restore the unity of action which the Broederbond so desperately desired.[15]

Apartheid

From the beginning of the eighteenth century, antedating the development of the civil religion by a hundred and fifty years, white racism has been a constant factor in Afrikaner history. At least since the establishment of the first Boer Republic in Natal in 1839, this white racism has been expressed in terms of an ideal of segregation and a reality of white domination and black labor. The dichotomy between ideal and reality was mirrored in the very Biblical imagery used by the frontier farmers. On the one hand, the black South African was a Canaanite and thus subject to the ban; on the other hand, he was a son of Ham and so destined to be a hewer of wood and drawer of water for his white compatriot.

Despite this ambiguity, the main point was clear—there was to be no equality between black and white in any area where the Afrikaner had his say. Nor should we make the error of assuming that the English-speaking white South African was particularly liberal by comparison. The Natal representatives at the South African convention before Union were in fact more discriminatory than the Cape Afrikaners. Indeed, the policy of separate development was first fully worked out among English-speaking South Africans in Natal, David Welsh (1971) argues. Smuts proposed a policy of segregation at Oxford in 1929. General Hertzog's segregatory solution to the "native problem" won support in 1936 of all but eleven members of the South African parliament; of the eleven who rejected Hertzog's proposals, three—Hofmeyr, F. S. Malan, and R. J. du Toit—had Afrikaans names and the remainder were English-speaking. In terms of sheer racism,

[15] Both Gluckman (1963) and Coser (1956) make a convincing case for the unifying functions of cross-cutting social conflict.

Smuts' newspaper, *Die Volkstem*, differed little from *Die Vaderland* of Hertzog. For instance, it commiserated with the white South African boxer, Don McCorkindale, because he had to fight a Canadian black, one Larry Gaines, for the empire title: "There will be sympathy in the Union for McCorkindale," said the editorial, "because he appears to be conscious of the fact that he will have to hold high the name of the South African white man" (*Die Volkstem*, January 26, 1932). Although it is possible to discern a certain uneasiness in many English pronouncements on racial issues, the same could be said of those by Cape Afrikaners. The Cape N.G., for example, was able between 1824 and 1857 to counter several efforts on the part of frontier congregations to segregate white from non-white members. But in the latter year, the synod was finally driven to sacrifice what it deemed a Christian principle to "the weakness of some" (cf. Ritner, 1967). Despite such evidence of liberal qualms, white men's fears of black South Africans prevailed. Over and over in parliamentary debates on the "color question," white South Africans expressed fears of miscegenation, such as did N. J. van der Merwe in 1936:

> It is not a struggle to oppress the native, or to put our foot on the necks of the coloured people, but it is a struggle to maintain the existence of the white race in South Africa. It is felt that if there is once political equality, that things will not stop there. They will go further, and continue on economic and social lines. It is felt that you will ultimately have social equality, which in the long run it will not be possible to stop, and if you have social equality, you subsequently get mixing of the blood, and the ruin of the white race [Tatz, 1962, p. 76]

This sexual component of white anxiety was easily expressed in civil-religion terms through the theme of the Afrikaner woman. Indeed, one of the major Nationalist weapons in the 1938 election was the argument that widespread miscegenation would inevitably result from the United party policy of allowing mixed marriages. *Die Transvaler* produced a poster depicting the pure Voortrekker woman and below her a mixed couple. Hertzog's lieutenant, Pirow, however scotched that imputation with consummate skill by condemning the poster as an insult to the moral purity of the Afrikaner woman. Nonetheless, Nationalist policy exploited the libidinal well of racial prejudice at every possible juncture.

Miscegenation and the Afrikaner woman aside, there were grounds in the civil theology itself for arguing the simple supremacy of white Afrikaners in South Africa. The covenant at Blood River was, after all, a proof that God favored white civilization, or at least white Afrikaners; and the Day of the Covenant, with such symbolic connotations, became a favorite venue for important statements on "native policy" by such men as General Hertzog and E. G. Jansen, who eventually was Malan's first minister of native affairs. Generally however, Geloftedag speeches did not argue white superiority—they assumed it. When speakers referred to "the black threat," it was usually to blame British imperialism for thwarting Afrikaner segregation policies rather than to express fear of black domination per se.

When Dr. Malan explicitly invoked fear of black domination at Blood River in 1938, he did not talk of development for black men along black lines. Rather he described the predicament of urban Afrikaners as a second Blood River. Furthermore, Malan stressed the desperation of the city migrants precisely because he believed they *could* be helped. This speech was significant, too, in that Malan introduced into the rhetoric of the civil religion an assumption which had underlain Nationalist policy since 1915. He explicitly conceded that white domination was based on white privilege rather than on innate superiority. For the first time, it was publicly admitted that given equal opportunities, black men could compete successfully with whites. At the same time as he acknowledged this, however, Malan also stressed that such equality of opportunity should not be allowed. A separate Afrikaner nation had a right to existence because "the fortunes of the Afrikaner People are not in the hands of men or of other Peoples but in the hands of God." Was there not a contradiction, then, in even mentioning the black threat? No—for God's elect were never exempt from suffering, but were preserved in spite of it. As Malan said on a later occasion:

It is through the will of God that the Afrikaner People exists at all. In his wisdom he determined that on the southern point of Africa, the dark continent, a People should be born who would be the bearer of Christian culture and civilization. In his wisdom He surrounded this People by great dangers. He set the People down upon unfruitful soil so that they had to toil and sweat to exist upon the soil. From time to time he visited them with droughts and other plagues.

But this was only one of the problems. God also willed that the Afrikaans People should be continually threatened by other Peoples. There was the ferocious barbarian who resisted the intruding Christian civilization and caused the Afrikaner's blood to flow in streams. There were times when as a result of this the Afrikaner was deeply despairing, but God at the same time prevented the swamping of the young Afrikaner People in the sea of barbarianism. [*Die Transvaler*, December 16, 1942]

The preservation of "white civilization" was thus associated with the continued existence of the Afrikaner People. This equation of the Afrikaner *volk* with white Christian civilization in South Africa was firmly entrenched in the civil faith during the 1940s, and not a Geloftedag went by without its mention. Emphasis fell not on the content of "white civilization," but rather on the perpetuation of Afrikanerdom.

The published conclusions of the 1944 F.A.K. Volkskongres on Afrikaner racial policy justified apartheid on the grounds of centuries of Afrikaner experience, scientific proof, and Biblical witness (*Inspan*, October 1944). Professor Cronje adduced scientific evidence before the congress which demonstrated irrefutably, he believed, that miscegenation led to racial decline (*Die Volksblad*, September 30, 1944). Totius addressed the meeting on the religious bases of apartheid. Because racial differences are grounded in the ordinances of creation, argued Totius, racial integration is not only foolish, it is sinful. Apartheid is thus justified, because God calls the Afrikaner to implement it for the well-being of black and white alike. Racial separation is thus not only a Boer tradition, it represents the Divine Will.

I have deliberately emphasized the negative aspects of Nationalist racial policy here because they surely constituted the major source of its popular appeal. Any discussion of apartheid in relation to election results must necessarily emphasize "the preservation of the white race." The remark of the Legum's white liftman after Malan's victory in 1948, "From now on a kaffir is a kaffir again," reflected a typical ordinary Afrikaner's conception of apartheid (Legum and Legum, 1964). In this sense, perhaps J. G. Strydom was the politician who spoke most directly to Afrikaner grassroots. He appealed to color consciousness, apartheid and white domination:

> If the European [white] loses his color sense, he cannot remain a White man. . . . On the basis of unity you cannot retain your sense of color if there is no *apartheid* in the everyday social life, in the political sphere or whatever sphere it may be, and if there is no residential separation. . . . South Africa can only remain a white country if we continue to see that the Europeans remain the dominant nation; and we can only remain the dominant nation if we have the power to govern the country and if the Europeans, by means of their efforts, remain the dominant section. [Tatz, 1962, p. 133]

Hancock, in his life of Smuts, argues that color was a particularly important factor in the elections of 1924 and 1929, and that what Malan learned from these elections was mirrored in his development of the Nationalist platform in 1948 (Hancock, 1968, p. 499). This is a misconception. Color had been a major factor in every election since 1915, and would continue to be a strong source of appeal to white South African voters. The reason that color appears especially crucial in the elections of 1924 and 1948 is that Smuts was in power during those elections, and there was apparently some doubt in the popular mind as to his steadfastness on that question. In 1948, the fact that the liberal Hofmeyr was Smuts' avowed successor was an important consideration for the voters.[16] On the other hand, as Hancock points out, republicanism was a definite deterrent to the marginal voter, and Malan played this down before 1948 (Hancock, 1968, pp.

---

[16] For an intelligent analysis of the problem posed to the United party by Hofmeyr's views on the race issue, see the memorandum submitted by E. G. Malherbe to Smuts in 1949 (Hancock, 1968, pp. 513-514). Perhaps, though, Malherbe had a personal animus against Hofmeyr (cf. Paton, 1963, pp. 345-346).

499-500). He had no need to emphasize it—the faithful knew his position by that time. A. J. R. van Rhijn, who headed the Republican Fighting Fund during the middle forties, admitted to me that he was better able to raise money for the party by mentioning the fact that white women were dancing with black men in Cape Town, than by stressing the republican issue. In his own words, "the small man might give for the republic, but men of wealth feared the issue. Advocate Erasmus geared Nationalist policy to the color issue after I had spoken to him about this."

However, the purpose of this chapter is to analyze the 1948 election only to the extent of seeing how certain issues in the election had roots in earlier years and in civil-religion themes. The year 1944, for example, provides typically representative instances of political appeals to color, to the racial consciousness of Afrikaners and, indeed, of all whites. *Die Volksblad* (June 24, 1944) made an issue of the instruction given to clerks in the department of labor to call Africans "Mr.," "Mrs.," and "Miss." There was an outcry about a welfare conference to which non-whites were invited (*Die Transvaler*, August 25 and August 31, 1944; and *Die Volksblad*, August 31, 1944). A mission conference of the N.G. called for apartheid (*Die Burger*, November 27, 1944), and the F.A.K. called a volkskongres on the racial issue. The racial theme then dominating the party as well as the cultural movement was summed up in an editorial by Professor H. M. van der Westhuizen in *Die Vaderland*:

> Of all the great ideals of the Voortrekkers their stance on color remains the key to the future which awaits South Africa. As bearers of a Christian religion and *weltanschauung*, of European civilization and white blood, of Afrikaans-Dutch forms of life, of the Boer culture and of culture in general, the generations of the Voortrekkers can always continue to exist in us and in our posterity and can grow to fullness if we hold today inexorably to the way which they have shown us. . . .[*Die Vaderland*, December 15, 1944; cf. *Die Burger*, December 15, 1944]

Despite the personal and ideological quarrels which rocked Afrikanerdom during the war years, certain issues helped to counter such divisions. If the issue of mother-tongue education served to unite Afrikaner intellectuals in their identity over against English, the racial outlook defined the National party as the legitimate inheritor of the Voortrekker traditions over against the blacks. Finally, its opposition to communism confirmed the party as the People's bastion against both liberal English and threatening black and drew the Dutch Reformed churches firmly into its sphere.

Communism

Fear of anglicization and of the black Africans had long been inherent in the emotional presuppositions of the civil religion; and for all their differences in interpretation and prescription on the basis of that civil faith, Afrikaner believers stood together in the face of such elemental threats. Fear of communism (the "red threat") provided a similarly basic exigency which could unite all Afrikaners (cf., e.g., *Inspan,* October 1946). Furthermore, since communism advocated racial equality and was envisaged as the inevitable concomitant of British imperialist liberal capitalism, anti-communism combined both anti-British and anti-black sentiment of the civil religion.

Each social metaphysical strand within Afrikanerdom was able to employ its own logic and language in defining communism as a major threat. For the Dutch churches, communism represented "atheistic materialism" (*Die Volksblad,* June 13, 1941; *Kerkbode,* September 29, 1943 and May 16, 1944); for the neo-Fichteans it represented "atomistic individualism;"[17] for the Kuyperians it represented an idolatrous attempt to transcend the separate spheres of authority laid down in the ordinances of creation (Stoker, 1941, pp. 93-104); and for all Afrikaners the Communist disregard for racial differences was a thrust at the very heart of their ethnic existence.[18] The National party had thus to unite these multiple anti-Com-

[17] The argument here was that communism represented a mechanical unity of individuals within a social class as opposed to the organic unity of the nation (cf. *Die O.B.,* January 15, 1947).

[18] See Diederichs' speech reported in *Die Burger* (July 7, 1938), and also the National party pamphlet of E. H. Louw, *Die Kommunistiese Gevaar.*

munist forces within Afrikanerdom in support of a single anti-Communist organization (the party itself) and to identify its major parliamentary opponents, in particular the government of General Smuts, with the Communist threat.

On the industrial Witwatersrand, a specifically anti-Communist organization arose in response to this need. It was directly precipitated by agitation in Germiston against the multi-racial Clothing Workers Union, headed by Solly Sachs. Sachs, an ex-Communist Jew with radically socialist and non-racist views, led a trade union made up largely of Afrikaans-speaking women and was a prime target for the Christian National attack. Since Sachs personally had been instrumental in improving conditions for his workers, however, his Clothing Workers Union was less susceptible than the Mine Workers Union to outside assault. Before the war, the Blackshirts of Albert Hertzog's Nasionale Raad van Trustees, were committed to what proved no more than fruitless acts of violence against Sachs' union (Naude, 1969, chapter 5). Despite occasional snipes from Afrikaans newspaper editors (cf. *Die Transvaler*, May 12, 1943; and *Die Volksblad*, May 14, 1943), little other action was mounted against Sachs' union until the beginning of 1944, when a clothing factory in Germiston employed several colored workers.

Although these new colored employees were isolated from their white fellow workers, the latter discovered their existence after several days; and a number of them immediately called on the others to strike. Prompt support was forthcoming from Dr. Van Rensburg of the O.B. (*Die Vaderland*, March 4, 1933), but the executive of the Clothing Workers Union refused to consider a strike and even dismissed two of the white workers who had led the racist rebellion in Germiston. Since there was a "closed shop" agreement in the clothing industry, these women lost their jobs.

According to Sachs, the dismissed women first contacted leaders of Albert Hertzog's Reform Organization, who suggested that the Dutch Reformed churches be approached and urged that any action taken should "appear to be under the aegis of the Afrikaner churches and that no word of the Reformers must be mentioned" (Sachs, 1953). Meanwhile one of the Reformer leaders called upon several Afrikaans ministers to discuss the matter with them. According to the ministers, however, one of their number was approached for help by one of the expelled workers, who was a faithful member of his congregation. Whatever the truth of the matter (and the two accounts are not necessarily contradictory), fifteen Dutch Reformed ministers attempted to attend a meeting of the Clothing Workers Union in Johannesburg that had been called to review the trouble in Germiston. They were refused admission on the grounds that they were not members of the union, and an undignified struggle ensued between the Garment Workers' shop stewards and the ministers and their supporters—but to no avail for those seeking entrance (*Die Volkstem*, March 22, 1944).

The affair became a national issue. On the insistence of the National party, it was debated for several days in parliament, although to little purpose, since the United party refused to interfere in the internal affairs of a trade union. The matter reverted to the churches. Ministers of all three Dutch Reformed churches addressed a protest meeting in Germiston (*Die Volksblad*, March 27, 1944) to announce the formation of an Enlarged Church Committee, consisting of ministers and lay members of the three synodal Commissions for Social Evils of the Dutch Reformed churches. This church committee issued an appeal, which obtained immediate support from van Rooy of the F.A.K. and Diederichs of the R.D.B., and which urged

> all ministers throughout the land to take leadership and, if need be, to establish powerful committees from all organizations and persons,
>
> 1. who wish to save white civilization and pure Protestant Christendom;
> 2. who wish to help our mothers and daughters who are placed on an equal level with coloureds in their struggle to keep the color bar, and in their need since some of them have already been thrown onto the street;
> 3. who wish to fight the outspoken principles and practices of the present Clothing Workers Union which believes in equality between white and non-white (decidedly in conflict with the principles of the Church grounded in God's Word). [*Inspan*, April 1944]

The Editor of *Die Volksblad* made explicit the implication of the third point in this appeal by speaking of the "Communist dictatorship of the trade unions" (*Die Volksblad*, March 30, 1944).

An issue had thus emerged, or been manufactured, on which Afrikaners could unite on behalf of the Afrikaner "wife and mother" in opposition to Communist racial equality. Churches, party and major voluntary associations could herein agree with little difficulty. As William Nicol observed:

> The church was not being used for politics, but took action solely on behalf of its members. . . . The church was not acting against lawful trade-unions. . . .The great principles which must be protected were that right must prevail and injustice be righted, that there must be racial apartheid and that the trade unions must be purified. . . . The workers in the factories should organize themselves in a white union. . . . The infiltration of the Communist idea is fatefully active in destroying the Christian principle of our church. The church will forcefully resist that Communist tendency at all times, and it is the calling of a Christian state to support the church in that struggle.
> [*Die Volksblad*, March 27, 1944]

Indeed, when the Reverend A. B. du Preez of Waterval was sued for libel by Solly Sachs, he read from the church law on the duties of a minister and then "emphasized that the church regards communism and race mixing as the most important social evils against which the church is especially called to fight" (*Die Vaderland*, September 7, 1945).

Despite the state's refusal to intervene in the Clothing Workers Union, the Enlarged Church Committee continued to agitate, publicizing the Germiston struggle with its full and ultimate implications. These latter were set forth in a pamphlet, which appeared on May 30, 1945, entitled *Blank Suid-Africa Red Uself!! Ondersteun die blanke fabriekster en die drie Afrikaanse Kerke in hulle stryd om die behoud van die kleurskeidslyn en die Christendom* ("White South Africa Save Yourself!! Support the White Clothing Worker and the Three Afrikaans Churches in Their Struggle for the Maintenance of the Color Bar and Christendom").

In June 1944, the Broederbond took action, establishing the Blanke Werkers se Beskermingsbond ("White Workers'

Protection Society") to fight the Communist evil within the trade unions. The organization opened its membership to all white Christians who sought to help maintain white civilization in South Africa. In order to achieve this end, it worked "to mobilize the People as a whole in order to root out the cancer of our ethnic life . . . especially present in the trade unions. The "healthy white unions" which it nurtured and encouraged would not be governed by leaders who used their power to propagate foreign ideologies or to support a South African political party.

> With regard to the relationship between white and non-white workers, the Bond supports a clear establishment of which work-spheres should be reserved for whites and which for non-whites; no undesirable contact between white and non-white workers in their work-spheres; and no mixed trade union membership for whites and non-whites. [*Inspan*, April 1947]

The executive committee of the society included Verwoerd, Diederichs, Ben Schoeman, Jan de Klerk, and four Dutch Reformed ministers, as well as Daan Ellis, leader of Albert Hertzog's miners' Reform movement, which now seems to have moved from Hertzog's sphere of influence to that of Verwoerd (cf. van der Walt, N. G. S., diary entry, February 20, 1947). The ideology of the society was specifically neo-Fichtean; and Diederichs, writing in its monthly journal, *Die Blanke Werker* ("The White Worker"), preached a neo-Fichtean version of the sacred history.

The political importance of Afrikaner racist associations of workers has sometimes been exaggerated.[19] However, there is no doubt that their anti-Communist activities, involving even the Afrikaans churches, was grist for the Nationalists' mill. In October 1946, the Dutch Reformed churches held a great congress, where all Christians were called to unequivocal opposition to communism. The congress appointed a commission to rally the churches and other sympathetic organizations to fight communism "with all permissible means." Members of this commission included P. J. S. de Klerk, the pro-party Kuyperian; Diederichs of the R.D.B;

---

[19] See Jan de Klerk's speech in *Hansard* (February 6, 1957), for instance.

Jan de Klerk of the Blanke Werkers se Beskermingbond; and Piet Meyer of the O.B. In opposition to Communism, at least, Afrikanerdom was once more fully united (*Die Burger*, October 10, 1946).

Once Afrikanerdom had been mobilized on specifically anti-Communist grounds, the National party wished to identify the United party as furthering the aims of communism. This intention was made easier because Stalin had been an "ally" during the war and because the government had turned a deaf ear, even to clerical appeals, in the Germiston trade union dispute. In 1945, the party held an anti-communist united congress in Johannesburg, at which delegates were subjected to harassment from members of the Springbok Legion, an ex-servicemen's association. Some of those ex-servicemen were Communist, a fact that Malan did not ignore. "We accept the challenge of communism," he declared boldly as Nationalist youth armed with clubs patrolled the hall (*Die Burger,* September 19, 1945). When, in 1948, the Springbok Legion and the Labor party joined with Smuts in an anti-Nationalist electoral front, the identification was substantiated.

The roots of the National party victory in 1948 thus extended back into the final years of the war, when Broederbonders in the party, in the churches, and in the cultural organizations began to heal the disastrous schism of 1941 by lending their energies to common goals. I do not wish to imply that this Broederbond campaign was the sole cause of the 1948 Afrikaner triumph, nor do I argue that the Broederbond ever "controlled the party"—at least before Verwoerd's day. Other factors were most certainly at play. The inefficiency of Smuts' government and the inevitable difficulties of return to normalcy after the war were against the United party, even as Malan's tactically superb coalition with Havenga and the Afrikaner party was able to gain several seats for the Nationalist coalition. Ententes between individual Nationalist candidates and the O.B. should not be overlooked, either, in assessing the causes of the electoral swing.[20]

---

[20] Although Stultz (1974) omits discussion of O.B.-party ententes, he provides a very thorough analysis of the 1948 election, including local issues which were decisive in individual constituencies.

According to *Die O.B.*, 35 candidates, of whom 27 were elected, entered into such ententes. It claimed that in nine of the winning constituencies, the O.B. vote made the difference. Among those who came into parliament with O.B. support were Dr. Diederichs and Henning Klopper (*Die O.B.*, June 2, 1948). Verwoerd almost certainly lost in Alberton because he refused O.B. support,[21] whereas B. J. Vorster, who had been a Stormjaer, lost in Brakpan by two votes because of H.N.P. opposition to his standing for the Afrikaner party. O.B.-party agreements were entered into in express defiance of Malan's instructions,[22] and the O.B. received no thanks for its support.

The National party won with a bare majority of five seats. The victory owed no small thanks to the civil religion, to Christian National ideology, and to the Broederbond's practical assistance. On the other hand, once the Afrikaners had won power, the civil religion rapidly proceeded to lose its bite, blunted by pragmatic priorities and the development of a bureaucratic party machine. Indeed the theme of righteous suffering which underlay the civil religion could not readily accommodate an unexpected triumph. Now the Broederbond began to degenerate into a movement whose main purpose was to feather the nests of its members. Neither Malan nor Strydom, while prime minister, made any move to found the long-awaited republic. This Verwoerd achieved by referendum in 1961, but the constitution of his new republic remained essentially what it had been since Union—a far cry from the Boer oligarchy which he had so strongly urged during the war years.

In one sphere, however, Verwoerd applied the logic of Christian Nationalism with unflagging rigor. It was no longer Afrikaner exclusivism but the policy of separate development which evoked the ideological fervor of Afrikaner intellectuals

[21] However, he was afterwards rewarded by Malan with an appointment to the senate.

[22] When I interviewed P. J. Hugo, who had taken Paarl with the help of the O.B., he felt the need, even twenty-one years later, to justify his entente with the O.B. "The Doctor was very angry," he told me, "but what else could I do? I could not have won without O.B. support."

in the 1950s and 1960s. It is in the zeal with which Verwoerd and his associates pursued this second ideal and the high-handedness of their treatment of non-whites that the most lasting effects of the old civil faith may be seen.

13

Conclusion: Ideology, Separate Development, and the Post-Republican State

Social scientists tend to use concluding chapters as opportunities for casting the results of their researches in a more generalized or comparative theoretical context. So here the political victory might quite convincingly be described as the beginning of an "Afrikaner Revolution" in South Africa; Verwoerd could be classed as the Afrikaner Robespierre and the present (Vorster) regime as the Afrikaner Thermidor. However, I concur with Max Weber that comparisons in social science are useful only insofar as they illuminate the peculiarity of each constellation of events, whose interest lies precisely in its unique consequences. Yet the "natural history" approach to social phenomena tends to obliterate just such particularities.

This study, then, aims not at illustrating yet another general theory but primarily at understanding Afrikaners during the period of their rapid ascendance to power. However, a study which attempts an interpretation of Afrikanerdom before 1948, if it has any validity, ought surely to illuminate current events in Afrikaner-dominated South Africa. Not that the findings of my research could lead to an invariable prediction of present tensions and contradictions in Afrikanerdom. Rather what I have described as occurring during the 1930s and 1940s should give sense and coherence to any examination of present trends. Let us then test the preceding analysis against a brief overview of consequential contemporary events.

Two of the most important areas of South African life since 1948 have been particularly molded by the force and power of the Afrikaner civil religion and Christian National ideology. We mentioned in the previous chapter that separate-development theory channeled off much of the ideological fervor which before 1948 was largely committed to the cause of Afrikanerdom. At the same time, the movement for the realization of the Afrikaner eschaton retained its grassroots commitment—especially in the Transvaal. But with the achievement of the Republic of South Africa in 1961, the problem of defining English-Afrikaner relations within the new state became a fountain of conflict and disruption.

Separate Development Policy

Traditionally, South African racial policy has been based on the determination of white South Africans to retain all political power and so to prevent economic competition from black Africans. These goals, whites came to believe, could best be met through residential segregation. Wherever physical contact continued between the races, the subordination of black to white has been clearly defined by law and custom. Helping to sustain white social dominance are norms regulating face-to-face contact with blacks—such as calling them by first names, speaking authoritatively to and of them in their presence or within easy earshot, expecting deference, and so on.

The social mastership of whites is buttressed by their economic position. We have already noted how industrialization, with wide-scale migration of unskilled whites to the cities, threatened the Afrikaners' sense of security. Hence the appeal of General Hertzog's policy of "civilized labor" and racial segregation, which guaranteed economic privileges to whites as well as radical residential separation of blacks, on the grounds that the latter should "develop on their own lines within their own areas." The favorite justification for this pragmatic protectionism was the unquestioned superiority of "white civilization." It is to the advantage of both native and European, Hertzog declared, that the white man guarantee his own "national existence and his civilization. . . . In South Africa 'European' is synonymous with civilization; and the extinction of the white man must inevitably be the extinction of civilization" (*Hertzog Gedenkboek*, 1965, p. 242).

Hertzog's native policy was consistent with his white politics. Even as the two white streams, English and Afrikaner, must flow apart until the latter had achieved full equality with the former, so, too, must there be separation between black and white until the former should develop to the level of the latter. The gap between black and white with regard to culture was so great, however, that Hertzog proposed that separation be political as well as social, and physical as well as cultural:

> As against the European the native stands as an eight-year-old against a man of mature experience—a child in religion, a child in moral conviction; without art and without science; with the most primitive needs and the most elementary knowledge to meet these needs. . . .

> Differences exist in ethnic nature, ethnic custom, ethnic development and civilization and these differences shall long exist. On account of these differences there will necessarily be differences in ethnic requirements, which will cry out for different handling—with regard to legislation no less than administration. . . . [*Hertzog Gedenkboek*, 1965, p. 238]

The policy of segregation and white domination would apply only during the black man's "minority," however:

> When he achieves his majority in development and civilization, and stands on an equal level with the white man, his adulthood will be acknowledged. Then the time will have come to take his claim to political rights into consideration, and further, to establish the relationship which he will have with the European.

> What concerns us today is to draw up the necessary measures for the transition period between now and then—to throw up a bridge for the native during the period of transition between the period of semi-barbarism and that of civilization.

> What will happen after that, how the relationship between native and European will be established then—that we must leave to the future. [*Hertzog Gedenkboek*, 1965, pp. 238-239]

What criteria would be used to assess the passage of the African to his majority, Hertzog never made explicit. Clearly white domination was here to stay for many years, and this was doubtless the most important factor for his supporters. Yet Hertzog himself did not regard culture as an invariable exponent of race. The earliest statement of his race policy, when it was least tainted by political compromise, granted to Coloureds political equality with white South Africans.

> The Coloured people, he said, were in many respects closer to the Whites, and differed fundamentally from the Africans. Their outlook was White, not African; further they spoke the mother tongue (Afrikaans). In their case there could be "no question of segregation" . . . "It was always clear to me that if we want to do justice to the Coloured person we should have to include him among the Whites industrially, economically, and politically. . . ." [Tatz, 1962, p. 46]

Hertzog was careful to allay white fears of miscegenation by insisting that socially, the Coloureds themselves "seek no association with Whites." But basically Hertzog was no simple racist. He was a liberal nationalist and, for all his stress on the importance of different ethnic streams, he never lost sight of the necessity of civic unity in South Africa as a whole. The black's "coming of age" lay far in the future, yet ultimately the logic of Hertzog's political philosophy must have forced him to concede the possibility of political rapprochment between black and white streams in a common South African society.[1]

The recommendations of the Fagan Commission, upon which the United party based its racial platform in 1948, were not radically different from General Hertzog's policy. The Fagan Report concluded that the process of economic interdependence in South Africa had made the country "the common home of races differing so radically from one another that there can be no question of assimilation," and yet so intertwined that "the European and native communities should be accepted as being permanent and as being parts of the same big machine." In response to this dilemma, the

[1] A 1958 speech by the present South African State President, J. J. Fouche, lends support to my interpretation of Hertzog's native policy (cf. *Hertzog Gedenkboek*, 1965, pp. 31-42, especially pp. 41-42).

report proposed a two-stream policy of racial and ethnic coexistence (Fagan report cited in Tatz, 1962, pp. 127-130).

Christian National Afrikaners, on the other hand, accepted the explicit premise that that interdependence which had made South Africa "the common home" of different races and cultures could be countered only by radical racial and cultural segregation. The 1944 F.A.K. Volkskongres on Afrikaner racial policy decided that "it is in the interest of both white and non-white in South Africa that a policy of apartheid be followed so that non-white ethnic groups will also have the opportunity to develop according to their own nature, in their own area, and ultimately to obtain full control over their own affairs there." At the same time it stated that "it is the calling and duty of the white race in South Africa to ensure that control of the state and full authority over national affairs in white areas shall remain in the hands of whites in the future" (*Inspan*, October 1944). The policy of apartheid thus contains both a negative defensive aspect that insists on continued white dominance, and a positive revolutionary aspect that denies the inevitability of a multi-racial society and proposes to realign "the whites and the Bantu nations which have become interwoven in this part of Africa . . . on their separate and natural evolutionary courses by means of a dynamic programme of national reconstruction" (Rhoodie, 1969, p. 63).

Analysis of "positive apartheid" is complicated by the fact that the National party came to power on the appeal of defensive or "negative apartheid." In the Nationalist's first ten years of office, most of the apartheid legislation passed by the party involved careful and full legal definition of the white racial domination which had long been an integral part of the South African way of life. These laws set specific limits to racial contact in housing, education, employment, entertainment, sport, amenities, and of course, sexual relations either within or outside of marriage (Horrell, 1971a). Such legislation gave rise to increasingly militant reactions from non-whites, which in turn led to more repressive legislation without regard to language, culture, creed, or color (Horrell, 1971b).

When Dr. Verwoerd became prime minister in 1958, however, he openly recognized the injustice of continued white domination—especially since other states in Africa were rapidly moving toward independence.

> [We] cannot govern without taking into account the tendencies in the world and in Africa [he said]. We must have regard to them. We are . . . taking steps to ensure that we adopt a policy by which we on the one hand can retain for the white man full control in his areas, but by which we are giving the Bantu as our wards every opportunity in their areas to move along a road of development by which they can progress in accordance with their ability. [Pelzer, 1966, p. 243]

Verwoerd suggested that the British Commonwealth might serve as a model for future relations between white South Africa and the new black South African states (or Bantustans) his policy would create.

Verwoerd's policy of granting political control to black South Africans in their own areas was not simply a pragmatic response to outside pressure, however.[2] The prime minister was an extremely prominent member of the Broederbond, and his statement above reads like the conclusions of the 1944 F.A.K. Volkskongres. There is a drive towards logical and moral consistency in Verwoerd's race policy which stems from the deliberations of intellectuals in the Broederbond. The ideological underpinnings of this doctrine of "positive apartheid" (or, as Verwoerd called it "the theory of separate development") were concisely encapsulated in the policy statement M. D. C. de Wet Nel, minister of Bantu Administration and Development, made when he introduced the Promotion of Bantu Self-government Bill before the House

---

[2] In presenting his plans for the Transkei to the cabinet, however, Verwoerd stressed heavily the pragmatic advantages of the policy:

> He explained that 1962 could become a crisis year for South Africa. He wished therefore to show to the world something great and new, which would confirm the just intentions of the government's Bantu policy and also provide a basis for the western members of the U.N. to prevent action against South Africa in the U.N. [Schoeman, 1973, p. 225]

Notice that he took for granted the moral righteousness of the policy.

of Assembly in May 1959 (*Hansard,* May 18, 1959, cols. 6001-6024):[3]

> The philosophy of life [*lewensbeskouing*] of the settled white population in South Africa, both English-speaking and Afrikaans-speaking[4] in regard to the color or racial problem . . . rests on three main basic principles.. . . The first is that God has given a divine task and calling to every People in the world, which dare not be destroyed or denied by anyone. The second is that every People in the world, of whatever race or color, just like every individual, has an inherent right to live and to develop. Every People is entitled to the right of self-preservation. In the third place, it is our deep conviction that the personal and national ideals of every individual and of every ethnic group can best be developed within its own national community. Only then will the other groups feel that they are not being endangered. . . . This is the philosophic basis of the policy of apartheid. . . . To our People this is not a mere abstraction which hangs in the air. It is a divine task which has to be implemented and fulfilled systematically. [*Hansard,* May 18, 1959, cols. 6001-6002]

The ideological context for the revolutionary aspect of apartheid theory is thus not simple racism, but those ethnic and cultural differences which are so crucial to Afrikaner Christian Nationalism. Black South Africans as a group are unfortunately bound together by only two bonds "their color" and "their hatred of the white man," said de Wet Nel. It is the racism of previous white policy which has led to such black nationalism, "the monster which may still perhaps destroy all the best things in Africa" (*Hansard,* May 18, 1959, col. 6007). The best antidote to such racial nationalism, he said, is to foster positive cultural nationalism.

> There are things greater which must bind Peoples together . . . the spiritual treasures, the cultural treasures of a People. These are the fine things which have united other Peoples in the world. Thus we say that our basis of approach is that the Bantu too will be linked together by traditional and emotional bonds, by their own language, their own culture, their ethnic particularities. I am convinced that for this mea-

[3] I refer to the English edition of *Hansard* although inaccuracies in translation have necessitated certain alterations in the text.

[4] Notice that de Wet Nel assumes that English-speaking South Africans also accept the Christian National ideology.

sure I shall receive the gratitude of the Bantu throughout South Africa. [*Hansard*, May 18, 1959, col. 6018]

The Zulu is proud to be a Zulu and the Xhosa proud to be a Xhosa and the Venda is proud to be a Venda, just as proud as they were a hundred years ago. The lesson we have learnt from history during the past three hundred years is that these ethnic groups, the whites as well as the Bantu, sought their greatest fulfillment, their greatest happiness and the best mutual relations on the basis of separate and individual development ... the only basis on which peace, happiness and mutual confidence could be built up. [*Hansard*, May 18, 1959, col. 6002]

The major premises of positive apartheid are thus Christian National. The principle of physical separation is conceived not simply as enforced white domination by means of racial segregation, but rather as insurance that the black "nations" in South Africa develop along their own ethnic lines to enable them to become "Peoples" in the sense in which Afrikanerdom became a "People" during the 1930s and 1940s. De Wet Nel was thus promising to black South Africans what Afrikaner Nationalist intellectuals had fought so hard for after Union—cultural, economic, and even some political independence. He believed that his policy created "for the Bantu the possibility of bringing to fullest fruition his personal and national ideals within his own ethnic sphere (*binne eie volkskring*)"; for such was the experience of the Afrikaner People, based upon its sacred history and the Kuyperian and neo-Fichtean principles of Christian Nationalism. "We grant to the Bantu," he said, "what we demand for ourselves" (*Hansard*, May 18, 1959, col. 6023).

If the white man is entitled to separate national existence, what right have we to deny that these Peoples have a right to it also? Let us be honest and fair. Moreover nationalism is one of the forces which puts into motion the best things in the spirit of a human being. Nationalism is one of the forces which has led to the most beautiful deeds of idealism and sacrifice and inspiration. Should the Bantu not have it? It is the nationalist who has learned to appreciate the cultural assets of other Peoples. . . . It will always be my task not only to respect these things of the Bantu, but to assist them to develop it as something beautiful and something which is in the interest of South Africa. It is our task to create channels along which these matters may develop, so that we may have cooperation instead of racial clashes. [*Hansard*, May 18, 1959, col. 6007]

The true believer in positive apartheid is thus certain that full achievement of its goals will answer equally the purpose of negative apartheid; that "it will ward off those factors which may possibly plough the white man under" (*Hansard*, May 18, 1959, col. 6023). Whatever racist and repressive measures of negative apartheid the black man now suffers, these injustices are temporary, borne in the interest of ultimate racial harmony, possible only through Christian National development of each ethnic group to its fullest potentiality.

One would be wrong to construe the policy of separate development as an attempt to return the African peoples to their tribalism.[5] Verwoerd insisted again and again that the purpose of the policy was to permit full industrial development in the black African areas but not at the expense of "Bantu national principles." We are reminded of Deiderichs' neo-Fichtean pamphlet, *Nasionalisme as Lewensbeskouing* (1936). Our reader will recall that Diederichs defined the "nation" in both static and dynamic terms, as both a community of feeling and a unity of commitment to a common calling. A nation involves both agreement on a common set of principles and the struggle to realize these principles along its own lines in all areas of life. The unity of a nation is thus not a static unity, but a growing, evolving one, and development is the process by which the national self realizes the potentiality of its unique calling. "[It] should not be forgotten that the form of government lies at the heart of every phase of ethnic development," said de Wet Nel, "I cannot imagine ethnic development without a dynamic form of government" (*Hansard*, May 18, 1959, col. 6006). Whether the Bantustan governments can be classified as in fact dynamic is beside the point here.[6] De Wet Nel certainly classified them in such neo-Fichtean terms.

[5] This is the argument of Ellen Hellman (1957) and, to an extent, David Welsh (1972).

[6] Note the influence of L. J. du Plessis and Afrikaner republicanism on de Wet Nel's formulation here. In fact, the governments

The form of government of every nation is the locomotive which takes the whole community along the road of development. . . . By means of this Bill we want to . . . give back to the Bantu this lifeblood of development . . . because we believe the Bantu should develop. . . . Every People in the world finds its highest expression and fulfillment in managing its own affairs and in the creation of a material and spiritual heritage for its posterity. We want to give the Bantu that right also. The demand for self-determination on the part of the non-white nations is one of the outstanding features of the past decade. . . . These matters are the steam-power of a People's soul and no safety-valve in the world can smother them forever. The late Dr. Malan described it pithily . . . once when he said that one might just as well stop the southeast gale with a sieve as suppress the national sentiment of a People. That applies to the Bantu also. [*Hansard*, May 18, 1959, col. 6006]

The Tomlinson commission made recommendations about certain aspects of tribal culture, which it suggested should be modified under the new dispensation.[7] As a result of questionnaires sent to all mission churches, the commission concluded that the development of the Bantu and Bantu areas demanded both "a characteristic Bantu culture" and "a characteristic form of vital expression within the Christian religion" (Tomlinson Commission, 1955, p. 159).[8] "Certain Bantu customs" such as witchcraft "are in conflict with the Christian religion" and are hence "undesirable;" other "good features" should be preserved or altered to conform with

---

of the Bantustans are little more than regional local authorities.

[7] The Tomlinson Commission was established in 1949 "to conduct an exhaustive inquiry into and to report on a comprehensive scheme for the rehabilitation of the native areas with a view to developing within them a social structure in keeping with the culture of the native and based on effective socio-economic planning (Tomlinson Commission, 1955, p. xviii). Its very terms of reference were thus neo-Fichtean.

[8] Many eminent scholars would agree with Tomlinson that the "reluctance" of the Bantu to develop might be converted through Protestant Christianity into "spontaneous and purposeful action" (cf. Eisenstadt, 1968). They would hardly agree, of course, that "the Christian religion is . . . a miraculous power which has radically affected the lives of the Bantu in such a way that no natural scientific explanation can be found for the transformation which has taken place in their lives" (Tomlinson Commission, 1955, p. 153).

Christianity (Tomlinson Commission, 1955, p. 159). But elimination of any of the Bantu institutions, especially certain aspects of their religion, insisted Ellen Hellman (1957), would upset the functional interrelatedness of Bantu society. Her critique of the Tomlinson report is, however, based on the assumptions of structure-functionalist social anthropology,[9] and factual criticism is meaningless if the protagonists disagree on fundamentals. On neo-Fichtean presuppositions, development of the black nations of South Africa would obviously lead to changes in black African society. Such changes might even in time involve the destruction of tribalism,[10] for Afrikaners know full well that their own society has changed radically in the course of urbanization and industrialization. Indeed, the whole effort of the Broederbond has been to further such changes, but at the same time to ensure that development does not bring abandonment of basic Christian National principles, the spirit by which Afrikaner culture is defined.

The F.A.K. Volkskongres and the Tomlinson Commission pushed the analogy between Afrikanerdom and the black African Peoples so far as to include a "Christian" as well as "national" future for black Africans. Accepting that national development is possible only within the context of Christian—indeed Calvinist—faith (cf. Nel, 1942), the Volkskongres reasoned that the "coming of Christian belief and morality is absolutely essential for the . . . extension of the different native tribes to Christian National unities" (*Inspan*, October 1944; cf. Tomlinson Commission, 1955, pp. 153-154). On neo-Fichtean grounds alone, this proposition cannot but seem a most arrogant imposition (perhaps somewhat like a group of Englishmen deciding that Afrikaner national development should take place in accordance with liberal principles), for neo-Fichteans assume the priority of the ethnic or cultural sphere over all others—even the religious. However,

[9] A useful if extraordinarily arrogant critique of social anthropological structure-functionalism is Jarvie (1964).

[10] The cabinet seriously debated the immediate introduction of "one man, one vote" in the Transkei in 1962 (Schoeman, 1972, p. 225). This would, of course, have effectively demolished the system of governments by chiefs.

as we have seen, Kuyperians like Stoker were attacking the neo-Fichteans in the 1930s on the grounds that all spheres—whether of work, family, church, nation, or state, whether individual, social, or cultural—were equally sovereign, subject only to God's absolute sovereignty.[11] But Stoker's doctrine of interdependence (*Koers*, December 1962) and Piet Meyer's assumption that conflict between spheres was unlikely because of "organic ties" within "the totalitarianism of the *volksbeweging*" (Meyer, 1942b, p. 12) caused Afrikaner Christian Nationalists, especially within the O.B., to blur this important distinction between neo-Fichteanism and Kuyperianism. They elevated the ethnic ordinances of creation above the other spheres, but the God of Calvin remained sovereign even within the sphere of the People. Hence black African development would necessarily be Christian as well as national.

During the Afrikaner struggle for control of South Africa, neo-Fichteans and Kuyperians worked together; but once in power, the implicit contradictions in their social metaphysics led to disagreement over the implementation of the ideology of separate development. How would black Africans develop along their ethnic lines? Migrant labor is an essential part of separate development, but it wrings radical disruption in the sphere of the family. Men who come to work in town have to leave their families behind in the "homelands" and live in hostels constructed for single men. This situation kindles much conscience-searching on the part of Afrikaner churchmen, who felt led to condemn this aspect of the policy in 1966 (*Studiestukke*, 1966, pp. 39-43). In a journal entitled *Woord en Daad*, published in Potchefstroom, certain Gereformeerde churchmen have for some years been expressing severe doubts about the whole separate development notion.

Ironically enough, the majority of South African blacks *do* claim allegiance to Christianity. However, statistics show that only some 3 percent of the non-whites of South Africa

[11] In fact, Kuyper himself believed that the conflict between the various spheres helped to ensure a balance of powers, which in turn guaranteed basic civil rights under the law.

are members of the three Afrikaans churches—that figure having been attained "after more than a century since we recognized the call 'to spread the Gospel of Light'" (van Jaarsveld, 1963, p. 26). Almost all such spreading of the gospel to black South Africans has been undertaken by overseas-financed missionary societies, whether Anglican, Methodist, Congregational, interdenominational or other (cf. du Plessis, J., 1965). For this reason, the form of Christianity accepted by most black Africans has been evangelical, rather than Calvinist, stressing admission of individuals to the universal church of Christ rather than the establishment of autogenous churches. Until 1953, almost all black African education was controlled by such missions with egalitarian and multi-racial ideals. As a result, indigenous black African "nationalism" has tended to stress common citizenship for all individuals in a multi-racial state rather than the ethnic pluralism peculiar to Afrikaners (cf. Meer, 1971; Walshe, 1970, pp. 7-10, 158-163). Thus the imposition of Christian Nationalism upon black South Africans implies not so much Christianization as a shift from a universalist to an exclusivist Christian tradition.

The missions, as representatives of "British philanthropic liberalism," have long been anathema to adherents of the Afrikaner civil faith. It is hence not surprising that the earliest positive apartheid measure should have been the Bantu Education Act of 1953. Following the recommendations of the Eiselen commission, this act centralized all black African education under the Native Affairs Department, thus neutralizing the liberalizing effects of missionary endeavor. The act specified that education for black South Africans should ensure "the development of a modern progressive culture, with social intitutions which will be in harmony with one another and with the evolving conditions of life to be met in South Africa" (cited in Duminy, 1967, p. 8). The Eiselen commission had set out certain "guiding principles" for the achievement of these aims: adequate "mass-based" schools "with a definite Christian character;" mother-tongue medium of instruction; parental say in running, and increasingly in financing, the schools; and "the maximum development of

the Bantu individual, mentally, morally, and spiritually"
(Tatz, 1962, p. 145).

The Eiselen commission was clearly urging the application
of Christian Nationalism to black Africans. Indeed, Dr. W.
W. M. Eiselen, chairman of the Eiselen commission, was not
only Verwoerd's secretary of native affairs, but the major
architect of the Broederbond theory of separate development.
The son of a missionary, Eiselen had in turn been lecturer
in Bantu languages at Stellenbosch, chief inspector of native
education in the Transvaal, and professor of anthropology
at Pretoria before his appointment as chief administrator of
the positive apartheid department in the new Afrikaner
government.[12] As early as 1929, when he addressed the Philosophical Union at Stellenbosch University, Eiselen interpreted General Hertzog's contemporary legislative proposals on
the "native question" from a "positive" standpoint.

> Because we refuse as government and People to recognize
> Bantu culture, because we measure the natives with the
> measure of European culture and on that basis classify them
> as raw or civilized, for that reason we are all, albeit uncon-
> sciously, apostles of assimilation. . . . The native wishes to
> stop being a "nigger" [*kaffer*] and to become a "man"—we too,
> under similar circumstances, would do the same. [Engelbrecht,
> J., 1959, p. 7]

General Hertzog's policy of segregation would be ludicrous,
he insisted, if it simply divided South Africa into a "civilized"
and a "barbaric" sphere. Eiselen's respect for the ethnic
particularity of black as well as white elements in the population was mirrored in his genuine concern for the preservation
of Bantu languages and culture.

> It will be clear to everyone that the factors which favor the
> continued existence of the Bantu languages (Holy Writ,
> schools, literature) do not weigh up against those against it
> (white opposition to third official language, multiplicity of
> Bantu languages). But there is one factor, and that the most
> important, which I have not yet mentioned. That is the will
> of a People to stand on guard [*handhaaf*], to remain immortal
> as a People. If such a will exists, then it can operate only

[12] Eiselen's appointment was made on the insistence of Broederbond parliamentarians despite the recommendation of the Public
Service Commission (cf. Schoeman, 1972, pp. 43-44).

through the medium of a unique ethnic language. From the history of the Boer People we learn how a People can retain its identity despite insuperable difficulties and enormous economic disadvantages.

The future will teach us whether the Bantu have a sufficient ethnically conscious stratum to persist and win for their languages a firm and abiding place in South Africa. From our side we can do much to encourage these Peoples in their struggle for cultural existence if we try to understand and respect their language and culture. [Eiselen, 1934]

With Verwoerd the master of racial policy and Eiselen his administrative aide-de-camp, the National party began to move slowly in the direction laid out in the policy statement of the 1944 Volkskongres. So important were Broederbond intellectuals in the theoretical formulation of positive apartheid that Verwoerd did not trouble to discuss the bill for promotion of Bantu self-government in the National party caucus before proposing it in parliament. Why should he? The main principles of the bill had been approved by the "People" at the 1944 Volkskongres:

In order to give the natives sufficient opportunities freely to realize their national aspirations, they must be provided with separate areas which will be administered and developed initially for them and eventually by them as self-ruling native areas in which the whites may have no rights of citizenship. [*Inspan*, 1944]

Apparently Verwoerd and Eiselen both construed the recommendations of the Volkskongres as their mandate for the positive aspects of apartheid policy.

The paternalism of Eiselen, at least, was fostered by his anthropological interests, and perhaps also by German missionary theology of the interwar years, which advocated the *Volkskirche* doctrine (van der Walt, I. J., 1963, pp. 39-81). There can be no doubt of his love for and the genuineness of his commitment to what he conceived to be the welfare of Bantu-speaking South Africans. Eiselen was never a racist; throughout his career he continued to insist that ethnic rather than racial dfferences were most important in South Africa (Eiselen, 1964). His retirement from the post of secretary of Bantu administration and development in 1960 possibly stemmed to some extent from general disillusionment. A confidential memorandum which he sent to his department in April 1959 proposed a bold move to quicken the practical application of separate development policy:

> In my judgment we have now come to the point where we must answer the question as to whether that road to overall Bantu development in the Transkei has really been opened. And I think that we must answer in the negative. Possible natural development is being retarded by the government by retaining strategically favorable places for whites. Thus I think that the time is at hand to declare open the white islands in Bantu areas. By so doing we do not eliminate the white, but we take from him his preferential position in the Bantu area and open the way for the Bantu gradually to take over. [Engelbrecht, J., 1960, p. 312]

This recommendation was never carried out. In an interview with a French journalist, Eiselen explained why:

> The government would like to do precisely what you have said: give the Bantu full rights in the Reserves; but, my dear sir, you can't imagine the bitterness of our internal political struggles. The opposition criticizes us when we put into practice what they demand in theory, that is to say, when we improve the lot of the Bantu. The farmers lose sight of our aim, they do not think ahead. When the state purchases land for the Bantu they say: Perhaps it is my farm they are going to buy up tomorrow. Our people . . . only think of their daily comfort. They accept the theory. But at the same time they want comfort. Obviously a generous theory and unchallenged comfort are incompatible. [cited in Scholtz, G. D., 1964, pp. 70-71]

Eiselen implied in this statement that white vested interest is the major factor hindering the full implementation of positive apartheid along Christian National lines. What he failed to mention is that there is an ideological strand in positive apartheid theory itself which is racist rather than ethnic in its rationale.

The foremost proponent of this racist strain in separate development theory was Geoff Cronje, whose ideas derive directly from National Socialist ideology within the O.B.[13]

[13] In December 1942, L. J. du Plessis, then policy head of the O.B., called a great Studielaer ("conference") which was attended by Broederbond intellectuals who were O.B. sympathizers. Copies of the papers presented to this conference are extant in the O.B. archives. Cronje's book, *'n Tuiste vir die Nageslag* ("A Home for Our Posterity"), published in 1945 by the O.B. press, seems to have

Whereas Cronje argued for total separation as strongly, perhaps more strongly, than Eiselen, his rationale stems from fear of miscegenation and the demise of the white race, rather than a primary concern for the ethnic heritage of the Bantu Peoples. Whereas Eiselen consistently held that "our task in South Africa is not the solution of a race problem but the creation of effective arrangements for the peaceful coexistence of different ethnic groups (*volksgroepe*)" (Eiselen, 1964, p. 9), Cronje argued that "the crux of South African racial questions . . . exists above all in that racial contact has led to racial mixing and that racial conflict has been born from the superior position of the whites [and the inferior position of the non-whites]" (Cronje, 1947, p. 70).

With the rapprochment between Broers after 1943, the O.B. (Cronje) faction was largely integrated into the Eiselen-disposed contingent.[14] Cronje addressed the 1944 Volks-kongres on the dangers of racial mixing, and the conclusions of the congress reiterated the calling and duty of the white race—not the Afrikaner volk—and summoned the whites to stand on guard against miscegenation. Thus, from its inception, the social metaphysical assumptions of positive apartheid were confused. Does the perceived imperative for separate development arise from biological differences or cultural pluralism? In fact, major public proponents of apartheid have tended to shift their ground depending on the argument, thereby creating an ideological system which is riddled with inconsistencies.[15] A recent American visitor to South Africa

---

been based on the deliberations of the 1942 Studielaer, as well as on earlier articles by P. J. Schoeman, P. J. Coertze, and J. P. de Vos published in *Wapenskou*.

[14] The South African Bureau for Racial Affairs (SABRA) appears to have given organizational expression to the Eiselen version of positive separate development. Founding members included Dr. T. E. Donges, Dr. Diederichs, Rev. G. B. A. Gerdener, and Dr. Eiselen himself. An earlier version of SABRA was Die Afrikanerbond vir Rassestudie ("Afrikaner Association for Race Studies") founded in the Transvaal in 1935 with M. D. C. de Wet Nel as secretary (cf. *Die Volkstem*, October 4, 1935).

[15] For a useful analysis showing up these contradictions see Slabbert (1971). Note, however, that he uses the term "ethnic" as equivalent to my use of "racial." I retain the term "ethnic" for what he calls "cultural politics."

reported that his "quest across South Africa slowly turned into a search for a definition of 'big' apartheid, a coming to terms with it, and an attempt to judge its sincerity or falseness, its efficiency or applicability. But it seemed at every turn to become more elusive, more of a will-o'-the-wisp, vanishing just as I thought I had seen its face . . ." (Hoagland, 1972, p. 147). Perhaps one clue to the puzzle lies in the fact that cultural pluralism is a morally acceptable reality, whereas racism is not; and protagonists of apartheid tend to justify racism on the grounds of cultural pluralism. Small wonder at Hoagland's confusion!

One of the most difficult questions in discussing apartheid theory is where Verwoerd stood on the spectrum between race and ethnicity? For if Eiselen was the major architect and administrator of positive apartheid, implementation of the policy in the legislative assembly was the responsibility of Verwoerd. Careful scrutiny of his collected speeches (Pelzer, 1966) reveals that Verwoerd actually shifted his position during the course of his parliamentary career. While minister of native affairs, Verwoerd was closely associated with Eiselen; and his public pronouncements reflected a sincere, if typically paternalistic concern for "Bantu" development. His famous 1954 statement on Bantu education itself conformed to the ethnic ideals and proposals of positive apartheid a la Eiselen.

> It is the policy of my department that education should have its roots entirely in the native areas and should be based on the native community and spirit [*gees*]. There Bantu education must be able to give itself complete expression and there it will have to perform its real service. The Bantu must be guided to serve his own community in all respects. There is no place for him in the European community above the level of certain forms of labor. Within his own community, however, all doors are open. [Pelzer, 1966, pp. 83-84]

This statement does not differ in philosophy from editorials Verwoerd wrote in *Die Transvaler* during the 1940s on mother-tongue education for Afrikaners, under such headings as "Save the Soul of the Child," and so on. Even so, his above speech broadly categorized "European" and "Bantu" into two distinct racial entities.

When Verwoerd became prime minister in 1958, this racist cast of his thought became increasingly apparent. In 1960, just after the Sharpeville affair, when some members of his cabinet were urging concessions to Africans,[16] he spoke of the danger that South Africa might "fall from the grasp of the white man together with everything that he has brought to this country which he loves" (Pelzer, 1966, p. 373). He cautioned that "you have not only to take into consideration the rights of the Bantu, of the black man in Africa, but ... there is also a white man in Africa to consider." Nor did he scruple to insist on the pre-eminence of the white way of life above that of the more numerous and less fortunate others.

> The white man brought civilization to this country and everything that the Bantu is inheriting today with us, was created by the knowledge and diligence of the white man. It is true that the black man took part in it, mostly as the laborer. We realize the value of that part and wish to see that he is repaid for what he has done for the country. But if we had not been here or cared for them throughout the hundreds of years, they would have perished of hunger or murdered one another and might not have been in existence today. [Pelzer, 1966, p. 377]

> May the white man, may the white nations of the world, including Britain, never lose their hold, intellectually and otherwise. If they try to abdicate and to surrender on our behalf, then in the long run the flood of color will not only overwhelm us but will reach their country in the years to come and eventually overwhelm them as well. [Pelzer, 1966, p. 369]

Verwoerd was thus moving from emphasis on "Bantu" rights to progress along the lines of their own culture to the necessity for preservation of European civilization, specifically associated with race. As though to underscore his abandonment of the ethnic argument, Verwoerd began to urge white unity, regardless of differences in history and culture.

> We have been living for many years with division and strife between English-speaking and Afrikaans-speaking people. This struggle has been born out of our history. But what is important for the people of South Africa at present is something more than history. . . . We grant all the nations of the world

[16] Schoeman makes special mention of Paul Sauer in this connection (cf. Schoeman, 1972, pp. 198-211).

national pride, and the past from which they have sprung. But besides history there is the present, a present which passes quickly away, and then there is the future. In that future we see the revolution of Africa and the growing problems of South Africa. For the sake of the future we must stand together as whites. [Pelzer, 1966, p. 381.]

The wheel had come full circle; Verwoerd was now using the arguments of General Hertzog that whites must stand together. The contradictions in the ethnic argument for separate development became increasingly obvious. Continued insistence on separate Bantu-speaking ethnic entities came more and more to look like a policy of divide-and-rule. Small wonder that Eiselen resigned to live among his beloved Bantu-speaking people as high commissioner to the Tswana "People." Verwoerd, on the other hand, set the seal upon his racist course by scotching a movement in the Cape to accept the culturally Afrikaner Coloureds into the white fold. Henceforth "positive separate development" on Christian National grounds was never to recover its original innocence and ardor.

It is not within the purpose of this study to provide a detailed critique of the policy of separate development. That has been ably done elsewhere.[17] However, I shoud be untrue to myself and to my reader were I to avoid all comment on the application of separate development.

Suffice it to say, then, that Afrikaners are wont to state that there are but two alternatives in South African racial policy—assimilation and total (territorial) separation. They fail to mention a third possibility, which in fact describes the reality of the South African situation as it is at present—that of white domination.[18] Contemporary South Africa constitutes a white racist oligarchy with the "Bantu Homelands" little more than a source of labor for white industry on or outside their boundaries. Repressive legislation, including the

[17] See, for example, Ben Marais (1964), British Council of Churches (n.d.); Carter, Karis, and Stultz (1967); Rhoodie (1969, chapter 12); and SPRO-CAS (1972).

[18] Cronje (1947) mentions the alternative of "permanent white supremacy" but dismisses it as immoral, impractical, and a betrayal of the calling of the white man!

lifting of habeas corpus, and retroactive laws have become part of the South African way of life. Professor John Hansen showed in 1962 that Coloured and African children were dying at fifteen and twenty-five times the rate of white children (*Cape Argus*, October 31, 1962). Correspondingly, life expectancy for white males is 65 years, as compared to 36 years for black Africans (SPRO-CAS, 1972, pp. 18-24). However many such figures one wishes to cite, he cannot illustrate the total human loss and deprivation in a state which dictates the inferiority and powerlessness of the majority. I do not wish to suggest that any governing policy in South Africa can necessarily avoid considerable human suffering, whether for white or black or both. However, unless the South African government can show more responsible returns from separate development, one cannot but conclude that the whole endeavor is a monstrous hoax.

In 1954, the Tomlinson Commission recommended that £ 60 million be spent on the industrial development of the "homelands" during the next ten years. This would enable 50,000 additional black Africans to find employment in the homelands each year. The government rejected this recommendation and proposed instead a Bantu Investment Trust which was capitalized initially at £ 500,000 (about U.S. $1,400,000). This effectively drew the teeth of the commission's proposals. Between 1960 and 1966, according to the minister of Bantu administration, R1,000,000 (about U.S. $1,540,000) had been invested in this trust in establishing 35 industries in the Bantu areas. These industries employed a total of 37 whites and 945 black Africans. Dr. Rhoodie calculates that, with inclusion of the border industries, approximately 2,000 additional work opportunities have been created annually for homeland dwellers since 1958 (Rhoodie, 1969, p. 341). Since Rhoodie's study, a measure of white investment has been permitted in the "Bantu areas" but

---

[19] All National figures for black Africans are estimates—almost certainly too low. The estimate of black African life expectancy is based on 1948 figures from the Witwatersrand, where African standards of living are at least as high as anywhere else in the country.

the Industrial Conciliation Act and the Wage Act have, as far as Africans are concerned, been suspended in the homelands (thus allowing employers to pay lower wages and dispense with normal forms of benefits for their African workers) whilst non-Africans in the homelands are still covered.... At Babelegi, a female sewing machinist starts at R3 per week instead of the R7.50 laid down by the Industrial Council for the Clothing Industry for the Transvaal. At the same time a 45-hour week is worked instead of the normal 40 hours. . . . Employers do not have to contribute to provident or medical benefit funds for their workers. . . . The possibilities of capital formation within the homelands remain meagre. [SPRO-CAS, 1972, p. 77]

By 1970, the Bantu Investment Trust had invested a total of R13 million (about U.S. $18 million) in the homelands.

Meanwhile, since 1960, the South African expenditure on "security and public order" has more than doubled and the defense budget has risen from R44 million (U.S. $61.6 million) in 1960-1961 to R257 million (about U.S. $349.2 million) in 1970-1971 (SPRO-CAS, 1972, p. 44). Comparison of these figures with those of Bantustan investment is perhaps the most poignant indicator of the failure of the policy of separate development and the most damning indictment of the present South African society. Part of the *raison d'etre* of separate development is to ensure "peace and harmony," yet we see the South African government buying order with guns!

Yet, because the policy of separate development originated from "a deep and honest conviction which flows from historical experience and which is based on the Christian principles underlying the approach of our People" (de Wet Nel: *Hansard*, May 18, 1959, col. 6023), because it rose from "a sort of mystical foundation" (de Villiers Graaff: *Hansard*, May 18, 1959, col. 6026), Afrikaner intellectuals, churchmen, and Broers even now find it very difficult to abandon the course and admit the realities of South African race relations. Separate development remains for the true Afrikaner believer what their "errand into the wilderness" was to the New England Puritans; it is his mission and calling, his salvation and his justification. De Wet Nel—even as John Winthrop[20]—

[20] Winthrop's own words were:

For we must consider that we shall be as a city upon a hill, the eyes of all people upon us. If we deal falsely with God, saw the work of his community as a divinely appointed task which would prove an example to other nations in the world. Speaking before the final vote on the Bantu Self-Government Bill, he said:

> The calling of this small white nation is to give the world the basis and pattern on which different races can live in peace and safety in the future, each within its own national circle. That is the prescription for the solution of the racial problem not only in Africa but throughout the world. . . .[Carter, Karis, and Stultz, 1967, p. 61]

The civil religion, which was developed by the leaders of an ethnic group trying to establish their identity as a body politic, was to become the logic of a system justifying the oppression of another group. One can but speak of this as one of the exquisite ironies of history—an irony that is distressing for those who continue to believe in the Afrikaner's mission and that is agonizing for black South Africa.

The Republic and After

Political triumph for the National party in 1948 was a surprise to both supporters and opponents. The narrow margin of the election victory implied that the exigencies of retaining power would override those of ideology for Nationalists during the following decade. The National party closed ranks, presenting a granite facade to the world. Malan moved cautiously on contentious issues in order to retain the support of Havenga and his moderates. The first fully Afrikaner cabinet, made up largely of Cape Nationalists whom Malan could trust, was quite acceptable to Havenga. The republican issue was shelved, despite Strydom's outspoken chagrin expressed in both cabinet and caucus; and the apartheid program limped along, with E. G. Jansen unwilling to dismiss liberal civil servants like D. L. Smit and Edgar Brookes (Schoeman, 1973, pp. 40-48). In addition, Malan's new minister of education, A. J. Sals, explicitly rejected the F.A.K. policy

---

not only will He descend upon us in wrath, but even more terrible, He will make us "a story and a byword throughout the world, we shall open the mouths of enemies to speak evil of the ways of God and all professors for God's sake." [cited in Miller, 1964, p. 11, spelling modernized]

Even so, says the critic of separate development, even so!

statement on Christian National education which had been issued on the eve of the 1948 election.[21]

Malan's reluctance to press for national application of Christian National principles was not, however, based simply on the pragmatic intent of retaining moderate support for the party. Malan was himself a liberal nationalist, a true believer in the civil religion, but with no specific attachments to either Kuyperian or neo-Fichtean interpretations of Christian Nationalism. Although a convinced republican, he preferred to wait until he could ensure that the new republic would remain happily within the British commonwealth (Schoeman, 1973, pp. 9-20). Antagonism between Cape and Transvaal Nationalists, an undercurrent in the party at least since the 1930s began to run high once more, but was not allowed to interfere with the party's primary goal of retaining political control in South Africa.[22]

Malan's successor, J. G. Strydom, was of course a Transvaaler and a fiery republican, but once he had achieved the

[21] This Christian National program for education, drawn up by the Kuyperian wing of the Broederbond, stated firmly that the object of education for Afrikaans-speaking children must be "the propagation, protection and development of the essentially Christian and National character of our nation." True to its Kuyperian origins, however, the document insisted that "the National principle must always be under the guidance of the Christian principle" (cf. Vatcher, 1965, pp. 288-301, for a translation of the complete text). Despite its rejection by Malan's cabinet the Transvaal National party congress accepted the program and the T.O. adopted its recommendations with enthusiasm. Since prominent members of the T.O. were rapidly promoted to inspectorates under the new regime, and Broers of the T.O. wrote the textbooks for the 1950s, a careful analysis of history texts and syllabi in the Transvaal (Auerbach, 1965) has little difficulty demonstrating that the ideals of Christian National education have increasingly been realized there. It is perhaps worth mentioning that most of Albert Hertzog's **Herstigte support apparently stems from young Transvalers raised** in this Christian National educational tradition.

[22] Information on internal affairs in the National party during the first twenty years of its rule has been culled largely from Schoeman (1973). This book, clearly based on the private diaries of Albert Hertzog and written by the top Herstigte journalist, tends to play up divisions within the party. It also overstresses the doings and feelings of *verkrampte* parliamentarians. If this bias is kept in mind, I see no reason to question the account on matters of fact.

premiership even he seemed loath to move on the republican issue.[23] The National party, even in its Gesuiwerde days, had always insisted that a republic could come only on "the broad base of the will of the People," and Strydom hesitated to risk popular support by pressing for the necessary constitutional change.[24] Many ardent Afrikaners must have felt that they would never live to see the day of the republic. In an effort to hasten its advent, the executive of the Broederbond planned to form a special cell in order that member M.P.s might continue to attend Bond meetings during the months of the parliamentary session. Strydom, himself a Broer, quashed this effort, however, by his strongly voiced disapproval of Broederbond interference in politics. According to Strydom, "the Broederbond must attempt to conquer trade and the attorney's profession for the Afrikaner. Even as the church, the Broederbond must abstain from stepping into political terrain" (Schoeman, 1973, p. 120). Despite Albert Hertzog's retort that "one of the most important tasks of the Broederbond is to ensure that the Afrikaner's government remain always on that course which is in the interest of Afrikanerdom and which will ensure the continued existence of Afrikanerdom" (Schoeman, 1973, p. 120), Strydom prevailed. The proposed parliamentary section never formally met.

But in 1958, Dr. Verwoerd succeeded Strydom as prime minister. He had long been a member of the Broederbond executive, and his first speech in parliament as premier affirmed his commitment to the republic:

> This has indeed been the basis of our struggle all these years: nationalism against imperialism. This has been the struggle since 1910: a republic as opposed to the monarchical connection. . . . We stand unequivocally and clearly for the establishment of the republic in the correct manner and at the appropriate time [Pelzer, 1966, p. 180, translation corrected][25]

[23] For an account of the lobbying which accompanied Strydom's election—from the verkrampte point of view—see Schoeman (1973, pp. 76-100).

[24] The source for this opinion is Verwoerd's introduction to van Jaarsveld and Scholtz (1966).

[25] Pelzer's collection of Verwoerd's speeches is invaluable (Pelzer 1966). However, the English translations range from poor to simply

The new republic, based on the "broad will of the People," including all whites, would thus conform to party tradition rather than to the exclusively Afrikaner ideals of the Broederbond elite. Verwoerd assured parliament that the new republic would not be based on the 1942 Broederbond draft constitution.

> That is something which was composed by a group of young intellectuals as a rendition of their ideas. I was associated with these people. . . . The National party is not and was not in any way connected with it. . . . This is a document which has never been accepted by the National party and, if I have anything to say in the matter, will not form the basis of any republican constitution in the future. [Pelzer, 1966, pp. 168-169]

At the Blood River celebrations of 1958, Verwoerd carefully charged his speech with the old rallying symbols of the civil faith:

> Although we no longer trek, we say like the Voortrekker of yore, "we can still fight." And we shall fight even though we might perish. We shall do battle for the survival of the white man at the southern tip of Africa and the religion which has been given him to propagate here. And we shall do it just as they did—man, woman and child. We fight not for gold or goods. We fight for the life of our People. . . . Why should whites have been led to the southern tip of Africa three hundred years ago? Why was half of the country unoccupied, why could small numbers of people so increase and spread over the whole country? Why could they, in spite of their Moordkrans and Italeni, also gain their Blood River? How could they undergo their wars of independence and, win or lose, yet survive as a nation? Why was all that given to us if there was no purpose in it? And I believe this to be the purpose—that we should here be an anchor and a stay for western civilization and the Christian religion. [Pelzer, 1966, pp. 209-211]

The "People" for which the Voortrekkers lived and died, according to Verwoerd, were not specified as Afrikaners but labeled "the white race."

When Verwoerd announced the republican referendum on January 20, 1960, he stressed again—even as had Malan in 1933—that a republic would foster a common white civic

---

misleading. I have corrected the references against the Afrikaans edition. Page citations continue to apply to the English edition.

sentiment. He proposed no essential change in the Union constitution. The president should have no active sovereignty but, like the British monarch, should function as "the unifying factor in our national life. . . . The [present] monarchy will always be the background for division. If we want to develop a common national sentiment we must have a head of state who comes from our midst and whom we respect" (Pelzer, 1966, p. 330).

On October 5, 1960, when the referendum was held, 90.73 percent of the white electorate turned out to vote. Verwoerd had rightly calculated his appeal to the civil faith, and the republic achieved a majority of 74,580 votes out of a total of some 1.6 million. Although a small percentage of English-speakers voted for the republic, what is most impressive was the overwhelming breadth of Afrikaner support. The aged, the sick, the halt and the lame struggled to the polling booths to lend their support to the Afrikaner dream. The F.A.K. organized a great Thanksgiving at the Voortrekker Monument, complete with oxwagon, scholar-chorus, national flag, and women who came forth from the audience bearing great bunches of flowers. Homage was paid there to Paul Kruger, General Hertzog, Malan, and Strydom. Verwoerd was the featured speaker:

> It is the day of answered prayer; it is the coming of the republican dawn; it is the sun breaking through the morning mist that we commemorate here. Through so many years we longed and prayed for this moment, and now it is here. As it behooved us, we entered the struggle of the referendum as a praying People, and notwithstanding the depth of our desire and the earnestness of our heart's wish we could as praying People still say: "Thy will be done!" And it is thus so much more moving today to know what it is that that will was. [Pelzer, 1966, pp. 32-424]

Can Verwoerd have forgotten the old General at Monument-koppie in 1939 (and his own anti-English editorials at that time) when he concluded:

> We have risen above pettiness and selfishness. Patriotism, fellow-citizenship, friendship, all have become of more importance to us. The English-speaking and the Afrikaans-speaking sections have become like the new bride and the bridegroom

who enter upon the new life in love to create together and to live together as life-mates. [Pelzer, 1966, p. 427]

The old ethnic interpretation of the sacred history was inevitably becoming an inclusively racist one. Piet Meyer, now Broederbond chairman, and Albert Hertzog, among others, charged Verwoerd (but in private) with sacrificing the ideal of Afrikaner dominance to the exigencies of racial politics. But Verwoerd stood firm on his insistence that the republic heralded a new South African English-Afrikaner rapprochment in the political sphere. Until his death he was able to maintain the loyalty of the Afrikaner elite by the sheer force of his character, the appeal of the policy of separate development, and of course, because he was an eminent Broer as well as party leader.

The difference between party and Broederbond leadership did not really surface until after Verwoerd's assassination in September 1966. Only weeks after Verwoerd's death, Piet Meyer spoke to the Broederbond executive of his deep-seated uncertainties over the future of Afrikanerdom:

> Since the founding of the republic the integration of English-speakers and Afrikaans-speakers has been consciously preached and furthered by our politicians on the basis of the principles of the National party. The result has been that Afrikaners are extending this necessary and desirable political cooperation into other areas of life without formulating a clearly defined foundation and goal. This leads necessarily to the increasing anglicization of Afrikaners rather than the Afrikanerization of English-speaking South Africans. [Serfontein, 1970, p. 42]

Anglicization, continued Meyer, involved the sacrifice of Afrikaner Christian Nationalism, with its Calvinist roots, for English egalitarian liberalism and economic capitalism. The only solution he saw was a policy of deliberate Afrikanerization of English-speakers so that English South Africans would eventually accept Christian National ideals, the Afrikaans language and Afrikaner history as their own. English could be retained as South Africa's international language.[26] These

---

[26] According to Verwoerd's 1958 speech, the clause in the 1942 draft constitution which relegated English to the status of a second language derived directly from the constitution of the Irish Repub-

goals had been recognized as the official Broederbond political program since 1934 (although the relegation of English was not quite so clearly stated in J. C. van Rooy's and L. J. du Plessis' 1934 program), and were framed as well in the draft republican constitution of 1942. Likewise the principles of the Herstigte ("Reconstituted") National Party formed by Albert Hertzog in 1969,[27] were essentially the same as those of Meyer and the 1942 draft constitution. These Herstigtes were soundly thrashed by the National party in a nationwide election in 1970, however, which is symptomatic of the gradual and ever-increasing movement away from Afrikaner exclusivism.

In the first place, popular opinion since the republic—especially among younger Afrikaners—has been in favor of cooperation with the English. Survey results show that the majority of young Afrikaners desire full integration with English-speakers. It is impossible to know how many Nationalist members of parliament are secretly sympathetic to the Herstigtes—probably quite a number of the old guard—but in the face of changes in voter opinion they are unlikely to to give unqualified support to the old Broederbond policy of Afrikanerization. Even in the heyday of the Gesuiwerde party, politicians were very cautious on this issue. The Afrikaans press itself—with more or less vigor—dubbed the Herstigte line as narrow, unenlightened, and chauvinistic.[28] The term *verkramp* ("the narrow ones") came to be applied to the old Christian Nationalist position, and its critics dubbed themselves *verligtes* ("the enlightened ones"). The debate is no longer between rival social metaphysical interpretations of Christian Nationalism, but rather the very continuance

---

lic. It owed its origin to the violation of Afrikaans by Smuts' wartime government and had no applicability since the defeat of that government in 1948. He added, "we, who have experienced the suppression of our language and the opposition that that evokes will be the last to deny another man his language rights' (Pelzer, 1966, p. 170).

[27] Serfontein (1970) is an excellent account of the conflicts within the National party immediately prior to the Herstigte breakaway.

[28] For differing accounts of the press battle, see Serfontein, (1970, pp. 219-230), and Schoeman (1973, pp. 101-112).

of the ideology itself. The achievement of the republican destiny means that Afrikaner intellectuals must now rethink their destiny. The alternatives seem to be either a more exclusively Afrikaner ethos within the republic or liberal cultural nationalism for Afrikaners within a broader South African context.

Verligtes, who stand to the left of Afrikaner public opinion, are drawn from three main spheres—the artistic, business, and ecclesiastical. Afrikaner artists have repeatedly rebelled against censorship from Christian National *verkramptes*. These *verligte* artists claim as their spiritual progenitor N. P. van Wyk Louw, the most brilliant Afrikaner writer of the 1930s and 1940s and one of the best of the twentieth century's narrative poets.[29] Writing in the 1930s after *samesmelting*, Louw maintained that he stood for Malanite nationalism at the same time that he proclaimed what he later called "liberal nationalist" art. He opposed to "parochial art," which is emphemeral and situation-bound, his universalistic passion for beauty. In genuinely universal art, he said, "the concept of limited ethnic particularity must disappear before the concept of full humanity within an ethnic connection. . . . Our task is more difficult than that of poets in other nations; they obtain as a gift what we have to win with bitterness every day: the right to be fully human within the confines of your own cultural group" (Louw, 1959, p. 13 and p. 30). Literature of genius, Louw recognized, could not be born within a narrow Christian National *laager* of multiple organizations nor flourish when constantly invigilated by a self-appointed elite. Yet creativity naturally ferments within a national context:

> It is the national duty of the artist to steep his whole being in the blind passion and yearning of his group; to transform all which is undefined or purely intellectual into a concrete image in his own heart; and then simply to render that image beautifully in his work. That is all, but also the best, that he can do in the struggle of his People. Not through hollow phrases, not through the most fiery rhetoric, not through

[29] For those who do not read Afrikaans, the recent English translation of van Wyk Louw's *Raka* may help to sustain my judgment on this point.

commemorative verses at each ethnic celebration, shall he serve his cause, but through absolute beauty. [Louw, 1959, p. 29]

An influential group of Afrikaner writers and painters, now called the *Sestigers* ("those of the sixties")[30] appeared in the 1960s, inspired by the ideals of van Wyk Louw and his circle. They and their followers firmly rejected *verkramptheid*. These are the true *verligtes*, and although their numbers are small, their influence spreads far beyond the confines of their own group.

When the Broederbond proffered promising business careers to bright young Afrikaners in order to Afrikanerize the realm of "Hoggenheimer" and subvert it to the good of the People, they did not forsee that ardent young Broers like Anton Rupert would one day become business tycoons with minds of their own. It is not that they so much "sold out" Afrikaner ideals or lost their ethnic sense of calling, but that the Afrikaner destiny is now seen in the context of Africa as a whole. Rupert, for example, is willing to devote funds and energy to the development of Lesotho; and largely from pressure of business men of his ilk, the government has now instituted an "outward" policy which theoretically ignores race in international relations.

In the previous section we spoke of the publicly expressed doubts of Afrikaner churchmen about the racist aspect of separate-development theory and the immorality of maintaining migrant labor in particular. Recent theological developments within the N.G. have now gone so far as to question the entire *volkskerk* position. Earlier adherence of the *volkskerk* section of the N.G. to the Christian National cause stemmed more from pragmatic concern for survival of church and People than from theological justification. Not only on ethnic matters, but on racial segregation as well, the *volkskerk* N.G. was far more concerned with Afrikaner survival than with theology. In reply to the question whether it was not unChristian to boycott Indian dealers, for example,

---

[30] Andre Brink (1970) is an assessment of the cultural situation in South Africa by one of the most radical of the Sestigers.

Ds. T. C. de Villiers resorted to the pragmatic argument of ethnic preservation:

> There is the principle of *self-protection*. That every living being has the right to protect himself is a law of nature which no thinking person can doubt. The capacity to do so was given by the Creator to every being—certainly with the intention that he use it.
>
> Scripture teaches that every People has at least the right to protect itself. The history of Israel—under guidance of the Higher Hand—shows that clearly. Every person is obliged to care for and protect his house and his posterity in every area. . . . Your first duty is to your own people. . . . Charity begins at home. Your first duty is to your own house, your own environment, your own People. . . .
>
> You may not hate or persecute anyone, but your first duty is to protect and help your children, your posterity, your own People. [*Inspan*, June 1948]

Such logic was hardly acceptable to the consciences of thoughtful Afrikaner theologians, especially once the practical exigencies of the drive for power had dropped away. In 1961, a group of Dutch Reformed theologians published a collection of essays entitled *Delayed Action* in which they refuted on biblical and moral grounds all arguments for apartheid. They also challenged the identification between church and People, which had served *volkskerk* men with ad hoc justification for accepting the entire civil faith. Said Ds. M. J. Redelinghuys:

> We Afrikaners have always cooperated closely in the fields of church and politics in the fight for recognition, preservation, and extension of our language, culture, etc. We have worked together so closely to free ourselves from English domination that the ideal of Church and State has virtually become one. This ideal and aim is not in the first instance the sovereignty of God, but the freedom of a strong Afrikaner people. . . . From a historical point of view this attitude of the church in South Africa is understandable. Prophetically, however, it can never be defended. . . . We as a people and we as a Church have turned Afrikaner Nationalism, and with it Apartheid, into an idol. We bow low before it. An idol is . . . something we make the be all and end all of life and for this reason it becomes the yardstick by which everything finally is measured. With whom have we the most in common? With a black

Christian or a white heathen, even if he is an Afrikaner and a Nationalist? If we are really honest with ourselves our reply would reveal to us that nationalism has become more important to us than the Lord Jesus Christ. Who, generally speaking, not formally but in reality, is honoured most at our celebrations of the Day of the Covenant and at our national festivites, God or our national heroes and the Afrikaner People? [*Delayed Action*, pp. 96-97]

Delayed Action was but the beginning of a comprehensive theological reconsideration of the whole question of the relation between church and People—especially in the N.G. In 1966, a special commission submitted to the Cape synod a searching report (*Studiestukke*, 1966), which challenged the very basic assumptions of the *volkskerk* position. The commission stood firmly for autochthonous churches; it urged that the gospel be preached in culturally relevant terms and lauded the cultural diversity of God's creation. However, it declared "an *eternal* ethnic destiny and existence is given to no People, no more than any People has received an eternal promise. The ethnic destiny of each People (Afrikaners included) is historically limited and its ethnic existence is temporary" (*Studiestukke*, 1966, p. 35). The continued existence of a separate People is morally acceptable only insofar as it "contributes to the progress of God's kingdom." The church, which "has been called by God's special grace to serve Him in a particular way," works within the locus of a People and is itself a new People, formed by faith—not by descent and cultural ties. If church and People "coincided, then one could speak of *volkskerk*—which is not found in the Scriptures" (*Studiestukke*, 1966, p. 35). The commission then proceeded to a distinction borrowed from Kuyper: "In spite of intimate connection, Church and People each have a unique structure and are hence sovereign in their own spheres (*sowerein in eie kring*)." The church must not become too intimately involved in the affairs of the People; in fact a church which expresses approval or disapproval in favor of any "party, People or ethnic section within the state, renounces its unique spiritual calling" (*Studiestukke*, 1966, p. 36). Those parts of the commission report which are here quoted   were   accepted   without   alteration   by   the synod of the Cape N.G. I do not wish to imply that the N.G. has become a hotbed of *verligtheid*. It has not. On the other hand, ready theological acceptance of congruence between the Afrikaner's Christianity and his civil faith can no longer be sustained. Prophetic condemnation of ethnic heresy is a potential legitimate weapon of the church—however little it may be applied.

Hertzog's new Herstigte Party has thus to face not only a moderate majority electorate and the opposition of the Afrikaans press, but also increasing *verligtheid* in business, church, and artistic circles. These *verligtes* represent a minority within Afrikanerdom; on the other hand, they are members of the elite and thus carry weight far out of proportion to their numbers. More important for the political prospects of Albert Hertzog's *verkramptes* than *verligte* opposition, however, is the fact that John Vorster continues to rule the National party and hence dominate the political scene.

Vorster is no *verligte*. A relatively junior member of the Broederbond, he was minister of justice and the strong-arm man in Verwoerd's cabinet. Parliamentary *verkramptes* supported his election as prime minister because they were impressed by his firm stand against communism and his commitment to "law and order." But Vorster was not nurtured in the ethnic tradition of the old National party. His first political mentors were not Malan and Verwoerd but Oswald Pirow and Hans van Rensburg—firmly anti-Communist, deeply republican, authoritarian, but relatively uncommitted to the ideals of Christian National Afrikaner exclusivism. Vorster has no objection to association with English-speakers who share his principles. Thus he has followed even more openly Verwoerd's policy of rapprochment of all white South Africans in opposition to the black African majority. There is a sense in which Vorster is taking the country back to the policies of the old General Hertzog—not the liberal democratic Hertzog of Havenga and the Afrikaner party, but the authoritarian National Socialist Hertzog of Pirow and the New Order.

If this is a valid judgment of Vorster's position, then one must consider the current suppression of dissent in South Africa as stemming from ideological conviction. Continued insistence on separate-development policy and outward-looking sports and diplomatic policy, however, strike one as more pragmatic responses to present political exigencies. Genuine *verligtheid* is quite as abhorrent to the current South African regime as *verkrampheid*—although less threatening. South Africa under Vorster is thus becoming a more traditionally authoritarian state than ever before—at least for whites. While this is a depressing prospect for the tiny genuine white opposition (mostly located in the English-speaking universities and the professions), there is some comfort in the thought that authoritarian, as opposed to idelogically totalitarian regimes,[31] tend to be somewhat more flexible in response to political and economic exigencies precisely because they are less bound by principles.

[31] Authoritarian regimes are intent on preserving the usually oligarchal status quo. Totalitarian regimes attempt to alter the status quo in accordance with ideological prescriptions.

Theoretical and Methodological Appendix

This study was originally intended to demonstrate the importance of the Afrikaner civil faith in the 1948 election victory of the National party in South Africa. The Afrikaner civil religion I conceived as a constellation of symbols held fairly universally and consistently by Afrikaners at least since the end of the Anglo-Boer War in 1902. I intended to demonstrate conclusively the independent role of belief systems in a particular instance of social action.

In the course of my research, I discovered that Afrikaner beliefs were neither unchanging nor universally accpted. In fact, the notion of "belief systems" as "independent variables" in social change now seems to me to be misconceived. Although beliefs and rituals constitute a dimension of reality for individuals and groups, they are nonetheless continually modified in response to conditions. However, since "conditions" are themselves perceived and responded to within a context of meanings, the crucial importance of ideas and beliefs, despite their relative fluidity, is self-evident.[1] Adequate sociological analysis must hence probe the significance of those meanings which are constitutive for an actor in the particular situation in question. My aim in this study thus became a description of certain Afrikaner beliefs which I am convinced were and are constitutive for Afrikaner politics.

Since my discussion employs certain terms which are either unfamiliar or highly ambiguous in social scientific discourse, I shall briefly define my use of *civil religion*, *social metaphysics*, and *ideology*. *Religion* I take to mean a set of symbols, whether words, objects, or ritual actions, which serve to assist an individual or group in meeting the ultimate problems of the human predicament. That is to say, a religious symbol system represents an attempt

---

[1] I have recently attempted a general statement of my current theoretical position (Moodie 1974), which relies heavily on the writings of Max Weber and the theories of George Zollschan (cf. Zollschan and Hirsch, 1964, part 2).

to meet the fundamental human questions of identity and destiny, like "Who are we?" and "Where are we going?" or "Why do things happen to *us*?" Because religious questions are ultimate, growing out of the universal human condition, religious symbols transcend everyday realities and yet impinge upon them, transforming one's perceptions with intimations of the infinite.[2] *Civil religion*[3], as I define it, denotes the religious dimension of the state. As such, it is invariably associated with the exercise of power and with the constant regeneration of a social order; it provides a transcendent referent for sovereignty within a given territory. The ultimate nature and destiny of political power is thus connoted in the symbols of the civil faith and re-enacted by civil ritual. The origins, the extent and limits, and the final purpose of political sovereignty are all thereby set within the context of ultimate meaning; aspirations to sovereign power and the exercise of sovereignty are given transcendent justification.

A caveat is perhaps necessary here. I do not assume that all citizens accept equally a given civil faith. Civil religion has its high priests and its local ministers, its true believers, its nominal adherents and its heretics, just like any other religion. It may appeal differently to different social classes: in fact, certain classes in a society may entirely reject the reigning civil faith. If the civil religion attempts to be inclusive, then different, even contradictory, aspects may be emphasized by various groups within the state. For instance, in the English civil religion of the eighteenth century the notion of *noblesse oblige* and the conception of the freeborn Englishman seem to have been held at the same time.[4] Furthermore, like any religion, a civil faith changes. Not only is it variously interpreted in terms of different social metaphysical systems, but the very symbols of the civil faith themselves tend to alter over time—or their meanings may alter in conformity to new conditions.

Any distinction between personal and civil religion in traditional societies is purely analytic.[5] The first establishment of a formal civil faith, at least in the west, was achieved in the reign of Augustus Caesar, who therein consciously attempted to accommodate Rome's

[2] This definition of religion owes much to the work of Robert Bellah (1970) and Clifford Geertz (1966).

[3] Robert Bellah (1970, pp. 168-189) is a brief and somewhat unsystematic description of the American civil religion, which makes no attempt at definition.

[4] The symbol of the "Norman yoke," however, was invoked in certain circles to demonstrate that these notions were contradictory (cf. Hill, 1964).

[5] This is certainly true of ancient Israel. Jaeger (1945) seems to me a moving and convincing description of the religion of the Greek *polis* as inextricably both civil and personal.

development from republic to empire. The social metaphysical basis
of this imperial civil religion was the traditional Roman conception
of the *res publica*, the common good, which incorporated the notions
of justice and order.[6] The civil theology of Rome's civilizing mission
found its noblest rhetorical expression in Virgil's *Aeneid*:[7]

> To achieve his purpose of glorifying Rome and her ruler, Virgil
> served himself heir to traditions which formed a precious
> appanage among the national possessions. His Roman reader
> could enter into this heritage with him. He could realize how
> the national life was enriched through the stimulus given to
> Roman patriotism when genius created pictures of a noble past
> half mythic, half real, which, like an eternal and silent monitor
> of the present, offered the surest guarantee of an exalted
> future." [Duff, 1960, p. 337]

So long as they accommodated to this magnificent imperial civil
faith, the religions of the empire could in theory maintain their
separate courses. In fact, as the empire disintegrated, under pressures both internal and external, a desperate effort was made to
graft Christianity onto the civil religion.[8] Although Augustine
stoutly refused to concede any ultimacy to the state, eastern
Christianity recognized the sacredness of imperial rule. In the west,
the Holy Roman Empire survived for almost a millenium as a myth,
sealing the legitimacy of various warring dynasties and nurturing
medieval apocalypticism (cf. Cohn, 1957). The development of the
nation-state (cf. Cobban, 1969, pp. 23-38), however, eventually destroyed that nebulous political base which remained to the Holy
Roman civil religion.

Nation-states may be divided into two categories, depending on
whether stress is laid on the political or cultural idea of the nation
(cf. Cobban, 1969, pp. 118-129). National civil religions are correspondingly either inclusive or exclusive; their referent is either
existing state power or the political aspirations of ethnic groups
within the state. The rise of class consciousness in industrial
societies further complicates the character of a civil faith. The one

[6] This notion had recently been restated clearly and with fine
style by Cicero (cf. Cochrane, 1957, pp. 27-73).

[7] If I may transpose Cochrane (1957. p. 65), Aeneas is the
voortrekker of antiquity; his followers the Great Trek of antiquity;
while the organized society of the empire is the Graeco-Roman
counterpart to the South African republic of the Afrikaner People;
"subject, it may be added, to limitations and threatened by dangers
which confront all societies in which consecrated egoism ... disguises
itself as the love of God."

[8] This was certainly true of Theodosius and to a lesser extent
of Constantine, (cf. Cochrane, 1957, part 2).

necessary characteristic of civil religion remains that it should have reference to power within the state, and yet transcend such power through focus on its ultimate conditions. Civil religion thus provides both justification for power, and, at the same time, a potential basis for criticism of those who exercise power. It serves as a symbolic universe, within the boundaries of which articulation may take place for a body politic, however defined.

For purposes of analysis, I distinguish between religious or belief-symbols, and cognitive or idea-symbols. When speaking of the latter, I prefer to use the term *social metaphysics* or, alternatively, social philosophy. Social metaphysics describes a consistent conceptual scheme which attempts to describe the nature of social and political reality, in other words a social ontology. A religious believer, when pushed back to the ultimate source of his faith, is confronted with an emotionally held and irreducable affective experience. A social philosopher, on the other hand, if pushed back to the roots of his analysis, emerges with certain irreducible intellectual postulates upon which his entire system is constructed.

A social metaphysics on the one hand defines the unit of social analysis. This may be the individual, family, nation, social class, or even mankind as a whole. On the other hand, it concerns itself with the question of distribution of power. Should power be vested in an elite—defined in ethnic, interest, or other terms—or should it be vested in the majority of individuals or indeed in a single individual? Whatever the basis of power, practical questions, like the protection of minorities, constitutional limitations upon the "sovereign will," apparatus for exercise of power, etc., become relevant.

An example of a social metaphysical system is Thomism, in which the unit of social analysis is an organic Christendom and power is distributed hierarchically. With the breakdown of medieval Europe, two conflicting systems of social metaphysics came into being, namely corporativism and liberalism. Liberalism assumed the individual to be the basic unit of social analysis,[9] whereas corpora-tivism chose to retain the organic emphasis of Thomism but to apply it less universally. Thus the corporate unit might be defined in terms of aristocratic elitism (e.g., Burkianism or German conser-vatism[10]), in terms of the state (e.g., Hegelianism or Mussolini's

[9] Hobhouse (n.d.) is a classic statement of liberalism. Notice that in speaking of liberalism and conservatism I am referring to systems of ideas, social metaphysical schemes, and not to attitudes. Political scientists often talk past one another because they fail to make this basic distinction. It is precisely because of this distinction between political attitudes and systems of political ideas that Louis Hartz (1955) is able to speak sensibly of "conservative liberalism."

[10] Mannheim (1953) is the best analysis of German conservatism (cf. also Marcuse, 1960, pp. 360-388). Mosse (1964) describes in an

fascism), in ethnic [11] terms (e.g., neo-Fichteanism [12], German National Socialism, or Zionism), or in class terms (as in Marxism—although Marx's proletarian corporativism implies a universalist utopia). Liberals, while agreed on the concept of the individual as the basic unit of social analysis, are divided on the issue of the distribution of power. Power, for liberals, may be vested in a sovereign individual (as in Hobbes), in constitutional representation of property owners (as in Locke), or in the "general will," the "will of the People" (as in the liberal nationalism of Rousseau).

Although civil religion and social metaphysics may be analytically differentiated, for any given individual they tend to be mingled in a single symbolic universe. The term *ideology* I restrict to prescriptive articulations derived from such a symbolic universe. [13] Ideology thus transforms civil faith and social metaphysics into directives or a program for political action. Insofar as an ideology taps the civil faith of a given group, to that extent the group will be more easily mobilized into social action. To overlook the civil religion in an analysis of ideology is to overlook one of the most important factors, especially in the reception of the ideology by nonelites. [14] E. P. Thompson's (1966) discussion of the development of English working class ideology and its operation in English political life is enormously strengthened, for example, by his treat-

---

appallingly unsystematic manner the civil religious byways of history by which this conservative doctrine was restated in National Socialist terms.

[11] My use of the term "ethnic" is throughout indebted to the illuminating discussion by Akzin (1964, pp. 29-37).

[12] Neo-Fichteanism, as I use it in this study, corresponds most closely to the nationalist doctrines described in Kedourie (1961). The fact that, in my opinion, Kedourie's definition of nationalism is too narrow in no way detracts from the excellence of his analysis.

[13] The major source for my understanding of ideology is Brzezinski (1962). I discovered Alasdair MacIntyre's definition of ideology (1971, pp. 5-6) some time after drafting this appendix. However, his "three key features" of ideology, might perhaps be held to correspond respectively to my social metaphysics, ideology and civil religion, although I chose to define them within a more narrowly political context.

[14] Barrington Moore (1965) might have benefited from greater attention to the Russian civil religion. Walzer's (1965) argument too, would have been much strengthened, especially with regard to the gentry, had he included in his discussion of the "traditional political world," an analysis of the civil religion which defined the English gentleman's sense of identity. In Little (1969) the author does unearth certain of the assumptions of the English gentleman's civil religion, especially in his analysis of the Anglicans and Coke. However, since such elements obscure the contrast between Puritans and Anglicans, which he seems to want to maintain at all

ment of Methodism and of the English civil religion, which he calls the "rhetoric of liberty."

In this book I have deliberately avoided the term "nationalism" as an analytic concept, largely because of the basic ambiguity of learned discussion on the subject. Scholars seem unable to decide whether the term refers to the nation-state or to primordial ethnic loyalties, which may or may not be identified with the nation-state. That this ambiguity is inherent in the thought of liberal nationalists themselves is clear in my discussion of the ideas of General Hertzog. I have restricted my use of "nationalism" to a certain type of social metaphysic (liberal or constitutional nationalism) and its corresponding ideology.

The above conceptual apparatus—indeed, my own "social metaphysical" framework—must be validated in actual research. Concepts are essentially tools for analysis of social reality. As such, they should be applied where useful, remaining flexible and always subordinate to the primary task, which is to describe clearly and meaningfully. To borrow a sentence from J. H. Hexter: "The way social change in fact took place is something we may find out about by *using* our framework; it is not and *ought not to be* something to be found *in* the framework" (Hexter, 1961, p. 16).

---

costs, he tends to relegate the civil faith to some analytic limbo, whence it emerges only implicitly to negate his entire argument about Coke and the common law.

References

The most important sources for my research were the six major Afrikaans newspapers, which published verbatim reports of political and "cultural" speechs speeches as well as extensive commentary on such affairs. I read all these newspapers from 1929 (or the date of first publication) through 1949 (or the date on which publication ceased). Each served as the mouthpiece of a prominent political figure, who in turn represented one of several rival social metaphysics. *Die Burger* represented the opinions of D. F. Malan, *Die Volkstem* those of General J. G. Smuts, *Die Vaderland* those of General J. B. M. Hertzog (and later of N. C. Havenga), and *Die Transvaler* those of J. G. Strydom and H. F. Verwoerd. Evidence suggests that *Die Volksblad* represented most faithfully the opinions of the Broederbond elite. Of all the major newspapers, *Die Oosterlig* remained the least interesting, for it followed unequivocally the National party line with only slightly stronger Nazi leanings during the early war years. The newspapers thus represent the full spectrum of Afrikaner political opinion of these years, from the liberalism of Smuts and Hertzog through the solid conservative nationalism of Malan to the more extreme views of Strydom and Verwoerd. In addition, for the lunatic fringe in the Transvaal during the 1930s, I consulted all copies of *Die Weste* available in the State Library in Pretoria; for the A.N.S., available copies of *Wapenskou*; for the O.B., the complete holdings of *Die O.B.* in the Potchefstroom University Library; and for Pirow's New Order, bound copies of *Die Anti-Kommunis* in the library of the University of South Africa.

I supplemented the newspapers with selected articles from the journals *Die Huisgenoot, Inspan, Koers, Kerkbode,* and *Die Nuwe Brandwag* and relevant debates in *Hansard.* In addition, I spent long hours in the South African Public Library in Cape Town reading its collection of school annuals (from about 25 Afrikaans schools) and the journals of the Afrikaans universities. Also in the South African Public Library were several Dutch Reformed congregational magazines, which reflected strong church support for the Reddingsdaadbond as well as great diversity of theological opinion.

The only relevant unpublished sources available to me were the holdings of the O.B. archives in Potchefstroom University Library, which contained, in addition to fragmentary minutes and study-reports, the fascinating diary of N. G. S. van der Walt; and the local National party minute books held by the Political Archives at the University of the Orange Free State in Bloemfontein. With occasional exceptions, these proved rather unilluminating. The papers of D. F. Malan at Stellenbosch University are unfortunately not yet available to researchers. Fortunately, the biographers of General Hertzog and N. J. van der Merwe quote extensively from diaries and private papers. (Since the English edition of van den Heever's life of General Hertzog is somewhat abridged, I chose to quote and consult the original Afrikaans version.)

Interviews with Afrikaner politicians and intellectuals were most fruitful, especially on the knotty problem of the Broederbond. After my work on the newspapers, I was oftentimes as well if not better informed than my subjects. Since many of them had no idea how much I was able to glean from their accounts and some of those who were most frank might be embarrassed if I were to name them, it seems best not to list their names. Certainly the greatest disappointment of my entire research effort was my failure to meet Dr. A. L. Geyer. He was editor of *Die Burger* from 1925 to 1948, through most of which period he kept a personal diary, and was also Dr. Malan's closest confidant. He invited me to spend a weekend on his farm, which would have given us ample time to talk, but on the preceding Thursday, he suffered a stroke and went into a coma from which he never recovered.

Secondary sources are referred to throughout the book. However, I should like to make special mention of two works. First, Roberts and Trollip (1947) was an essential starting point. Of all the many works in Afrikaner history which are now out of print, this one most deserves to be reprinted. Despite the florid style and a tendency to underrate the importance of developments in Afrikanerdom before 1939, it is an extraordinarily well-documented study, packed with perpicious insights. Stephanus du Toit has an interesting review of this book in *Koers* (June 1948). For the view, which I share in part, that it tends to overemphasize the role of the party at the expense of the O.B. see *Koers* (August 1948), where A. J. van Rooy replies to du Toit's review.

Second, I was able to study Newell Stultz's *Afrikaner Politics in South Africa* in manuscript. The care with which he analyzes the 1948 election has meant that I was able to make a number of assumptions which I should otherwise have had to sustain independently. The lack of an adequate study of *samesmelting* explains the detail which was necessary at that point in my account.

Two important unpublished sources on which I relied in the conclusion are Engelbrecht's collection of Eiselen's papers and the entire thirteen volumes of the Tomlinson Commission report. Tatz led me to the most important parliamentary debates on apartheid. There are innumerable statements by Afrikaner intellectuals in justification of South Africa's racial policy and even more critiques by opponents of the white oligarchy, many of which miss the mark completely in handling Afrikaner arguments. Recent accounts by J. H. P. Serfontein and Beaumont Schoeman prove most illuminating on current Afrikaner infighting. Most useful of all in understanding both the policy of separate development and contemporary Afrikanerdom, however, has been my intimate acquaintance with the events, personalities and ideologies of the 1930s and 1940s and the general ground plan of the Afrikaner civil religion. However, even the most informed evaluations of the sweeping changes which are currently taking place in Afrikanerdom are speculative at best.

Newspapers

All consulted in the State Library, Pretoria.
Die Burger, 1929-1949 (occasional earlier issues).
Die O.B., 1942-1949.
Die Oosterlig, 1936-1943.
Die Republikein, see *Die Weste*.
Die Suiderstem (occasional issues).
Die Transvaler, 1937-1949.
Die Vaderland, see *Ons Vaderland*.
Die Volkstem, 1929-1949 (occasional earlier issues).
Die Weste (after 1934, became *Die Republikein*), 1925-1938 (incomplete).
Ons Vaderland (after 1932, became *Die Vaderland*), 1929-1949.
The Star, occasional issues.

Journals

All consulted in the State Library, Pretoria, unless otherwise indicated.
Besembos, Student journal, Potchefstroom University for Christian higher Education, 1930-1945.
Die Handhawer, Journal of the Handhawersbond, 1930-1932 (South African Public Library, Cape Town).
Die Huisgenoot, occasional issues.
Inspan, Journal of the F.A.K., 1941-1950.
Die Kerkbode, Journal of the N.G. church. (occasional issues).
Koers, Theological journal published in Potchefstroom. Major mouthpiece for Kuyperian Calvinism. 1929-1950.
Die Stellenbosse Student, Student journal, Stellenbosch University, 1930-1950.
Wapenskou, Journal of the A.N.S., 1934-1939 (incomplete), and 1939-1945 (complete in Potchefstroom University Library).

Wellington Teachers' Training College Annual Magazine. 1920-1940 (South African Public Library, Cape Town).

Woord en Daad, Gereformeerde theological journal, occasional issues.

Journals of local Dutch Reformed congregations

All consulted in South African Public Library, Cape Town.

Nederduits Gereformeerd

Beaufort-West (*Die Boodskapper*)

Dordrecht

Johannesburg East (*Irenenuus*)

Johannesburg West (*Ons Huisvriend*)

Zeerust

Gereformeerd

Pretoria East (*Die Kerkstem*)

High School Annuals

All consulted in South African Public Library, Cape Town.

Bethal (Hoogenhout-Hoërskool)

Bethlehem

Bloemfontein (Sentrale Hoërskool)

Boshof

Ceres

Ermelo

Heidelberg (*Volkie*)

Heilbron

Johannesburg (Helpmekaar Hoërskool, including *Gedenkuitgawe*, 1921-1942.)

Klerksdorp

Mooreesburg

Paarl

Potchefstroom (*Ons Jaarblad*)

Wolmaranstad

Zeerust (*Die Zeeruster*)

National party local branch minutes

All unpublished and deposited in the Political Archives, Bloemfontein

Bedford

Cape Town, Tuine branch

Leliedal, Ondergrootrivier branch

Malmesbury

Murraysburg

Olifantshoek

Paarl

Piketberg
Queenstown
Steytlerville
Victoria West
Wellington

Books, Pamphlets and Journal Articles

Akzin, Benjamin, 1964. *State and Nation*. London: Hutchinson University Library.

Albertyn, C. R., n.d. *My Eie Kerk*. Johannesburg: Armesorgkommissie van die N. H. of G. Kerk, Transvaal.

Auerbach, F. E., 1965. *The Power of Prejudice in South African Education*. Cape Town and Amsterdam: A. A. Balkema.

Antonissen, Rob, 1965. *Die Afrikaanse Letterkunde van Aanvang tot Hede*. Third revised edition. Pretoria: H.A.U.M. First ed., 1955.

Bekommerd (pseudonym), 1935. *Christus die Deur, die Twee Rigtings van die Calvinisme*. Cape Town: H.A.U.M. Originally published as a series of articles in *Die Kerkbode*.

Bellah, Robert, 1970. *Beyond Belief*. New York: Harper and Row.

Beyers, Coenraad, 1929. *Die Kaapse Patriotte*. Cape Town: Nasionale Pers.

Boodt, C. P., 1939. *De Reformatie van het Calvinistisch Denken*. S'Gravenhage: De Bres.

Booyens, Bun, 1959. *Die Lewe van D.F. Malan: die eerste veertig jaar*. Cape Town: Tafelberg.

Brink, André, 1970. "Some Aspects of Culture and Apartheid." In *Anatomy of Apartheid*, edited by Peter Randall. Occasional Publication No. 1. Johannesburg: SPRO-CAS.

British Council of Churches, n.d. *The Future of South Africa*. London: S.C.M. Press.

Brzezinski, Zbigniew, 1962. *Ideology and Power in Soviet Politics*. New York: Praeger.

Bunting, Brian, 1969. *The Rise of the South African Reich*. rev. ed. Harmondsworth and Baltimore: Penguin Books.

Calvin, John, *Institutes. Institutes of the Christian Religion*, edited by John T. McNeill, translated by Ford Lewis Battles. Philadelphia: Westminster Press, 1961.

Campaign for Right and Justice, n.d. *The Afrikaner Broederbond by a well-known Afrikaner*. Johannesburg: Campaign for Right and Justice.

Carter, Gwendolyn; Karis, Thomas; and Stultz, Newell; 1967. *South Africa's Transkei: the Politics of Domestic Colonialism*. Evanston: Northwestern University Press.

Cilliers, A. C., 1939. *Quo Vadis*. Stellenbosch: Pro Ecclesia.

———, 1940a. *Volkseenheid, of Brollocks en Bittergal*. Stellenbosch: Pro Ecclesia.

———, 1940b. *Hertzog en Hereniging*. Stellenbosch: Pro Ecclesia.

Cloete, Henry, 1856. *Lectures on the Emigration of the Dutch from the Cape to Natal until 1843*. Cape Town: Solomon.

Cloete, T. T., 1963. *Die Wêreld is ons Woning nie*. Cape Town: Tafelberg.

Cobban, Alfred, 1969. *The Nation State and National Self-Determination*. New York: Crowell.

Cochrane, C. N., 1957. *Christianity and Classical Culture*. New York: Oxford University Press. First published 1940.

Coertze, P. J., Language, F. J., and van Eerden, B. I. C., 1943. "Die Oplossing van die Naturelle-Vraagstuk in Suid-Afrika." *Wapenskou*, April 1943, pp. 4-17; and June 1943, pp. 23-25.

Coetzee, Abel, 1937. *Die Opkoms van die Afrikaanse Kultuurgedagte aan die Rand*. Johannesburg: Afrikaanse Pers.

Coetzee, J. Albert, 1931. *Nasie-wording in Suid-Afrika*. Potchefstroom: Die Weste Drukkers.

———, 1944. *Politieke Groepering in die Wording van die Afrikanernasie*. Johannesburg: Voortrekkerpers.

———, Meyer, P. J., and Diederichs, N., 1941. *Ons Repubiek*. Bloemfontein: Nasionale Pers.

Cohn, Norman, 1957. *The Pursuit of the Millenium*. London: Secker and Warburg.

Cope, Jack and Krige, Uys, 1968. *The Penguin Book of South African Verse*. Harmondsworth and Baltimore: Penguin Books.

Coser, Lewis, 1956. *The Functions of Social Conflict*. Glencoe: The Free Press.

Cronje, Geoff., 1945. *'n Tuiste vir die Nageslag*. Johannesburg: Publicite.

———, 1947. *Regverdige Rasseapartheid*. Written in conjunction with William Nicol and E. P. Groenwald. Stellenbosch: C.S.V.

Davenport, T. R. H., 1965. *The Afrikaner Bond*. Cape Town: Oxford University Press.

Degenaar, J. J., 1969. "Nasionalisme." In de Klerk, W. A., Versveld, Martin, and Degenaar, J. J., *Beweging Uitwaarts*. Cape Town: Malherbe.

De Jongh, S. J., 1946. *Sonder Gewere*. Johannesburg: Publicite.

De Kiewiet, C. W., 1937. *The Imperial Factor in South Africa*. London: Oxford University Press.

———, 1941. *A History of South Africa: Social and Economic*. London: Oxford University Press.

Delayed Action! An Ecumenical Witness from the Afrikaansspeaking Church. Pretoria: N. G. Boekhandel.

Desmond, Cosmas, 1971. *The Discarded People*. Harmondsworth and Baltimore: Penguin Books.

De Vos, J. P., 1941. "Blank Suid-Afrika en die Administrasie van Naturelle: 'n Pleidooi vir absolute Teritoriale Segregasie." *Wapenskou*, November 1940, pp. 54-59.

De Waal, J. H. H., 1932. *My Herinnerings van ons Taalstryd.* Cape Town: Nasionale Pers.

Diederichs, Nicolaas, 1936. *Nasionalisme as Lewensbeskouing en sy verhonding tot Internasionalisme.* Bloemfontein: Nasionale Pers.

———, n.d. *Die Reddingsdaadbond,* Cape Town: Nasionale Pers.

Duff, J. Wight, 1960. *A Literary Histry of Rome: From the Origins to the Close of the Golden Age,* edited by A. M. Duff. New York: Barnes and Noble. First ed., 1909.

Duminy, P. A., ed., 1967. *Trends and Challenges in the Education of the South African Bantu.* Pretoria: van Schaik.

Du Plessis, E. P., 1964. *'n Volk staan op: die Ekonomiese Volkskongress en daarna.* Cape Town: Human and Rousseau.

Du Plessis, J., 1919. *The Life of Andrew Murray of South Africa.* London: Marshall Bros.

Du Plessis, J., 1965. *A History of Christian Missions in South Africa.* Cape Town: Struik.

Du Plessis, J. S., n.d. *President Kruger aan die Woord.* Bloemfontein: Sacum.

Du Plessis, L. J., Hugo, T. J., and Labuschagne, F. J., n.d. *Ons Volksideaal: drie lesings.* Bloemfontein: Nasionale Pers.

Du Plessis, L. J., 1941a. *Die Moderne Staat.* Stellenbosch: Pro Ecclesia.

———, 1941b. *Afrikanereenheid: Voledige verslag van die Eenheidskomitee se Voorsitter.* Bloemfontein: Nasionale Pers.

———, 1942. *Jeug en Toekomsstaat.* Stellenbosch: Wapenskou.

Du Plessis, Louis J., 1951. *Letters of a Farmer.* Privately published.

Du Plessis, Otto, n.d. *Die Nuwe Suid-Afrika: Die Revolusie van die Twintigste Eeu.* Cape Town: Nasionale Pers.

Durkheim, Emile, 1965. *The Elementary Forms of the Religious Life.* New York: The Free Press. First English ed., George, Allen and Unwin, 1926.

Du Toit, J. D. ("Totius"), 1962. *Versamelde Werke.* Vol. 8. Johannesburg: Dagbreek Boekhandel.

Du Toit, S. J., Malherbe, Gideon and Hoogenhout, C. P., 1895. *Die Geskiedenis van ons land in di taal van ons volk.* Paarl: du Toit. Second ed. First ed., 1877.

Eeufeestoesprake, 1842-1942. *Eeufeesalbum van die Nederduits Hervormde Kerk van Afrika.* Pretoria: Wallachs.

Eiselen, W. W. M., 1934. "Wat gaan van die Bantu-tale in Suid-Afrika word?" *Sending Instituut Jaarblad,* 1934.

———, 1964. "Die Aandeel van die Blanke ten Opsigte van die Praktiese Uitvoering van die Belied van Afsonderlike Ontwikkeling-Kultureel-Maatskaplike:" *Journal of Racial Affairs,* 1965.

Eisenstadt, S. N., ed., 1968. *The Protestant Ethic and Modernization.* New York: Basic Books.

Engelbrecht, J., 1959. *Die Naturellevraagstuk e.a.: 'n bundel re-*

ferate deur Dr. W. W. M. Eiselen. Roneoed. Pretoria, December 17, 1959.

Engelbrecht, S. P., 1946. *President Thomas Francois Burgers.* Pretoria: de Bussy.

———, 1951. *Geskiedenis van die Nederduits Hervormde Kerk van Afrika*, third ed. Cape Town: H.A.U.M. First ed. 2 vols., Pretoria: de Bussy 1920 and 1925.

Erasmus, L. J., n.d. *'n Volk Staan op uit sy As.* Johannesburg: Afrikaanse Pers.

Erikson, Erik, 1958. *Young Man Luther.* New York: W. W. Norton.

Euvrard, J. A., 1956. *Die Geskiedenis van die Pretoriase Afrikaanse Kultuurvereniging en sy voorlopers.* M. A. dissertation, University of Pretoria, 1956.

Fees by die Waens, 1939. *Gedenkalbum gewy aan die Sentrale Eeufees op 22 en 23 Oktober, 1938, in Bloemfontein.* Compiled by J. J. Kruger. Bloemfontein: Nasionale Pers.

Geertz, Clifford, ed., 1963. "The Integrative Revolution." *Old Societies and New States.* Glencoe: The Free Press.

———, 1966. "Religion as a Cultural System." *Anthropological Approaches to the Study of Religion*, edited by Michael Banton. London: Tavistock.

Gerdener, G. B. A., 1934. *Ons Kerk in die Transgariep. Cape Town: Nasionale Pers.*

Gluckman, Max, 1963. *Custom and Conflict in Africa.* Oxford: Blackwell. First ed., 1960.

Grove, A. P. and Harvey, C. J. D., 1962. *Afrikaans Poems with English Translations.* Cape Town: Oxford University Press.

Haller, William, 1957. *The Rise of Puritanism.* New York: Harper Torchbooks.

———, 1963. *Liberty and Reformation in the Puritan Revolution.* New York: Columbia University Press.

Hancock, W. K., 1962. *Smuts: The Sanguine Years.* Cambridge: Cambridge University Press.

———, 1968. *Smuts: The Fields of Force.* Cambridge: Cambridge University Press.

Hanekom, T. N., 1951. *Die Liberale Rigting in Suid-Afrika.* Vol. 1. Stellenbosch: C.S.V.

———, 1951a. *Kerk en Volk.* Johannesburg: N.G. Kerkuitgewers.

Hansard. Union of South Africa, House of Assembly Debates. Pretoria: Government Printer.

Hartz, Louis, 1955. *The Liberal Tradition in America.* New York: Harcourt, Brace and World.

Haywood, J. J., n.d. *Dr. J. F. J. van Rensburg en die Stormjaers.* Bloemfontein: Nasionale Pers.

Hellman, Ellen, 1957. "Tribalism in a Modern Society." *Race Relations Journal.* 24(1957): 1-11.

Hepple, Alexander, 1967. *Verwoerd*. Harmondsworth and Baltimore: Penguin Books.

Hertzog Gedenkboek, 1965. Edited by P. J. Nienaber. Issued by the Suid-Afrikaanse Akademie vir Wetenskap en Kuns. Johannesburg: Afrikaanse Pers.

Hexter, J. H., 1961. *Reappraisals in History*. Evanston: Northwestern University Press.

Hill, Christopher, 1964. *Puritanism and Revolution*. New York: Schocken Books.

Hoagland, Jim, 1972. *South Africa: Civilizations in Conflict*. Boston: Houghton Mifflin.

Hobhouse, L. T., n.d. *Liberalism*. New York: Henry Holt, Home University Library.

Horrell, Muriel, 1971a. *Legislation and Race Relations*. Revised ed., 1971. Johannesburg: South African Institute of Race Relations.

———, 1971b. *Action, Reaction and Counter-Action*. Johannesburg: South African Institute of Race Relations.

Houghton, D. Hobart, 1967. *The South African Economy*. Cape Town: Oxford University Press.

Institutes (see Calvin, John).

Impeta, C. H., 1964. *Kaart van het Kerklijk Nederland*. Kampen: Kok. First ed., 1961.

Jaeger, Werner, 1945. *Paideia: the Ideals of Greek Culture*. Vol. 1. New York: Oxford University Press.

Janson, Murray, 1967. *Die Kerk en die Ideologie*. Potchefstroom: "Die Evangelis."

Jarvie, I. C., 1964. *The Revolution in Anthropology*. London: Routledge and Kegan Paul.

Jooste, J. P., 1959. *Die Geskiedenis van die Gereformeerde Kerk in Suid-Afrika*. Potchefstroom: published by the author.

Jordan, Winthrop, 1959. *White over Black*. Baltimore and Harmondsworth: Penguin Books.

Kedourie, Elie, 1961. *Nationalism*. London: Hutchinson University Library; New York: Praeger.

Kerksaak, 1932. *Die Kerksaak tussen Prof. J. du Plessis en die N. G. in Suid-Afrika. 'n Woordelike Verslag van die Verigtinge. . .* Cape Town: Nasionale Pers.

Kestell, J. D., 1939. *My Nasie in Nood*. Bloemfontein: Nasionale Pers., Tweede Trek Reeks.

———, and van der Velden, D. E., 1912. *The Peace Negotiations between the Governments of Great Britain and the South African Republic and the Orange Free State*. Pretoria: de Bussy.

Kirstein, Jan, "Some Foundations of Afrikaner Nationalism." Honors dissertation, University of Cape Town, 1956.

Kleynhans, W. A., 1966. *Volksregering in die Z.A. Republiek: die*

Rol van Memories. Pretoria: van Schaik.

Koers in die Krisis, Vol. 1, 1935; Vol. 2, 1940; Vol. 3, 1941. Issued by the *Federasie van Calvinistiese Studentevereniginge in Suid-Afrika*. Stellenbosch: Pro Ecclesia.

Kotze, C. R., 1932. *Die Dwaling in Ons Kerk*. Bloemfontein: Nasionale Pers.

Krüger, D. W., 1960. *South African Parties and Policies, 1910-1960*. Cape Town: Human and Rousseau.

———, 1963. *Paul Kruger*. Vol. 2. Johannesburg: Dagbreek Press.

Kuyper, Abraham, 1899. *Calvinism*. Amsterdam: Honeker and Wormser, Stone Lectures.

Langenhoven, C. J., 1921. *Eerste Skoffies op die Pad van Suid-Afrika*. Cape Town: Nasionale Pers.

———, 1932. *My Aandeel in Ons Taalstryd*. Cape Town: Nasionale Pers.

Leipoldt, Louis, 1961. *Oom Gert Vertel en ander gedigte*. Cape Town: Nasionale Boekhandel. First ed., 1908.

Legum, Colin and Legum, Margaret, 1964. *South Africa: Crisis for the West*. New York: Praeger.

Le May, G. H. L., 1965. *British Supremacy in South Africa*. Oxford: Clarendon Press.

Le Roux, N. J., 1943. *Enkel-of Dubbel-Mediumskool*. Cape Town: Nasionale Pers.

Levi-Strauss, Claude, 1963. *Structural Anthropology*. New York: Basic Books.

Little, David, 1969. *Religion, Order and Law*. New York: Harper Torchbooks.

Louw, E. H., n.d. *Die Kommunistiese Gevaar*. Cape Town: Voorligtingsdiens van die H. N. P.

Louw, N. P. van Wyk, 1959. *Berigte te Velde*. Cape Town: Nasionale Pers.

———, 1968. *Raka*. English translation by Anthony Dawes. Cape Town: Nasionale Boekhandel.

MacCrone, I. D., 1937. *Race Attitudes in South Africa*. London: Oxford University Press.

MacIntyre, Alasdair, 1971. *Against the Self-Images of the Age: Essays on Ideology and Philosophy*. New York: Schocken Books.

Malan, D. F., 1911. "Taal en Nationaliteit." *Wij zullen handhaven*. Students Taalkonferentie, Stellenbosch, 6 and 7 April 1911. Bloemfontein: De Vriend.

Malan, D. G., Lategan, D., and van Rooyen, E. E., 1936. *Christus en Calvinisme: die ware toedrag van sake teenoor "Bekommerd" toegelig*. Stellenbosch: Pro Ecclesia.

Malan, F. S., 1933. *Ons Kerk en Professor du Plessis*. Cape Town: Nasionale Pers.

Malherbe, D. F. du T., 1942. *Afrikaner Volkseenheid*. Bloemfontein: Nasionale Pers., Tweede Trek Reeks.

References   311

Malherbe, E. G., 1943. *The Bilingual School*. Johannesburg: C.N.A.

Mannheim, Karl, 1953. "Conservative Thought." *Essays on Sociology and Social Philosophy*. Edited by Paul Kecskemeti. London: Routledge and Kegan Paul.

Marais, Ben, 1964. *The Two Faces of Apartheid*. Pietermaritzburg: Shooter and Shuter.

Marais, J. S., 1944. *Maynier and the First Boer Republic*. Cape Town: Maskew Miller.

———, 1961. *The Fall of Kruger's Republic*. Oxford: Clarendon Press.

Marcuse, Herbert, 1960. *Reason and Revolution*. rev. ed. Boston: Beacon Press. First ed., Oxford: Oxford University Press, 1941.

Meer, Fatima, 1971. "African Nationalism—Some Inhibiting Factors." *South Africa: Sociological Perspectives*, edited by Heribert Adam. London and New York: Oxford University Press.

Meyer, P. J., 1941. *Die Afrikaner*. Bloemfontein: Nasionale Pers., Tweede Trek Reeks.

———, 1942a. *Demokrasie of Volkstaat*. Stellenbosch: A.N.S.

———, 1942b. *Die Toekomstige Ordening van die Volksbeweging in Suid-Afrika*. Stellenbosch: A.N.S.

———, 1943. *Arbeidersordening in die Volksbeweging*. Stellenbosch: A.N.S.

———, n.d. *Die Stryd van die Afrikanerwerker*. Johannesburg: Publicite.

Miller, Perry, 1961. *The Puritan Mind: The Seventeenth Century*. Boston: Beacon Press. First ed., New York: The Macmillan Company, 1939.

———, 1964. *Errand into the Wilderness*. New York: Harper Torchbooks. First ed., Cambridge, Mass.: Harvard University Press, 1956.

Moberg, David, 1961. "Social Differentiation in the Netherlands." *Social Forces*. 39(1961): pp. 333-337.

Moll, A. M., n.d. (a). *Sowereine Onafhanklikheid. My Politieke Belydenis*. Potchefstroom: A. H. Koomans.

———, n.d. (b). *Die Onafhanklikheid van Suid-Afrika*. Potchefstroom: A. H. Koomans.

Moodie, T. D., 1974. "Toward a Dynamic Conception of Social Order." *Social Change: Conjectures, Explorations and Diagnoses,* edited by George Zollschan and Walter Hirsch, second ed. Cambridge, Mass: Schenkman.

Morgan, Edmund S., 1966. *The Puritan Family*. New York: Harper Torchbooks. First ed., Cambridge, Mass.: Harvard University Press, 1950.

Mosse, George, 1964. *Crisis of German Ideology: Intellectual Origins of the Third Reich*. New York: Grosset and Dunlap.

Muller, C. F. J., 1948. *Die Britse Owerheid en die Groot Trek*. Cape Town: Juta.

———, 1960. *Waarom die Groot Trek geslaag het.* Pretoria: University of South Africa.

Muller, Tobie, 1913. *Die Geloofsbelydenis van 'n Nasionalist.* Stellenbosch: Afrikaans Taalvereniging.

Murray, A. H., n.d. *The Political Philosophy of J. A. de Mist, Commissioner-General of the Cape, 1803-1805: A Study in Political Pluralism.* Cape Town: H.A.U.M.

National Party, n.d. *Politieke Toespraak.* Cape Town: Nasionale Pers.

———, 1942. *Ons Party en die O.B.* Cape Town: Nasionale Pers.

Naude, Louis, 1969. *Dr. Albert Hertzog, die Nasionale Party, en die Mynwerkers.* Pretoria: Nasionale Raad van Trustees.

Nel, B. F., n.d. *Ons Jeug en sy Nasionale Vorming.* Bloemfontein: Nasionale Pers.

———, 1942. *Naturelle-Opvoeding en Onderwys.* 2 vols. Bloemfontein: Nasionale Pers., Tweede Trek Reeks.

Nepgen, C. C., 1938. *Die Sosiale Gewete van die Afrikaans-sprekendes.* Stellenbosch: C.S.V.

Neumann, F. L., 1966. *Behemoth: The Structure and Practice of National-Socialism.* New York: Harper Torchbooks. First ed., New York: Oxford University Press, 1944.

Nicol, William, 1942. "Die Strydende Skool." *Helpmekaar Höerskool Gedenkuitgawe, 1921-1942.*

———, 1958. *Met Toga en Troffel: Die Lewe van 'n Stadspredikant.* Cape Town: N. G. Kerkuitgewers.

Nienaber, G. S. and Nienaber, P. J., 1941. *Die Geskiedenis van die Afrikaanse Letterkunde.* Pretoria: van Schaik.

O.B., 1942a. *Die Ossewabrandwag: Vanwaar en Waarheen.* Pretoria: Ossewabrandwag.

———, 1942b. *Gesonde Huisgesinne Bou 'n Lewenskragtige Volk!, Amptelike Gesinsbeleid van die Ossewabrandwag.* Stellenbosch: Pro Ecclesia.

———, 1944. Kommandant-General's Annual Report. Potchefstroom: O.B. Archives, unpublished.

Oberholster, J. A. S., 1956. *Die Gereformeerde Kerke onder die Kruis in Suid-Afrika.* Cape Town: H.A.U.M.

Oelofse, J. C., 1964. *Die Nederduitse Hervormde Kerk en die Afrikaner Broederbond.* Krugersdorp: N. H. W. Pers.

Opperman, D. J., 1949. *Die Joernaal van Jorik.* Cape Town: Nasionale Pers.

———, ed., 1967. *Groot Verseboek.* Cape Town: Nasionale Pers. First ed., 1951.

Ossewa Gedenkboek, 1940. *Die Gedenkboek van die Ossewaens op die Pad van Suid-Afrika.* Cape Town: Nasionale Pers.

Paton, Alan, 1964. *Hofmeyr.* Cape Town: Oxford University Press.

Pelzer, A. N., 1966. *Verwoerd Speaks.* Johannesburg: Afrikaanse Pers.

Pienaar, E. C., 1926. *Taal en Poesie van die Twede Afrikaanse Taalbeweging.* Cape Town: Nasionale Pers. First ed., 1921.

Pienaar, S. W., ed., 1964. *Glo in U Volk: D. F. Malan as Redenaar, 1908-1954.* Cape Town: Tafelberg.

Pirow, Oswald, 1941. *Nuwe Orde vir Suid-Afrika.* Pretoria: Christelike Republiekeinse Suid-Afrikaanse Nasionaal Sosialistiese Studiekring. First ed., 1940.

Potgieter, P. J. J. S., 1972. *"Op die Voorpunt van die Tye." Hooftrekke van die Staatkundige Denke van L. J. du Plessis.* Potchefstroom: Pro Rege.

Preller, Gustav, 1909. *Piet Retief.* Ninth ed. Pretoria: van Schaik. First ed., 1906.

Raad van Kerke Handelinge, 1951. *Handelinge van die Twee-en-twintigste Vergadering van die Raad van die Kerke, 16 Mei, 1951.* Johannesburg: Voortrekkerpers.

Reitz, F. W., 1900. *A Century of Wrong.* London: Review of Reviews.

Rhoodie, N. J., 1969. *Apartheid and Racial Partnership in Southern Africa.* Pretoria: Academica.

Ritner, Susan Rennie, 1967. "The Dutch Reformed Church and Apartheid." *Journal of Contemporary History.* 2, (1967), no. 4.

Roberts, Michael, and Trollip, A. E. G., 1947. *The South African Opposition, 1935-1945.* Cape Town: Longmans Green.

Sachs, Solly, 1953. *The Choice before South Africa.* London: Turnstile Press.

Scannell, J. P., ed., 1965. *Keeromstraat 30.* Cape Town: Nasionale Pers.

Schoeman, B. M., 1973. *Van Malan tot Verwoerd.* Cape Town and Pretoria: Human and Rousseau.

Schoeman, P. J., 1941. "Territoriale Segregasie." *Wapenskou,* June 1941, pp. 34-35.

Scholtz, G. D., 1941. *Generaal Christiaan Frederick Beyers.* Johannesburg: Voortrekkerpers.

———, 1942. *Die Rebellie, 1914-1915.* Johannesburg: Voortrekkerpers.

———, 1944. *Dr. Nicolaas Johannes van der Merwe, 1888-1941.* Johannesburg: Voortrekkerpers.

———, 1956 and 1960. *Die Geskiedenis van die Nederduitse Hervormde of Gereformeerde Kerk van Suid-Afrika.* Cape Town: N. G. Kerkuitgewers.

———, 1964. *'n Swart Suid-Afrika?* Cape Town: Nasionale Boekhandel.

———, 1969. *Die Ontwikkeling van die Politieke Denke van die Afrikaner.* Johannesburg: Voortrekkerpers.

Scholtz, J. du P., 1939. *Die Afrikaner en sy Taal.* Cape Town: Nasionale Pers.

Sentrale Propaganda-Komitee vir 'n Christelike-Republikeinse Politiek in Suid-Afrika, 1945. *Die Stryd vir 'n Christelike-Republikeinse Politiek in Suid-Afrika.* Potchefstroom.

Serfontein, J. H. P., 1970. *Die Verkrampte Aanslag*. Cape Town and Pretoria: Human and Rousseau.

Simons, H. J., and Simons, R. E., 1970. *Class and Colour in South Africa, 1850*-1950. Harmondsworth and Baltimore: Penguin Books.

Slabbert, F. van Zyl, 1971. "Cultural and Ethnic Politics in the Apartheid Ideology." *Towards Social Change*, Report of the Social Commission of the Study Project on Christianity in Apartheid Society. Johannesburg: SPRO-CAS.

Smit, A. P., 1966. *Kuruman Gedenkalbum*. Cape Town: Nasionale Pers.

Smit, F. P., 1951. *Die Staatsopvattinge van Paul Kruger*. Pretoria: van Schaik.

Smith, E. W., 1949. *The Life and Times of Daniel Lindley*. London: Epworth Press.

Smith, J. A., 1917. *Brit en Boer (van Slagtersnek tot Jopie Fourie): uit die geskiedenis van die laaste honderd jare (1814-1915)*. Cape Town: Nasionale Pers.

Spoelstra, B., 1963. *Die 'Doppers' in Suid-Afrika, 1790-1899*. Cape Town: Nasionale Pers.

SPRO-CAS, 1972. *Power, Privilege and Poverty*, Report of the Economics Commission of the Study Project on Christianity in Apartheid Society. Johannesburg: SPRO-CAS.

Steyn, H. A., n.d. *Moedertaal-Onderwys: Afrikaans vir die Afrikaner*. Bloemfontein: Nasionale Pers.

Steyn, H. J., 1929, *Die Status van die Unie getoets aan die Beginsels van Suid-Afrikaanse Nasionalisme*. Potchefstroom: *Die Weste* Drukkery.

Stoker, H. G., 1941. *Die Stryd om die Ordes*. Potchefstroom: Calvyn Jubileum Boekefonds.

Studiestukke, 1966. *Studiestukke oor Rasse-Aangeleenthede van die N.G. Kerk in Suid-Afrika met die besluite van die Sinode van die Kaapse Kerk vir voorlegging aan die Algemene Sinode van die N.G. Kerk op Donderdag, 13 Oktober 1966 en die volgende dag in Bloemfontein*. Cape Town: N.G. Kerk in S.A. (Kaapse Kerk).

Stultz, Newell M., 1974. *Afrikaner Politics in South Africa, 1934-1948*. Berkeley and Los Angeles: University of California Press.

Swart, Marius, 1961. *Geloftedag*. Cape Town: H.A.U.M.

Tatz, C. M., 1962. *Shadow and Substance in South Africa*. Pietermaritzburg: Natal University Press.

Thom, H. B., 1965. *Die Lewe van Gerrit Maritz*. Cape Town: Nasou. First ed., Cape Town: Nasionale Pers. 1947.

Thompson, E. P., 1966. *The Making of the English Working Class*. New York: Vintage Books.

Thompson, L. M., 1960. *The Unification of South Africa*. Oxford: Clarendon Press.

————, 1969a. "Co-operation and Conflict: The Zulu Kingdom and Natal." *The Oxford History of South Africa*, by Monica Wilson and Leonard Thompson. Oxford: Clarendon Press, 1: 334-390.

————, 1969b. "Co-operation and Conflict: The High Veld." Wilson and Thompson, *op. cit.* 1: 391-446.

————, 1971. "Great Britain and the Afrikaner Republics, 1870-1899." Wilson and Thompson, *op. cit.* 2: 287-324.

Tomlinson Commission, 1955. *Summary of the Report of the Commission for the Socio-Economic Development of the Bantu Areas within the Union of South Africa.* U.G. 61/1955.

Tomlinson, Gordon, 1956. *Herrineringe van 'n Jong Turk.* Cape Town: Nasionale Pers.

Van den Heever, C. M., 1944. *Generaal J. B. M. Hertzog.* Johannesburg: Afrikaanse Pers.

Van der Meiden, A., 1968. *De Zwarte Kousen Kerken.* Utrecht: Amboboeken.

Van der Merwe, P. J., 1937. *Die Noordwartse Beweging van die Boere voor die Groot Trek (1770-1842).* The Hague: van Stockum.

————, 1938. *Die Trekboer in die Geskiedenis van die Kaapkolonie (1657-1842).* Cape Town: Nasionale Pers.

Van der Post, Laurens, 1955. *The Dark Eye in Africa.* London: Hogarth Press.

Van der Walt, A. J. H., 1944. *'n Volk op Trek.* Johannesburg: Publicite.

Van der Walt, I. J., 1963. *Eiesoortigheid en die Sending.* Potchefstroom: Pro Rege-Pers Beperk.

Van der Walt, N. G. S. *Diary.* Potchefstroom: O.B. Archives, unpublished.

Van Jaarsveld, F. A., 1941. *Die Eenheidstrewe van die Republikeinse Boere.* Johannesburg: Impala Opvoedkundige Diens.

————, 1959. *Die Afrikaner en sy Geskiedenis.* Cape Town: Nasionale Pers.

————, 1961. *The Awakening of Afrikaner Nationalism, 1868-1881.* Cape Town: Human and Rousseau.

————, 1962. *Die Tydgenootlike Beoordeling van die Groot Trek, 1836-1842.* Pretoria: University of South Africa.

————, 1963. *The Afrikaner's Interpretation of South African History.* Cape Town: Simondium.

————, 1963a. *Die Beeld van die Groot Trek in die Suid-Afrikaanse Geskiedsksywing 1843-1899.* Pretoria: University of South Africa.

Van Jaarsveld, F. A. and Scholtz, G. D., 1966. *Die Republiek van Suid-Afrika: Agtergrond, Ontstaan en Toekoms.* Johannesburg: Voortrekkerpers.

Van Oostrum, O., 1936. "Republieke het oorlog verloor maar Afrikanderdom het gewen." *Vaderland,* February 14, 1936.

Van Rensburg, Hans, 1956. *Their Paths Crossed Mine: Memoirs of the Commandant-General of the Ossewa-Brandwag.* Johannesburg: C.N.A.

Van Rooyen, J. J., 1956. *Die Nasionale Party*. Cape Town: Hoofraad van die Nasionale Party.

Van Schoor, M. C. E., 1963. *Die Nasionale en politieke bewuswording van die Afrikaner in immigrasie en sy ontluiking in Transgariep tot 1854*. Pretoria: South African Archives Yearbook.

———, and van Rooyen, J. J., 1960. *Republieke en Republiekeine*. Cape Town: Nasionale Pers.

Van Schoor, M. C. E., Malan, S. I., and Oberholster, J. J., 1964. *Generaal C. R. de Wet*. Bloemfontein: Nasionale Vrouemonumentkommisie.

Van Tonder, J. J., 1961. *Viertien Gedenktekens van Suid-Afrika*. Cape Town: Nasionale Pers.

Van Wijk, Theo, 1963. "Die Uitgang van die Agtiende Eeu." *Die Hervertolking van Ons Geskiedenis*, by F. A. van Jaarsveld, Theo van Wijk, C. F. J. Muller and G. D. Scholtz. Pretoria: University of South Africa.

Vatcher, W. H., 1965. *White Laager, the Rise of Afrikaner Nationalism*. New York: Praeger.

Verwoerd, H. F., n.d. *Red die Afrikaans-Mediumskole*. Johannesburg: Voortrekkerpers.

Walker, E. A., 1934. *The Great Trek*. London: Black.

Walshe, Peter, 1970. *The Rise of African Nationalism in South Africa*. Berkeley and Los Angeles: University of California Press.

Walzer, Michael, 1965. *The Revolution of the Saints*. Cambridge, Mass.: Harvard University Press.

Welsh, David, 1971. "The Growth of Towns." *The Oxford History of South Africa*, Edited by Monica Wilson and Leonard Thompson. Oxford: Clarendon Press. 2: 182-284.

———, 1972. "The Cultural Dimension of Apartheid." *African Affairs*, January 1972, 71: 35-53.

Wendel, Francois, 1963. *Calvin: The Origins and Development of his Religious Thought*. London: Collins.

Wolff, Kurt H., 1950. *The Sociology of Georg Simmel*. Glencoe: The Free Press.

Wypkema, A., 1939. *De Invloed van Nederland op Ontstaan en Ontwikkeling van de Staatsinstellingen der Z. A. Republiek tot 1881*. Pretoria: de Bussy.

Zolberg, Aristide, 1972. "Moments of Madness." *Politics and Society*, Winter, 1972.

Zollschan, George, and Hirsch, Walter, 1964. *Explorations in Social Change*. Boston: Houghton Mifflin.

Index

Adams, James Luther, 106n
African nationalism, 271
Afrikaans language movement. *See*
Language movement (Afrikaans)
Afrikaner: as defined by J. B. M.
Hertzog, 73-74, 76; by Tobie Mull-
er, 85; by D. F. Malan, 84-85; by
Joon van Rooy, 111; by Piet
Meyer, 163-164
Afrikaner Broederbond. *See* Broe-
derbond
Afrikanerization, 113-114, 162, 164
Afrikaner Nasionale Studentebond
(ANS), 161n, 227, 232n; founded
1933, 155
Afrikaner national self-con-
sciousness. *See* National con-
sciousness
Afrikaner party, 221, 228, 257. *See
also* Havenga, N. C.
Afrikaner trade unions. *See* Trade
unions
Afrikaner Woman, image of. *See*
Woman
Akzin, Benjamin, 75, 299n
Albertyn, J. R., 69, 170
Albertyn, P. K., 69-70
Althusius, 74
Anglicization, 4, 10, 46, 69, 105, 203,
240
Anglo-Boer War. *See* Boer War
ANS. *See* Afrikaner Nasionale Stu-
dentebond
Anti-semitism, 15, 162, 165-168
Antonissen, Rob., 41, 107
Apartheid (separateness): Afrikaner-
English, xi, 15, 21, 243-244; black-
white, 21, 29n, 228; early glimmer-
ings of in National party, 81; as
issue in 1940's, 245-251; the will of
God, 248, 253-254; post-1948, 263-
281

A.T.K.V. (Afrikaanse Taal en Kul-
tuurvereniging—S.A.S. en H.), 176
Auerbach, F. E., 382n
Augustine, 297
Augustus Caesar, 296
Authoritarianism, xi, 292-293; de-
fined 293n

Baker, John A., xi
Balfour Declaration, 91-94, 123
Basson, J., 166
Beets, Nicolaas, 53
Bekommerd, in defence of Murrayite
theology in the N.G., 62-65, 68
Beliefs, discussed theoretically, 295,
298
Bellah, Robert N., xi, 97, 296n
Beyers, General C. F., 9, 10, 37n, 81,
82, 93, 117
Beyers, Coenraad, 30n
Biblical principles, 65, 104, 218-219,
226; justifying apartheid, 248, 290
Blaaukrantz, massacre at, 6, 12, 13,
16, 18, 178, 224, 284. *See* Woman,
Concentration camps
Black threat, 15, 247
Blanke Werkers se Beskermings-
bond, 254-256
Blood River (1838), 6, 7, 15, 18, 27,
67, 93, 117, 178, 181, 195, 198-201,
206, 223, 224, 247, 284. *See* Gelofte-
dag, Covenant Oath
Boer War, 185, 284; of 1881, 7-8, 27,
31, 93, 117; of 1899-1902, 9-10, 12,
18, 19, 32-36, 41, 93, 116, 117, 223,
234, 240, 295
Boodt, C. P., 61
Booyens, Bun, 10n, 40, 62, 70, 72, 74,
82
Boshoff, P. J. J., 187n
Bot, A. K., 244n
Botha, General Louis, 9, 10, 36, 37n,

F